Case Studies
in Business Ethics

second edition

Case Studies
in Business Ethics

Edited by

Thomas Donaldson

Georgetown University

A. R. Gini

Loyola University of Chicago

PRENTICE HALL, Englewood Cliffs, New Jersey 07632

Library of Congress Cataloging-in-Publication Data

Case studies in business ethics / edited by Thomas Donaldson and A.R.
Gini. -- 2nd ed.
        p.   cm.
    ISBN 0-13-116211-X
    1. Business ethics--Case studies.   I. Donaldson, Thomas,
. II. Gini, A. R.
HF5387.C36   1990
174'.4--dc20   89-36667
                                                     CIP

Editorial/production supervision and
  interior design: Jan Stephan
Cover design: Marianne Frasco
Manufacturing buyers: Ray Keating and Mike Woerner

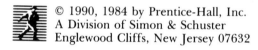 © 1990, 1984 by Prentice-Hall, Inc.
A Division of Simon & Schuster
Englewood Cliffs, New Jersey 07632

Printed in the United States of America

10 9 8 7 6 5 4 3 2 1

ISBN 0-13-116211-X

Prentice-Hall International (UK) Limited, *London*
Prentice-Hall of Australia Pty. Limited, *Sydney*
Prentice-Hall Canada Inc., *Toronto*
Prentice-Hall Hispanoamericana, S.A., *Mexico*
Prentice-Hall of India Private Limited, *New Delhi*
Prentice-Hall of Japan, Inc., *Tokyo*
Simon & Schuster Asia Pte. Ltd., *Singapore*
Editora Prentice-Hall do Brasil, Ltda., *Rio de Janeiro*

To
John Donaldson
Guido A. Gini

Contents

Preface

Not long ago the term *business ethics* was reserved for simple cases of fraud or honor. Customers complained about business ethics when they were victimized by bait-and-switch advertising, and corporate presidents boasted of business ethics in Christmas speeches and annual reports. But more recently the term has acquired greater complexity and sophistication. It has come to refer not only to matters of fraud and public relations, but to a growing field of study that encompasses standards of professionalism, corporate decision-making structures, and the interface between ethical theory and economic practice. Even as more and more business schools are introducing courses in business ethics, scholars in the humanities and social sciences are expanding the boundaries of research into the field.

In its evolution toward greater sophistication, business ethics has shed its "antibusiness" reputation. Repeatedly pointing the finger of blame—at the latest corporate watergate, at the most recent insider trading scandal or managerial fiasco—has come to be recognized as having limited pedagogical value. Such knee-jerk indignation promotes ethical simple-mindedness and avoids many of the deeper problems that vex even the most conscientious of managers.

In the face of this rising tide of academic interest in business ethics, it was inevitable that teachers and scholars would seek out better and more challenging case studies. *Case Studies in Business Ethics* is an attempt to fill that need by collecting into a single package some of the better case studies available. This book contains cases that deal not only with ethical failures, but with ethical successes, and each case attempts to confront the reader with the same complex value trade-offs that characterize real-life business decision making. Its cases are also designed to complement the new, more philosophically oriented approach taken in contemporary business ethics courses. Most instructors will want to use the book in conjunction with other materials dealing with specific topics in ethics, business, and economics. For those who wish to learn more about teaching with the aid of cases, we have provided an introductory essay that explains the case method and shows its special application to ethics. Each case study is followed by a set of discussion questions highlighting issues in the case. A set of questions marked by an asterisk indicates that we, and not the original author, formulated the questions.

It would be hard to sufficiently thank all those who helped design, prepare, and critique this book. These people include Jeanne Huchthausen, Ray O'Connell, Manuel Velasquez, and Pat Werhane. Special thanks go to Jeffrey A. Barach of Tulane University and Michael S. Pritchard of Western Michigan University for their careful reading of the manuscript. Research assistant Marci Lehe provided invaluable editorial advice and production editors Pattie Amoroso and Jan Stephan saved us from numerous embarrassments while doing a thoroughly professional job. Special thanks also have to be extended to Cynthia Rudolph for diligence in preparing the final manuscript, Caroline Carney and Helen Brennan for their advice and support and the Oak Park Public Library for its up-to-date holdings and professional courtesy.

Thomas Donaldson
A. R. Gini

Case Studies
in Business Ethics

Introduction
to Ethical Reasoning*

Thomas Donaldson
Patricia H. Werhane

What is the basis for making ethical decisions? Should Joan challenge Fred the next time he cracks a chauvinist joke? Should John refrain from lying on his job application despite his temptation to do so? What, if anything, should make Hillary decide that eating meat is corrupting, whereas vegetarianism is uplifting? It is obvious that the kind of evidence required for an ethical decision is different from that needed to make a nonethical one; but what is the nature of the difference? These questions give rise to a search for a *method* of ethical justification and decision making, a method that will specify the conditions that any good ethical decision should meet.

To see how such questions arise concretely, consider the following case.[1]

> Some years ago, a large German chemical firm, BASF, decided to follow the lead of many other European firms and build a factory in the United States. BASF needed land, lots of it (1,800 acres), an inexpensive labor pool, almost 5 million gallons of fresh water every day, a surrounding area free of import taxes, and a nearby railroad and ocean port. Obviously, only a handful of locations could meet all these requirements. The spot the company finally picked seemed perfect, an area near the coast of South Carolina called Beaufort County. It purchased 1,800 acres.
>
> South Carolina and Beaufort County were pleased with BASF's decision.

*This article is a revised version of one appearing in Thomas Donaldson and Patricia H. Werhane, eds., *Ethical Issues in Business* 2nd ed. (Englewood Cliffs, N.J.: Prentice-Hall, 1983) pp. 5–17.

The surrounding area, from which the company would pick its workers, was economically depressed and per capita income stood well below the national average. Jobs of any kind were desperately needed. Even the Governor of South Carolina and his staff were eager for BASF to build in South Carolina, and although BASF had not yet finalized its exact production plans, the State Pollution Central Authority saw no problems with meeting the State pollution laws. BASF itself said that although it would dump chemical byproducts into the local Colleton River, it planned not to lower the river's quality.

But trouble started immediately. To see why, one needs to know that Beaufort County is the home of the internationally famous resort area called "Hilton Head." Hilton Head attracts thousands of vacationers every year—most of them with plenty of money—and its developers worried that the scenic splendor of the area might be marred by the air and water pollution. Especially concerned about water pollution, resort developers charged that the proposed chemical plant would pollute the Colleton River. They argued that BASF plants in Germany had polluted the Rhine and, in Belgium, the Schelde River. Further, they noted that on BASF's list of proposed expenditures, pollution control was allocated only one million dollars.

The citizens of Beaufort County, in contrast to the Hilton Head Developers, welcomed BASF. They presented the company with a petition bearing over 7,000 signatures endorsing the new plant. As one local businessman commented, "I would say 80 percent of the people in Beaufort County are in favor of BASF. Those who aren't rich." (William D. McDonald, "Youth Corps Looking for Jobs," *The State*, February 23, 1970.)

The manager of BASF's U.S. operations was clearly confronted by an economic and moral dilemma. He knew that preventing massive pollution was virtually impossible and, in any case, outrageously expensive. The eagerness of South Carolina officials for new industry suggested that pollution standards might be "relaxed" for BASF. If it decided to go ahead and build, was the company to push for the minimum pollution control it could get away with under the law? Such a policy might maximize corporate profits and the financial interests of the shareholders, while at the same time it would lower the aesthetic quality of the environment. It might make jobs available to Beaufort County while ignoring the resort industry and the enjoyment of vacationers. Moreover, the long-term effects of dumping chemicals was hard to predict, but past experience did not give the manager a feeling of optimism. Pollution seemed to be not only a business issue, but a *moral* one. But how should the manager sort out, and eventually decide upon, such a moral issue?

To solve his moral problem, BASF's manager might try a variety of strategies. He might, for example, begin by assuming that he has three basic options: (1) Build with minimal pollution control; (2) build with maximal pollution control; or (3) do not build.

Then, he might reason

The consequences of option 1 will be significant but tolerable water pollution, hostility from the Hilton Head Developers, high short-term corporate profits, and satisfied shareholders.

The consequences of option 2 will be unnoticeable pollution, no complaints from the Hilton Head Developers, high pollution-control costs, low profits, and unsatisfied stockholders.

The consequences of 3 will be approval from the Hilton Head Developers, low short-term profits (while a search for a new location is underway), strong disapproval from the local townspeople.

My job from a *moral* perspective is to weigh these consequences and consider which of the alternatives constitutes a maximization of good. Who will benefit from each decision? How many people will be adversely affected and in what ways?

Or the manager might reason

Both BASF Corporation and I are confronted with a variety of *duties, rights,* and *obligations.* First there is the company's obligation to its stockholders, and my duty as manager is to protect the economic interests and rights of our stockholders. Next there are the rights of those Beaufort residents and visitors in the area to clean air and water. Finally there are the rights of other property owners in the area, including the Hilton Head Developers, not to be harmed unreasonably by other industries. There is an implied obligation to future generations to protect the river. And finally, there are broader considerations: Is this an act I would want others to do? What kind of moral example will I be setting?

My job from a *moral* perspective is to balance and assess these duties, rights, and obligations, and determine which have priority.

Finally, the manager might reason

I cannot confront a moral problem from either the abstract perspective of "consequences," or of "duties, rights, and obligations." Instead, I must use a concrete concept of *human nature* to guide my deliberations. Acts that aid persons to develop their potential human nature are morally good; ones that do the opposite are bad.

I believe that the crucial potentialities of human nature include such things as health, knowledge, moral maturity, meaningful employment, political freedom, and self-respect.

My job from a *moral* perspective is to assess the situation in terms of its harmony or disharmony with these basic concepts of human potential.

Notice how different each of these approaches is. The first focuses on the concept of *consequences;* the second on *duties, rights, and obligations;* and the third on *human nature.* Of course, the three methods may overlap; for example, applying the concept of "human nature" in the third approach may necessitate referring to concepts drawn from the first and second, such as "consequences" and "rights," and vice versa. Even so, the approaches reflect three classical types of ethical theory in the history of philosophy. Each has been championed by a well-known traditional philosopher, and most ethical theories can be catagorized under one of the three headings. The first may be called *consequentialism*, the second, *deontology*, and the third, *human nature ethics.*

CONSEQUENTIALISM

As its name implies, a consequentialist theory of ethical reasoning concentrates on the consequences of human actions, and all actions are evaluated in terms of the extent to which they achieve desirable results. Such theories are also frequently labeled *teleological*, a term derived from the Greek word *telos*, which means "end" or "purpose." According to consequentialist theories, the concepts of right, wrong, and duty are subordinated to the concept of the end or purpose of an action.

There are at least two types of consequentialist theory. The first—advocated by only a few consequentialists—is a version of what philosophers call ethical egoism. It construes right action as action whose consequences, considered among all the alternatives, maximizes *my* good—that is, action that benefits *me* the most or harms *me* the least. The second type—advocated by most consequentialists—denies that right action concerns only *me*. Rather, right action must maximize *overall* good; that is, it must maximize good (or minimize bad) from the standpoint of the entire human community. The best-accepted label for this type of consequentialism is *utilitarianism.* This term was coined by the eighteenth-century philosopher Jeremy Bentham, although its best-known proponent was the nineteenth-century English philosopher John Stuart Mill. As Bentham formulated it, the principle of utility states that an action is right if it produces the greatest balance of pleasure or happiness and unhappiness in light of alternative actions. Mill supported a similar principle, using what he called the "proof" of the principle of utility—namely, the recognition that the only proof for something's being desirable is that someone actually desires it. Since everybody desires pleasure or happiness, it follows, according to Mill, that happiness is the most desirable thing. The purpose of moral action is to achieve greatest overall happiness, and actions are evaluated in terms of the extent to which they contribute to this end. The most desirable state of affairs, the greatest good and the goal of morality, said Mill, is the "greatest happiness for the greatest number."

While later utilitarians accept the general framework of Mill's argument, not all utilitarians are hedonists. That is, not all utilitarians equate "the good" with pleasure or happiness. Some utilitarians have argued that in maximizing the "good," one must be concerned not only with maximizing pleasure, but with maximizing other things, such as knowledge, moral maturity, and friendship. Although it could be claimed that such goods also bring pleasure and happiness to their possessor, it is arguable whether their goodness is ultimately *reducible* to whatever pleasure they bring. These philosophers are sometimes called pluralistic utilitarians. Still other philosophers have adapted utilitarianism to modern methods of economic theory by championing what is known as preference utilitarianism. Instead of referring to the maximization of specific goods, such as pleasure or knowledge, preference utilitarians understand the ultimate foundation of goodness to be the set of preferences people actually possess. One person prefers oysters to strawberries; another prefers rock music to Mozart. Each person has a set of preferences, and so long as the set is internally consistent, it makes no sense to label one set morally superior to another. Preference utilitarianism thus interprets right action as that which is optimal among alternatives in terms of everyone's preferences. Disputes, however, rage among preference utilitarians and their critics over how to specify the meaning of *optimal*.

Bentham and Mill thought that utilitarianism was a revolutionary theory, both because it accurately reflected human motivation and because it had clear application to the political and social problems of their day. If one could measure the benefit or harm of any action, rule or law, they believed, one could sort out good and bad social and political legislation as well as good and bad individual actions.

But how, specifically, does one apply the traditional principle of utility? To begin with, one's race, religion, intelligence, or condition of birth is acknowledged to be irrelevant in calculating one's ultimate worth. Each person counts for "one," and no more than "one." Second, in evaluating happiness, one must take into account not only present generations, but ones in the future. In calculating the effects of pollution, for instance, one must measure the possible effects pollution might have on health, genetics, and the supply of natural resources for future generations. Third, pleasure or happiness is measured *en toto* so that the thesis does not reduce to the idea that "one ought to do what makes the most persons happy." Utilitarianism does not reduce to a dictatorship of majority interests. One person's considerable unhappiness might outweigh the minor pleasures of many other persons added together. Utilitarians also consider the long-term consequences for single individuals. For instance, it might be pleasurable to drink a full bottle of wine every evening, but the long-term drawbacks of such a habit might well outweigh its temporary pleasures.

Finally, according to many utilitarians (such as Mill), some pleasures are *qualitatively* better than others. Intellectual pleasure, for example, is said to be higher than physical pleasure. "Better to be Socrates unsatisfied," writes Mill, "than a pig satisfied." The reasons that drove Mill to formulate this qualitative distinction among pleasures are worth noting. Since Mill believed that the optimal situation was one of "greatest happiness for the greatest number," than what was he to say about a world of people living at the zenith of merely *physical* happiness? If science could invent a wonder drug, like the "soma" in Aldous Huxley's *Brave New World,* that provided a permanent state of drugged happiness (without even a hangover), would the consequence be a perfect world? Mill believed not, and to remedy this difficulty in his theory, he introduced *qualitative levels* of happiness. For example, he said that the happiness of understanding Plato is "higher" than that of drinking three martinis. But how was Mill to say *which* pleasures were higher? Here he retreated to an ingenious proposal: When deciding which of two pleasures is higher, one should poll the group of persons who are experienced—that is, who know *both* pleasures. Their decision will indicate which is the higher pleasure. Ah, but might the majority decision not be wrong? Here Mill provides no clear answer.

Modern-day utilitarians divide themselves roughly into two groups: *act utilitarians* and *rule utilitarians*. An *act* utilitarian believes that the principle of utility should be applied to individual acts. Thus one measures the consequences of each *individual action* according to whether it maximizes good. For example, suppose a certain community were offered the opportunity to receive a great deal of wealth in the form of a gift. The only stipulation was that the community force some of its citizens with ugly, deteriorated homes to repair and beautify them. Next, suppose the community held an election to decide whether to accept the gift. An act utilitarian would analyze the problem of whether to vote for or against the proposal from the standpoint of the *individual voter*. Would an individual's vote to accept the gift be more likely to maximize the community's overall good than would a vote to the contrary?

A *rule* utilitarian, on the other hand, believes that instead of considering the results of specific actions, one must weigh the consequences of adopting a *general rule* exemplified by that action. According to the rule utilitarian, one should act according to a general rule which, if adopted, would maximize good. For example, in the hypothetical case of the community deciding whether to accept a gift, a rule utilitarian might adopt the rule "Never vote in a way that lowers the self-respect of a given class of citizens." She might accept this rule because of the general unhappiness that would ensue if society systematically treated some persons as second-class citizens. Here the focus is on the general rule and not on the individual act.

Critics raise objections to utilitarianism. Perhaps the most serious objection is that it is unable to account for justice. Because the utilitarian concentrates on the consequences of an action for a majority, the employment of the principle of utility can be argued to allow injustice for a small minority. For example, if overall goodness were maximized in the long run by making slaves of 2 percent of the population, utilitarianism seemingly is forced to condone slavery. But clearly this is unjust. Utilitarianism's obvious response is that such slavery will not, as a matter of empirical fact, maximize goodness. Rule utilitarians, as we have seen, can argue that society should embrace the rule "Never enslave others," because following such a principle will, in the long run, maximize goodness. Even so, the battle continues between utilitarians and their critics. Can utilitarianism account for the widely held moral conviction that injustice to a minority is wrong *regardless* of the consequences? The answer is hotly contested.

Another criticism concerns the determination of the good to be maximized. Any consequentialist has the problem of identifying and ranking whatever is to be maximized. For a utilitarian such as Mill, as we have seen, the problem involves distinguishing between higher and lower pleasures. But for pluralistic utilitarians, a similar problem exists: What is the basis for selecting, for example, friendship and happiness as goods to be maximized and not, say, aesthetic sensitivity? And even granted that this problem can be solved, there is the future problem of arbitrating trade-offs between goods such as happiness and friendship when they *conflict*. When one is forced to choose between enhancing happiness and enhancing friendship, which gets priority? And under what conditions?

An interesting fact about consequentialist reasoning is that most of us employ it to some degree in ordinary decisions. We weigh the consequences of alternatives in choosing colleges, in deciding on a career, in hiring and promoting others, and in many other judgments. We frequently weigh good consequences over bad ones and predict the long- and short-term effects of our choices. We often even cite consequentialist-style principles—for example, "No one should choose a college where he or she will be unhappy," or, "No one should pollute the environment when his or her action harms others."

However, for a variety of reasons including the objections to utilitarianism mentioned earlier, some philosophers refuse to acknowledge consequentialism as an adequate theory of ethics. They argue that the proper focus for ethical judgments should not be consequences, but moral *precepts* —that is, the rules, norms, and principles we use to guide our actions. Such philosophers are known as deontologists, and the next section will examine their views.

DEONTOLOGY

The term *deontological* comes from the Greek word for "duty," and what is crucial according to the deontologist are the rules and principles that guide actions. We shall discuss here two approaches to deontological ethical reasoning that have profoundly influenced ethics. The first is that of the eighteenth-century philosopher Immanuel Kant and his followers. This approach focuses on duty and universal rules to determine right actions. The second—actually a subspecies of deontological reasoning—is known as the "social contract" approach. It focuses not on individual decision making, but on the general social principles that rational persons in certain ideal situations would agree upon and adopt.

Kantian Deontology

Kant believed that ethical reasoning should concern activities that are rationally motivated and should utilize precepts that apply universally to all human actions. To this end, he opens his treatise on ethics by declaring

> It is impossible to conceive anything at all in the world, . . . which can be taken as good without qualification except a *good* will.[2]

This statement sums up much of what Kant wants to say about ethics and is worth unraveling. What Kant means is that the only thing that can be good or worthwhile without any provisos or stipulations is an action of the will freely motivated for the right reasons. Other goods such as wealth, beauty, and intelligence are certainly valuable, but they are not good *without qualification* because they have the potential to create both good and bad effects. Wealth, beauty, and intelligence can be bad when they are used for purely selfish ends. Even human happiness—which Mill held as the highest good—can, according to Kant, create complacency, disinterest, and excessive self-assurance under certain conditions.

According to Kant, reason is the faculty that can aid in the discovery of correct moral principles; this it is *reason,* not *inclination,* that should guide the will. When reason guides the will, Kant calls the resulting actions ones done from "duty." Kant's use of the term *duty,* turns out to be less formidable than it first appears. Kant is simply saying that a purely good and free act of the will is one done not merely because you have an *inclination* to do it, but because you have the right reasons for doing it. For example, suppose you discover a wallet belonging to a stranger. Kant would say that despite one's inclination to keep the money (which the stranger may not even need), one should return it. This is an act you know is right despite your inclinations. Kant also believes you should return the wallet even when you believe the *consequences* of not returning it are better. Here his views are at sharp odds with consequentialism. Suppose that the stranger is known for her stinginess, and you plan to donate the money to a children's hospital. No matter. For Kant, you must return the wallet. Thus the moral worth lies in the act itself and not in either your happiness or the consequences brought about by the act. Acts are good because they are done for the sake of what is right and not because of the consequences they might produce.

But how do I know what my duty is? While it may be clear that one should return a wallet, there are other circumstances in which one's duty is less evident. Suppose you are in a six-person lifeboat at sea with five others and a seventh person swims up? What is one's duty here? And how does one even know that what one *thinks* is right *is* right? To settle such problems, Kant claims that duty is more than doing merely what you "feel" is right. Duty is acting with *respect for other rational beings.* It almost goes without saying, then, that "acting from duty" is not to be interpreted as action done in obedience to local, state, or national laws, since these can be good or bad. Instead, "duty" is linked to the idea of universal principles that should govern all our actions.

But is there any principle that can govern *all* human beings? Kant believes the answer is yes, and he calls the highest such principle the "categorical imperative." He formulates the categorical imperative in three ways (although we shall only consider two formulations here). The first formulation, roughly translated, is

> One ought only to act such that the principle of one's act could become a universal law of human action in a world in which one would hope to live.

For example, one would want to live in a world where people followed the principle "Return property that belongs to others." Therefore one should return the stranger's wallet. We do not, however, want to live in a world where everyone lies. Therefore, one should not adopt the principle "Lie whenever it seems helpful."

The second formulation of the categorical imperative is

> One ought to treat others as having intrinsic value in themselves, and *not* merely as means to achieve one's ends.

In other words, one should respect every person as a rational and free being. Hitler treated one group of persons as nonpersons in order to achieve his own ends, and thus he acted contrary to the categorical imperative. Another instance of treating persons as means would occur if a teacher looked up the grade records of new students to determine how to assign grades in her own class. She would be treating students as if they had no control over their destinies. Such actions are immoral according to Kant because they fail to respect the inherent dignity of rational beings.

Ethical reasoning for Kant implies adopting principles of action and evaluating one's actions in terms of those principles. Even Kant grants that the evaluation is sometimes difficult. For example, there is the problem of striking the proper level of generality in choosing a principle. A principle that read, "If one is named John Doe and attends Big State University and has two sisters, then he should borrow fifty dollars without intending to repay it," is far too specific. On the other hand, the principle "You should always pay your debts" might be too general, since it would require that a starving man repay the only money he possesses to buy a loaf of bread. Because of the problem of striking the proper degree of generality, many modern deontologists have reformulated Kant's basic question to read: "Could I wish that everyone in the world would follow this principle *under relevantly similar conditions?*"

As with utilitarianism, critics challenge deontological reasoning. Some assert that fanatics such as Hitler could at least *believe* that the rule "Persecute Jews whenever possible" is one that the world should live by. Similarly, a thief might universalize the principle "Steal whenever you have a good opportunity." Moreover, a strict interpretation of deontological ethical reasoning is said to allow no exceptions to a universal principle. Such strict adherence to universal principles might encourage moral rigidity and might fail to reflect the diversity of responses required by complex moral situations. Finally, critics argue that, in a given case, two principles may conflict without there being a clear way to decide which principle or rule should take precedence. Jean-Paul Sartre tells of his dilemma during World War II when he was forced to choose between staying to comfort his ill and aging mother, and fighting for the freedom of France. Two principles seemed valid: "Give aid to your father and mother," and "Contribute to the cause of freedom." But with conflicting principles, how is one to choose? Nevertheless, deontological ethical reasoning represents a well-respected and fundamentally distinctive mode of ethical reasoning, one which, like consequentialism, appears in the deliberations of ordinary persons as well as philosophers. We have all heard actions condemned by the comment, "what would it be like if everyone did that?"

The Contractarian Alternative

Kant assumes that the categorial imperative is something all rational individuals can discover and agree upon. A different version of deontology is offered by many philosophers who focus less on the actions of individuals, and more on the principles that govern society at large. These include two philosophers whose writings appear in our book: the seventeenth-century political philosopher John Locke and the twentieth-century American philosopher John Rawls. They and others try to establish universal principles of a just society through what might be called "social contract thought experiments." They ask us to imagine what it would be like to live in a situation where there are no laws, no social conventions, and no political state. In this so-called state of nature, we imagine that rational persons gather to formulate principles or rules to govern political and social communities. Such rules would resemble principles derived through the categorical imperative in that they are presumably principles to which every rational person would agree and which would hold universally.

Locke and Rawls differ in their approach to establishing rules or principles of justice, and the difference illustrates two distinct forms of contractarian reasoning. Locke argues from a "natural rights" position, while Rawls argues from a "reasonable person" position. Locke claims that every person is born with, and possesses, certain basic rights that are "natural." These rights are inherent to a person's nature, and they are possessed by every one equally. Like other inherent traits, they cannot be taken away. They are, in the words of the Declaration of Independence, "inalienable." When rational persons meet to formulate principles to govern the formation of social and political communities, they construct a social contract that is the basis for an agreement between themselves and their government, and whose rules protect natural rights. Rights, then, become deontological precepts by which one forms and evaluates rules, constitutions, government, and socioeconomic systems. While many philosophers disagree with Locke's view that each of us has inherent or *natural* rights, many do utilize a theory of human rights as the basis for justifying and evaluating political institutions.

Rawls adopts a different perspective. He does not begin from a natural rights position. Instead, he asks which principles of justice rational persons would formulate if they were behind a "veil of ignorance"—that is, if each person knew nothing about who he or she was. That is, one would not know whether one were old or young, male or female, rich or poor, highly motivated or lazy, or anything about one's personal status in society. Unable to predict which principles, if picked, will favor them personally, Rawls argues, persons will be forced to choose principles that are fair to all.

Rawls and Locke are not in perfect agreement about which principles would be adopted in such hypothetical situations, and more will be said about their views later in the book. For now it is important to remember that the social contract approach maintains a deontological character. It is used to formulate principles of justice that apply universally. Some philosophers note, however, that from an original position in a "state of nature" or behind a "veil of ignorance," rational persons *could* adopt consequentialist principles as rules for a just society. Thus, while the social contract approach is deontological in style, the principles it generates are not necessarily ones that are incompatible with consequentialism.

In the moral evaluations of business, all deontologists—contractarians included—would ask questions such as the following:

1. Are the rules fair to everyone?
2. Do the rules hold universally even with the passage of time?
3. Is every person treated with equal respect?

What may be missing from a deontological approach to ethical reasoning is a satisfactory means of coping with valid exceptions to general rules. Under what circumstances, if any, are exceptions allowed? Deontologists believe that they can answer this question, but their solutions vary. Suffice it to say that deontologists, just as utilitarians, have not convinced everyone.

HUMAN NATURE ETHICS

According to some contemporary philosophers, the preceding two modes of ethical reasoning exhaust all possible modes. That is to say, all theories can be classified as either teleological or deontological. Whether this is true cannot be settled here, but it will be helpful to introduce briefly what some philosophers consider to be a third category, namely the *human nature* approach.

A *human nature* approach assumes that all humans have inherent capacities that constitute the ultimate basis for all ethical claims. Actions are evaluated in terms of whether they promote or hinder, coincide with, or conflict with these capacities. One of the most famous proponents of this theory was the Greek philosopher Aristotle. In Aristotle's opinion, human beings have inherent *potentialities,* and thus human development turns out to be the struggle for self-actualization, or in other words, the perfection of inherent human nature. Consider the acorn. It has the natural potential to become a sturdy oak tree. Its natural drive is not to become an elm or a cedar or even a stunted oak, but to become the most robust oak tree possible. Diseased or stunted oak trees are simply deficient; they are instances of things in nature whose potential has not been fully developed. Similarly, according to Aristotle, persons are born with inherent potentialities. Persons, like acorns, naturally are oriented to actualize their potentialities, and for them this means more than merely developing their physical potential. It also means developing their mental, moral, and social potential. Thus, human beings in this view are seen as basically good; evil is understood as a deficiency that occurs when one is unable to fulfill one's natural capacities.

It is important to understand that the concept of human nature need not be an individualistic one. According to Aristotle, persons are "social" by nature and cannot be understood apart from the larger community in which they participate. "Man," Aristotle wrote, is a "social animal." For Aristotle, then, fulfilling one's natural constitution implies developing wisdom, generosity, and self-restraint, all of which help to make one a good member of the community.

The criterion for judging the goodness of any action is whether or not the action is compatible with one's inherent human capacities. Actions that enhance human capacities are good; those that deter them are bad unless they are the best among generally negative alternatives. For example, eating nothing but starches is unhealthy, but it is clearly preferable to starving.

This theory puts great emphasis on the nature of persons and obviously, how one understands that "nature" will be the key to determining both what counts as a right action and how one defines the proper end of human action in general. Aristotle argued that intelligence and wisdom are uniquely human potentialities and consequently that intellectual virtue is the highest virtue. The life of contemplation, he believed, is the best sort of life, in part because it represents the highest fulfillment of human nature. Moral virtue, also crucial in Aristotle's theory, involves the rational control of one's desires. In action where a choice is possible, one exercises moral virtue by restraining harmful desires and cultivating beneficial ones. The development of virtue requires the cultivation of good habits, and this in turn leads Aristotle to emphasize the importance of good upbringing and education.

One problem said to affect human nature theories is that they have difficulty justifying the supposition that human beings *do* have specific inherent capacities and that these capacities are the same for all humans. Further, critics claim that it is difficult to warrant the assumption that humans are basically good. Perhaps the famous psychoanalyst Sigmund Freud is correct in his assertion that at bottom we are all naturally aggressive and selfish. Third, critics complain that it is difficult to employ this theory in ethical reasoning, since it appears to lack clear-cut rules and principles for use in moral decision making. Obviously, any well-argued human nature ethic will take pains to spell out the aspects of human nature which, when actualized, constitute the ultimate ground for moral judgments.

CONCLUSION

The three approaches to ethical reasoning we have discussed—consequentialism, deontology, and human nature ethics—all present theories of ethical reasoning distinguished in terms of their basic methodological elements. Each represents a type or model of moral reasoning that is applicable to practical decisions in concrete situations. Consider, for example, the case study with which we began our discussion, involving BASF and its proposed new plant. As it happened, BASF chose option 3 and decided to build elsewhere. In making his decision, did the BASF manager actually use any or all of the methods described above? Although we cannot know the answer to this question, it is clear, as we saw earlier, that each method was applicable to his problem. Indeed, the three methods of moral reasoning are sufficiently broad that each is applicable to the full range of problems confronting human moral experience. The question of which method, if any, is superior to the others must be left for another time. The intention of this essay is not to substitute for a thorough study of traditional ethical theories—something for which there is no substitute—but to introduce the reader to basic modes of ethical reasoning that will help to analyze the ethical problems in business that arise in the remainder of the book.

NOTES

1. "BASF Corporation vs. The Hilton Head Island Developers," in *Business and Society*, Robert D. Hay, et. al., eds. (Cincinnati: South-Western Publishing Co., 1984), pp. 100–12.

2. Immanuel Kant, *Groundwork of the Metaphysic of Morals*, trans. H. J. Paton (New York: Harper & Row, 1948, 1956), p. 61.

The Case Method

Thomas Donaldson

Professor Gragg of the Harvard Business School, himself a master of the case method, once said the belief that knowledge can simply be "told" and passed on is "the great delusion of the ages."[1] Gragg's remark concurs with the view of Socrates, the Greek philosopher, whose well-known style of teaching was never a one-way street, with the instructor talking and the student listening, but rather a two-way exchange in which the student actively participated by questioning, searching, and answering. Thus the fundamental basis of the case method, the belief that knowledge cannot simply be "told," is in step with an age-old norm of good teaching. And it is a norm that for centuries has been recognized as valid by philosophers. One should not be surprised, then, to learn that the case method is gaining wide acceptance even outside schools of business. Philosophers, theologians, and social scientists are using it to confront issues of public policy, distributive justice, and ethics.

The purpose of this essay is to describe the case method, its strategies and aims, and to apply it to the teaching of ethics.

THE CASE METHOD: A DIFFERENT STYLE OF LEARNING

"You can lead a person to the university," someone once quipped, "but you can't make him think." What too often passes for learning is the repetition of facts by students during standardized exams. The case method, however, does not allow a student the luxury of memorizing a body of accepted wisdom. Rather, it forces the student to confront a set of facts that demands analysis; and these facts, the student soon discovers, are not understood by the application of memorized truths.

Thus, a philosophy of education undergirds the case method—namely, that people must be taught to think well in the presence of new situations and to arrive at reasoned courses of action. In this way the method emphasizes *judgment* as much as *understanding*. Moreover, it attempts to develop skills of judgment that can be applied to situations in the real world. Although it varies from practitioner to practitioner, the case method may be defined as a method of instruction that confronts students with descriptions of realistic human events, and then requires the students to analyze, evaluate, and make recommendations about those events.

What is known today as the case method began at Harvard University in 1908 with the opening of the new business school. The business school's first catalog stated that the "problem method" would be utilized "as far as practicable." After years of struggle and experimentation, the case method reached maturity at Harvard from 1919 to 1942 under the encouragement of the dean of the business school, Wallace Donham. It was during these years that the method became the trademark of the Harvard Business School, a position it retains to this day.

THE ROLE OF THE INSTRUCTOR

Just as there is no such thing as a "typical" case, there is no such thing as a "typical" case-method teaching style. Each instructor develops his or her own questions, responses, and style. Certain pedagogical virtues, however, are obvious, such as approachability, enthusiasm, and articulateness.[2]

The responsibilities of the instructor using a case-method approach have been summed up as follows:

1. Assign cases for discussion
2. Act as a responsible member of the group delegated to provoke argumentative thinking
3. Guide discussions through remarks and questions toward points of major importance
4. Take a final position on the viewpoints at the end of the discussion *if* the instructor chooses[3]

Sometimes an instructor has a remarkable teaching experience in which it is necessary only to ask an opening question—"Mr. Y, would you begin our discussion?"—and the class is off and running. More frequently, the instructor must help the discussion through contributions of his or her own. To accomplish this, the instructor may

1. Ask further questions
2. Restate and reconstruct what has been said
3. Voice his or her own opinions and draw upon his or her knowledge of fact[4]

To open a discussion, an instructor may ask such questions as

Do you see a problem in this case? If so, what is it?
Would someone volunteer to give us a brief sketch of the facts in the case?
(Or simply) What's happening in this case?

Once the discussion is underway, the instructor may invite a student to play the part of one of the managers who has a central role in the case. Thus, the instructor might ask, "What would you do if you were Mr. Jones?" Indeed, unless an instructor pushes a student to speak in terms of decisions, the advantage of the case method may be undercut as the discussion regresses into a fragmented series of general observations.

Discussion leaders frequently summarize or attempt to interpret a student's remark. Doing so has a double advantage: It helps to confirm what the student actually meant, and it helps to ensure that other students interpreted the remark correctly. In a surprisingly large number of cases, the student will want to qualify a remark once it has been interpreted by the instructor. This has the welcome consequence of encouraging the student to reflect upon both the nature of the view being expressed and the reasons for it.

Professor Andrews has summarized the role of the instructor as follows:

The instructor provides the impromptu services which any group discussion requires. He keeps the proceedings orderly. He should be able to ask questions which . . . advance . . . group thinking and at the same time reveal the relevance of talk that has gone before. . . . He needs the sense of timing which tells him that a discussion is not moving fast enough to make good use of available time or is racing away from the comprehension of half the class. . . . He exercises control over an essentially "undirected" activity, but at the same time he keeps out of the way. . . . Since unpredictable developments always distinguish real learning, he examines his class rather than his subject. His workshop is not the study but the classroom. . . . He must himself be a student.[5]

An instructor may block a direct question from a student. When a student asks a specific question about the material, the instructor may decide that to answer the question would stifle the thinking of other students. Hence the instructor may reply by saying "Well, what does the class think?" or "My opinion is X, but is that really the right opinion?" Here the attempt is to turn the question into a catalyst rather than a retardant of the ongoing discussion.

The following are sample questions asked by case-method instructors:

> Where does this idea lead?
> You said X. May I add Y?
> Do others disagree?
> Do you mean X?
> Do you have more to say about Y?
> Do you think that is true in all cases?
> How does that apply to the situation in the case?
> Is your point related to Ms. Y's?
> What does that have to do with the bigger question?[6]

An instructor can do more than ask questions. He or she can identify unstated assumptions that one of the participants is making and hold them up to the class for inspection. Or if a discussion is really dragging, the instructor may frankly ask the class what's wrong and attempt to generate discussion about the *process* of the discussion itself. (Sometimes this will have surprising results.) Blackboards can be used to list options, relevant facts, pros and cons, and assumptions.

When a discussion is well under way, it is not unusual for an instructor to retire to an inconspicuous place and simply observe.

THE ROLE OF THE STUDENT

In the case method, the active cooperation of the student is essential. Previous schooling habituates a student to the role of receiver. In the case method, this previous schooling must be undone; the student must learn the habit of being active, of being a force in the teaching process. Hence the student must master a number of skills. First he or she must learn to synthesize material on his or her own. Although infrequently an instructor's summary of the main lines of the preceding discussion will help the student to integrate important aspects of the discussion, ordinarily the act of synthesis must be undertaken by the student. Equally important, the student must learn to separate irrelevant from relevant information. (Cases are frequently constructed intentionally to contain both kinds.) Finally, the student must invest sufficient time in preparing a case to make the discussion productive. With other methods, a failure to prepare is problematic; with the case method, it is disastrous.

Sometimes students benefit from discussing a case in a small, preclass group. In such a group they often discover crucial items around which ordinary group discussions will turn; moreover they gain experience in the presentation of ideas.

Discouragement is routine when students begin the case method. They jump to the conclusion that they are making no progress because they are accustomed to defining "progress" differently. After discussing the first case or two, they recognize that not all issues have been resolved, and may be left with a sense of incompleteness, like hearing a piece of music with no resolving chord. Gradually, however, they will experience a growing confidence in their ability to analyze complex case materials and, in turn, a growing conviction of the value of the case method. At this stage it is not uncommon for the original skepticism to turn to an uncritical endorsement of the method.

THE CASE METHOD APPLIED TO ETHICS

Any given method is related to the function and object of the method's activity. Thus, we should begin by noting—as Aristotle and others have before us—that the end or aim of ethical enquiry is different from that of empirical enquiry. Whereas the goal of empirical enquiry is factual or empirical knowledge, the goal of ethical enquiry is ethical insight. By "ethical insight" I mean insight about good and bad, right and wrong, and permissible and impermissible behavior. We want to be able to distinguish false or irrational convictions (e.g., that of first-century Romans that when a slave owner was killed by one of his slaves, *all* of his slaves should be executed) from correct ones (e.g., the more modern conviction that this Roman custom was unfair). Although ethics intersects frequently with matters of taste, and hence involves a certain amount of relativity, the very possibility of ethical insight recognizes a difference in the truth status of the belief that torturing children for sport is permissible, and the belief that it is not.

Ethical and empirical knowledge must be distinguished because although they both may be kinds of knowledge, they not only have different subjects but different epistemological foundations. The belief that salt is soluble in water is a piece of empirical knowledge because it is known through experience. It depicts a "fact," and if one were to doubt it, the proper response would be to take a pinch of salt and throw it into water. But the belief that patricide is wrong is an *ethical* belief, not an empirical one, and doubters may well not be persuaded by undertaking the "experiment" of killing their fathers. Indeed, it is difficult to see just what killing one's father could possibly "prove" about the rightness or wrongness of patricide.

The reasoning necessary to make sense of ethical issues has a different logic from that of empirical reasoning. Consider the traditional distinction offered by philosophers such as Aristotle and Aquinas between practical and theoretical reasoning. The end of theoretical reasoning is a general concept, while that of practical reasoning is an action. Thus, using theoretical reasoning I might conclude from the fact that all ravens I have seen are black to the general proposition that all ravens are black. Or I might reason from the premises that all healthy corporations have a strong corporate culture, and that the XYZ Corporation is a healthy corporation, to the deductive conclusion that the XYZ Corporation has a strong corporate culture. Both would be pieces of theoretical reasoning.

However, in practical reasoning, the tables are turned. I reason from the acknowledgment of a general value or desire to a practical action, and I do so typically through a process of means-ends reasoning. Thus, given that I hold the value of "honoring valid contracts," and that I believe that giving you a check in the amount of $10,000 is a means of "honoring a valid contract," my reasoning may lead me to write you a check in the amount of $10,000.

Notice that I have employed means-ends reasoning; that is, I reason that writing the check is a *means* of honoring the contract, but that my process of reasoning is not deductive in nature. The necessary conclusion that is characteristic of deductive reasoning is absent in practical reasoning. For although writing a check for $10,000 is one means of achieving my value, it may not be the only means. I might similarly honor the contract by giving you $10,000 in cash, or by arranging to release you from a prior debt. So whereas the conclusion that "XYZ Corporation has a strong corporate culture" is necessarily true if the premises, "All healthy corporations have a strong corporate culture" and "XYZ Corporation is a healthy corporation" are true, it does not follow necessarily that *if* I hold the value of honoring valid contracts and *if* I believe that writing you a check is a means of honoring a valid contract, I *will* write you a check. It does not even necessarily follow that I *should* write you a check.

Practical reasoning occurs in a variety of contexts, not only those dealing with ethics. It occurs whenever one employs means-ends reasoning as a guide for action. Yet ethical reasoning, in contrast to nonethical reasoning, has another identifying feature: It necessarily involves evaluation of ends and principles as well as means. If I assume that I want to sell a given piece of property and reason about the best means of selling it, I am using a practical, though not necessarily ethical, mode of reasoning. Ethical reasoning also requires that I deliberate about the act of selling itself, and that I evaluate whether the end of selling the piece of property is morally justified. This feature adds to the complexity of business decisions enormously. For insofar as we can assume that the end or guiding principle of a corporation is the maximization of profit, our reasoning about corporate behavior is simplified. Moral analysis, however, requires that at least from time to time the corporate goal of profit maximization itself come under scrutiny.

Let us now apply our conclusions about ethical reasoning to the matter of teaching business ethics through cases.

The first thing to notice is that adapting the case method to ethics is relatively easy because this method emphasizes practical reasoning, which is a crucial component of ethical reasoning. Cases traditionally have been used to hone a student's judgment in concrete business situations. They emphasize means-ends reasoning and can be used to do the same when the ends are not only market share and profits, but fairness and corporate integrity. A major pedagogical difference between traditional business subjects and that of ethics, however, stems from ethics' concern with ends and principles. Because ethics requires investigation of values to be achieved as well as the means used to achieve them, cases must be adapted to evaluate broader issues. As we shall see, this implies a difference in the structure of cases and the style of pedagogy.

To begin with, teaching ethics requires a different selection of cases. Cases must be structured to raise issues about ends and principles, and this implies a backing away from the traditional insistence, associated with the Harvard case method, that every case must pose a decision-making problem confronted by an individual manager. A case dealing with the FDA's decision to ban the manufacture of Laetrile may not yield to the traditional format of "What should manager A do now?" Yet it may be a good case nonetheless if it confronts students with some of the difficult trade-offs between the liberties of individual actors in a market, and the (supposed) well-being of consumers.

Nor is the enormous detail championed by some case-method practitioners always necessary. Whereas practical reasoning always occurs in the context of a maze of facts, reasoning about ends sometimes thrives in rarefied atmospheres. Consider, for example, the following "case," which is only two sentences long:

> Two equally qualified candidates, one of whom is a black female and the other a white male, have applied for a job. Should the prospective employer hire the black female?

Admirably brief, these two sentences could serve as the focus of a highly profitable, hour-long discussion.

Cases alone are not sufficient when teaching business ethics and should be augmented by theoretical material. The examination of ends and principles is enhanced by reference to the inquiries of others. Whereas it may be possible to gain a reasonable sense of good marketing practice merely through an analysis of cases (although I have my doubts even here), it is nearly impossible to do so in the case of ethics. Again, unlike empirical disciplines, basic ethical knowledge owes little to experience per se. Like mathematics, ethics requires sustained reflection on specific concepts. Thus, just as teaching mathematics would be impossible through an approach involving nothing but cases, so too would ethics. One benefits greatly by examining the theoretical investigations of specialists in the field of ethics, and it follows that any casebook should be supplemented by theoretical materials.

Even as the structure of cases must be adapted to the teaching of ethics, so too must the instructor's teaching style. The "neutrality" of the instructor is a well-respected fixture of the case method in its ordinary setting. Should instructors be similarly neutral when teaching ethics? Although the answer is somewhat a matter of opinion, there seems little reason for sacrificing openness in ethical contexts. We are reminded of the long-standing Socratic irony: Socrates believed that virtue could not be taught, yet he spent his life teaching virtue. The solution to the seeming paradox, of course, is that Socrates believed that one teaches ethics in a quite different manner than one teaches other disciplines. One does not convey facts to the student; instead one plays the role of midwife, attempting to engage the student in a process of reflection that will yield ethical understanding. The truths of ethics cannot be drummed into one's head; rather they must instead be discovered and respected by oneself. Otherwise, they cannot be "known" in a meaningful sense.

Because of this, the instructor must struggle to preserve his or her own openness in the face of the student's own investigations. But openness should not be confused with moral relativism. As the philosopher Ralph Barton Perry notes, it "is easy to raise doubts, to point out the ignorance and conflicting evidence that beset the mind on every side. It is well to do this and an honest and trained mind will do it . . . (but) if beliefs are demolished, they should be built again, or others built in their place."[7]

Openness does not imply that there are no givens in ethics. As in any practical sphere, some things can be assumed: We can assume that murder, torture, and the intentional harming of innocents is bad, and that fairness and happiness are good. Documents such as the United Nation's *Universal Declaration of Human Rights* are good examples of how much we have in common even with peoples of distant lands and different tastes. Signed by virtually every country in the world, the *Declaration* lays down a basic floor of values that deserve the name "universal": rights to freedom, adequate medical care, safe working conditions, participation in government, and the ownership of property. So too, an instructor teaching ethics can make certain basic assumptions about values without compromising his pedagogical openness.

In empirical science, success implies that we have discovered the structure of the subject—and finally of the world itself—by perception and experiment. In ethical theory, success implies that we in some sense create the structure of the world, and that we do so in the image of a design that is beautiful and not ugly. As the German philosopher Immanuel Kant once remarked, "Things in nature act according to laws; only people act in accordance with the *concept* of laws." In business, people should be guided by concepts not only related to profitability and efficiency, but of professional integrity, responsibility, and fairness. The latter concepts demand an attention to ends and principles that is uncharacteristic of traditional case-method technique. Thus case-method instructors must make a concession to the unique demands of the discipline of ethics.

SHORTCOMINGS OF THE CASE METHOD

The case method is not foolproof. Like any other method, it is susceptible to the foibles and failings of those who use it and, badly handled, produces classroom disasters. At its worst, the method becomes a boring exposure to the prejudices of others.

Cases necessarily oversimplify business situations. Whereas cases can imitate reality by demanding decisions on the basis of incomplete facts (no real-world decision maker has *all* the facts), cases are at odds with reality in presenting a "static" rather than a dynamic decision-making context. A case presents a situation in which the action has already occurred, but everyday situations unfold gradually, and every hour brings fresh information to the decision maker. Hence the skills of knowing when to seek new information, and of knowing when the proper moment has arrived to make a decision, are not developed by the case method.

Essential to a good case discussion is adequate discussion time. A case done hurriedly is an unrewarding experience in which most of the analysis is either superficial or wrong. At first, students may find the discussion of many problems in a short time stimulating. But soon the frustration of approaching case after case without in-depth analysis will bring discouragement with the entire method.

Finally, although the case method is an excellent method for most students, one or two students may benefit little if at all. However, this is not a characteristic drawback of the case method per se, since every approach to teaching misses some students. Indeed, a special advantage of the case method is that it can bring to life a joy in learning for students who have been turned off by traditional methods.

STRUCTURING THE LEARNING EXPERIENCE

The following are suggestions for designing a case discussion process.

Lecturing in Conjunction with Cases

Depending on the style and preference of a given instructor, a lecture may precede or follow a case discussion. Most instructors in business ethics courses use cases only as one part of their course, with lectures and discussions of theoretical material constituting the remaining parts.

Time

A case may occupy a full class period or, in the instance of exceedingly long and complicated cases, two or more periods. Two or three short cases can sometimes be discussed in an hour. Even the shortest of cases (perhaps a paragraph or two in length) will usually require twenty minutes of discussion time.

Call Lists

Some instructors work entirely with volunteers, but others call on specific students, especially in the beginning, to get things moving. Calling on students increases pressure on them to be prepared, although some instructors and students find such pressure uncomfortable and distracting. Of those who do call on students, many use "call lists" containing the names of participants and their frequency of participation. Near the end of a discussion, an instructor may stop recognizing volunteers and move to call on those who haven't yet participated.

Assigning Additional Work

The usual assignment for students is to read and study the case carefully. With complicated cases, instructors sometimes ask for a brief written analysis to be submitted on the day of the discussion.

Role Playing

Role playing is a device sometimes used to simulate a living situation. Choosing an opportune moment, the instructor invites a student (or students) to assume the role of a participant in the case. In a case dealing with government regulation, for example, one student may remark that the corporation's best option is to stall the regulatory agency. The teacher, knowing that other students do not agree with this strategy, may ask, "Does anyone want to play the role of the regulator?" When someone accepts the invitation and responds directly to the student who advocates stalling, the former student has a chance to respond directly to the regulator. Such exchanges can enliven a discussion and reveal difficulties that otherwise might be glossed over.

Concluding Evaluation

At the end of a discussion, some instructors will ask for a vote among various options that have been explored in the discussion. This is not to affirm that correct answers are simple products of democratic vote, but to indicate how others have interpreted the points made in the discussion.

Grading

The method of grading, of course, is the prerogative of the instructor. Most instructors, however, try to form a general impression of a student's performance and then record it either after each class discussion or at one or two points during the semester.

Students may also be given exams that ask them to analyze cases in a written essay. In ethics courses where theoretical material is being covered in addition to cases, it is common to ask students to analyze a case by using concepts drawn from the theoretical readings.

The case method, though not foolproof, offers clear rewards. Socrates' insight that moral truth cannot simply "be told" is reflected in the case method's emphasis on analysis, discussion, and decision making. Like any method, it is subject to the failings of its practitioners. Like any method, it must be carefully adapted to the special territory it covers. But handled properly it can spark the search for skills and values of utmost human import. It can, perhaps more effectively than any other method, demonstrate the need for intellectual solutions to practical problems.

NOTES

1. Charles I. Gragg, "Because Wisdom Can't Be Told," in *The Case Method at the Harvard Business School*, ed. Malcolm P. McNair (New York: McGraw-Hill, Inc., 1954), p. 10.

2. Kenneth R. Andrews, "The Role of the Instructor in the Case Method," in *The Case Method at the Harvard Business School*, ed. Malcolm P. McNair (New York: McGraw-Hill, Inc., 1954), p. 99.

3. Gragg, "Wisdom Can't Be Told," p. 12.

4. Andrews, "Role of the Instructor," p. 105.

5. Ibid., 98–99.

6. Ibid., 105–6.

7. Ralph Barton Perry, *The Citizen Decides: A Guide to Responsible Thinking in Time of Crisis* (Bloomington: Indiana University Press, 1951), Chapter VII.

SUGGESTED SUPPLEMENTARY READINGS

ANDREWS, KENNETH R., ed. *The Case Method of Teaching Human Relations and Administration.* Cambridge, Mass.: Harvard University Press, 1953.

ANDREWS, KENNETH R. "The Role of the Instructor in the Case Method," in *The Case Method at the Harvard Business School*, ed. Malcolm P. McNair. New York: McGraw Hill, Inc., 1954, pp. 98–109.

CANTOR, NATHANIAL B. "Learning Which Makes a Difference," in *To Study Administration by Cases*, ed. Andrew Towl. Cambridge, Mass.: Harvard University Press, 1969, pp. 153–58.

COPELAND, MELVIN P. "The Genius of the Case Method in Business Instruction," in *The Case Method at the Harvard Business School*, ed. Malcolm P. McNair. New York: McGraw-Hill, Inc., 1954, pp. 25–33.

GLOVER, JOHN D., AND RALPH M. HOWER. "Some Comments on Teaching by the Case Method," in *The Case of Teaching Human Relations and Administration*, ed. Kenneth R. Andrews, Cambridge, Mass.: Harvard University Press, 1953, pp. 13–24.

McNAIR, MALCOLM P., ed. *The Case Method at the Harvard Business School.* New York: McGraw-Hill, Inc., 1954.

STENZEL, ANNE, AND HELEN FEENEY. *Learning by the Case Method.* New York: The Seabury Press, Inc., 1970.

1

Communication in Business: Truth-Telling Misinformation, and Lying

Unlike the ancient cynic Diogenes, who is said to have searched the streets of Athens for an honest man, modern cynics have special fears about the world of business. Business, they say, is a medium in which honesty cannot flourish; the two repel each other like oil and water. The cases in this section deal with hard choices in business that are made more complicated by the fact that they revolve around questions of communication and honesty. Does business have a special set of rules covering the issue of truth-telling? Are these rules more lenient than those that exist in the non-business world?

The issue of truth-telling in business is far broader than that of whether to lie to the boss about one's expense account. It reaches into questions of misleading advertising, reporting procedures for complex government regulations, issues of public health and product safety, and bargaining styles during negotiation sessions. It is probably fair to say that no aspect of business life is completely free of the issue of truth-telling. In turn, every business manager should strive to develop and correct his or her own view of acceptable business communication.

Although even the most callous tend to grant that business requires a minimal level of honesty, disputes arise about the extent to which business requires adherence to strict principles of truth-telling. At one end of the spectrum of views, we find the claim that business is analogous to the game of poker and that, just as bluffing is acceptable in poker, so a certain amount of deception is acceptable in business.[1] When the automobile company Avis claims, "You have a friend at Avis," no one seriously believed it; rather, it is acceptable puffery. Similarly, when a gentleman in his fifties suspects that he may be discriminated against because of his age when applying for a job, then his lying about how old he is, is acceptable bluffing.

At the opposite end of the spectrum are views like that of the philosopher Immanuel Kant which condemn any lie, however small. Kant is quick to distinguish a lie from what he calls a false statement, thus distinguishing between a genuine lie and merely a false statement in a game (where doing so is part of the game), or a false statement when being tortured by a malicious enemy. Thus a few false statements are not lies. But with these exceptions, Kant insists that falsehoods are never justified.[2] Even when someone is planning to make bad use of requested information, and even when the consequences seem to justify it, Kant argues that one must refrain from lying. One *can* remain silent, of course, but one must never lie. Kant views his analysis as extending throughout the entire range of human activities, including both the world of personal affairs and business.

The cases in this section deal with truth-telling in a variety of contexts. The Litton Industries, Inc. case considers the issue of honest versus misleading advertising, especially when claims by advertisers are made on the basis of surveys commissioned by the company itself. The two cases on Manville's high product liability losses and subsequent bankruptcy proceedings examines the question "What did Manville really know and when did they know it?" Finally, "Italian Tax Mores" considers the issue of truth-telling in the context of Italian culture, a culture that at least appears to condone financial dishonesty.

NOTES

1. See Albert Carr, "Is Business Bluffing Ethical?," *Harvard Business Review* (January–February, 1968).

2. Immanuel Kant, "Ethical Duties Towards Others: Truthfulness," rpt. *Ethical Issues in Business,* ed. Thomas Donaldson and Patricia Werhane (Englewood Cliffs, N.J.: Prentice-Hall, Inc., 1983).

Case Study
Litton Industries, Inc.

Kenneth L. Bernhardt
Larry M. Robinson

INTRODUCTION

Fridays were always the worst day of the week for Marc Stillwell. As an Administrative Law Judge for the Federal Trade Commission, he frequently considered his workload burdensome, but Fridays always seemed the worst. While many civil servants spent the afternoon clearing off their desks preparing to start off fresh the following Monday, Stillwell was cramming his briefcase with case files and court briefs that would require his attention over the weekend. He felt he would be lucky if he could spare the time to watch a little football on Sunday, judging by the bulge in his briefcase.

The Litton Industries case decision had to be made soon, and as the presiding administrative law judge he would have to prepare a detailed decision, including his reasoning for the conclusions reached. The FTC staff attorneys and the Litton attorneys had both filed their final statements containing their arguments and findings of fact, and he would have to sort out from these conflicting documents what was actually correct.

Although it was not surrounded by the heavy publicity that characterized some of the more dramatic cases on which he had worked in the past, the Litton case was important because it contained some important issues concerning the use of surveys in advertising, and the increasing use of comparisons between competitors in advertising with actual names of competitors being used. He knew it was FTC policy to encourage advertising that uses factual data, such as that obtained from surveys, and that the agency also wanted to encourage comparative advertising. At the same time, he had to decide, in this case, if these goals conflicted with another FTC policy—that no advertising should be unfair or deceptive.

In addition to deciding if Litton had engaged in unfair or deceptive advertising and if they had adequate substantiation for the claims made, he also had to determine an appropriate remedy if the company was found guilty. A proposed order had been recommended by the FTC staff attorneys, and he would have to decide if that was reasonable or whether some other order would be better.

THE COMPANY

Litton Industries, Inc., was founded in November 1953 as a small electronics firm in San Carlos, California. Revenues that year were less than $3 million. By the end of fiscal 1978, Litton was the ninety-ninth largest U.S. corporation, with revenues exceeding $3.65 billion.[1] But Litton's management still held to a strategy laid out in the company's first annual report:

> The company's management [has] planned to first establish a base of profitable operations in advanced electronic development and manufacturing. Utilizing this base, the plan contemplates building a major electronics company by developing new and advanced products and programs and by acquiring others having potential in complementing fields. . . . This plan is designed to establish strong proprietary product values and a "broad base" on which to grow—a profitable balance between commercial and military customers and an integrated but diversified line of electronic products.[2]

By 1980, Litton had grown to become a widely diversified, international industrial conglomerate with 175 manufacturing and research facilities in the United States and around the world, employing over 90,400 people. The corporation produced such products as business computer systems, business furniture, calculators, copiers, Royal typewriters, Sweda cash registers and POS/retail information systems, machine and hand tools, material-handling systems, specialty metal products, electronic components, biomedical equipment, paper and printed products, medical professional publications (including the *Physicians Desk Reference*), textbook publications, airborne navigation systems, electronic signal surveillance equipment and so on. Litton's Ingalls Shipbuilding subsidiary built U.S. Navy destroyers and nuclear submarines.

. . . Litton Industries produced primarily commercial, industrial, and defense-related products. However, the company's Electronic and Electrical Products division successfully produced and marketed at least one major consumer good—microwave ovens.

Litton's history in electronic technology allowed the company to be one of the first manufacturers of consumer model microwave ovens. By 1979, the company was the largest manufacturer with a 25 percent market share. Amana, a division of the Raytheon Corp., and another early pioneer in the microwave cooking field, was the second largest producer with 20 percent of the market, followed by Sharp, General Electric, and Tappan with 15, 10, and 10 percent shares, respectively. Litton's microwave sales contributed almost $180 million in revenues to the company in 1978.

PRIMARY DEMAND

Until 1978, microwave oven sales for the industry had been increasing at an annual rate exceeding 45 percent and it was estimated that by 1985 almost 50 percent of American households would be using the product. Microwave ovens were capable of handling over 80 percent of a household's normal cooking.

Demand for microwaves began to fall off sharply in mid-1978, surprising analysts who expected sales to begin to decline only after market penetration of America's 80 million households exceeded the 20 percent level. In the first six months of 1978, unit sales were only 14 percent ahead of the same period in the previous year. Comparatively, the growth rate for the first six months of 1977 was 43 percent. This represented a shakeout period in the industry, with two manufacturers, Farberware and Admiral, dropping out of the American microwave market.

Industry experts generally concurred on several reasons for the unexpected slump. By 1978 there were 35 different manufacturers with microwave models on the U.S. market. The proliferation of brands, each with its own array of special features, was believed to have injected a great deal of confusion into consumer purchasing decisions. The complicated controls on many of the models also was believed to have scared off potential buyers.

Because it was a new and fairly expensive product, the proper marketing strategy called for knowledgeable salespeople to explain and demonstrate the microwave oven's many uses. Industry analysts pointed out that by 1978 most dealers were not putting enough effort into actual cooking demonstrations and other "push-type" marketing strategies. This became especially true as mass merchandise retail chains began selling the product. Such stores had neither the time nor the trained salespeople to devote to the kind of personal selling required for such a product.

Although it remained slightly ahead of the industry, with a 20 percent growth rate in 1978, Litton felt the effects of the general sales slump. The company reacted aggressively. The 1978 advertising budget already had been increased by 13.5 percent to over $21.5 million. To counter declining demand, the 1979 ad budget was increased to about $50 million. The company decided to stress product education as the key to market growth, and a large portion of the budget was earmarked for sales training, dealer promotions, and in-store demonstrations. Over 2,000 home economists were hired across the country to demonstrate the product in appliance and department stores, shopping malls and grocery chains.

The Federal Trade Commission Complaint

On January 31, 1979, the Federal Trade Commission formally issued a complaint against Litton stating that some of their earlier advertisements constituted "unfair and deceptive acts or practices in or affecting commerce and unfair methods of competition in or affecting commerce in violations of Section 5 of the Federal Trade Commission Act."[3] The complaint concerned a series of 1976 and 1977 ads in such publications as *Newsweek* and *The Wall Street Journal* that featured the results of an "independent" survey. The FTC charged that the ads claimed that:

1. The majority of independent microwave oven service technicians would recommend Litton to their customers.
2. The majority of independent microwave oven service technicians are of the opinion that Litton microwave ovens are superior in quality to all other brands.
3. The majority of independent microwave oven service technicians are of the opinion that Litton microwave ovens require the fewest repairs of all microwave brands.
4. The majority of independent microwave oven service technicians have Litton microwave ovens in their home.[4]

The FTC stated that such claims were deceptive and unfair and that there was "no reasonable basis of support for the representations in those advertisements, at the time those representations were made."[5]

The FTC formally alleged that the survey in no way could be described as "independent." They claimed that Litton hired Custom Research, Inc. to conduct the survey but that Litton designed the survey instrument and analyzed the results themselves and that Custom Research had only engaged in telephoning the respondents who were selected from a list of names supplied by Litton.

The FTC also claimed that the list of respondents were drawn exclusively from a list of Litton-authorized microwave service agencies. The surveys also failed to show that the respondents knew enough about competing brands of microwave ovens to make a comparison to Litton's ovens. The Commission also stated that the base number of respondents was too small to have any statistical significance.

In summary, "the sample surveyed was not representative of the population of independent microwave oven service technicians and the survey was biased . . ."[6]

The filing of the FTC complaint was accompanied with the usual notice stating the time and place of an administrative hearing at which Litton would have to show cause why it should not be subject to a cease-and-desist order. Litton did not choose to enter into a consent agreement, whereby the company would not have admitted any of the charges and would have negotiated an order outlining an agreed upon remedy.

At the time the complaint was originally issued, a Litton spokesperson made the following public response to the charges:

> We employed an independent research firm to survey our authorized independent microwave service agencies numbering over 500 throughout the U.S. Litton surveyed only those servicemen who repaired at least two brands of ovens, and tabulated their response only as to the brands they serviced. Litton feels the claims made in the ads, that up to 80 percent of the servicemen would recommend purchase of Litton microwave ovens, were accurately represented, and that the FTC's concerns are unfounded.[7]

THE FEDERAL TRADE COMMISSION

The Federal Trade Commission is an independent law-enforcement agency charged by the Congress with protecting the public—consumers and businesspeople alike—against anticompetitive behavior and unfair and deceptive business practices.

The Commission has authority to stop business practices that restrict competition or that deceive or otherwise injure consumers, as long as these practices fall within the legal scope of the Commission's statutes, affect interstate commerce and involve a significant public interest. Such practices may be terminated by cease-and-desist orders issued after an administrative hearing, or by injunctions issued by the Federal courts upon application by the Commission.

In addition, the FTC defines practices that violate the law so that businesspeople may know their legal obligations and consumers may recognize those business practices against which legal recourse is available. The Commission does this through the *Trade Regulation Rules and Industry Guide* issued periodically as "do's and don't's" to business and industry, and through business advice—called Advisory Opinions—given to individuals and corporations requesting it.

When law violations are isolated rather than industrywide, the FTC exercises its corrective responsibility also by issuing complaints and entering orders to halt false advertising or fraudulent selling or to prevent a businessperson or corporation from using unfair tactics against competition. The Commission itself has no authority to imprison or fine. However, if one of its final cease-and-desist orders or Trade Regulation Rules is violated, it can seek civil penalties in Federal court of up to $10,000 a day for each violation. It can also seek redress for those who have been harmed by unfair or deceptive acts or practices. Redress may include cancellation or re-formation of contracts, refunds of money, return of property, and payment of damage.

The Commission defines its role, in its literature, as:

> ... protecting the free enterprise system from being stifled or fettered by monopoly or anti-competitive practices and protecting consumers from unfair or deceptive practices.[8]

DECEPTIVE PRACTICES

Deceptive or fraudulent trade practices affecting consumers have centered around the misuse of advertising. The trend in the agency has been to identify and counter the more subtle forms of false advertising. Businesses, in arguing against the FTC's jurisdiction, have relied heavily on the First Amendment's protection, specifically freedom of speech. In 1976, the U.S. Supreme Court held in *Virginia State Board* v. *Virginia Citizens Consumer Council* that:

> Although an advertiser's interest is purely economic, that hardly disqualifies him from protection under the First Amendment. . . . It is a matter of public interest that [private economic] decisions, in the aggregate, be intelligent and well informed. To this end, the free flow of commercial information is indispensable.[9]

The Court was reaffirming the First Amendment rights of business enterprises through the right of the public to know facts relevant to decision making in the marketplace.

The Supreme Court, however, held in *Bates* v. *State of Arizona* in 1977 that this First Amendment protection of advertising was entirely dependent upon its truthfulness. "The public and private benefits from commercial speech derive from confidence in its accuracy and reliability."[10] In other cases, the courts have gone on to say that truthfulness in advertising includes completeness of information, as well as the absence of misleading or incorrect information.

The key legal requirement of advertising is that the advertiser have a "reasonable basis" to substantiate the claims made before an ad has been run. Not having a reasonable basis beforehand has been found by the courts to be a violation of Section 5 of the FTC Act as an unfair marketing practice, even if the ad is not deceptive.

It has long been argued that the FTC's simple enforcement power to issue cease-and-desist orders in regard to false advertising was largely ineffectual, since it occurred after the fact and offered no remedial sanctions. Unscrupulous advertisers could get by with a simple admonition to "go and sin no more." Recently, however, the FTC has been increasing the use of such remedial actions as corrective advertising, the most severe of possible penalties facing legitimate marketers.

In 1975, for example, the FTC ordered the Warner-Lambert Co. to include a corrective message in their next $10 million of advertising. The message would have to say that Listerine was not effective against colds and sore throats, a statement which contradicted the company's earlier advertising. The Commission argued that if, under Section 5(b) of the FTC Act, it had:

> . . . the authority to impose the severe and drastic remedy of divestiture in antitrust cases in order to restore competition to a market, surely it had the authority to order corrective advertising to restore truth to the marketplace.[11]

On April 3, 1978, the Supreme Court upheld the FTC order by denying a request to review a lower court's decision.

The FTC, as a rule, has required corrective advertising only when it found that such ads are necessary to present to the public "the honest and complete information" about an advertised product to dispel "the lingering effects of years of false advertising."[12] Without such measures, advertisers would:

> . . . remain free to misrepresent their products to the public, knowing full well that even if the FTC chooses to prosecute, they will be required only to cease an advertising campaign which by that point will, in all likelihood, have served its purpose.[13]

SUMMARY OF THE FTC'S ARGUMENTS AGAINST LITTON

In a national advertising campaign that stretched over a year and a half in at least 26 states, Litton Microwave Cooking Products promoted the results of a survey of microwave oven service technicians (see Figure). The advertisements represented the majority of service technicians as recommending Litton microwave ovens on the basis of quality, fewest repairs, and ease of repairs. These advertisements are held by the Federal Trade Commission to be unfair and deceptive in that the survey as conducted does not substantiate the advertisements' claims.

The survey is represented as an independent survey conducted by Custom Research, Inc. In fact, Litton designed the survey, developed the

Quality is No.1 at Litton!

76% of the independent microwave oven service technicians surveyed recommend Litton.

Litton Model 419
microwave oven.

Litton leads all brands.

PREFERENCE FOR SPECIFIC BRANDS AMONG TECHNICIANS SERVICING THOSE BRANDS				AVERAGE PREFERENCE FOR LITTON VS. ALL COMPETITION – (weighted average)
Brand To Brand	Litton vs. G.E.	Litton vs. Amana	Litton vs. Magic Chef	
Which Microwave Oven Brand would you recommend to a friend?	59% vs. 23%	66% vs. 18%	81% vs. 1%	76% vs. 8%
Which Microwave Oven Brand is easiest to repair?	68% vs. 5%	65% vs. 8%	71% vs. 0%	72% vs. 4%
Which Microwave Oven Brand is the best quality?	48% vs. 16%	50% vs. 26%	69% vs. 1%	63% vs. 9%
Which Microwave Oven Brand requires fewest repairs?	38% vs. 22%	42% vs. 24%	59% vs. 3%	53% vs. 12%
Which Microwave Oven Brand do you have in your home?	48% vs. 19%	59% vs. 18%	70% vs. 5%	67% vs. 10%

Among independent technicians servicing Litton and competitive microwave ovens, an average of 76% of those surveyed said they would recommend Litton to a friend. And an average of 63% identified Litton brand ovens as having the best quality.

You'll find it in our full line of advanced countertop microwave ovens, double-oven and combination microwave ranges.

And in such Litton features as Vari-Cook® oven control, Vari-Temp® automatic temperature control and new Memorymatic™ microwave program cooking. Innovative ways to microwave more foods better.

Need any more reasons to buy Litton? Ask your Litton dealer for a microwave cooking demonstration. For his name and number, call us right now, toll free **800-328-7777.**

Respondents represent independent microwave oven service agencies, who service at least two brands of microwave ovens, (one of them Litton) and do not represent a factory owned service agency. Percentages add to less than 100% due to other responses (other brands and no preference).
© 1976 Litton Systems, Inc.
*Survey conducted by Custom Research, Inc. Complete survey results available on request.

LITTON
Microwave Cooking
1405 Xenium Lane No. Minneapolis, Minnesota 55440

Litton... changing the way America Cooks.

questionnaire, provided the sampling frame, and analyzed the results. Custom Research personnel made the actual phone interviews.

Errors existed in the survey design, which biased the results of the study, thus precluding the results being projected to the population of service technicians as represented in the ads. Litton was aware of these biases prior to the implementation of the ad campaign, but ran the advertisements anyway. A memorandum, sent to executives by Litton's manager of marketing analysis, noted that the surveys were likely to be biased and recommended that the source of the sample be kept confidential. The sample used for survey was limited to those service technicians on a list of 500 Litton-authorized service agencies. No attempt was made to draw a sample from technicians authorized to service other brands of microwave ovens.

Only one technician from each agency and the technician selected by the person answering the phone was interviewed. Even with this limited, easily accessible sample, response rates were between 42 and 47 percent. Little was done to improve the response rate, and what was done is uncertain since no written instructions were provided for interviewers.

With the majority of respondents authorized only by Litton, their familiarity with Litton products would tend to bias their responses. In addition, no screening was conducted to determine if the respondent had recently or ever serviced Litton or the brand compared, thereby failing to establish a level of expertise necessary for answering the questionnaire.

With the survey biased to the point that it cannot be held to substantiate the advertisements' claims, the FTC has proposed an order for Litton Industries, the parent corporation, and all divisions, to cease and desist advertisements and representations based on faulty survey techniques or testing. This "strong order," which refers to all of Litton's consumer products and representations, is necessary to "protect the public interest and to deter respondents from future unfair and deceptive acts."

SUMMARY OF LITTON'S DEFENSE

The original complaint in this action challenged certain advertisements run by Litton Industries as being in violation of Section 5 of the Federal Trade Commission Act. The complaint was preceded by a two-year investigation of a limited number of magazine and newspaper ads run October through December of 1976 and August and September of 1977.

Complaint counsel has not met the burden of proving that the advertisements were "deceptive" within the meaning of Section 5. Complaint counsel and their witnesses did nothing more than identify "potential" deviations from *ideal* survey procedures that "might" have influenced the survey results. The procedures used were perfectly reasonable, were in accord with generally accepted survey practice, and yielded reliable results.

Even if one were to assume that a technical violation of Section 5 has occurred, the unintentional, minor nature of any such violation, and the public policy implications of the proposed order dictate that no order should be issued. The proposed order covers all products of Litton Industries. As such, it is punitive in nature, sweeping far beyond the violations, if any, that occurred.

In essence, the complaint charges that the ads contained three categories of representations: (1) alleged representations concerning the actual superiority of Litton microwave ovens over competitor brands, (2) alleged representations concerning the opinions of the "majority" of independent microwave oven service technicians relative to the superiority of Litton microwave ovens over competitive brands, and (3) alleged representations that the Litton surveys "proved" the first two representations. Only the third category is alleged to be false and misleading. Complaint counsel did not seek to prove that Litton was *not* superior to competitive brands on the attributes listed or even that independent service technicians were *not* of that opinion. The main issue was not the specific allegations in the ads but, rather, the sufficiency of the surveys upon which the ads were based.

The key issues, then, are (1) whether the ads were interpreted by the readers of those ads in the manner alleged in the complaint, and if so, (2) if the survey provided a "reasonable basis" for any representations that were made. On both issues, complaint counsel bears the burden of proof. A careful examination of the record reveals that complaint counsel misconceived the nature of their burden of proof and fell far short of meeting it. What the record does reveal is that Litton Industries attempted in good faith to conduct reliable surveys aimed at guiding its future marketing and engineering decisions. The surveys were designed and conducted in a manner that would lead to results upon which a "reasonably prudent businessman" could rely.

The surveys were designed and conducted as part of the business planning function at Litton. Specifically, the surveys were in response to advertising and point-of-sale literature by Amana, which directly and implicitly raised questions concerning the quality of Litton microwave ovens. These Amana ads emphasized the fact that Amana had received an exemption from a warning label requirement and caused certain Litton dealers to question the quality of Litton microwave ovens. As a result of the Amana ads, Litton dealers began encountering problems on the sales floors. Their concerns were communicated to Litton management.

The problems caused by Amana's attacks on the quality of Litton microwave ovens persisted. As a result, product quality became a frequent subject of discussion. The Litton Marketing Division President and Litton Microwave Consumer Products President became very concerned that perhaps the quality of Litton microwave ovens was in fact deteriorating and that they were not being adequately informed. Thus, in the early spring of 1976, Litton decided to investigate the quality of Litton microwave ovens through market research studies.

It was only after Litton conducted its studies for internal management purposes and analyzed the results that the idea of incorporating the results into advertising germinated. That possibility was not even seriously considered until September 1976. In fact, the ads were not included in the advertising budget for 1976–1977. As a result, special approval had to be obtained from the President of Litton Microwave Consumer Products in order to prepare the ads.

The advertising copy that ultimately emerged from the surveys presented the results fairly, at a level of detail so complete that it threatened their effectiveness as an advertising tool. The decision to present the data fully was made so that the ads would withstand any subsequent scrutiny.

This case was chosen by Federal Trade Commission staff as a "test" case for establishing industrywide standards for the advertising of survey results and for the procedures which must be followed in such surveys. Indeed, the Commission press release announcing the issuance of the complaint identified it as a test case that would set standards for advertising surveys and tests. Thus, the key issue is whether Litton had a "reasonable basis" upon which to make the claims included in the ads.

NOTES

1. "The Forbes 500s," *Forbes* (May 14, 1979), 234.

2. Litton Industries, Inc., *Annual Report, Fiscal 1978*, p. 4.

3. Federal Trade Commission Complaint, Docket No. 9123 (January 31, 1979), p. 5.

4. Ibid., p. 2.

5. Ibid., p. 4.

6. Ibid.

7. "Litton Industries, Inc.'s Microwave Oven Ads Deceptive, FTC Says," *Wall Street Journal* (February 2, 1979), 4.

8. This section is based on *Your FTC: What It Is and What It Does*, pamphlet published by the Federal Trade Commission, Washington, D.C.

9. William Sklar, "Ads Are Finally Getting Bleeped at the FTC," *Business and Society Review* (September 1978), 41.

10. Ibid., p. 42.

11. "Corrective Ad Order Not Anti-Free Speech: FTC," *Advertising Age* (September 13, 1976), 2.

12. Ibid.

13. Ibid.

QUESTIONS FOR DISCUSSION*

1. Did Litton's decision to survey only independent authorized Litton microwave service agencies result in "deceptive and unfair" claims? *Was* Litton making "deceptive and unfair" claims?

2. Should Litton be ordered by the FTC to air "corrective" advertising?

3. How should Litton executives respond to the current charges?

Case Study
Manville: The Ethics
of Economic Efficiency?

A. R. Gini

On Friday, July 30, 1982, a short article appeared on page four of the *Wall Street Journal* announcing that yet another company, UNR Industries Inc. of Chicago, had filed for Chapter 11 of the Federal Bankruptcy Code of 1978. Given the present state of the economy the public notification of a bankruptcy proceeding is hardly a novel occurrence. However, the circumstances leading to the UNR petition were certainly far from usual.

At the time of filing UNR assets exceeded $200 million, with debts totaling only about $100 million. While sales had marginally declined, 4.2% in the second quarter of 1982, yearly sales figures were expected to remain relatively strong. UNR chairman, David S. Leavitt, said that the company was forced to file for bankruptcy because of the nearly 17,000 suits filed against it in regard to their asbestos pipe insulation product line. Although the company had stopped manufacturing asbestos insulation in 1970, the suits seek damages for alleged injuries and wrongful deaths supposedly attributable to exposure to the insulation. Mr. Leavitt claimed that the company simply could not survive the burden of the costs of all the present and possible future litigation.[1] While the general business community probably paid little or no attention to UNR's plight, their predicament did not go unnoticed by the Denver-based Manville Corporation, the nation's, if not the world's, single largest producer of asbestos and asbestos products.

On Thursday, August 26, 1982, the Manville Corporation (formerly Johns-Manville) and its principal American and Canadian affiliates filed for reorganization under Chapter 11 in the United States District Court for the Southern District of New York. Manville's unexpected bankruptcy petition stunned the financial community, surprised Congress, shocked their creditors, suppliers, and customers, outraged those who had filed damage suits against them, and raised a complex tangle of legal, political, and ethical issues that will have far-reaching implications for millions of Americans. The drama of the Manville announcement stems from the fact that this is the same Manville Corporation that last year earned $60.3 million on sales exceeding $2 billion with an unencumbered net worth of $1.1 billion. This is the same Manville that ranks 181 on the Fortune 500 list of American corporations. And this is the same Manville that has been traditionally included in the 30 companies used to calculate the prestigious Dow Jones industrial average, the most watched indicator of prices on the New York

Stock Exchange. While there are many factors in the equation that resulted in Manville's final decision, like UNR's unprecedented decision less than a month earlier, Manville Chairman John A. McKinney angrily announced that this company could no longer sustain or survive the blitz of "toxic torts" that it was now facing.

Many of Manville's critics have claimed that Manville, and by implication UNR, is acting in an immoral and illegal manner. They are held to be immoral insofar as their critics feel that they are using the "bankruptcy boom" as a means of avoiding just compensation for those who have truly been injured or killed due to excessive or abusive exposure to asbestos. Manville is accused of acting illegally in that the spirit and purpose of the 1978 Bankruptcy Act is being violated because no company has ever filed for Chapter 11 given the size of their assets, their net worth, and their yearly sales figures. Other observers suggest that this is much too simplistic a response to the situation and that whatever the final merits of Manville's petition the factors involved in their decision warrant a careful and detailed analysis.

Asbestos is a naturally occurring mineral found in various concentrations across the earth's surface. Asbestos is the best known member of a family of fibrous silicate minerals, which share the common attribute of being able to be separated into relatively soft, silky strands. Because of its high tensile strength, superior flexibility, and durability and because of its resistance to fire, heat, and corrosion, asbestos finds broad use in many essential applications. In all, asbestos is a component in more than 3,000 industrial and consumer products. It is an essential ingredient in plastics, textiles, roofing tiles, brake linings, insulation and fire wall materials, cement water and sewerage pipes, and vinyl floor coverings. Because it is plentiful in nature and relatively inexpensive in cost, asbestos continues to be widely used. According to the Bureau of Mines, 349,000 metric tons of asbestos was used to make various products in this country in 1981.

Industry spokesmen are quick to point out that its unique combination of properties makes asbestos superior to any other natural or man-made fiber. After more than a decade of intense well-financed research for an asbestos substitute, none has been found that works as well or makes as much economic sense. Robert Clifton, asbestos commodities specialist for the National Bureau of Mines, stated that while there are substitutes for practically every application in which asbestos is used, they are either inferior, more costly, or contain serious health hazards.[2]

Like many of the naturally occurring materials, asbestos may also pose a health hazard unless properly handled. Today there is little doubt that excessive exposure to airborne asbestos fiber can cause disease, principally of the respiratory tract. Some forms of asbestos consist of fibers so small that 1,600 particles can occupy the space of a single human hair. Because of their minute size and needle-like shape asbestos fibers can be inhaled into the lungs; and because they are relatively indestructible they may be substantially resistant to the body's normal defense mechanisms.[3]

The insidious aspect of asbestos-related illness is that they have an incubation period of 10 to 40 years. Diseases of this type are usually referred to as "delayed emergence diseases." Asbestos has been primarily associated with three forms of respiratory illness: asbestosis, mesothelioma, lung cancer. Asbestosis is a chronic and sometimes fatal lung disease characterized by extensive scarring of the lung tissue and progressive shortness of breath much like emphysema. This disease has a latency period of 10 to 20 years. Mesothelioma is a fatal if rare cancer of the chest or abdomen lining. Its average latency is 25 to 40 years. Asbestos-related lung cancer is a highly virulent and always fatal form of the disease which has a latency period of 20 to 40 years. Moreover, modern research has also suggested a link between asbestos fibers and cancer of the gastrointestinal tract, larynx, and kidney.

In a recent statement in *Newsweek* magazine Dr. William Blot of the National Cancer Institute claims that excessive exposure to asbestos fibers "appears to be the greatest single source of occupational cancer."[4] Medical specialists estimate that over the past 40 years 9 to 20 million Americans have been exposed to large amounts of asbestos in the workplace and that *at least* 5,000 cancer related deaths directly linked to asbestos will occur annually until the end of the century. According to Manville, the major occupational groups that may have been exposed to excessive amounts of asbestos in the past are divided into three categories: (1) Workers in mines, mills, and factories where raw asbestos was used; (2) Insulation workers who worked with non-bonded or non-encapsulated asbestos-containing products; (3) Workers exposed to asbestos while in government controlled naval shipyards.[5]

For all intents and purposes the origins of Manville's present predicament begins with this country's preparation for World War II. Because of its fire resistant qualities, asbestos was extensively used in government owned or controlled shipyards in the production of 6,000 new warships and freighters and the refitting of 65,000 other vessels. Over 4 million workers were directly exposed to clouds of asbestos dust in their race to build and repair America's naval arsenal.[6] While it is the case that after the war asbestos came to be looked upon as the "miracle mineral" and was extensively used throughout the construction industry, the shipyard workers remain the largest single group exposed to the possible effects of asbestos poisoning. It is from this group that Manville is experiencing the largest number of lawsuits and claims.

By the summer of 1982 Manville was being sued at the rate of 500 new cases a month. Having already settled 3,500 suits at a cost of over $50 million[7] and with 16,500 suits still pending, Manville commissioned a study by Epidemiology Resources, Inc., a small, Boston based, health data research company, to determine how many new lawsuits would probably be filed against them. The report was filed on August 4, 1982, and it forecast by the year 2009 Manville could conservatively expect another 32,000 suits. Together these pending and probable suits could cost the company anywhere between $2 to $5 billion, budgeting $40,000 per settlement based on the assumption of a modest rate of inflation and an average win/loss ratio.

While many critics contend that Manville's figures are an excessive extrapolation, a number of independent authorities maintain that Manville's figures are not only conservative but very low estimates indeed. Dr. Irving J. Selikoff, chief of Environmental Health at Mt. Sinai Hospital in New York and a leading authority on asbestos-related disease, claims that Manville is vastly underestimating their future rate of litigation and probable liabilities. According to Dr. Selikoff's figures, from 1940 to 1980 about 27 million workers were exposed to asbestos. He claims that while only a fraction of those exposed developed cancer, the number of cancer deaths among asbestos workers exceeds the average in the population by 8,000 to 10,000 a year. This means, said Dr. Selikoff, that the total liabilities to Manville and other asbestos companies could reach $40 to $80 billion![8]

Based on the "Epidemiology Resources Report" and after an intensive review by a "blue-ribbon committee," Manville's board of directors announced their decision to file for reorganization under Chapter 11 of the Bankruptcy Act. In filing for reorganization Manville has won at least a temporary respite from its legal woes. Although the company will continue operating during the reorganization, all suits now pending are frozen and no new suits can be filed. While the company develops a plan to handle its liabilities, it is up to the bankruptcy courts to deal with all present claims as well as establishing guidelines for the handling of any future claims.

In a full-page interview that appeared as an ad in 21 major newspapers one day after the bankruptcy filing, Manville Chairman John A. McKinney contended that while the decision to apply for Chapter 11 was a dramatic one, he stressed that the company was not in a desperate manner. "This is not a financial failure," McKinney emphasized.

> Nothing is wrong with our business. Filing under Chapter 11 does not mean that the company is going out of business and that its assets will be liquidated. Lawsuits are the problem. We will continue to manufacture and ship high quality products and provide the same services, as always.[9]

McKinney went on to say that he was personally angered by and opposed to the decision to file for bankruptcy, but he agreed with the board of directors that there was no other logical recourse legally left to the company.

Mr. G. Earl Parker, Manville Senior Vice-President, in testimony before a "House Subcommittee on Labor Standards" on September 9, 1982, itemized the four chief reasons that forced Manville to the bankruptcy courts:

1. to avoid the largest tort litigation ever witnessed;
2. federal standards in regard to accounting principles and requirements;
3. legal disputes with insurance companies;
4. the federal government's unwillingness to establish a compensation fund for asbestos victims.[10]

The first two points are interconnected. With Manville being faced with the possibility of a minimum of $2 billion in litigation costs and liabilities, the company found itself, at least on paper, in a difficult financial position. As John McKinney pointed out, the company's net worth is only $1.1 billion. Therefore, if Manville did not file for bankruptcy

> we would have to strangle the company slowly, by deferring maintenance and postponing capital expenditures. We would also have to cannibalize our good businesses to just keep going. . . . We would have to mortgage our plants and properties and new credit would be most difficult and expensive to obtain.[11]

Because Manville is a publicly-held company it is required to comply with certain accounting requirements. Federal law states that a company is supposed to estimate the costs of all current and probable litigation whenever possible and create a reserve fund for the liability in an amount equal to the estimated costs. Given the volume of present and projected litigation facing Manville, it is clearly impossible for them to establish such a fund even on a liquidation basis. "Without court protection," McKinney insisted, "the lawsuits, one way or another, would cripple us."[12]

Perhaps the last appreciated factor in the equation that led Manville to Chapter 11 is the long disputes it has been having with its major insurance carriers. According to Manville spokesman John Lonnquist, "Except for one company, all are essentially withholding payments."[13] The insurance industry has been split into two warring camps by the flood of asbestos-related lawsuits that led Manville to declare bankruptcy. Some insurance experts suggest that it is the insurance industry's war, more than any other factor, that has prompted the bankruptcy filing. At the heart of the insurance battle is the question of whether an insurer's liability begins when the workers were exposed to asbestos or when the asbestos-related disease manifests itself, typically many years after exposure. As one might expect, insurance firms who covered the asbestos manufacturers in the early years favor the manifestation theory. And the insurers who have written coverage for the asbestos industry more recently are fighting for the exposure theory. Manville's problem is that as long as the insurance companies are fighting among themselves about whose policies cover what, Manville must use its corporate assets to pay both the fees and damages involved in all suits. For its part, Manville is presently suing all its insurers (27 companies); they are asking that all outstanding claims be paid as well as $5 billion in punitive damages.[14]

No matter what the other reasons that have led Manville to apply for Chapter 11, in so doing it clearly hopes to encourage the support and active participation of the federal government in establishing a compensation program for all asbestos victims. Up until now the government has steadfastly denied responsibility and refused to participate in any further compensation fund beyond the presently mandated compensation programs.[15] John McKinney vigorously rejects the allegation that Manville is simply seeking a federal "bailout" vis-á-vis Chrysler or the railroads. Manville maintains that the government should pay a large portion of the asbestos claims for three reasons:

1. The government was the chief contractor for the shipyards and the major employer of the asbestos-exposed workers.
2. The government established the specifications for all aspects of the sale and use of asbestos in wartime shipbuilding.
3. Since the war the government has been responsible for the establishment and policing of all safety standards regarding asbestos.[16]

Manville insists that it has always conformed to government standards and that it always tried to establish company regulations that reflected the latest word in scientific achievement. Tragically for many workers, however, it has taken decades for the medical/scientific community, industry, and the government to obtain the broad knowledge we have today. The public literature has reported since the 1930s that factory workers exposed to 100 percent raw asbestos fiber experienced an increased risk of contracting a pulmonary fibrosis that has come to be called asbestosis. But there was no reason to believe that any worker faced a health risk from using finished asbestos products, and there was no reason to believe that workers faced any health risks other than asbestosis.[17] In 1964 Dr. Irving Selikoff of Mt. Sinai School of Medicine in New York reported the results of a study of insulation workers and changed everyone's understanding of the extent of potential health problems from excessive exposure to asbestos. Dr. Selikoff's findings showed that exposure to asbestos from products such as asbestos insulation, even though below the accepted standard, heightened the risk of disease among insulation workers. In addition, he showed that there was a markedly increased risk of lung cancer in asbestos insulation workers who smoked cigarettes. Studies since then have supported Dr. Selikoff's findings.[18]

Given this information and the new standards that have evolved, Manville is convinced that asbestos can and is being used safely. Today's disease problems, Manville contends, are a legacy of the past when the state of medical knowledge concerning asbestos was inadequate. Therefore, while Manville recognizes that it has participated in the mistakes of the past, the company feels that the government has been a full partner in these errors. As a partner Manville is willing to share costs with the government in the establishment of a statutory compensation program to aid all those who have contracted an asbestos disease. According to John McKinney, without such a program there will be no help for present and future victims of asbestos, and there will be no way to save the Manville Corporation from going defunct!

After all is said and done, the central issue in this case for most people is not that Manville is filing for Chapter 11 to avoid immediate and future liability, but that Manville is alive, doing well, highly solvent, and not even close to closing up shop and yet it is filing for bankruptcy! Manville claims that just because their actions are unprecedented (save for UNR) and highly unorthodox, it does not follow that they are acting in an immoral or illegal fashion. Manville officials insist that filing for bankruptcy was unavoidable and in the best interest of its stockholders, employees, and creditors. Moreover, they feel that in the long run their decision will better benefit the victims of asbestos-related diseases. Earl Parker testified that only by filing now could Manville ensure that the asbestos disease claimants will receive the money owed them in the coming decades.[19] Manville Chairman John McKinney insists that Chapter 11 is the only orderly way possible for the company to treat everyone fairly. He emphasized that Manville's failure is really our court and legislative systems' failure to provide a reasonable way to compensate victims of an unexpected occupational health catastrophe. McKinney is firmly convinced that Manville's problems are America's problems and the government should and must help![20]

In all candor it must be remembered that Manville's actions are not without danger. To the extent that Manville is using Chapter 11 as a shelter against the rush of asbestos litigation, the company is nevertheless taking a risky gamble. Manville must now operate under the eye of a federal bankruptcy judge, and, said Lawrence King, Professor of Law at New York University, "once you file, there is always a risk of liquidation." "It is not yet clear," said King, "that the bankruptcy proceeding will succeed in mooting the claims against Manville."[21] No one really knows how Manville's decision to apply for Chapter 11 will ultimately affect the status of the litigation and claims now in the courts. The only thing that is clear is that each decision in the Manville controversy will be breaking new legal ground each step of the way, whether it be in regard to Manville itself, the asbestos industry in general, government regulations and responsibilities, and/or the future status of public health and environmental policy.

AN UPDATE

Reorganization Gives Manville New Life Amid Asbestos Suits
Christopher Elias
Insight
August 1, 1988

Perhaps as soon as late August, Denver's Manville Corp. will emerge from bankruptcy proceedings that have lasted six years and cost the company $100 million in fees for lawyers and other professionals. When the last appeal has been made and the last legal argument has ended, the bankruptcy of Manville, once New York-based Johns-Manville Corp., undoubtedly will go down as one of the most complicated and successful ever. Instead of a corpse, Manville will be a going business, deeply in debt to be sure, but alive and earning money.

Its 550-page reorganization plan filed under Chapter 11 of the Federal Bankruptcy Code is already being counted among the most imaginative, since it reconciles the interests of an extraordinary number of disparate creditors with claims far greater than the total assets of company. Instead of wiping out shareholders, which could easily have occurred, the plan lets them hang on, though they must accept a dilution of the value of their holdings by as much as 98 percent, while relinquishing governance of the company to two trusts and ultimate control to a group of banks supplying new working capital of more than $200 million. . . .

In outline, the reorganization plan requires Manville to fund enormous known and unknown potential liabilities, resulting largely from asbestosis, a disease often contracted by people working with and around asbestos products sold by Manville for decades. . . .

Under its reorganization plan Manville has accepted an obligation of at least $2.5 billion and agrees to pay out as much as 20 percent of its earnings for as long as they "are needed to provide compensation for personal injury and property damage caused by asbestos." The plan also provides money for commercial creditors, including 12 banks, and Manville suppliers.

The plan enables the company to remain viable by setting up two independent trusts to administer and pay claims, freeing the company to tend to its diversified businesses. The separation, a pragmatic one agreed to by a variety of claimants, is essential if Manville is to fund claims initiated years, even decades from now. To shield the company from lawsuits bypassing the two trusts, Burton R. Lifland, chief judge of the U. S. Bankruptcy Court in New York, issued an injunction prohibiting further suits after the reorganization is consummated.

The injunction was a departure from Bankruptcy Code and is considered unique by lawyers, since the effect is to extend some of the protection of bankruptcy to a company no longer in bankruptcy. The order might be challenged one day, since doubt exists that future claims against Manville can be discharged before the fact by a Bankruptcy Court.

"It was the most imaginative bankruptcy proceeding yet," said attorney Roy Babitt, a retired New York bankruptcy judge and former associate of Lifland. "It shows that the bankruptcy system is working."

At Manville's headquarters, Chief Executive Officer W. Thomas Stephens, credited as one of the chief architects of the reorganization along with New York lawyer Leon Silverman, is jubilant. Legal opposition to the reorganization is winding down. Two groups of claimants may yet appeal to the Supreme Court, imposing new delays. But, as early as Aug. 25, six years from the day Manville declared its bankruptcy, Stephens might be able to start running the company without Lifland's approval of management decisions. . . .

. . . . the plan separates Manville's operating companies from direct involvement in claim procedures. It establishes two trusts, one to pay asbestos-related personal injury claims, the other to pay claims related to property damage. The personal injury trust is being funded with an estimated $2.5 billion over the next 20 to 25 years. Insurance companies will contribute $615 million to the funding and the firm will contribute $150 million in cash as well as a $50 million interest-bearing note. It will also contribute the proceeds from the sale of $1.65 billion in bonds payable over 25 years and "an interest" in a second, $150 million bond. The company will double the 24 million shares outstanding and contribute half the total to the trust, which one day could own as much as 80 percent of Manville's outstanding shares. For as long as needed, the personal injury trust will also receive as much as 20 percent of Manville's net earnings. . . .

We are going to come out of this smokin', there's no doubt about it," says the Arkansas-born Stephens, an engineer by training, a logger in his youth and former president of Manville's Forest Products Group. . . .

Last year, Stephens's first complete year as chief executive officer, Manville's earnings rose 102 percent, to $164.1 million, as sales rose only from $1.9 billion to $2 billion. Most of these earnings, however—$91.5 million—was devoted to advance funding of the personal injury trust that will be born when the 130-year-old company emerges from bankruptcy. That charge reduced 1987 net earnings to about $72.6 million from $81.2 million in 1986. . . .[22]

NOTES

1. *Wall Street Journal,* July 30, 1982, p. 4.

2. *New York Times,* September 2, 1982, Sec. D, p. 2.

3. *Compensating Workers for Asbestos-Related Disease,* Asbestos Compensation Coalition, 1981, p. 1.

4. *Newsweek,* September 6, 1982, pp. 54, 55.

5. *Asbestos, Health and Johns-Manville,* Johns-Manville Corporate Relations Department, September 1981, p. 5.

6. "Kirkland & Ellis Report: The Government's Legal Responsibilities," Manville Corporate Relations Department, September 8, 1982.

7. *Time,* September 6, 1982, p. 17.

8. *New York Times,* August 31, 1982, Sec. A, p. 13.

9. *New York Times,* August 27, 1982, Sec. D, p. 3.

10. "The Testimony of G. Earl Parker, U.S. House of Representatives," Manville Corporate Relations Department, September 9, 1982.

11. *New York Times,* August 27, 1982, Sec. D, p. 3.

12. Ibid.

13. *Science News,* September 18, 1982, Vol. 122, p. 183.

14. *New York Times,* September 7, 1982, Sec. D, p. 2.

15. *Sci Now,* September 18, 1982, Vol. 122, p. 182. *New York Times,* September 10, 1982, Sec. D, p. 1.

16. "Kirkland & Ellis Report: The Government's Legal Responsibilities," Manville Corporate Relations Department, September 8, 1982.

17. "The Testimony of G. Earl Parker, The Senate Subcommittee on Courts," Manville Corporate Relations Department, November 19, 1982.

18. *Asbestos, Health and Johns-Manville,* Johns-Manville Corporate Relations Department, September 1981, p. 6.

19. "The Testimony of G. Earl Parker, U.S. House of Representatives," Manville Corporate Relations Department, September 9, 1982.

20. *New York Times,* August 27, 1982, Sec. D, p. 3.

21. *Newsweek,* September 6, 1982, p. 55.

22. In effect, what this means is that Manville will be the first company to be operated primarily for the purpose of generating money for people injured by one of its products.

According to Manville's CEO, W. Thomas Stephens, "The whole Manville reorganization is driven by the rights of the future claimants, and that's what's unique about it." Estimates of the number of asbestos claims that may ultimately be filed run to 50,000 or more. (*New York Times, National Edition,* July 30, 1988, pp. 17,18).

QUESTIONS FOR DISCUSSION

(See questions: "When Did Johns-Manville Know?)

When Did Johns-Manville Know?

Jeff Coplon

Even if the Manville Corp. is thrown out of bankruptcy court, Ted Kowalski and his fellow plaintiffs will be fighting uphill to collect on their damage suits. To date, New Jersey workers have been shunted to workers' compensation in cases of job-related illness or injury; no one has ever successfully sued an employer in civil court.

But in California, the state Supreme Court ruled in 1980 that the family of a dead J-M employee could sue the company for "fraud and conspiracy" in concealing the dangers of long-term exposure to asbestos.

By 1981, under the same principle, several judges throughout the country had ordered six-figure punitive awards to people outside the company who had taken sick after handling J-M products. In one case, a widow of a Cleveland insulation worker won $350,000 in punitive damages, in addition to $500,000 in compensatory damages.

For the victims in Manville, then, the legal issue is this: what did J-M know, and when did the company know it?

In its defense, J-M says it protected its own workers from asbestosis as best it could since the 1930s, that it followed the U.S. Public Health Service standard set in 1938, and that it was aware of no cancer threat until 1964.

But a growing body of evidence suggests otherwise—that J-M knew more than it admits, and that it deliberately suppressed medical information from its workers in Manville.

The first case of asbestosis was reported in 1907 in England, followed by conclusive medical research in 1930 and documentation of a link with lung cancer in 1934. In this country, the Journal of the American Medical Association reported on asbestosis in 1928—the same year Prudential Insurance suspended all policies on the lives of asbestos workers.

In the 1930s, J-M responded by taking annual chest X rays at the

Manville plant and partially funding a study of asbestosis at Saranac Lake. But at the same time, recently disclosed correspondence between officers at J-M and other asbestos firms shows they sought to keep the bad news from spreading.

In December 1934, after reviewing galley proofs of the Saranac Lake study, J-M attorney Vandiver Brown requested revisions: "All we ask is that . . . none of the unfavorable [aspects] be unintentionally pictured in darker tones than the circumstances justify." The study was duly revised.

In 1942 an outside attorney named Charles Roemer met with Brown. After his cousin, a doctor at a Paterson asbestos plant, found "lung changes" among many workers, Roemer approached J-M "to see how they were handling the asbestos health problem."

The answer, included in a sworn affidavit taken from the 83-year-old Roemer last September, pulled no punches: "Vandiver Brown stated that Johns-Manville's physical examination program had, indeed, also produced findings of X-ray evidence of asbestos disease among workers exposed to asbestos and that it was Johns-Manville's policy not to do anything, nor to tell the employees of the X-ray findings. Vandiver Brown went on to say that . . . if Johns-Manville's workers were told, they would stop working and file claims against Johns-Manville, and that it was Johns-Manville's policy to let them work until they quit work because of asbestosis or died as a result of asbestos-related diseases".

In 1952, Dr. Kenneth Smith, J-M's medical director, asked company executives to place a warning label on some asbestos products, which he felt could be dangerous to insulation workers. Their reply, he attested in a 1975 deposition, was that the corporation "is in business . . . to provide jobs for people and make money for stockholders, and they had to take into consideration the effects of everything they did and if the application of caution label would cut out sales, there would be serious financial implications." The warning labels were deferred until 1964.

In 1950 Dr. Nicholas Demy, a Somerset radiologist, found asbestos fibers imbedded within the lung cancer of a deceased J-M worker—demonstrating a link the industry would deny for 14 more years. Subsequently, J-M refused to supply Demy with occupational histories he needed to pursue the lead.

When it was clear the controversy over asbestos would not blow over, J-M was selective as to what research it backed. When Dr. Maxwell Borow, a surgeon at Somerset Medical Center, asked for $3500 in 1966 to mount an exhibit on the worst Manville cancer of all, the company declined: "They said they were not prepared to admit a causal relationship between asbestos and mesothelioma."

Even as the conflagration raged full blast, some say the company shrank from sounding an alarm. According to Wilber Ruff, a former J-M manager at its Pittsburgh, California, plant, company doctors were barred until 1971 from telling workers about their X rays or referring them to outside specialists.

"The company did not want to talk about these things and get employees upset," Ruff testified before Congress, "until such time as we knew our ground."

Few people will question a doctor who tells them they're healthy. It's what they want to hear, after all, that all will be well in the morning. And in a company town like Manville, filled with immigrants who spoke little English, the doctor was a man of learning, a high authority. If he said the X ray showed nothing, they must be fine. They weren't much for complaining.

"They're good people, strong people, with strong beliefs," said Ted Kowalski. "Someone took advantage of their goodness."

That remains true today. For all the hoopla and network specials about the lethal white fiber, there is no research to determine why certain workers are susceptible to asbestosis and related cancers, or how they might get sick under current workplace conditions.

"Neither the companies nor the insurance companies nor the government have shown the slightest interest in finding out how these diseases occur," said Dr. Irving Selikoff, the Mt. Sinai researcher whose 1964 paper was the first accepted by J-M. "One side says the other should pay for it. There's been no interest. So people will continue to die."

QUESTIONS FOR DISCUSSION

1. Is Manville telling the truth about its knowledge of the health factors involved in excessive exposure to asbestos? Is it true that officers of the company were unaware of the connection between asbestosis and certain other respiratory diseases, including cancer? Or is it true, as many of J-M's critics contend, that company officers conspired for more than 40 years to both deny and cover up any knowledge of the long-term ill effects of working with and around asbestos and asbestos products?

2. If it is true that Manville did conspire to cover up any knowledge of ill effects of asbestos, is the company justified in petitioning the government for its support in establishing a compensation program for asbestos victims?

3. In regard to general product liability, how far back can claims be made against a company? More importantly, is it just to sue a company when, at the time, it acted legally, cautiously, and in good faith?

4. Given that Manville was simply the producer/supplier of a product and not the contractor, designer, or an agent in charge, is the federal government justified in denying further responsibility?

5. A major by-product of Manville's actions may be the restructuring of the legal responsibilities of industrial insurance carriers. Specifically, how does an insurance company determine a valid claim, and when may a company decide to deny or withhold a claim?

6. Can the 1978 Federal Bankruptcy Act be used as a means of seeking relief from possible future claims and liabilities?

Case Study
Italian Tax Mores

Arthur L. Kelly

The Italian federal corporate tax system has an official, legal tax structure and tax rates just as the U.S. system does. However, all similarity between the two systems ends there.

The Italian tax authorities assume that no Italian corporation would ever submit a tax return which shows its true profits but rather would submit a return which understates actual profits by anywhere between 30 percent and 70 percent; their assumption if essentially correct. Therefore, about six months after the annual deadline for filing corporate tax returns, the tax authorities issue to each corporation an "invitation to discuss" its tax return. The purpose of this notice is to arrange a personal meeting between them and representatives of the corporation. At this meeting, the Italian revenue service states the amount of corporate income tax which it believes is due. Its position is developed from both prior years' taxes actually paid and the current year's return; the amount which the tax authorities claim is due is generally several times that shown on the corporation's return for the current year. In short, the corporation's tax return and the revenue service's stated position are the opening offers for the several rounds of bargaining which will follow.

The Italian corporation is typically represented in such negotiations by its *commercialista*, a function which exists in Italian society for the primary purpose of negotiating corporate (and individual) tax payments with the Italian tax authorities; thus, the management of an Italian corporation seldom, if ever, has to meet directly with the Italian revenue service and probably has a minimum awareness of the details of the negotiation other than the final settlement.

Both the final settlement and the negotiation are extremely important to the corporation, the tax authorities, and the *commercialista*. Since the tax authorities assume that a corporation *always* earned more money this year than last year and *never* has a loss, the amount of the final settlement, i.e., corporate taxes which will actually be paid, becomes, for all practical purposes, the floor for the start of next year's negotiations. The final settlement also represents the amount of revenue the Italian government will collect in taxes to help finance the cost of running the country. However, since large amounts of money are involved and two individuals having vested personal interests are conducting the negotiations, the amount of *bustarella*—typically a substantial cash payment "requested" by the Italian revenue agent from the *commerciolista*—usually determines whether the final settlement is closer to the corporation's original tax return or to the fiscal authority's original negotiating position.

Whatever *bustarella* is paid during the negotiation is usually included by the *commercialista* in his lump-sum fee "for services rendered" to his corporate client. If the final settlement is favorable to the corporation, and it is the *commercialista*'s job to see that it is, then the corporation is not likely to complain about the amount of its *commercialista*'s fee, nor will it ever know how much of that fee was represented by *bustarella* and how much remained for the *commercialista* as payment for his negotiating services. In any case, the tax authorities will recognize the full amount of the fee as a tax deductible expense on the corporation's tax return for the following year.

About ten years ago, a leading American bank opened a bank subsidiary in a major Italian city. At the end of its first year of operation, the bank was advised by its local lawyers and tax accountants, both from branches of U.S. companies, to file its tax return "Italian-style," i.e., to understate its actual profits by a significant amount. The American general manager of the bank, who was on his first overseas assignment, refused to do so both because he considered it dishonest and because it was inconsistent with the practices of his parent company in the United States.

About six months after filing its "American-style" tax return, the bank received an "invitation to discuss" notice from the Italian tax authorities. The bank's general manager consulted with his lawyers and tax accountants who suggested he hire a *commercialista*. He rejected this advice and instead wrote a letter to the Italian revenue service not only stating that his firm's corporate return was correct as filed but also requesting that they inform him of any specific items about which they had questions. His letter was never answered.

About sixty days after receiving the initial "invitation to discuss" notice, the bank received a formal tax assessment notice calling for a tax of approximately three times that shown on the bank's corporate tax return; the tax authorities simply assumed the bank's original return had been based on generally accepted Italian practices, and they reacted accordingly. The bank's general manager again consulted with his lawyers and tax accountants who again suggested he hire a *commercialista* who knew how to handle these matters. Upon learning that the *commercialista* would probably have to pay *bustarella* to his revenue service counterpart in order to reach a settlement, the general manager again chose to ignore his advisors. Instead, he responded by sending the Italian revenue service a check for the full amount of taxes due according to the bank's American-style tax return even though the due date for the payment was almost six months hence; he made no reference to the amount of corporate taxes shown on the formal tax assessment notice.

Ninety days after paying its taxes, the bank received a third notice from the fiscal authorities. This one contained the statement, "We have reviewed your corporate tax return for 19— and have determined that [the lira equivalent of] $6,000,000 of interest paid on deposits is not an allowable expense for federal tax purposes. Accordingly, the total tax due for 19— is lira _____." Since interest paid on deposits is any bank's largest single expense item, the new tax assessment was for an amount many times larger than that shown in the initial tax assessment notice and almost fifteen times larger than the taxes which the bank had actually paid.

The bank's general manager was understandably very upset. He immediately arranged an appointment to meet personally with the manager of the Italian revenue service's local office. Shortly after the start of their meeting, the conversation went something like this:

GENERAL MANAGER: "You can't really be serious about disallowing interest paid on deposits as a tax deductible expense.

ITALIAN
 REVENUE SERVICE: "Perhaps. However, we thought it would get your attention. Now that you're here, shall we begin our negotiations?"[1]

NOTE

1. For readers interested in what happened subsequently, the bank was forced to pay the taxes shown on the original tax assessment, and the American manager was recalled to the United States and replaced.

QUESTIONS FOR DISCUSSION

1. Would you, as the general manager of the Italian subsidiary of an American corporation, "when in Rome" do as other Italian corporations do or adhere strictly to U.S. tax reporting practices?

2. Would you, as chief executive officer of a publicly traded corporation (subject to Securities Exchange Commission rules, regulations, and scrutiny), advise the general manager of your Italian subsidiary to follow common Italian tax reporting practices or to adhere to U.S. standards?

2

Pollution
and Environment

The Eskimo and some subcultures in India regard pollution as a philosophical concept. For such persons, to pollute is to injure the harmony that exists between people and nature. Hence, one should avoid polluting not only the physical environment but also one's social environment. In western Europe and the United States, we have tended to view pollution more narrowly. We have defined it largely in a physical manner, referring primarily to air pollution, water pollution, radiation pollution, waste-disposal pollution, and noise pollution. Although the first case in this chapter deals with both the physical and the social ramifications of pollution, in the other three cases we shall adapt the narrower concept and construe pollution to mean "the presence in the environment of a substance produced by human beings that renders the environment less fit for life." Notice that this definition is sufficiently broad to accommodate pollution inside the workplace as well as outside it.

Concern about pollution mushroomed during the 1960s with the appearance of such books as Rachel Carson's *Silent Spring,* a chilling forecast of the destruction that pesticides such as DDT could bring to bird and animal populations. During the 1960s, not only were DDT and other pesticides restricted by congressional legislation, but broad regulatory mechanisms were also established under such acts as the Clean Air Act and the Clean Water Act. Unfortunately, for Congress to put legal teeth into its legislation sufficient to force business into compliance, these acts were forced to wait until the early 1970s and the passage of the Clean Air Amendments Act and the Clean Water Amendments Act.

An economic concept crucial to an understanding of pollution issues is that of an *external cost*. Economists define external costs as *costs of production borne by someone other than the producer*. Under this definition, the production of steel would involve both external and internal costs. Producing steel requires iron ore, coal, and skilled labor. These are all internal costs, since they are borne directly by the producer. But steel production also typically involves the discharge of pollutants such as sulfur dioxide and sulfur trioxide into the atmosphere, and such pollutants are notorious for defacing and weakening steel and marble structures. And since the structures damaged are typically not owned by the steelmaking firms themselves, these costs must be counted as external ones. From an ethical point of view, then, the push is to make external costs internal. In other words, the push is either to require the steel company to compensate those who are harmed by the pollution, or—as is usually done—to require the company to pay for pollution-control devices sufficient to deter pollution damage.

Becoming clearer about pollution issues requires a healthy sense of realism. The goal of *zero discharge*—in other words, no pollution at all—is probably a dream. Pollution experts note that the cost of eliminating pollutants from a given production process is inversely and exponentially related to the percentage of pollution remaining. That is, as a manufacturer spends money to control pollution, the first 50 percent of the pollution is relatively inexpensive to eliminate; but eliminating each remaining percentage point of pollution is dramatically more expensive. Indeed, for many production processes, eliminating 100 percent of the pollution is infinitely expensive, or, practically speaking, impossible.

The cases in this section focus on the question of the extent to which corporations must exercise internal moral responsibility, in addition to simply following laws in regard to environmental use. The "Cumberland Gasket" case deals with an in-plant pollutant, asbestos, and Cumberland Company's attempt to restrict harm to workers while maintaining reasonable profit. In the "Hooker Chemical and Plastics" case, the reader is confronted with a complex web of environmental problems and managerial dilemmas occurring in the context of what we have come to know as the "Love Canal" problem. Finally, the "Diablo Canyon" case deals with a celebrated attempt by critics of the nuclear power industry to block the introduction of a nuclear power generating plant. In addition to issues of managerial responsibility, it also raises the public policy issue of the extent to which our society should limit nuclear facilities.

Case Study
Cumberland Gasket Co., Inc.

Herman Gadon
Dwight R. Ladd

"It's my problem and I've got to live with it," said Fred Barlow, Vice President and General Manager of the Maryland Division of Cumberland Gasket Co., Inc. "There are thirty people out there in the plant working with asbestos, and even with all of the precautions we have taken, some of them may develop symptoms of asbestosis or lung cancer." Mr. Barlow went on to observe that the real moral issue for him was related to the fact that most of the scientific evidence of serious consequences from inhaling asbestos dust was based on asbestos miners and other workers around raw asbestos, while only a relatively modest amount of asbestos was used in the Maryland Division. "My trouble is," he said, "that I just cannot be sure how serious it is."

The Maryland Division of Cumberland Gasket Co., Inc. manufactured a wide range of gaskets, washers and other non-metallic fittings and parts which were primarily used in petroleum processing equipment such as pumps and valves. Some of these parts and fittings were made of asbestos because of the latter's exceptional resistance to wear and heat. The parts were relatively inexpensive, but unusually critical components of the equipment in which they were used. Failure of one of these small parts could shut down an oil well or cause serious oil spillage. Thus, Cumberland's products were of substantial importance. The parts in question were manufactured in two plants of Cumberland, Maryland. In 1977, the Maryland Division had sales of about $20 million. Cumberland, which in other plants in Michigan and California made parts for the automotive industry, had sales of about $60 million in 1977.

CUMBERLAND AND FRED BARLOW

Cumberland Gasket Co., Inc. had been formed in 1970 by the merger of three smaller companies. While the primary goal behind the merger was to enable the companies involved to serve better an increasingly dispersed nationwide market, the divisions, which were generally equivalent to the predecessor companies, retained a great deal of autonomy. The general

This case was made possible by the cooperation of a business firm which remains anonymous. It was prepared by Professors Herman Gadon and Dwight R. Ladd, University of New Hampshire, Whittemore School of Business and Economics, and is intended to provide a basis for classroom discussion and not to illustrate effective or ineffective administrative practices. Reprinted with permission.

managers of each Division, who were Vice-Presidents of Cumberland, were primarily responsible for the profitability of their divisions. Thus, Mr. Barlow had the authority to decide what was best for his division, although he would also be responsible for the consequences.

Fred Barlow had been Vice President at the Maryland Division of Cumberland Gasket for three years. His career had been marked by determination to do well and to move on to more challenge when he felt he had come to grips with the ones he faced when he first took a job. Now 34, he had gone to work for a bearing manufacturer after he had finished high school. He worked there for a year to get enough money to get through college, went to college for a year, ran out of money, went back to the bearing manufacturer and finished his Bachelor's degree at night. After completing college, he acquired an MBA in an evening program. When he was 22 he became works manager of the bearing company. At 24 he left that company and joined a larger one that made electromagnetic laminations and stampings. First employed as production control manager, he became manufacturing manager before he left at the age of 27 to manage a division of a company that sold to libraries. At the age of 30 he came to Cumberland Gasket Co., Inc. as Manufacturing Vice President. Two years later the company merged and he became a corporate officer and general manager of the Maryland Division.

Shortly after he joined Cumberland, Mr. Barlow read a book entitled *The Expendable American* by Paul Brodeur. The book described the hazards of breathing asbestos dust, and documented the long struggle to impose maximum exposure standards. The book convinced Fred Barlow that working with asbestos could be a major health hazard, and he concluded that dealing with that hazard should be one of his major responsibilities.

THE PRODUCTS

About 15% of the Maryland Division's sales were of products containing asbestos. These products ranged from tiny washers and gaskets to relatively large vanes used in air compressors. All of these were parts which had to fit snugly with metal surfaces against which they moved, while also being resistant to heat and having a certain amount of give. The production process began with sheets of canvas and asbestos laminated with resin compounds which were purchased from another manufacturer. At the Maryland plants, the laminated sheets were sawed, cut or drilled into the desired shapes and sanded as necessary. These operations created the exposure to dust which concerned Mr. Barlow.

ASBESTOS

Asbestos is a mineral which is impervious to heat and fire, and which can be separated into fibres which, like wool, can be carded, spun and woven or felted. It can also be crushed into powder and mixed with other substances such as paint or patching plaster. These qualities of asbestos mean that it has a multitude of applications in industry and consumer products. Some commonplace applications are brake linings, electrical insulation, washers, gaskets and shingles.

Asbestos was known and used in classical times—as lamp wicks, for example—but widespread use began with the industrial revolution. For some applications—automotive brake linings, for example—there is no known substitute for asbestos. Unfortunately, it has been generally known since the beginning of this century that asbestos—or more specifically, inhaled asbestos fibres—is a principal cause of certain, almost invariably fatal diseases. One of these is asbestosis which is the scarring of the tissues of the lungs which ultimately results in the victim being unable to breathe. Lung cancer is also a likely result of inhaling asbestos as is mesothelioma, malignant tumors of the lining of the chest cavity. Asbestos-related diseases are of the sort which, in the absence of regular medical check-ups, appear only twenty or thirty years after exposure at which time they are generally untreatable. As yet, it is not known how much or how little exposure will cause one or another of these diseases, but it is clear that not a great deal of exposure is required and that build up of fibres in the body is cumulative and irreversible. Further, because asbestos fibres readily cling to other substances such as clothing or the skin, the dust can be widely dispersed. There is incontrovertible evidence that members of the families of asbestos workers have contracted these diseases in an abnormal degree even though they had never been near places where asbestos was handled.

REGULATION

Prior to 1972, the United States had no enforceable standard for maximum exposure to asbestos. In 1969, the American Conference of Governmental Hygienists recommended a minimum exposure standard of not more than twelve asbestos fibres longer than five microns in a cubic centimeter of air, over an eight-hour period.* In spite of its name, this organization was a privately funded, non-governmental agency, and thus adherence to the standard was entirely voluntary.

In 1970, Congress passed the Occupational Safety and Health Act which, among other things, empowered the Secretary of Labor to set safety standards. The act also created the National Institute for Occupational Safety and Health (NIOSH) and during 1970 and 1971, NIOSH publicized a number of earlier studies showing the health hazards associated with asbestos. Trade union officials and independent investigators urged that a minimum exposure standard of two, five micron fibres per cubic cen-

---

*A micron is equal to 1/5000th of an inch. It is about the smallest fibre length that can be measured without an electron microscope. It is estimated that the presence of two, five micron fibers in a cubic centimeter of air means the presence of up to 1000 smaller particles.

The average person will breathe in about eight million cubic centimeters of air in an eight-hour period.

timeter be instituted by the Secretary. This, incidentally, was the standard adopted by the British government in 1968. However, the Secretary chose, in early 1972, to impose a standard of five fibres. After continued controversy and public hearings, the two-fibre standard was promulgated in July, 1975, and in 1977 OSHA proposed a new limit of one-half of a five micron fibre per cubic centimeter of air. NIOSH, at the same time, was urging adoption of a standard of one-tenth of a five micron fibre.

THE FABRICATION DIVISION

The Maryland Division's operations were carried on in two separate plants. One was housed in the original nineteenth-century factory where Cumberland began, but the other, in which most of the asbestos processing took place, had been constructed in 1976. In the old plant, only some machines were fitted with dust collectors, and therefore asbestos products could only be worked on those machines—thereby considerably limiting flexibility in scheduling. In the new, one-story, windowless plant, dust was collected from all machines and deposited through a central evacuating system into plastic sealable bags. This meant that products containing asbestos could be worked on any machinery in the plant. Though more costly, the application of dust collection to all equipment in the new plant provided a cleaner total environment as well as more scheduling flexibility. The sealed plastic bags were removed by a small independent contractor and buried within 24 hours in the city's landfill dump.

Under OSHA regulations every employee working with asbestos was required to wear a mask. Mr. Barlow insisted on rigorous enforcement of the rules by ordering that the supervisor of any employee working with asbestos without a mask would be immediately suspended for a week. Though Mr. Barlow made frequent inspections, no one had ever been found without a mask. In the early days of Mr. Barlow's tenure, Cumberland's insurance carrier had made annual surveys of dust conditions. In 1976, Mr. Barlow had his own testing equipment purchased so that the plant could conduct its own tests every month. In the three inspections by OSHA, particles of asbestos at every machine in the two factories had always been below the OSHA standard of two fibres. In accordance with OSHA regulations, any employee working with asbestos was required to have his pulmonary functions tested and chest X-rayed under the direction of a physician at least once each year. The company was required to keep records of these medical tests of each employee for 50 years.

ATTITUDES ABOUT THE HAZARD

In spite of various precautions being taken, Mr. Barlow was not sure that enough was being done, or whether any exposure to asbestos was acceptable. Though scientific evidence of the effects of small dosage was still inconclusive, Mr. Barlow observed, "If a five micron fibre is dangerous, why is a 4.9 micron fibre OK?"

Though his peers were aware of, and concerned about, the dangers of working with asbestos, there were differences of opinion among them about what more could or should be done. Some were resigned to the realization that hazards are all about us anyhow and in some minimum sense unavoidable. Others equated the risk with no more than occasional smoking and raised the question whether tests on animals of massive exposure to substances could really be used to evaluate effects of very small, albeit continuous, exposure of humans to those substances. By and large they had concluded from all the facts as they knew them, that Cumberland's precautions provided workers with sufficient protection as well as early warning through regularly scheduled pulmonary inspections. This opinion was strengthened by the results of a study of the medical records of retired Cumberland employees who had died during the preceding 20 or so years. In no case was the cause of death apparently related to asbestos.

Mr. Barlow's greatest frustration was with the workers themselves, who, according to Mr. Barlow, "couldn't give a damn." Employees and others, Mr. Barlow felt, had seen so many ridiculous government regulations that they assumed that all government regulations were ridiculous.* Wiping the white asbestos dust off his finger after he had handled a small, in-process piece of asbestos laminated sheet, a supervisor, showing the casewriters through the plant, shrugged his shoulders and said he had resigned himself to the exposure as an unavoidable part of his job, though he worried about the effect on his wife and children. He noted the thin layer of dust on all surfaces in the plant in spite of elaborate dust collection equipment, and reflected about the consequences of asbestos particles carried home on his clothes and transferred to the clothes of other family members in the family wash.

Most customers (see below) were primarily concerned that asbestos and asbestos products were becoming more expensive and harder to get, but did not otherwise appear to be overly concerned about the health hazard since they only installed parts and did not machine, sand or saw them.

THE MARKET

When Mr. Barlow took over management of the Maryland Division, Cumberland Gasket Co., Inc. had two competitors for its asbestos-based products. About the time that the two-fibre OSHA standard was introduced in 1975, one of the competitors left the market for reasons not known to Mr.

---

*Mr. Barlow believed that contrary to much popular opinion, OSHA was good and effective. He observed that while OSHA had promulgated some silly and widely publicized regulations about the shape of toilet seats and the like, there was incontrovertible evidence that industrial injuries and accidents had declined since OSHA had come into existence. He was confident that these declines would not have occurred without OSHA.

Barlow. Thus, in 1978, only Cumberland and one other company were supplying the market. Mr. Barlow thought that the other company reflected concern for the hazards of working with asbestos when they stopped selling trimmed asbestos sheet in 1977. (Trimming creates dust.) He had heard rumors from customers and other sources that the last competitor was planning to leave the market.

The market for the asbestos-based products made by Cumberland was dominated by a few large companies. In addition, there were 20 to 30 very much smaller customers. Mr. Barlow felt that the primary concern of these customers, especially in the replacement market, was with price and delivery. Early in 1977, the price of asbestos had increased by 16% following just six months after a 10% increase. Because there were now only two producers left, Cumberland and its one competitor, it was becoming increasingly difficult for customers to get timely delivery. Because of the general lack of concern about the hazards of asbestos, very little work had been done on developing a substitute. (There are hazards other than those related to workers. One estimate holds that 158,000 pounds of asbestos fibre is put in the air each year from the wearing down of automotive brake linings.) Nor could Cumberland, a relatively small company, afford to do much pure R & D on its own. Du Pont had developed a substitute, which tends to be four to five times more expensive than asbestos, and was of inferior quality for some applications. The evidence of customer behavior was that they were unwilling to pay more for asbestos substitutes.

COMPANY POLICY AND ALTERNATIVES

In 1978, Cumberland's announced policy was to continue to manufacture asbestos as long as it could do so in compliance with OSHA or other standards, and as long as it could do so without further capital investment—unless the investment had a six-month or less payback. The investment limitation reflected management's view that standards very probably would be made more restrictive. Products using asbestos were always fully priced, including the costs of the air testing and special cleaning programs. Mr. Barlow would not discount products containing asbestos in order to promote other business. In his visits to and discussions with customers, he regularly tried to get them to try substitutes for asbestos, though with limited success. Mr. Barlow stressed the company's obligation to its customers and observed that Cumberland could not leave them without a source. Without Cumberland as a supplier, market demands could not be met. However, if the OSHA standard of one-half of a fibre were introduced, Mr. Barlow thought that Cumberland could not continue without major changes.

One possible change would be to move to a complete "white room," space-age environment. This would involve isolating equipment used in making asbestos from the rest of the plant. Employees using the equipment would have to make a complete change of clothing and to shower before leaving the room. Masks would still be required. In addition to the costs associated with clothing changes, etc., the white room would mean serious under-utilization of equipment, since the machines would only be used with asbestos material about 30% to 40% of the time. A "white room" would require an investment of $3/4 million and would raise operating costs by $100,000 a year. The Fabrication Division had $6,000,000 in assets. Another alternative would be to process all asbestos under water or other liquid. However, since asbestos is absorbent, product properties could change. Thus considerable research would have to go into developing the liquid used and testing the properties of the product after it had been processed in a liquid.

Processing in a liquid would eliminate dust but would substitute asbestos-bearing sludges. Interestingly, neither OSHA nor the State had any regulations preventing the company from dumping sludge containing asbestos into the river. (Eventually, asbestos in the water would be washed up on the banks, dry out and enter into the air.) The new Cumberland plant had a completely enclosed filtration system designed to prevent any discharge into the river. This system had not been required by law, but Mr. Barlow had included it when the plant was built, and even though it had added a substantial amount to the cost of the plant, top management had not questioned it.

The final option for Mr. Barlow and Cumberland was to leave the asbestos business entirely. As noted above, this would do irreparable harm to customers, and would raise the cost of many goods and services for society generally. Beyond this, there were serious financial consequences for the Cumberland company and its employees. Unless substitutes developed for asbestos involved materials and processes which were adaptable to Cumberland's capabilities, jobs in the plant would inevitably be lost. Furthermore, the Fabrication Division was only marginally profitable and the contribution of products containing asbestos was considerable. Loss of the asbestos business would place the division in a loss position—and would jeopardize the profitability of other divisions within the company.

Though Mr. Barlow had given considerable thought to the moral and business issues involved in Cumberland's processing of asbestos materials, he still faced unresolved questions and concerns about the extent of the hazards to which Cumberland's workers were exposed and of the ways in which he should respond to them.

QUESTIONS FOR DISCUSSION*

1. Should Mr. Barlow wait until more information is forthcoming about the long-range dangers of asbestos exposure at low levels before taking additional measures?
2. Does Mr. Barlow have an obligation to encourage stricter government standards?
3. What steps, if any, should Mr. Barlow take?

Case Study
Hooker Chemical and Plastics

Gary Whitney

Hooker Chemical and Plastics Corp. found itself in the middle of complex legal maneuverings involving 2.3 billion dollars worth of filed intents-to-sue in 1979 as a result of dumping chemical wastes sealed in steel drums near the Love Canal during the period of 1942 to 1953. In 1978, New York state declared a health emergency when 82 chemicals, eleven of them suspected carcinogens, were identified on the surface near the Love Canal. Abnormally high rates of birth defects, miscarriages, and liver disorders have been reported by Love Canal residents. Hooker officials deny any legal liability.

LOVE CANAL

The canal is adjacent to the Niagara River about four miles from the famous falls. It is in the city of Niagara Falls. The canal was dug in the 1890's to provide water and power for William J. Love's visionary scheme for a model industrial city. The canal was never finished and the model city never materialized. The immediate area ultimately did become heavily populated with industrial chemical plants. Carborundum, Union Carbide, Olin, Du Pont, Hooker, and a city water treatment plant were operating in the area in 1978.

The old canal appeared, in 1942, to be an ideal dump site for waste from Hooker's Niagara Falls plant. The area was sparsely populated and the canal was 10 feet deep, 60 feet wide, and 3000 feet long surrounded by an impervious clay soil. (Water transmission through clay is $\frac{1}{3}$ inch in 25 years.) Hooker obtained permission to use the canal for dumping in 1942 and subsequently acquired a strip 200 feet wide with the canal approximately in the center. The chemical wastes were sealed in steel drums and dropped in the old canal and covered with a layer of clay. Approximately 22,000 tons were deposited by 1953.

In 1953 Hooker closed the dump and sold the land to the city's Board of Education for one dollar. The dump was overfilled with clay. The board subsequently constructed a school on part of the land and sold the remainder to a developer who built and sold homes for families. None of the homes were built directly over the canal but it is believed during the pro-

This case was prepared by Professor Gary Whitney of the University of San Diego as a basis for class discussion rather than to illustrate either effective or ineffective handling of an administrative situation. Copyright © 1979 by Gary Whitney. Reprinted with permission.

cess of road construction some of the overfill was removed and distributed in the area.

In 1976, after abnormally heavy rains, the canal overflowed its underground banks and quantities of various chemicals oozed to the surface. Apparently the steel drums had corroded and leaked their contents which leached through the soil. In some places pools of chemicals sat on the surface. Near the canal, chemicals such as Mirex and lindane, banned for use as pesticides; plus chloroform, benzene, trichloroethane, toluene, tetrachloroethane, and 1,3,5, trichlorobenzene leaked into basements. EPA air monitors have recorded 250 to 5000 times the safe level of some chemicals.

The *New York Times* (Aug. 2, 1978, p. B 9) made this report.

> Karen Schroeder's backyard seems to be the lowest draining point for the waters leaching out of the fill. Her swimming pool was popped out of the ground by the rising water table, her whole garden killed, the redwood posts of her backyard fence [were] eaten away, and local authorities pumped 17,500 gallons of chemical filled water out of her yard in two days this year, water that even Chemtrol, the country's biggest waste disposal company refused to handle, she said. So it was trucked to Ohio and poured down a deep-well disposal site.
>
> Her dog died young and now her husband, Timothy, jokes that their daughter's Easter rabbit has become their miner's canary, "If it dies, we'll know to move away."

One expert, Dr. Beverly Paigen of Buffalo's Roswell Park Memorial Cancer Center noted that there were definitely elevated "rates of miscarriages, increased risks of birth defects, increased urinary tract problems, and a striking effect on the central nervous system." A more personal reaction is registered below.

> Jim Clark—an admittedly bitter man whose family has been plagued with medical problems and whose yard is littered with signs like one reading "Welcome to Chemical City"—is one resident who feels there's need for scientific studies.
>
> "My kidney just solidified and quit functioning," he said.
>
> "My four kids all display hyperactivity. We have three members of the family now who have skin problems. My one son quit growing at 12, developed an ulcer at 15 and he's an acute diabetic. My wife has cardiovascular problems and just everybody feels generally rotten." (*Palouse Empire News*, May 19, 1979, p. 2)

On August 2, 1978, New York State Health Commissioner Robert J. Whalen declared an emergency and on August 7, President Carter declared it a limited disaster area and sent Federal Disaster Administrator William H. Wilcox to investigate. Subsequently the state evacuated 239 families and purchased their homes for about $12 million.

Despite findings traces of the chemicals after taking 5000 soil samples, health investigators admit they can find no pattern to the chemical traces nor a direct indication that they are flowing from the dump.

RESPONSIBILITY

"We take moral responsibility, not legal liability," declared Bruce Davis, Executive Vice President of Hooker's industrial chemical group. "What do you expect us to do—put up signs and tell people not to buy houses here?" Elsewhere he is quoted as saying, "We've had no control of that property for 25 years." He also claimed that Hooker did not want to sell the land to the school board but did so only when the Board of Education threatened to condemn the land. Hooker included a clause in the deed to the Board noting the past use of the land and required that the school board assume risk of liability for any future claims that might result from the buried chemicals.

At the time the dumping occurred there were no federal or state statutes that controlled dumping of waste materials.

However, the dangers of the dumping did not become evident for the first time in 1978. In 1958, several children suffered chemical burns from playing near the closed dump. Hooker sent investigators who found chemical residues exposed apparently from material excavated to put a road through the site. The school was notified by Hooker but no further action was taken.

According to *The New York Times* (Jan. 21, 1979):

> In 1971, when almost every lot had a house on it, rainwater leaked into the canal bed, stirring up the chemicals. Drums broke open on the surface, creating three-foot pools of pesticide. Dogs and cats lost their fur and died. Children burned their feet. Five infants with birth defects were born at the southern end of the canal. The miscarriage rate went up.

RELATED ACTIVITIES

1972 (New York): At Hyde Park, also in Niagara Falls, where Hooker operated another chemical waste dump, the manager of an adjacent plant wrote to Hooker complaining of "an extremely dangerous condition affecting our plant and employees . . . our midnight shift workers has (sic) complained of coughing and sore throats from the obnoxious and corrosive permeating fumes from the disposal site."

1976 (New York): Mirex, which causes cancer in laboratory animals, was being discharged illegally by Hooker's Niagara Falls plant at a rate of one pound per day. In September 1976 the New York Department of Environmental Conservation banned consumption of seven species of fish from Lake Ontario warning they were contaminated with Mirex. In March 1977 Hooker released a study which reported a failure to find Mirex in 12 species of Lake Ontario fish; however, the Department of Environmental Conservation was not satisfied with the study.

1976/7 (Virginia): Suits of more than $100 million were filed by employees of Life Science who were exposed to Kepone dust. Symptoms ranged from severe trembling to sterility. Hooker was named as a defendant since it supplied certain raw materials used in the manufacturing process. In January 1977, the suit was settled out of court. The terms of the settlement were not disclosed. A spokesman for Occidental Petroleum (who acquired Hooker in 1968) said the settlement would have negligible impact on the earnings of Hooker.

1977 (Michigan): Hooker is ordered to pay $176,000 for discharging HCCPD, a building block for Mirex and Kepone pesticides in a lake.

1979 (Michigan): Michigan officials sued Hooker for air, water, and land pollution around its plant in Montague. State attorney general Frank Kelly calls Montague "an environmental time bomb." More than 30 chemicals have been identified on the site.

1979 (New York): In January the New York State Health Department surveyed residents near Hyde Park. In February, the town of Niagara Falls filed a $26 million suit against Hooker regarding its Hyde Park landfill dump.

QUESTIONS FOR DISCUSSION*

1. Is the distinction between "moral" and "legal" responsibility made by Hooker's vice president a valid one? If so, what is the extent of Hooker's "moral" responsibility?

2. Do companies ever have moral obligations to disclose information that places them in a bad light and even to finance a campaign to distribute that information widely? If so, under what conditions does the responsibility arise?

3. Is there "shared" accountability in the Hooker case? If so, which parties in the Hooker case share accountability?

4. How should Hooker managers respond to the problems as described in the case?

Case Study
Diablo Canyon:
Nuclear Energy and the Public Welfare

A. R. Gini

The Diablo Canyon Nuclear Reactor is located on a rocky cove just outside of San Luis Obispo, California and midway between Los Angeles and San Francisco. In September of 1981 Diablo Canyon was the scene of the final showdown between the Abalone Alliance (a coalition of anti-nuclear groups), the powerful Nuclear Regulatory Commission (NRC) and California's single largest producer of energy, the Pacific Gas and Electric Company (PG&E). The confrontation that ensued during the next three months was in fact the culmination of twelve years of protest and legal maneuverings which had kept the plant idle since its completion in 1979.

The Diablo reactor is the largest and most sophisticated of three nuclear plants to be designed and built by PG&E. The 735 acre shoreline site seemed to be an ideal location in 1968 when construction began. It was far from the big cities, had unlimited supplies of cooling water and the cost was put at a modest $350 to $450 million. To the nearby town of San Luis Obispo, population 40,000, it meant new jobs.

The plant itself is made up of two separate nuclear reactors and electric generating systems with the combined output of 2,200,000 kilowatts of electricity. The two units were designed to produce 33% of the projected energy resources of PG&E in the 1980s. It is estimated that once in operation the plant would save the equivalent of 20 million barrels of fossil fuels per year and over $2 billion in customer services charges in the first five years of operation.

PG&E has steadfastly claimed that the Diablo reactor was the cheapest, most efficient and ecologically safest means to meet the increasing volume of energy demanded by its customers. They maintain that the reactor is the finest example of the "state of the art" in the nuclear energy industry. PG&E claims that the plant contains every possible safety device, and that the construction of the plant was designed to take into account the geological abnormalities of the California coastline. Specifically, they claim to have intentionally designed and "over constructed" the plant in order to withstand a 6.75 earthquake as measured on the Richter scale. The was done in order to compensate for any possible "ripple effects" from seismic reactions emanating from three major fault zones located between 15 and 60 miles due east of the plant (Sur-Nacimiento Fault Zone, Rinconada Fault and San Andreas Fault).

At the time construction began there was no organized anti-nuclear power movement and environmental groups voiced little or no opposition. Utility officials predicted that the plant could start producing electricity within two to four years. These projections, however, proved to be at least five years off the mark as one series of design and construction problems after another added both to the postponement of the completion date and to increased building costs. PG&E's difficulties were multiplied when in 1973 geologists discovered an active fault (Hosgri Fault) in the Pacific seabed just 2.5 miles west of Diablo Canyon. Both federal and state authorities ordered that the plant be structurally reinforced to withstand an earthquake of 7.5 magnitude. These modifications took nearly three years at a cost of well over $200 million. Further costs and delays were incurred in various lawsuits and injunctions as well as over 190 days of public hearings defending the safety of the plant. In March of 1979 yet a new setback occurred when the nuclear plant at Three Mile Island near Harrisburg, Pennsylvania was shut down by the NRC because of serious design errors, inadequate emergency procedures and deficiencies in operating techniques. The NRC immediately suspended the licensing of all new plants and ordered sweeping changes in equipment and operating procedures, changes that added $100 million to the cost of Diablo Canyon.

As a result of all of this, the initial projected costs of the plant zoomed from $350 million to well over $2.5 billion—an almost 800 percent cost overrun. In May of 1981 Barton W. Schakelford, president and chief operating officer of PG&E, estimated that his company was spending over $500,000 a day in interest charges alone on money borrowed to continuously up-grade a plant which has yet to produce one kilowatt hour of electricity.

By mid-1981 PG&E had completed "retrofitting" the Diablo reactor to meet the specifications of the NRC both in regard to the Hosgri Fault as well as the new requirements imposed on all plants because of the near tragedy of Three Mile Island. On July 17, 1981, PG&E announced that the "Atomic Safety and Licensing Appeal Board" of the NRC had found that "the (Diablo Canyon) plant (is) adequately designed to withstand any earthquake that can be reasonably expected." The NRC stated that its staff and their technical consultants had conducted the most "extensive and exhaustive" seismic review ever undertaken, and that they had complete confidence in the Board's decision.[1]

Even before this report had been issued Dr. John A. Blume, internationally recognized seismologist and primary consultant for PG&E, flatly stated that the containment structures at Diablo Canyon were the "strongest man-made structures in the world." Dr. Blume was convinced that no other building in the world was better designed or had more strength. He was confident that the plant would survive unimpaired a quake of an 8.25 magnitude.[2] Given all of this data a senior spokesman for PG&E stated that as far as the company was concerned all the evidence to date indicated that "Diablo Canyon is without question the most thoroughly studied power plant in the nation's history. The plant is safe from any earthquake that can occur in the area."[3]

Working from this body of evidence PG&E in August 1981 initiated procedures for petitioning the NRC for a "limited license" to begin the loading of atomic fuel into one of the plant's reactors and to commence with low level (5% capacity) power testing operations. After the successful completion of these preliminary tests PG&E would be eligible to apply for a full commercial operator's license. If all went well the plant manager, Robert Thornberg, felt that the facility could be generating electricity by January of 1982.

However, the opposition was simply not convinced of the overall safety of the plant, and the anti-nuclear forces under the direction of the Abalone Alliance began to activate plans for a final assault on Diablo. The Abalone Alliance was formed in 1977 and although its roots are in California it grew to become the parent body for a nationwide coalition of 58 anti-nuclear organizations. It takes its name from the thousands of abalone mollusks that were killed during the testing of the plant's cooling system. While the alliance was organized to protest the completion of the Diablo

Canyon reactor the overall goals of the group are much larger. As Claude Steiner, a spokesman for the alliance, put it, "Our purpose goes beyond blockading Diablo; we want to halt all U.S. nuclear power development."[4] Specifically, the alliance believes that all nuclear energy is inherently unsafe because of the complexity of their overall systems, the problems involved with the disposal of radio-active wastes and because of the possibility, no matter how slim, of a "melt down" or uncontrolled nuclear accident. The alliance also believes that nuclear reactors are inextricably linked to the nuclear armaments race, at least insofar as the fissionable material needed to make an atomic bomb comes from reprocessing the uranium in spent fuel rods into plutonium. And finally, the alliance believes that the Diablo Canyon site is a certain disaster simply waiting for an opportunity to occur!

The alliance contends that PG&E's initial decision in 1968 to build the plant within 60 miles of three separate fault zones may ultimately be proven to be a well-warranted risk, for which PG&E took all necessary precautions. However, they feel that the utility's decision in 1973 to carry on with construction after the discovery of the Hosgri Fault just 2.5 miles to the west is both morally indefensible and technically impossible to justify. The site, they argue, is simply too dangerous. They appealed to the federal government to deny any form of license to PG&E because of the serious seismic, emergency preparedness and related safety issues that still remained to be explored and resolved. The alliance felt that if one must be built, there are much better places to build nuclear plants. Dr. John Gofman, a nuclear industry expert from the University of California Medical Center in San Francisco, claims that the plant is unsafe because quakes are too unpredictable in regard to their duration and intensity. He argues that if the NRC allows the Diablo plant to operate, then in effect it is saying that "people in this area are expendable and that they are willing to write us off." Professor Gofman went on to suggest that the best-laid plans of mice and men have gone wrong so often that if they had any common sense, they wouldn't build a plant there![5]

In September 1981 after one year of intensive preparation, numerous successful rallies publicizing the events, and countless grass-roots organizational meetings, the various forces, factions and friends of the alliance began to arrive at a thirty acre tent village set up on private property northeast of the plant. Their strategy was to blockade the plant compound by land and sea. The blockade was to include groups of people scaling the entrance gate, groups of individuals lying down in the middle of the access roads to the plant and a mini-fleet of rubber rafts and scuba divers who would try to penetrate the plant's perimeter along the coastline. It was their hope to make the plant's start-up as difficult as possible and to stop the loading of the atomic fuel which is the first necessary step for the proposed low level power testing. The alliance, however, was determined to keep violence from marring the demonstrations. They adopted a code which prohibited property damage, verbal or physical violence and the carrying of weapons while taking part in any form of protest. Their goal was to focus world attention on what was happening at Diablo Canyon. However, the leaders of the alliance realized from the beginning that their blockade was nothing more than a "symbolic effort." The blockade was "symbolic" in two senses:

1. The atomic fuel necessary for testing had already been stored in the plant for a period of five years, and, therefore, the chances of stopping the actual loading operations were very small.
2. The plant area was being patrolled and protected by an estimated 1,000 local police, state sheriffs and the National Guard. The leaders of the protest realized that at best their efforts could forestall but not entirely prohibit the operational status of the plant.

By September 14, the tent city had only grown to 3,000 people. This figure was far below the 30,000 that the alliance had initially estimated. Officials of PG&E were overjoyed by the sparse turnout of protestors. They felt that such a small turnout helped to substantiate their belief that the Abalone Alliance only represented a minority opinion in regard to nuclear energy and that most people had confidence in PG&E claims for the safety of the twin reactor complex. Fearful of losing their momentum the leaders of the alliance announced that the blockade of Diablo would begin on the morning of September 15. On the first day of the blockade the press clearly outnumbered the protestors and only 300 people were arrested for blocking or scaling the facility's entrance. It was also estimated that twenty-five more people were arrested for trespassing after reaching the beach front side of the plant in rafts. In no way did the protestors deter the busing of 700 PG&E workers into the plant. As far as the plant manager was concerned, "It was business as usual around here!"[6] The police also grew in confidence after the first encounter. They felt that the protestors were unorganized and undermanned and that they, the police, would be able to handle all eventualities. Nevertheless, they warned that they would remain on the scene. "If it lasts a month," said Glen Craig, commissioner of the California Highway Patrol, "we are prepared to deal with it for a month."[7]

By September 18, the ranks of the alliance had already dwindled to approximately 1,500 people and yet each day the number of people arrested grew. Although few new people were joining the protestors, the same group of people kept getting re-arrested. By the end of the month while less than 300 protestors remained at the campsite, over 1,893 arrests had been made. Yet even with these disappointing figures, the Abalone Alliance vowed to continue its vigil. PG&E at this point felt that it had survived the gauntlet of trial by public opinion and had won. Now all that was needed was approval by the NRC to begin testing.

Approval by the NRC came on September 21 when the full board unanimously voted to grant PG&E a license to test the first of its two reactors. Work began immediately at the plant on a final checklist in preparation for the loading of atomic fuel and preliminary testing. Suddenly, PG&E was beset with a series of unexpected reversals. On September 28, PG&E announced that fuel loading would be delayed because "a discrepancy" had been found in a checklist stress analysis of part of the plant's containment structures. By the very next day PG&E was forced to admit that the start up of the Unit One reactor would be "indefinitely suspended" after finding that the structural supporter of Unit One did not conform to the design plans as approved by the NRC. To simplify, when PG&E upgraded the seismic support systems around the reactors after the discovery of the Hosgri Fault, the reconstruction plans intended for Unit One were in fact used on Unit Two and vice versa. The critical point is that the possible seismic stress that each reactor could absorb would be different because they are approximately 200 feet apart. This seemingly minor separation would mean that each reactor would be exposed to a different degree of "vertical earthquake motion." Therefore, it is possible that the containment structures could be damaged, thereby violating the integrity of the reactor's cores. The containment structures in question are also part of the reactor's heat removal system. This system, in addition to its normal role in dispersing residual heat when a reactor is shut down for refueling, functions as a back-up cooling device in the event of a nuclear accident.

This first unexpected setback was by no means the end of PG&E's problems. By October 1, the utility discovered serious design problems in four other systems within the reactor containment structure that are vital parts of a network of devices necessary to shut down or cool off the reactor in case of emergency. October 2 brought yet new disclosures by PG&E of structural errors in the support systems that hold the electronic cables attached to the reactors. Officials indicated that the improper construction of the cable supports could result during an earthquake in the loss of the electrical power needed to control the reactors and their emergency monitoring devices. The *coup de grace* came on October 24 when James Hanchett, a spokesman for the San Francisco office of NRC, announced that PG&E was unable to demonstrate that the weights it calculated for the equipment located in the reactor areas were correct. If these calculations were incorrect it would mean that the floors of the reactor areas were not sufficiently reinforced to sustain the trauma of a seismic shock. If the accusation was accurate the NRC felt that this error was potentially more significant and more dangerous than any of the mistakes that had been earlier identified at the Diablo Canyon plant.[8]

Throughout all of this PG&E had voluntarily postponed all testing procedures as a precautionary measure, but steadfastly maintained that even if these errors had gone undetected the plant would not have been endangered because of the extremely conservative design criteria used.[9] Officials of PG&E including its president claimed before the press and the NRC that the problems were ultimately minor ones isolated to one area of the plant, and that repairs could be completed within a matter of months so that testing could resume.

The response of the Abalone Alliance to these claims was expected. One member of the alliance stated that the discovery of these errors "affirms what we have been saying all along—that the plant is structurally not safe."[10] The alliance felt that PG&E's overall response to the situation typified the disregard that the utility has for public safety and welfare. What PG&E really is interested in is recouping and making a profit on the more than $2.5 billion they have invested into the Diablo project. As far as the alliance is concerned, PG&E has been both cavalier and criminal in its construction of so delicate a plant so close to a fault.

From the first report by PG&E of the discovery of a "slight discrepancy" in September, the NRC began to analyze and re-analyze all the relevant data. NRC officials were dispatched from their offices in Washington and San Francisco to Diablo Canyon for an endless series of on-site inspections. At the same time PG&E officials were being summoned to Washington to explain and justify the various discoveries as they occurred. By November the newly installed chairman of the NRC, Nunzio J. Palladino, called for a closed-door session of the commission to study "the many structural deficiencies that have come to light." Following three days of debate, on November 19, Mr. Palladino announced that "the commission doesn't like what it's seen" and because it does not feel that PG&E can live up to "efficiency standards" and "quality control" requirements the NRC has voted to suspend the license of the Diablo Canyon reactor.[11] One board member of the NRC, Peter A. Bradford, asserted that the reported "discrepancies" at the Diablo reactor had been a "first rate screw-up" since day one. He found it unbelievable that so many errors could occur in the most controversial area of the most controversial plant in the country.[12] The action to suspend the license of PG&E represents the first time a license to load fuel has been revoked, and it makes Diablo Canyon the most conspicuous and embarrassing reversal that the nuclear energy industry has suffered to date.

Clearly, throughout this prolonged multilateral confrontation the NRC tried to walk a fine line between public safety on the one hand and the danger of a huge financial loss by PG&E on the other. The NRC's other major concern was the ripple effect that the Diablo decision would have on the entire industry. Finally, in early October of 1981 President Reagan ordered the NRC and its chairman to speed up procedures for the licensing of nuclear plants so that the time from first blueprint to the start of electricity production, now as long as 14 years, could be cut to six to eight years. Also, Reagan ordered the NRC to work with industry on developing safe methods for the permanent disposal of nuclear wastes.[13] The motivation behind the president's pro-nuclear policy statement was to make America more energy independent, to create a more amiable climate for the construction of atomic plants and to take some pressure off the financially strapped industry.

Since the March 1979 accident at Three Mile Island the growth of nuclear power has been slowing steadily and in some places in the country completely stopped. In the months preceding the final NRC ruling on Diablo Canyon at least ten atomic plants closed or had their completion plans terminated because of design problems, escalating costs and public concern about location and safety. With the setback at Diablo Canyon most experts now feel that it is highly questionable whether the President's program will bring relief to the atomic industrial community.

On December 1, 1981, at the annual conference of the Atomic Industrial Forum, Mr. Palladino told executives of the nation's utilities and builders of nuclear power plants that while excessive governmental regulations are partially responsible for the present position of atomic energy, they too were responsible because of their poor workmanship and the "inexcusable" standards of quality assurance programs. "During my first five months as NRC chairman," said Palladino, "a number of deficiencies in some plants have come to my attention which show a surprising lack of professionalism in the construction and preparation for operation of nuclear facilities. The responsibility for such deficiencies rests squarely on the shoulders of management." Palladino went on to say that "there have been lapses of many kinds—in design analyses resulting in built-in design errors, in poor construction practices, in falsified documents, in harassment of quality control personnel and in inadequate training of reactor operators. Quality cannot be inspected into a plant," Mr. Palladino said. "Quality must be built into the plant. All of you, I am sure, would say that you know this, but the practices at some plants do not confirm that the importance of this principle is always understood."

Mr. Palladino went on to suggest that because of Three Mile Island and Diablo Canyon "the industry and the NRC have suffered a loss of credibility that can only be regained over time. The responsibility for regaining public confidence rests with the utilities who finance and operate the plants and the construction companies that build them, as well as with government regulators." He called on the utility companies to examine their policies on quality control. He stressed that just as all utilities have certified independent financial audits of their fiscal activities, there should also be similar audits of their quality control measures. "I believe," said Mr. Palladino, "that credibility will be regained if the future brings safe and economic nuclear power along with (the) elimination of shoddy workmanship and poor practices. Well managed utilities cannot afford to let the poor performers jeopardize public safety and undermine public confidence in the industry."[14]

Whatever the ultimate outcome of Mr. Palladino's chastisement, the future of the Diablo Canyon nuclear power plant remains in doubt. If nothing else, the confrontation at Diablo Canyon has served to make the American public aware of the benefits, issues and dangers at stake in the use of atomic energy. For some, Diablo Canyon has been a valuable lesson from which the entire industry can profit and grow. For others, Diablo Canyon symbolizes the end of an overly ambitious and expensive experiment. As one cynical observer put it, "At the present time, nuclear power is dead in the United States. The economics and politics of it rule out the construction of more plants."[15]

AN UPDATE

After meeting all the retrofitting requirements of the NRC, in the fall of 1983 Unit I of the Diablo Canyon nuclear power plant was granted a limited license to commence low-power testing. On November 2, 1984, the

NRC granted Unit I a full operating license and the plant began producing electricity for commercial use on May 7, 1985. In the same month of that year, Unit II was granted a limited license and in August 1985 was granted a full license and began commercial production on March 13, 1986.

According to Ron Weinberg, PG&E public information officer, the final cost for the Diablo Canyon plant exceeded $5.8 billion but has already proven to be a good investment. In its first year of full operation, the plant manufactured 25 percent of all the electricity produced by PG&E. As of this writing, the plant generates a combined output of 2,250,000 kilowatts of electricity and serves 2,250,000 customers in northern and central California. Moreover, Weinberg stated, the company takes special pride in the fact that in 1986 *The Institute of Nuclear Power Operations,* an industry watchdog group based in Atlanta, Georgia, listed the Diablo Canyon plant as one of the six best operated and managed nuclear reactors in the country.

NOTES

1. *Diablo Canyon Info,* PG&E Public Information Department, July 17, 1981.
2. "PG&E Interviews Dr. John A. Blume," PG&E Public Information Dept., 1981.
3. *New York Times,* August 24, 1981, sec. 2, p. 10.
4. *Maclean's: Canada's Weekly News Magazine,* September 28, 1981, p. 40.
5. *Newsweek,* August 10, 1981, p. 51.
6. *New York Times,* September 15, 1981, sec. 4, p. 28.
7. *Newsweek,* September 28, 1981, p. 38.
8. *New York Times,* October 25, 1981, sec. 1, p. 24.
9. *New York Times,* November 4, 1981, sec. 1, p. 18.
10. *New York Times,* September 30, 1981, sec. 1, p. 20.
11. *New York Times,* November 20, 1981, sec. 1, p. 1.
12. *New York Times,* October 1, 1981, sec. 1, p. 1.
13. *Time,* October 26, 1981, p. 18.
14. *New York Times,* December 12, 1981, sec. 1, pp. 1 and 19.
15. *U.S. News & World Report,* April 6, 1981, p. 59.

QUESTIONS FOR DISCUSSION*

1. In light of the Diablo Canyon experience, what special responsibilities, if any, do you think the managers of utility companies planning atomic plants have to the general public?

2. Should the U.S. government refuse to allow utility companies to build atomic power generating plants?

3. Evaluate the way in which PG&E responded to its critics. Evaluate the approach of the critics to PG&E.

3

Business
and Government

The relationship between business and government varies dramatically from country to country. In some countries, such as Japan, close cooperation occurs between corporations and the government. The corporations are interested in profit and long-term economic security, while the government is interested in public welfare and political success. Their interests coincide at vital points. Hence the Japanese government plays an active role in determining business policy and providing capital investment for promising industries. In the United States, the situation is different: Businesspersons are suspicious of governmental policies and motives and rely to a great extent on the impersonal, largely nonpolitical forces of the market.

Nevertheless, the spectacular success of U.S. business during the last 150 years has occurred in the context of both "hands-on" and "hands-off" government policies. It is a myth that the U.S. government during the nineteenth century adopted a fully laissez-faire, "hands-off" philosophy. The U.S. government provided vast sums to encourage the building of the nation's system of canals and railroads. We are reminded that Eli Whitney, nearly broke after inventing the cotton gin and failing to patent it, relied on the government to introduce the first interchangeable parts system. He persuaded the government to allow him to manufacture muskets for the army, which, in contrast to those in operation, would contain parts exactly like those in other muskets. (When he showed ten muskets to President Adams and offered to disassemble them and reassemble them with exchanged parts, the president was dumbfounded.)

When business has required support, the government has sometimes conveniently forgotten its ordinary slogans of laissez-faire, but when business has required independence, the government has backed off. The U.S. government has never, as had the seventeenth-century government of King Louis XIV, suffocated commerce beneath the weight of bureaucracy and regulations. Businesspeople complain today about government interference, but one must remember that the U.S. government has, perhaps more than any other throughout history, endorsed the benefits of a free-market philosophy.

Three major classifications of law affect corporate behavior. These are

1. Procedures allowing citizens to bring suit against corporations
2. Laws affecting the relationship between corporations and their stock holders
3. Legislation establishing special regulatory agencies and policies

All three of these have expanded dramatically since the early part of the twentieth century.

Consider, for example, the final category. Everyone knows that regulatory agencies have mushroomed in the United States since the 1920s, but few people know how dramatic that change has been. The list of government regulatory agencies whose principal business is to control U.S. corporations is too lengthy to repeat. Among its more prominent listings are the Food and Drug Administration (FDA), the Equal Employment Opportunity Commission (EEOC), the Federal Trade Commission (FTC), the Federal Communications Commission (FCC), the Federal Aviation Administration (FAA), the Securities and Exchange Commission (SEC), the Consumer Product Safety Commission (CPSC), the Environmental Protection Agency (EPA), the Federal Energy Administration (FEA), the Federal Power Commission (FPC), the Federal Reserve System (FRS), the Interstate Commerce Commission (ICC), and the Nuclear Regulatory Commission (NRC). For each of these there exists accompanying congressional legislation that authorizes certain activities and sets limits on others.

Two issues concerning government and business must be distinguished. One is the general public policy issue of to what extent government should become involved in business. In other words, it is a question of deciding when the overall advantages of government involvement are outweighed by the rights of business participants to pursue business activities freely, or when those advantages are outweighed by a tendency to show unfair favoritism toward some business interests and not others. The Laetrile case focuses on the line that separates justified consumer and producer freedom on the one hand from justified public involvement in the welfare of the consumer on the other.

The second issue is centered squarely not on government policy, but on how managers should respond to government policy. In "Business and Political Action," we encounter the problem many business administrators face when they know that some government initiatives will help their own business. Should they contribute to PACs (Political Action Committees) that make campaign contributions to individual legislators? If so, should they ask for restrictions on the use of those funds?

Besides government's involvement in the marketplace to regulate business practices and standards, it is also involved as a direct consumer of goods and services. The area in which the government has traditionally spent the largest percentage of its buying dollars is on weapons and military hardware. As a consumer, albeit an extraordinary one, the government is open to all the benefits and drawbacks of the marketplace and therefore must proceed ever mindful of a central proposition of free economic life—caveat emptor! The last piece in this section, "Defense Contracts," is not a case per se but is instead an overview essay on some of the most recent issues and scandals involved in defense spending and the awarding of military contracts.

Case Study
Laetrile:
The FDA and Society

Thomas Donaldson
Carol J. Fritz

The Food and Drug Administration (FDA) has often found itself at the focal point of public attention; sometimes it has been the recipient of loud and vigorous praise, as when it prevented the sale of dangerous meat products, and sometimes it has been bitterly criticized, as when it allowed thalidomide to be used by expectant mothers. But by the summer of 1977, the FDA was facing one of its most difficult battles with public opinion. By then, it was clear that the FDA's official stand on the controversial cancer cure, Laetrile, had stiff opposition. Not only did hundreds of thousands of cancer sufferers believe they should be able to take Laetrile, but a number of state legislatures had expressed their disagreement with the FDA by passing laws which legalized Laetrile in their own states. It was a problem which was slipping far beyond the simple issue of Laetrile's medical effectiveness; now people were charging that the FDA's ban was a denial of a fundamental right to free choice as guaranteed by the U.S. Constitution.

Ever since the thalidomide scare in the early 1960s, the FDA has been required by law to license only substances which are both safe and effec-

This case was prepared by Thomas Donaldson, Loyola University of Chicago. Recent developments and study questions were added by Carol J. Fritz. Reprinted with permission.

tive.[1] As a result, the FDA was bound to look at Laetrile not only in terms of its safety to users—and it *did* appear to be safe—but also in terms of its effectiveness. The FDA was convinced that Laetrile, which it calls the world's "most tested cancer cure," was absolutely worthless for the purpose of curing cancer. But there was, as might be expected, vehement disagreement from the pro-Laetrile forces. To further complicate matters, the FDA had recently incurred hostile reaction for its unpopular attempt to remove saccharin, an artificial sweetener, from the market after numerous tests indicated that when given to rats in extremely large doses, it contributed to the development of cancer. But the agency could hardly have anticipated the hostile reaction which followed from weight-watchers who used saccharin and manufacturers who made their living selling it. The FDA had hit a new low in popularity, and its ban on Laetrile was making matters worse.

By June of 1977, FDA head Donald Kennedy began to wonder how long his agency could remain effective in the face of mounting criticism. Commissioner Kennedy had already personally organized a team of four experts, which was ready to travel at the shortest notice to provide testimony against Laetrile at public hearings.[2] But the tide of sentiment in favor of the drug was not to be stopped by such measures. Indeed, pressure was beginning to mount for a public trial of Laetrile, where it would be administered to humans instead of rats, in order to respond to the advocates' challenge that only human tests could establish its effectiveness. Even Dr. Franz Ingelfinger, respected editor of the *New England Journal of Medicine*—who himself was a cancer sufferer—was beginning to suggest publicly that a human test of Laetrile would do more to bury it than any public criticism from the Food and Drug Administration. The level of public confidence in the FDA had reached a dangerous new low. What possible steps could Commissioner Kennedy take to alleviate the conflict?

Laetrile has a long and improbable history. Essentially obtained by concentrating the extract from apricot pits, it was not discovered in any ordinary way. In San Francisco during the 1920s a physician hoped to discover a special ingredient which would improve the taste of bootleg whiskey.[3] However, Dr. Ernst Krebs happened instead upon a strong apricot extract which seemed to have positive effects in the curing of cancer; or at least, it seemed to retard the growth of tumors in the rats with which Dr. Krebs experimented. Unfortunately, the extract did not appear to have the same remarkable effect on cancer in humans, and Dr. Krebs abandoned his project.

It remained for Ernst Krebs, Jr., a medical school dropout, to attempt to isolate the active ingredient in his father's apricot mixture. In 1944, he announced that he had succeeded in identifying and isolating the all-important cancer-curing element, which he named Laetrile.[4] There is, however, a strong doubt among professional chemists as to whether such a drug even exists. Following Kreb's own recipe, laboratory researchers have been unable to isolate anything other than the substance amygdalin, which chemists have known about for a long time and which has never been known to have any medical use. Interestingly enough, however, proponents of Laetrile use the expressions "Laetrile" and "amygdalin" interchangeably, recognizing no significant difference between them.

Krebs himself offers the most articulate version of how the drug presumably works. Laetrile contains, among other things, the poison cyanide, which works together with an enzyme found in many cancer cells called betaglucosidase. According to Krebs, the curative powers of Laetrile are simple to understand: The cyanide which it releases attacks the cancer tumor, while not affecting the ordinary, noncancerous cells. The normal cells are spared because they contain an enzyme called rhodanese, which detoxifies cyanide when present in moderate amounts.[5]

More and more, defenders of Laetrile are extending the claims of its benefits to include, not only positive effects against already established cancers, but also preventative powers against possible or future cancers. Thus, in many quarters of the pro-Laetrile movement, supporters are urging normal, healthy people to either take Laetrile pills or to eat foods which supposedly contain high amounts of the drug, e.g., carrots, lima beans, and beets. The movement to defend Laetrile has now become an established part of the regime of some health food devotees, and it is included along with organically grown food in their list of necessary health food substances.[6]

Apart from its possible cancer-curing benefits, Laetrile has a special advantage over conventional methods of cancer treatment, it is extraordinarily cheap. With the median cancer cure in 1973 standing at $19,000, Laetrile's price is almost insignificant in comparison: about $10 per injection and $1 per pill.[7]

The FDA has announced that Laetrile is the "most tested of all cancer cures." Indeed, an official bulletin states that every one of the scientific tests conducted on Laetrile (five studies by the National Cancer Institute alone) has shown that it has no effect against cancer whatsoever.[8] In addition to the strong opposition of the FDA, most other official medical organizations have proclaimed the drug's worthlessness: Laetrile's use is officially opposed by the American Medical Association (AMA), and spokespeople from the National Cancer Institute, the American Cancer Society, and the Sloan-Kettering Institute all denounce its effectiveness as a cancer cure.

However, some individual sufferers of cancer are willing to claim fantastic effects for the drug. For example, Hugh Wildermuth, a farmer from Akron, Indiana (age 59), was diagnosed as having muscle cancer and given a year or less to live by his doctors. Even after seven weeks of cobalt radiation therapy and after large doses of a conventional drug, actinomycin D, Mr. Wildermuth was regarded as an incurable case by his doctors. Instead of abandoning hope, however, he traveled to Tijuana, Mexico, where a group of rebel physicians operate a number of Laetrile clinics. At the Clinica Del Mar, Mr. Wildermuth received three grams of Laetrile each day through injections and later was placed on a "maintenance" program in which he ingested Laetrile pills. Three years later, Mr. Wildermuth's lymph nodes were shrunken and he claimed not to be suffering from cancer at all. Doctors, however, doubt that the cancer was cured by the Laetrile treatment, assuming it was cured at all. They suggest it is more likely that the traditional treatment he underwent before his trip was responsible for the recovery.[9]

Professional researchers and doctors are not convinced by the personal testimonials of Laetrile users. Doctors generally claim that the case histories of fantastic cures leave out important information. Surprisingly enough, one of the pieces of information which researchers often complain is missing is evidence that the person actually had cancer in the first place.

In the absence of concrete information from users, most doctors are inclined to accept the results of laboratory experimentation. A variety of scientific tests have been conducted by well-respected researchers which conclude that Laetrile is ineffective against cancer. The only apparent counterexample occurred during the early 1970s when researcher Kanematsu Sugiura, at Manhattan's famed memorial Sloan-Kettering Institute, used Laetrile in mice which had breast cancer. In the Laetrile-treated mice, only 21 percent showed spreading of the tumor to the lungs, whereas in those given salt solution, 90 percent did show signs of spreading. As might be expected, the pro-Laetrile faction views this test as representing important supporting evidence for their claims.

But in June 1977, Sugiura's original study was disavowed by Sloan-Kettering. Claiming that his original experiment was not "blind," in the sense that he knew which mice were receiving Laetrile and that he attempted to determine the existence of cancer with the naked eye (a very risky business), Sloan-Kettering requested a repeat of the original experiment. Indeed they requested not only a single repeat, but a double one, and this time Sugiura could find no significant difference between the spread of cancer in the two test groups. Although Sugiura still believes that Laetrile can be effective against cancer, the Sloan-Kettering Institute has stated publicly that "Laetrile was found to possess neither preventive . . . nor anti-metastatic, nor curative anti-cancer activity."[10] Lewis Thomas, the distinguished president of Sloan-Kettering, was more abrasive: "These are bad times for reason all around. Suddenly all of the major ills are being coped with by acupuncture. If it's not acupuncture, it is apricot pits."[11]

In an attempt to check more closely on the claims of individual Laetrile users, the FDA invited Dr. Ernesto Contreras, a former Mexican army doctor who now runs perhaps the largest Laetrile clinic, Clinica Del Mar, to submit a number of cases of his own choosing for inspection by medical authorities. Dr. Contreras responded by presenting twelve cases, which presumably represented Laetrile cures. But the findings of the FDA were not encouraging. Of the twelve cases, the FDA says, six had died, three couldn't be traced, and the remaining three all had been exposed to traditional treatment and therapy, including extensive surgery, radiation treatment, and conventional drugs.[12]

Laetrile is now produced in at least ten factories around the world, most of which were started by a special foundation, headed by Andrew McNaughton, which is at least nominally dedicated to the exploration of scientific concepts. McNaughton has himself been active in the Laetrile controversy since 1956, and it was he who started one of the largest and most profitable Laetrile clinics in Mexico, the Clinica Cydel, located in Tijuana. McNaughton's past history is not perfectly spotless: He was earlier convicted of fraud in a Canadian mining operation, and was accused by the U.S. Securities and Exchange Commission of making untrue statements in a Laetrile stock venture.[13] The Clinica Cydel and the Clinica Del Mar estimate that in 1977 7,000 patients will have been tested and treated as a part of the Laetrile program, at an average weekly cost of $350. The manufacturer of Laetrile for sale and distribution is also a profitable business. Most of the Laetrile imported to the United States is produced at the Cyto Pharma de Mexica, S.A., in Tijuana. Frankly admitting that they are in business to make a profit, the owners claim to look forward to an expanded U.S. market. Their factory is already quite profitable, however, and operates twenty-four hours a day while processing over six tons of apricot seeds a month.[14]

Many businesspeople in the United States have expressed interest in manufacturing Laetrile in this country. The market appears ready and growing, and consumers would be happy to avoid the almost 700 percent markup which is now given to blackmarket Laetrile entering the United States. Unfortunately for potential U.S. manufacturers, there appears to be little way of avoiding the FDA ban. Even if individual states legalized the manufacture and sale of Laetrile—which seems to be a possibility—the FDA still has control over all interstate traffic. Since most states do not produce apricots in the amounts necessary to manufacture Laetrile, importing the requisite apricot pits would constitute a federal legal infraction. Already some U.S. manufacturers of Laetrile, attempting to operate undercover, have been raided and closed.

Although admitting that Laetrile may not be damaging in itself, the FDA maintains that its use tends to make people seek worthless remedies instead of those which hold out some chance of success. This is undoubtably the argument the FDA tends to emphasize most. The syndrome, it argues, involves a patient being informed that he has cancer and that he must undergo painful, expensive, and possibly unsuccessful traditional methods of treatment. Shocked and afraid, the patient is ready to believe anyone who promises to relieve him of his disease in a cheap, painless manner. Persuaded by the promoters of Laetrile, the patient then stops pursuing traditional treatment in favor of a Laetrile cure. But because the cancer does not wait for the patient to be treated unsuccessfully by Laetrile, it happens that the patient is indirectly killed by the very remedy he hoped would save his life.

The FDA claims it knows about women with cervical cancer, which has a high rate of cure (about 65 percent), who have refused surgery in favor of Laetrile—and have died. Dr. De Vita of the National Cancer Institute has remarked, "Hardly a day goes by now that I don't hear of a case of a patient dying after leaving accepted treatment and taking Laetrile."[15]

On the other hand, the proponents of Laetrile argue that it is not a question of whether Laetrile works or not; instead it is an issue of freedom of choice. To deny a person the freedom to choose his own means of treatment is akin to denying him freedom of speech or freedom of worship. It is argued that denying citizens Laetrile constitutes a denial of a freedom guaranteed by the U.S. Constitution. How, defenders ask, can the FDA allow the American public to consume unlimited amounts of cigarettes, the use of which has been conclusively demonstrated to cause cancer, while denying people the right to use Laetrile, even though it has no known damaging effects and may very well constitute a cure of cancer? The position of the FDA, it is said, almost approaches the kind of Big Brotherism which is incompatible with a democratic government.

The opposition to the FDA's position on Laetrile was increasing so rapidly that by 1977 it appeared to be seriously challenging the authority of the agency. Not only state legislatures, but also individual judges had begun fighting back. By June 1977, seven states—Alaska, Arizona, Florida, Indiana, Nevada, Texas, and Washington—had all legalized Laetrile in one form or another. Some states had legalized both its sale and manufacture, whereas others had simply legalized its use under specific conditions. Also by the summer of 1977, it appeared that three more states would be soon joining the original seven, and legislation was pending in more than a dozen. In October 1976, the U.S. Court of Appeals, Tenth Circuit, in Denver ruled that the FDA's record on Laetrile was "grossly inadequate," and it refused to overturn lower court rulings which allowed patients to buy and transport Laetrile.[16] In addition, the court forced the FDA to listen to testimony from individual Laetrile users and to hold public hearings on the general subject of the drug's use. Even *The New York Times* had asked, in a column dedicated to the discussion of Laetrile, "Shouldn't people be allowed to choose their own placebo, for better or worse?" And Federal District Judge Luther Bohanon of Oklahoma City ruled that it was legal for certain terminally ill cancer patients to import Laetrile from Mexico.

More significantly from the standpoint of the FDA, there was strong and mounting pressure by the summer of 1977 to test the drug publicly through a controlled and well-supervised program which used humans instead of laboratory animals. Dr. Franz Ingelfinger, editor of the *New England Journal of Medicine,* argued that a public trial would do more to get rid of Laetrile than any official debunking. As he put it, "Forbidden fruits are mighty tasty, especially to those who hope that a bite will be lifegiving."[17] And Guy Newell, head of the National Cancer Institute, had recently indicated that his agency might be willing to undertake a clinical test of Laetrile, using humans, even though he considered it an "out-and-out fraud."[18] Finally, Laetrile users and proponents strongly supported human tests, especially since they thought Laetrile was more effective on humans than on rats.

RECENT DEVELOPMENTS

In July 1980, the National Cancer Institute (NCI) sponsored a clinical trial of Laetrile on humans at four medical centers in the United States. Preliminary results, from data coordinated at the Mayo Clinic, were made public on April 30, 1981, and showed no substantive benefit from Laetrile.[19]

The study treatment was developed in accordance with the writings of Laetrile practitioners, and several practitioners served as consultants. In addition to Laetrile, a program of "metabolic therapy" was used that included enzymes, vitamins, and minerals and a diet restricted in meat, animal products, refined flour, refined sugar, and alcohol. Thus, treatment was in keeping with current practice.[20]

Subjects were cancer patients with a broad spectrum of measurable tumors for which no other treatment had been effective, or for which no proven treatment existed. All subjects gave their informed consent. Cyanide levels in the blood were monitored, and in one case treatment was stopped when the level became dangerously high.[21]

Of the 156 patients for whom data have been reported, 90 percent showed progression of the disease within three months of the start of the Laetrile treatment, with 50 percent showing such evidence within one month; 50 percent died within five months; and only 20 percent still were alive at the end of eight months. One patient showed a partial reduction in tumor size that lasted for ten weeks, after which the tumor grew despite continued Laetrile therapy. Although 19 percent of those who had felt the effects of the disease prior to the Laetrile treatment claimed that they felt better at some point during the study, only 5 percent of those still in the study during the tenth week claimed any improvement. Results were consistent with those expected with a placebo or inactive medication.[22]

Although this study indicates that Laetrile does not seem to be effective in treating cancer, the fundamental question of freedom of choice, or of the extent to which the FDA should regulate one's medical treatment in a life-threatening situation, remains unanswered.

During the late 1970s, a new dimension was added, Diana and Gerald Green had moved to Massachusetts with their 21-month-old son Chad, so that the boy could be treated for leukemia at Massachusetts General Hospital. Dr. John Truman used chemotherapy treatments to keep the leukemia in a state of remission, first by injection and later by pills to be taken at home. When leukemia reappeared in blood tests, it was learned that the parents had not given the chemotherapy pills but had substituted Laetrile.[23]

When the parents refused to have chemotherapy reinstated, the matter was taken to court where Truman testified that without chemotherapy the boy would die. Upon this basis, the court made Chad a ward of the state for medical purposes only, leaving the boy in the custody of his parents. Chemotherapy began again, at state expense, and the boy improved. Treatment with Laetrile was denied because of its incompatibility with chemotherapy.[24]

The parents fled to Mexico with three-year-old Chad so that he could be treated at the clinic of Dr. Ernesto Contreras with a regimen of Laetrile, vitamins, health pills, and chemotherapy. Because of the incompatibility previously mentioned, signs of cyanide poisoning appeared in Chad, and Massachusetts Attorney General Francis X. Bellotti obtained a court order demanding the return of the boy. Kidnapping charges had been considered but were not made.[25]

The Greens, who were receiving financial support from the National Health Foundation, described by *Time* as a right wing California group that also opposed fluoridation of water, and from private citizens who felt that the state had no business in this matter, refused to bring the child back to Massachusetts.[26]

Chad Green died in Mexico nine months after being taken there. Unfortunately, no autopsy was performed. Therefore, it cannot be known with certainty whether the boy died from the normal progression of cancer or from a buildup of cyanide from Laetrile, or from some other cause.

When the parents of the dead child returned to Massachusetts, they faced civil and criminal contempt charges in Plymouth, Massachusetts. Former Assistant Attorney General Jonathan Brant told the court that with chemotherapy Chad might still be alive. The Greens apologized to the court and asked for forgiveness. Judge Francis Keating found the Greens guilty but gave no sentence, stating that, "Any further punishment beyond what had already been endured would certainly be unfair."[27]

This case received wide publicity. For some it represented a violation of freedom of choice in selecting medical treatment. For others it became a rallying point in efforts to keep Laetrile from being sold in the United States.

Another widely publicized case involved actor Steve McQueen. The world first learned of his fight against mesothelioma, a rare and deadly form of cancer that affects the tissues lining the chest and abdomen, in October 1980 when his voice, labored and rasping, was heard on Mexican radio praising the nonspecific metabolic therapy he was receiving at the Plaza Santa Maria General Hospital in Baja California (Mexico). "Congratulations," he said, "and thank you for helping to save my life."[28] This radio broadcast later was used on U.S. television with pictures of McQueen's two-bedroom cabana at the hospital, but without pictures of McQueen, whose features were said to have changed because of the disease.

McQueen was under a treatment devised by former Texas dentist William Donald Kelley that included Laetrile, vitamins, minerals, and a diet with large amounts of raw vegetables and little fish or chicken or meat.[29] Thus the regimen was similar to the diet and supplements tested by the NCI study.

November 1, McQueen left Mexico and returned to his ranch in Santa Paula, California. A *New York Times* report said that it was unclear whether he would return to the clinic.[30]

On November 7, 1980, McQueen underwent surgery in Juarez, Mexico, during which Dr. Cesar Santos removed a five-pound tumor from the abdomen, stating afterward that somebody should have operated on him immediately after the tumor was discovered. Although Santos felt that McQueen did not have much time to live, he decided to remove the tumor to relieve the pain from its pressure.[31]

McQueen died on November 7, at age 50, from heart failure following the surgery. This was three months after he had gone to Mexico for Laetrile and metabolic therapy.[32]

One wonders whether McQueen would have chosen different treatment if the results of the NCI tests of Laetrile and the metabolic diet, being conducted at that time, had been known, or if he would have taken this treatment anyway, knowing that the alternative was drugs and high-voltage radiation with almost certain death within a year.

NOTES

1. "Damn the Doctors—and Washington," *Time,* June 20, 1977, p. 50.

2. Ibid., p. 53.

3. "Laetrile, Should It Be Banned?" *Newsweek,* June 27, 1977, p. 50.

4. Ibid.

5. Ibid.

6. *New York Times,* April 17, 1977.

7. "Victories for Laetrile's Lobby," *Time,* May 22, 1977, p. 97.

8. *New York Times,* April 17, 1977.

9. "Laetrile, Should It Be Banned?" p. 52.

10. Ibid., p. 56.

11. "Victories for Laetrile's Lobby."

12. "Laetrile, Should It Be Banned?"

13. Ibid., p. 51.

14. Ibid.

15. "Damn the Doctors—and Washington," p. 54.

16. *New York Times,* February 18, 1977.

17. "Damn the Doctors—and Washington," p. 54.

18. Ibid.

19. *Clinical Study of Laetrile in Cancer Patients. Investigators' Report: A Summary,* press release, National Institutes of Health, National Cancer Institute, April 30, 1981.

20. Ibid.

21. Ibid.

22. Ibid.

23. "A Battle over Cancer Care," *Time,* February 12, 1979, p. 25.

24. Ibid.

25. Ibid.

26. Ibid.

27. "Ample Penalty: Defiance of Court is Excused," *Time,* December 22, 1980, p. 74.

28. M. Clark and R. Henkoff, "Strange Sort of Therapy," *Newsweek,* October 20, 1980, pp. 65–66.

29. Ibid.

30. "McQueen Leaves Clinic," *New York Times,* November 1, 1980, p. 50.

31. "Steve McQueen, 50, Is Dead of a Heart Attack after Surgery for Cancer," *New York Times,* November 8, 1980, p. 21.

32. Ibid.

QUESTIONS FOR DISCUSSION

1. Should an individual, given currently available information on the effectiveness of a form of therapy, have the right to exercise freedom of choice in accepting or

rejecting it? Should a distinction be made between the choice of therapy for a child (such as Chad Green) and for a consenting adult (such as actor Steve McQueen)? Should the nature of the disorder—that is, life threatening or not—make a difference?

2. What should be the role of a regulatory agency such as the FDA: to provide information for intelligent decision making or to regulate the availability of treatment? Would you answer differently if the treatment under question were merely ineffective, or if lack of safety were uncovered?

3. What role should the court system and Congress play in deciding medically related issues? Are there other organizations that should be involved?

Case Study
Business and
Political Action:
To PAC or Not to PAC?

Carol J. Fritz

Jessica Smythe, founder and chief executive officer of a chain of 17 hardware and hobby stores in a heavily populated midwestern state, had seen the firm grow in 15 years from a single store on a neighborhood shopping street to a corporation with assets of $9 million and annual sales of $22 million: 12 of the stores were located in large thriving suburban shopping malls, 2 were in urban neighborhoods undergoing a renaissance, and the remaining 3, including the original store, were in declining urban areas and undergoing a decrease in sales concurrent with a surge in operating expenses.

At its last meeting, the board of directors had voted to leave these last three stores in their present locations rather than move them to more profitable settings. This decision to become involved in efforts to rejuvenate the neighborhoods was motivated both by concern for the maintenance of urban neighborhoods and by the knowledge that renovation efforts in the two renaissance areas had produced heavy demand for hardware and other remodeling aids. In fact, Smythe had been able to purchase the paneling, stained glass, and fixtures from buildings scheduled for demolition in these areas and to resell them. Generally, they were sold as quick-

Copyright © 1982 by Pittmann Press. Reprinted with permission. Carol J. Fritz has received an Ed.D. and an M.B.A. She has both university teaching experience and national level corporate experience, and has served on a national advisory committee on legislation and public policy for a professional association in the health field.

ly as they could be put on display. In brief, neighborhood development was good for the corporation as well as for the city.

Each of the three declining areas had formed a neighborhood association, largely in response to the urging of the local merchants, and had sought public development funds with which to renovate the older buildings. Partly owing to financial entrenchment severely limiting the money available at all levels of government, and partly because of insensitivity to the needs of the communities on the part of their congressional representatives, available federal funds in the form of block grants were not forthcoming. It was apparent that the neighborhood associations had little political clout.

Smythe was certain that these congressmen had enough influence to obtain funding for the deteriorating areas and to have a suitable amount allocated to these development projects.

As Jessica Smythe pondered the insensitivity of locally elected officials to neighborhood interests, she was aware that the next congressional election was just six months away. Most likely, some form of political involvement was needed . . . perhaps in the form of campaign financing.

Smythe would like to see one congressman in particular defeated. Not only had he voted against the enabling legislation for neighborhood development funds, he also had refused to discuss the matter on her recent visit to his local office during the congressional recess.

The other two congressmen were neither antagonistic nor helpful, and Smythe felt that they would listen to reason once the political clout of one neighborhood group was established.

COMMUNITY CHARACTERISTICS

Smythe reviewed the strengths and weaknesses of the neighborhoods. All three were heavily populated with middle-aged and older adults with a common, foreign ethnic origin. They had remained in the neighborhood in which they had settled and raised their children, even though in many instances the children had moved away, leaving a customer base of individuals on fixed incomes. Other less affluent families had been attracted to the neighborhoods in recent years because of their close proximity to the urban center and because rental and home sales prices were reasonable.

Each neighborhood association wished to maintain the identify of the neighborhood; both the older and the more recent residents agreed about this. Furthermore, the residents cooperated with each other in keeping the neighborhood clean and in a modest state of repair. Each could point out specific improvements that had resulted from community effort: one or more homes that had been repainted using volunteer labor and paint supplied by an elderly homeowner, or porch steps replaced in similar fashion. However, the age of the homes and the lack of financial resources clearly indicated that outside funding was needed even to retain the status quo.

Faced with the prospect of seeing the neighborhoods decline further, and of losing the equity the residents and merchants had in their properties (frequently a high percentage of their total worth), everyone involved believed that each neighborhood group would be cohesive and would actively support a group effort. Smythe felt certain of this.

It would be possible to calculate the financial cost to the city of lost property, business, and sales and personal income taxes if local merchants and residents were forced to move from the area. Moreover, there would be increased costs for protection services to avoid property damage, fires in empty buildings, and crime on dark streets. It also was doubtful that any new enterprises could be found to move into the neighborhoods to occupy empty store spaces and to create new jobs.

The best approach appeared to be immediate action directed at elected officials, such as Congressman X.

CORPORATE POLITICAL ACTION

For a political action committee (PAC) to be formed, several things had to occur quickly. Jessica Smythe knew that her firm could provide administrative services for a PAC associated with it. However, she would need the support of the board of directors. Jessica Smythe owned 40 percent of the stock, but approval of the remaining stockholders would be critical.

Smythe knew of a firm of similar size that had raised $50,000 for a PAC, and she wondered how she might be able to accomplish such a goal. Funds could be solicited directly from stockholders and employees. Would employees from suburban areas and nearby cities where branch stores were located be willing to contribute funds? What type of internal network would be needed? Since PACs can solicit funds from individuals outside the parent organization twice a year, the Smythe PAC could approach merchants and residents within the area and appeal as well to civic-minded individuals from a wider geographic region.

If like-minded groups could be identified, such as party committees for candidates the PAC wished to support, the League of Women Voters, and perhaps groups interested in neighborhood preservation, the efforts of the Smythe PAC could be extended. Since the election was just six months away, the PAC might not be able to qualify as a multicandidate committee; therefore it would have to follow the dollar limitations established for individuals and other such groups acting in concert. Each candidate that was supported could receive $1,000 per election (primary, general, run-off); however, $5,000 could be given to any other committee in support of one or more candidates the PAC favored, and $20,000 could be given to a national party committee for use in congressional elections. Adding this together, the PAC could contribute $3,000 directly to the three congressional candidates it selected for the general election, as much as $20,000 to the party of the candidate opposing Congressman X, and $10,000 to two committees that loaned their support to the opposing candidate. Together, this meant that $33,000 could be allocated for contributions, and the remaining money used for the preparation of leaflets and for solicitation expenses.

There were additional considerations. To qualify eventually as a multicandidate PAC and be able to contribute $5,000 per candidate per election another time, it would be necessary to contribute to at least five federal candidates and to obtain funds from at least 50 individuals.

Would it be wise to plan for the long term and to qualify as a multicandidate PAC? Smythe knew that the 17 stores were scattered throughout 12 congressional election districts in the state and that some employees lived in still other districts. How would five candidates be selected for support? Should small amounts be given to a large number of candidates, with larger sums reserved for the three targeted districts? The uncle of one suburban store manager was running in a "safe" election. How much money should be diverted for his campaign? Would a wider dispersal of funds to include the suburbs hinder solicitation efforts from groups interested primarily in urban neighborhood preservation? There were five stores in urban areas, each in a different congressional district.

Of course, other types of PAC organization were possible. Each neighborhood association could form a PAC, but this would prevent the Smythe firm from providing administrative services. There was a national trade association of hardware dealers, but if support was sought from this group, other firms learning of these efforts might try to acquire a large share of the block grant money for areas they serve, even if they provided little support for the association PAC.

On another level, the effort could boomerang through negative publicity or through retaliatory action on the part of developers interested in tearing down the buildings and creating large office or apartment buildings.

Would Smythe company involvement in politics truly represent the interests and viewpoints of individual shareholders? To what extent should shareholders and employees decide what candidates to support?

Jessica Smythe had been asked to prepare a report for board consideration by the end of the week. What specific recommendations should she make?

QUESTIONS FOR DISCUSSION

1. What recommendations should Jessica Smythe make to the board of directors? Should a PAC be formed? Why or why not? What other alternatives should be considered, and on what basis do you accept or reject them?

2. If a PAC is formed by a business firm, what criteria should be used in deciding whether to apply for multicandidate committee status, in selecting the candidate(s) to be supported, in soliciting funds from individuals and other groups, and in deciding whether to expand the PAC to an organizational level beyond the firm?

3. In evaluating the level of political involvement in a firm, what factors must be considered? When is political involvement in the best interests of the firm? Of the stockholders?

Essay
Defense Contracts:
Operation Ill Wind

Karen Marquiss

"Operation Ill Wind" began with a single telephone call in September, 1986. A former Navy employee working for a defense contractor received a call from an industry consultant who offered for sale some confidential Pentagon information. The employee alerted the Naval Investigative Service and agreed to talk to the consultant while wearing a hidden microphone. Investigators then secured enough information to confront the consultant and convinced him to go undercover in talks with other consultants and a Pentagon official. This led to a huge network of bidding system corruption. The evidence pointed toward an underground economy where consultants trafficked in information about military contracts, allegedly bribing government employees for inside information in order to help their clients obtain valuable military contracts.

For two years investigators operated in secret. The probe combined the efforts of the F.B.I., the Justice Department and the Naval Investigative Service. After 290 days of court-authorized wire-tapping, the group overheard 4,764 conversations, of which 671 were deemed incriminating. Evidence indicated that 75 to 100 weapons contracts involving tens of billions of dollars were won either as a result of bribes paid to Pentagon officials or through collusion among contractors.[1]

On June 14, 1988, F.B.I. agents made a surprise search of Pentagon offices. Included in the search were the offices of two senior officials in the Pentagon and the home and office of the Navy's former chief researcher. Agents also searched the offices of fourteen military contractors and eleven independent defense consultants throughout twelve states in a sweeping effort to "insure the integrity of Government procurement programs."[2]

In the days to follow, a federal grand jury issued more than 250 subpoenas for documents and testimony from defense contractors, officials, and consultants. Twenty people in the Department of Defense, primarily Navy and Marine Corps officials, were under suspicion, as were fifty industry consultants and a number of large defense contractors. Evidence also pointed to potential involvement by at least two members of Congress.

This paper was written by doctoral student Karen Marquiss under the direction of Joanne B. Ciulla. Dr. Ciulla is a Senior Fellow at the Wharton School of the University of Pennsylvania, where she teaches courses in Business Ethics and Management. (Reprinted with permission.)

The scandal had developed into the most far-reaching fraud investigation in Pentagon history.

HISTORY

The scandal uncovered by "Operation Ill Wind" is not without precedent. It seems the "intertwining of arms and money is always accompanied by trouble."[3] Even the Romans encountered this kind of problem. Some 2000 years ago, Cicero warned of greed and corruption in a "garrison" state while receiving the equivalent of $85,000 in one year as colonial governor.[4]

Efforts to reform the contracting system in the United States date all the way back to the Revolutionary War when horses were sold to the Army more than once. Early in the twentieth century, government production plans nearly came to a halt because separate branches of the armed forces schemed and bribed to achieve individual goals under separate purchasing agencies.[5] In the post–World War II era, both weapons and the procurement process became more complex and costly. In 1955, the Hoover Blue-Ribbon Commission examined the defense system for evidence of waste, fraud and abuse, but its findings had little actual influence on defense purchasing. By the 1960's, Pentagon relations became so tainted by scandal that Defense Secretary Robert McNamara barred employees from even having lunch with suppliers.[6] In 1970 another attempt at reform came through the appointment of the Fitzhugh Commission. Results of this study were similar to its predecessor: Little impact was made on the system's fundamental operation.[7]

In the 1980s, procurement has been marked by even more complexity and inefficiency. The Justice Department set up a defense procurement fraud unit to monitor abuses in response to pressures from Congress. The unit primarily went after accounting irregularities and contract law cases where the government had been overcharged due to inflated material and labor costs. Despite the Justice Department's efforts, problems of overcharging remained commonplace. This was the era of the $600 toilet seat, the $7000 indestructible airborne coffee pot, and the $400 hammer.

An estimated $40 billion per year was wasted in military procurement. Outsized design, engineering and performance demands have increased the inefficiency factor. During the period from 1980 to 1985, the procurement budget more than doubled, rising from $45.7 billion to $96.8 billion. This represented a 139% constant dollar increase. Of this budget, sixty percent was channeled to major weapons systems.[8]

The vast availability of funds, coupled with a symbiotic relationship between industry and the Department of Defense (DOD), encouraged waste, fraud, and abuse. Nearly 57% of all Pentagon contracts were awarded with no competitive bidding, which provided a near monopoly for many defense contractors. In response to the situation, Congress increased legislation and the Defense Department beefed up regulations. The Reagan administration tried to increase competition for the granting of contracts by passing the Competition in Contracting Act which required the DOD to seek out two bidders for contracts whenever possible.[9]

THE REVOLVING DOOR

Thousands of military contracts were awarded each year at a cost of $150 billion. The Pentagon employs 50,000 designated contract officers and grants 62,000 contracts per day. There are over 300,000 military suppliers. About 30,000 pages of procurement regulations exist, issued by 70 offices. Defense activities are monitored by 55 subcommittees of 29 Congressional committees assisted by more than 20,000 staff and supporting agencies. Rules describing the way defense contracts are to be sought and awarded are bound into volumes that occupy almost one-quarter mile of shelf space![10]

Defense procurement is a peculiar business. There are many suppliers and one customer. The sellers work to shape customer demands and then lobby to make sure the customer hangs on to its power. Meanwhile, both sellers and the customer draw from the same pool of potential employees.[11] The private interests of the buyers and sellers are then juxtaposed with the public interest of national security.

Because the defense business is large and complicated, information comes at a huge premium. This explains the extensive use of consultants in the industry. According to a General Accounting Office study, the Defense Department spent $2.8 billion on consulting contracts in 1987 alone. This figure soars to $18.1 billion if the definition of "consultant" is expanded to include management review, technical assistance, special studies, and support and professional services.[12] Secretaries of Defense have traditionally recruited consultants from industry to assist as deputies within the department.

A familiar presence in the Pentagon, experienced consultants also possess the expertise needed by defense contractors. Consultants often have access to information and individuals in the Pentagon because many are ex–Defense Department employees. Their knowledge, judgement, experience, and contacts can help clients understand and interpret complex government rules and sharpen competitive bids. Top consultants command fees ranging from $1000 to $2000 a day. Still they remain in high demand by the defense industry.

Another common practice is for defense contractors to hire former Pentagon officials. In 1983 and 1984, of 30,000 employees that left the Pentagon, one-fifth went to work for contractors, and 82% had subsequent communication with the DOD. One-fourth had held jobs in the Defense Department that materially affected the contracting firms for whom they ultimately ended up working.[13]

Researcher Danielle Brian-Bland of the Project on Military Procurement in Washington explains why this phenomenon exists. "All the people who are in the Pentagon—especially the military—are in danger of losing their jobs at a relatively young age. As a result, they are always aware of the fact that the natural place for them to go to work is for one of the contractors." Later, they may rejoin the government in a higher level position. During the process they do not always "maintain the arms-length transactions that they should." Basically, Bland says, they are "all in the same business. It is to their advantage to keep these contacts flowing."[14]

One official said the situation demonstrates the "classic revolving door syndrome: guys in the Pentagon and guys who have left the Pentagon scratching each others' backs."[15] Other observers describe the tight-knit system as an "iron triangle," beyond the control of existing laws, where consultants operate at the "frontiers" of the law. There is often a murky line between information that is obtained legitimately and data that is gathered illegally. Defense Department regulations are not always clear on this issue.

What is clear is the variation of consultant methods and integrity. Labeled the "Beltway Bandits" (after the freeway that encircles the capital city and runs through newer suburban areas in Maryland and Virginia), most consultants in the Washington area are highly specialized. Some consultants perform technical studies and analyze data for both government and industry. Others exist primarily as conduits to the government bureaucracy. Still others have been described as "sleaze boutiques" that strictly traffic in information.[16]

THE BLUE RIBBON COMMISSION

In 1986, President Reagan authorized the Packard Blue Ribbon Commission to study the procurement system once again and suggest possible reforms. The study coincided with Congressional hearings on allegations of the existence of fraud and slush funds at the Pentagon. Hewlett-Packard founder David Packard was selected to head up the Commission, having served as former deputy defense secretary from 1969 to 1971.

The Packard Commission recognized the Defense Department's obligations to the armed forces, the taxpayers and the nation. It stressed the necessity of applying the highest standards of ethical conduct through the industry initiative. It recommended the appointment of a "czar of procurement" to institute "broad reforms" in the Defense Department. Tellingly, the first "czar," Richard Godwin, resigned after one year in the position, saying he found it "impossible" to change the procurement process.[17]

The Commission also recognized the "long-term mutual dependence commitment of suppliers and customer." The study suggested the Pentagon map out a "coherent military strategy" to end intraservice rivalry. Weapons would then be ordered over a two-year defense budget. Multi-year procurement contracts would be issued to stabilize production.[18] However, Defense Secretary Caspar Weinberger largely resisted the Packard Commission and its recommendations.

AN EARLY OMEN

Indications of wide-spread military-industrial espionage first came to light in 1984 when the Justice Department brought charges against GTE Government Systems Corporation and one of its consultants. In February, agents from the Defense Criminal Investigative Service called on GTE marketing executive Walter R. Edgington. When the investigators stated their purpose, Edgington surprised them. "You don't have to explain. I know why you're here," he responded as they inquired of his knowledge of an alleged theft of secret military documents. Mr. Edgington said that classified Pentagon office documents were commonplace at GTE. His first encounter had been in 1966 shortly after joining the firm, and he "had received a steady flow of secret data ever since." Mr. Edgington alleged, "Every major corporation gets the same material."[19]

In September, 1985 the Justice Department indicted Edgington, GTE, another GTE executive and consultant Bernie Zettl, a retired Air Force major who allegedly provided the firm with secret Pentagon documents. According to charges filed in the case, Zettl had been paid more than $120,000 in consulting fees over a four year period. Described as a "colorful" man, Zettl secretly funneled information to GTE via a post office box in California. The company revealed the nature of this contractual relationship in a memo that stated: "We do not want to list on paper the work that he is doing."[20]

GTE pleaded guilty to the possession of sensitive Defense Department documents which included budget reports, program objective memoranda, and five-year defense plans. The company was fined $590,000, while charges against Edgington and his colleague were dropped. The Zettl case remains unresolved. However, Major Zettl is reportedly in financial ruin and no longer in the consulting business.

In many respects the GTE incident foreshadowed the "Ill Wind" operation. Investigators in the GTE case found evidence that implicated at least 25 other major contractors and their consultants. For an unexplained reason, superiors stopped the inquiry and did not allow agents to pursue further leads. One agent called the ending of the inquiry "premature," and declared the case to be only the "tip of the proverbial iceberg."[21] In essence, the Defense and Justice Departments postponed the inevitable for nearly two years by stifling every investigative efforts.

BLOWING IN THE WIND

As undercover operants began to feel the "ill wind" blow in 1986, the defense industry faced several minor crises. The national budget for defense shrank under the weight of the federal deficit. Increased competition and more regulation began to squeeze the bidding process. Federal contracts were no longer easy prey.

To buffer these effects, contractors began to rely more extensively on outside consultants. At the same time, the industry sought to salvage their image by policing their own ranks. Forty-six contractors signed the "Defense Industry Initiative," an agreement which required companies to adopt a code of industry ethics. The firms pledged to "train their workers in ethical conduct" and "encourage whistle-blowing without fear of retribution."[22] Ironically, the initiative failed to stipulate standards of conduct in the gathering of sensitive data from the military. By the summer of 1988, thirty-seven of the forty-six firms were under investigation for contracting misconduct in the bribery scheme.

Three kinds of illegal activity emerged from the evidence gathered through wiretapping in Operation Ill Wind:

1. Consultants working for one company obtained confidential information on bids already submitted by other companies competing for the same contract. The information was supplied by Defense Department employees.
2. Officials changed contract specifications to make them more suitable to a particular company.
3. Companies competing for the same contract acted in collusion.

Pentagon officials were suspected of two primary acts:

1. Succumbing to bribes.
2. Rigging bids for either a promised position outside government or simply as a favor to a consultant or company.

Specific crimes under investigation included bribery, conspiracy, theft of government property, false statement to the government and violations of fraud and conflict of interest laws."[23] No charges were filed immediately. However, five Pentagon officials, fifteen consultants, nineteen companies and five company officials were either subpoenaed or subjected to searches. Approximately fifteen additional Pentagon employees also remained under suspicion.

Significant on the list were McDonnell Douglas, the nation's largest defense contractor, and UNISYS, the computer firm formed in the merger of Sperry and Burroughs corporations. Both were consulting clients of Melvyn Paisley, former chief researcher for the Navy, who had substantial contacts in both industry and the military. Paisley was quickly becoming the central figure in the Pentagon scandal.

THE PAISLEY TIE

When agents searched the home and office of Melvyn Paisley on June 14, 1988, they discovered stacks of classified Federal documents he had no security clearance to possess. The F.B.I. had bugged Paisley's consulting office and tapped his telephone as a result of Operation Ill Wind. The federal search warrant alleged that Paisley "relied upon government officials to provide Department of Defense contract information which is not available to the contracting public. Paisley then provided this information, for a fee or as part of his 'consulting contract'" to clients.[24] Agents had uncovered a "web" of Paisley's personal and professional contacts, some of whom were close to the center of the investigation.

To many, Paisley epitomized the Pentagon's old-boy revolving-door network. Before serving as assistant Navy Secretary for research, engineering and systems, Paisley worked for twenty-eight years for one of the nation's largest defense contractors, the Boeing Company. When he left the Pentagon in 1987, Paisley became a consultant. According to one high-ranking Pentagon official, Paisley, at age 63, had a bright future. "Mel Paisley is the kind of guy who's a star in the contracting and consulting world—the kind of guy who could easily earn $1 million a year."[25] Many colleagues and subordinates remembered him fondly. E. C. Grayson, a former Deputy Assistant Secretary of the Navy, described him as a "multi-faceted, brilliant guy, a total dynamo, a lot of fun, uninhibited—you couldn't help but like him."[26]

Paisley was a dramatic presence in the defense industry. He inspired "deep respect from some underlings" for his way of handling the Navy's weapons procurement program "with a damn-the-torpedo panache."[27]

One of Paisley's closest allies was John F. Lehman, Jr. The two men were first acquainted when Paisley was a Boeing vice-president and Lehman was a consultant to the aerospace company. They became fast friends, and Paisley followed Lehman to the Pentagon in 1981 when Lehman was appointed Navy Secretary. Together, they set out to design the "Navy of the future." They saw the Pentagon bureaucracy as a "socialist culture," and aggressively pursued Lehman's goal to build a 600-ship Navy fleet. During his tenure, Lehman cultivated his hard-nosed style and take-charge approach in an attempt to bring more competition to the contracting process.

Meanwhile, Paisley handled the Navy's weapons procurement program. Paisley had broad authority outside his role as research and development chief. Together, Lehman and Paisley earned the title of "bureaucratic swashbucklers." They abolished the Navy Materiel Command, a review agency for weapons programs and largely ignored "checks and balances" provided by the uniformed military and career civilians.

In 1986 Paisley told the House Armed Services Committee how he, Lehman and the Navy shipbuilding chief Everett Pratt drove down prices by increasing competition and forcing contractors to share more of the cost of weapons buying. "We are writing history," said Paisley. "We are changing things right now."[28] As an ex-military officer put it: "Paisley cut costs, but there were bodies strewn along the way: contractors, bureaucrats, and the military."[29]

Paisley's personal life mirrored his professional success. He was known as a "hard-charging, back-slapping bon vivant" with a "ready appreciation for gourmet food and vintage wines."[30] He and his young wife, Vicki, shared an elegant colonial home on a one-acre plot near the Hickory Hill estate of Ethel Kennedy and her family in McLean, Virginia. In Washington, he zipped around town in his bottle-green Jaguar XKE.

Yet there was another side to Paisley. A former co-worker claimed

"He was erratic. He would fly off the handle, storm around and get mad."[31] His past bulged with evidence that aroused suspicion about his character. According to *Who's Who in America,* Paisley told them he graduated from Massachusetts Institute of Technology with a Masters of Science in 1954. M.I.T. says he attended for one semester in 1953 and never received a degree. In his Navy biography he credited himself with shooting down nine enemy aircraft in World War II as a P47 pilot. The Air Force credits him with four kills and two one-half kills.

A myriad of abuses were invoked by Paisley while a Boeing executive and trouble-shooter. Former employees claimed that Boeing didn't pay bribes but Paisley did. Known for womanizing, Paisley was said to have hired prostitutes with company funds. He allegedly bugged the office of a competitor in 1970, and bragged of how he bribed military assistance teams overseas.[32] There was even talk of charging Paisley with the murder of his second of four wives who accidently died from an overdose of painkillers in the 1960s.

Paisley was sued in a civil case by the Justice Department for receiving improper severance pay from Boeing on termination of his employment. When he left the company to work for the Pentagon, his salary dropped from over $100,000 per year to $72,500. However, the deal was sweetened by a $183,000 "golden handshake" from Boeing. The Justice Department claimed the payment constituted a conflict of interest, but the case was never resolved.

Although Paisley had achieved results through cutting costs and streamlining the bureaucracy, some of his methods smacked of questionable tactics. According to one source, Paisley leaked confidential bidding information to rival contractors. For example, he took credit for forcing General Dynamics and McDonnell Douglas into jointly bidding on the A12 attack plane, a supersecret Bomber with stealth characteristics.[33]

At one point Paisley revised the bidding rules on a contract that favored UNISYS while his wife received $50,000 from a company formed by principal UNISYS lobbyist, William Galvin. The revisions concerned the $9 billion Navy Aegis contract, which had been a sole-source engagement for RCA since 1969. Under new law, RCA now had to share one-half of the contract with other companies. The second-source half was divided into six portions. With bids already submitted, Paisley suddenly decided the Navy should select only one second-source firm. Since UNISYS was the only contractor to originally bid for all six components, they automatically received the contract.

In an interesting twist, Representative Bill Chappell, Jr. pressured Paisley publicly to award the entire Aegis contract to UNISYS. The representative had reportedly received at least $20,000 over a period of four years from consultants linked to UNISYS.[34]

When Paisley left the Pentagon in March of 1987 Lehman granted special permission for Paisley to retain his security clearances. This gave Paisley continuing access to information on the most up to date weapons technology, which Paisley allegedly used in his consulting practice. The privilege was shortlived, though. Lehman resigned his post within a month and the new secretary ordered Paisley's clearance cancelled.

The resignations of Lehman and Paisley came as no surprise. Congress had passed an amendment to prohibit former government employees from working for a contractor if they had been closely involved in negotiations with that company during the last two years in government. The law took effect on April 15, 1987. "Hordes" of high-ranking officials left government service before the deadline.[35] Both men went on to open their own consulting firms.

After only a year in private practice, Paisley had built an "enviable client list" which included McDonnell Douglas, Martin Marietta Co., United Technologies Corporation and UNISYS, all industry giants. A few months later, he stood accused of bribery, conspiracy, and theft of government property. Authorities claimed he had used Pentagon inside information and his contacts to help clients win contracts with the government, as evidenced by telephone wiretapping.

Paisley had allegedly "passed inside information to help McDonnell Douglas win contracts to sell its F/A18 airplane to Switzerland, France and Korea, including details of a competing proposal by General Dynamics for its F16 airplanes.[36] Apparently Paisley told McDonnell Douglas to hire retired Admiral James A. Lyons as a consultant on the Korea sale. Lyons had just left his post as commander of the Pacific Command, which gave him access to top Korean military officers who were considering a major purchase of McDonnell Douglas jets.[37] Law enforcement officials were also looking into whether Paisley improperly aided clients at an earlier date while he was at the Navy.

AGAINST THE WIND

The findings of Operation Ill Wind led many to question the procurement system. As Senator John Warner put it, "We must ask if some part of our procurement process which, if not fostering, may be permitting an atmosphere in which this type of criminal activity could occur."[38] In a letter to Defense Secretary Frank Carlucci, Warner urged that "a review of the procurement process must begin immediately."[39]

David Packard showed concern as well. He told the armed services committee that "one could do as good a job awarding major contracts by throwing darts at the bidders." He claimed that one big reason the defense weapons buying went awry was "the attempt to impose competition in a situation where real competition is virtually impossible,"[40] because of the mutual dependence of contractors and the Pentagon.

Secretary Carlucci defended the process, claiming "the system works. We've got more than enough legislation."[41] "If you have bank embezzlement, you don't suddenly condemn the banking system, you look at ways to deal with those who are culpable."[42] Former Secretary Caspar Weinberger agreed: "The system is basically a good one. But a few rotten apples can do an awful lot of damage . . . we're at the mercy of the most dishonest person in a very long chain."[43]

President Ronald Reagan waxed philosophical: "I think anyone in a top position in government goes to bed every night with the knowledge that some place in the ranks there could be someone that is not playing fair."[44] He said he was "disappointed and upset," but added, "I think it should be understandable how such things can happen in something as big as our Government is."[45]

Vice President George Bush was indignant: "Corruption anywhere in government is bad enough, but these people . . . were not just stealing money from the Treasury, they were stealing money from our national defense and undermining our national security."[46] While Senator Dan Quayle claimed, "Unfortunately, we can't pass laws to eradicate crime or criminal intent," and described the situation as "simple greed, bribery and fraud."[47]

However, one of Weinberger's former Pentagon deputies blamed the crisis on the Defense Department's lack of leadership, saying "This is Cap's Irangate."[48] He explained that Weinberger had "left details of spending the $2 trillion he raised between 1981 and 1987 to subordinates the way President Reagan left details of trading arms to Iran for hostages to his deputies."[49] Weinberger's hands-off management style, lack of experience and decision to "distance himself from defense contractors" left a management "vacuum" which was filled by John Lehman and his staff, including the accused Melvyn Paisley, according to Pentagon careerists.[50]

Senator Charles E. Grassley charged Defense and Justice Department officials with "turning their backs" on the crisis. He accused officials of ignoring evidence of wide-spread fraud, and insisted "the public must be made aware of the fact that our Justice Department has been asleep at the switch."[51]

Contractor self-governance, a corner-stone of the Packard Commission recommendations, also received its share of criticisms. Joseph H. Sherick, retired DOD inspector general said, "I don't think the government can feel comfortable that self-policing will work. You have to believe human beings are human beings. That's why we have locks on doors."[52]

"We've entered into a culture of distrust," said Donald Hicks, a consultant who formerly served as Pentagon research chief. "We've got to stop feeling that everybody is a crook."[53] Senator J. James Exon was familiar with the preliminary evidence and insisted: "I want to see somebody go to jail."[54]

Others like Retired Rear Admiral Stuart Platt said, "When the dust settles on this, what I'd like to see is some kind of defense-consulting registration act."[55]

Secretary Carlucci warned against "hasty, piecemeal changes" as an answer to the Ill Wind scandal. He claimed: "There is simply no way to devise a system that is greed-proof."[56]

By September, 1988 the Defense Department had already issued "new, uniform conflict-of-interest regulations" for consultants and banned the signing on of any new consultants for the duration of the Reagan

Administration.[57] Late in 1988, as Congress braced for the changing of the guard in the White House and a new defense Secretary, the procurement reform was already underway.[58]

NOTES

1. "Can't Make Arms-Purchasing 'Greed-Proof,' Carlucci States," *The Los Angeles Times,* June 28, 1988, sec. 1. p. 14.

2. "FBI in Surprise Search of Pentagon and Suppliers," *The New York Times,* June 15, 1988, p. A1, col. 3.

3. "The Enemy Within," *U.S. News & World Report,* July 4, 1988, Vol. 105, p. 17.

4. Ibid.

5. "Military Scandal, Again," *Wall Street Journal,* June 27, 1988, p. 12 col. 4.

6. "The Defense Scandal," *Business Week,* July 4, 1988, No. 3059, p. 28.

7. "Military Scandal, Again," p. 12, col. 4.

8. "U.S. Fraud Probe Rekindles Military Waste Controversy," *Aviation Week and Space Technology,* Vol. 129, no. 1, p. 14.

9. "Drawing a Flak Attack," *Time,* Vol. 152, no. 4, p. 59.

10. "'84 Incident Omen of Defense Scandal," *The Los Angeles Times,* June 26, 1988, sec. 1, p. 24, col. 1.

11. "Pushing Defense Firms to Compete, Pentagon Harms Buying System," *The Wall Street Journal,* June 27, 1988, p. 4, col. 2.

12. "Consultant Fees Called Understated," *The Washington Post,* June 22, 1988, sec. 1, col. 1.

13. "The Enemy Within," p. 18.

14. "Probe Sheds New Light on Pentagon Consultants," *The Washington Post,* June 16, 1988, p. A16, col. 1.

15. "Pentagon Inquiry Hears of Payoffs from Contractors," *The New York Times,* June 16, 1988, p. A1, col. 6.

16. "'84 Incident Omen of Defense Scandal," sec. 1, p. 24, col. 1.

17. "The Enemy Within," p. 17.

18. "Competition in Defense Buying Costly to U.S.," *The Los Angeles Times,* July 31, 1988, part 4, p. 1, col. 1.

19. "'84 Incident Omen of Defense Scandal," sec. 1, p. 1, col. 1.

20. Ibid., sec. 1, p. 24, col. 1.

21. Ibid.

22. "Defense Firms' Self-Policing Hasn't Closed the Ethics Gap," *The Los Angeles Times,* July 31, 1988, sec. 4, col. 5.

23. "Pentagon Fraud Inquiry: What is Known to Date," *The New York Times,* July 7, 1988, Vol. 137, p. A1, col. 3.

24. "250 Pentagon Subpoenas Served," *The Washington Post,* June 17, 1988, p. A10, col. 1.

25. "Pentagon Purchasing Inquiry Examines Paisley's Actions While a Navy Official," *Wall Street Journal,* p. 3, col. 2.

26. "The Private Life of Melvyn Paisley," *U.S. News & World Report,* July 4, 1988, Vol. 105, p. 24.

27. Ibid., p. 23.

28. "Consultant Paisley's Method: Big Risks for Big Gains," *The Washington Post,* June 28, 1988, p. A5, col. 1.

29. Ibid.

30. Ibid.

31. Ibid.

32. "Paisley and the Pentagon," *Newsweek,* July 11, 1988, pp. 31, 33.

33. "The Private Life of Melvyn Paisley," p. 24.

34. "Paisley Change in Bidding Rules Aided UNISYS," *The Los Angeles Times,* sec. 1, p. 1, col. 5.

35. "'Buddy System' Can Circumvent Laws Governing Defense Contracts," *The Washington Post,* June 19, 1988, p. A12, col. 2.

36. "250 Pentagon Subpoenas Served," p. A10, col. 2.

37. "'84 Incident Omen of Defense Scandal," sec. 1, p. 25.

38. "Pentagon Inquiry Hears of Payoffs from Contractors," p. D6, col. 3.

39. "U.S. Alleges Defense Consultant, 'Steered' Jobs Valued at Billions to McDonnell," *The Wall Street Journal,* June 17, 1988, p. 13, col. 2.

40. "Competition in Defense Buying Costly to U.S.," sec. 4, col. 1.

41. "250 Pentagon Subpoenas Served," p. A10, col. 1.

42. "Can't Make Arms-Purchasing 'Greed-Proof,' Carlucci Says," sec. 1, p. 14.

43. "Pushing Defense Firms to Compete, Pentagon Harms Buying System," p. 1, col. 6.

44. Ibid.

45. "Pentagon Fraud Inquiry: What Is Known to Date," p. A1, col. 3.

46. "Pentagon Probers Study Two Legislators' Roles," p. A10, col. 1.

47. "Tinkering With Defense," *National Journal,* September 3, 1988, no. 36, p. 2178.

48. "Navy Chief Filled Vacuum at Pentagon," *The Washington Post,* June 19, 1988, p. 1, col. 2.

49. Ibid.

50. Ibid.

51. "Fraud Evidence Ignored, Senator Says," *The Washington Post,* June 21, 1988, p. A1, col. 4.

52. "Defense Firms' Self-Policing Hasn't Closed the Ethics Gap," sec. 4, col. 5.

53. "Pushing Defense Firms to Compete, p. 4, col. 4.

54. "Navy Chief Filled Vacuum at Pentagon," p. 1, col. 2.

55. "Pushing Defense Firms to Compete, Pentagon Harms Buying System," p. 1, col. 6.

56. "Can't Make Arms-Purchasing 'Greed-Proof,' Carlucci States," sec. 1, p. 14.

57. "Tinkering with Defense," no. 36, p. 2179.

58. Special thanks to Professor Joanne B. Ciulla for her assistance in the preparation of this case.

QUESTIONS FOR DISCUSSION

1. Do bribery, influence peddling, and industrial espionage take on even more onerous qualities when they occur in regard to military contracts and national defense spending?

2. Is the defense industry so complex and intertwined that there is little hope for real and long-lasting reform?

3. Are the statements of Ronald Reagan and Joseph H. Sherick (p. 96) an acceptance of the inevitable or an invitation to future corruption?

4. Is Secretary Carlucci's warning an accurate one: "There is simply no way to devise a system that is greed-proof"?

4

Employee-
Employer Relations

The relationship between employees and employers has undergone constant evolution. Today one would never see the kind of sign that was posted in a New York carriage shop in 1878, reading

> It is expected that each employee shall participate in the activities of the church and contribute liberally to the Lord's work . . . All employees are expected to be in bed by 10:00 P.M. Except: Each male employee may be given one evening a week for courting purposes. . . .[1]

Today's employees are better educated and bring to the workplace a higher set of expectations than their counterparts in the nineteenth century. Old organizational habits are confronting new demands, and in turn, new ethical problems.

Many modern theorists insist that employers must modify their attitudes toward employees and be willing to grant an expanding and increasingly well-defined set of "employee rights." Among the rights that such theorists champion are

1. The right of an employee to complain about dangerous products and practices without being penalized.
2. The right of an employee to participate in political and personal activities outside the workplace without being penalized.
3. The right of an employee to a hearing before being fired.
4. The right of an employee to refuse immoral orders without being penalized.

One of the most controversial employee-employer issues today is "whistle blowing." Whistle blowing is directly related to the first item in the list, since the right to "blow the whistle" is at bottom the right to complain about dangerous or immoral practices without being penalized. In other words, advocates of the right to whistle blowing argue that when employees write letters to local newspapers, or inform government authorities, or contact local television reporters in order to complain about company practices they believe are immoral, illegal, or dangerous, they should be protected from being fired or demoted as a consequence. Usually, the right to blow the whistle is assumed to cover only those who appeal to *external* media or authorities (ones outside the organization), and who have first attempted to use *internal* remedies. (Say, by reporting the problem to their superiors.)

Since the issue of whistle blowing is related to that of freedom of speech, one may wonder why so much controversy surrounds a right that presumably is already protected under the First Amendment of the U.S. Constitution. The reason is that, although the First Amendment protects the right of persons to free speech without suffering either government reprisal or the use of force by others to suppress one's speech, it has not—at least traditionally—been interpreted to protect free speech from *employer* reprisal. Indeed, this is an important fact not only about the right of whistle blowing, but of all other purported employee rights as well. People are in one sense always "free" to blow the whistle or refuse immoral orders. The tough question is whether they are free to do these things *and* not be penalized by employers.

Employers who object to the notion of "employee rights" offer two principal criticisms. First, they say that implementing employee rights will harm organizational efficiency. Management's hands would be tied, they say and unable to respond effectively to a company's primary responsibility—maintaining and increasing profits. Not all persons who complain to outside media and authorities are sincere, for example. Many are merely disgruntled troublemakers. Management must remain free to make decisions that it thinks best. Second, employers point out that employees are free to quit their jobs at any time they wish; why, then, should employees not be free to terminate employees when *they* wish? Employers do not demand a "good reason" before allowing an employee to quit; their ability to do so is simply a matter of individual freedom. Why then should employers always be required to offer a "good reason" when firing or demoting?

Over the past two decades, the law has become increasingly protective of employee rights in the United States, especially in the area of whistle blowing. The doctrine of "employment at will," a common-law principle allowing an employer to fire for good reason, bad reason, or no reason, continues to dominate court decisions, but its influence has steadily diminished. A series of court decisions in the late 1960s and early 1970s held that employees could sue employers who fired them as retaliation for whistle blowing *when that whistle blowing occurred either in a government organization or in a profit-making organization that conducted a majority of its work with the government.* In the late 1970s and early 1980s, courts appeared to be extending such employee privileges farther into the sphere of mainstream private business, but—at least at the time of this writing—it is unclear what the final position of the courts will be.

Besides the proposed rights already innumerated, some employees have argued in behalf of four more, namely

1. The right of an employee to be protected in the workplace from physical harm and infectious diseases.
2. The right of handicapped and chronically ill employees, who are able to fulfill their job requirements, not to be discriminated against because of their illness.
3. The right of worker participation and meaningful work tasks, as much as is possible, for every employee.
4. The right of an employee not to be discriminated against because of sexual identity or sexual orientation.

For those championing expanded rights for employees, there are two separate and distinct remedies available. One is to protect such rights through the law through tougher regulations and broader rights of access for employees to the judicial process. The other is to protect rights not through the law, but through internal managerial procedures, policies, and structures. Grievance committees, "open door" policies, quality circles, and employees' "bills of rights" are among the suggestions presently being tried by modern corporations. Those who take the former approach argue that business will never voluntarily police its own house; it must be forced by external pressures. Those taking the latter approach deny that corporations lack the potential for moral initiative, and they point to the obvious drawbacks of using laws and the courts to enforce moral standards: Doing so involves red tape, governmental confusion, and inefficiency.

The cases in this section raise an array of employee-employer issues. "AIDS in the Workplace" examines the issue of infectious diseases and handicapped employees in the workplace. The problems of free speech, whistle blowing and employment at will are explored in the "*Palmateer* v. *International Harvester Company*" and "Dan Gellert, Airline Pilot." Issues dealing with the extent of the employer's prerogative to fire is raised in "Small-Plant Layoff." "*Weber* v. *Kaiser Aluminum*" addresses the complicated issue of affirmative action. The concept of worker participation in management decision making is dealt with in "Harman International." "Vital Information at Complex" and "Management Dilemma" deal with the issue of how managers should respond to complex employee problems involving trade-offs between employee rights and organizational goals. "Sexual Discrimination at Eastern Airlines" is a case that deals with sex discrimination and the more complicated issue of reassigned sexual identity and its effects on an employee's performance on the job. Finally, "Walter Stanton: Employee Responsibility and the Use of Time" deals with the issue of how *employees* should respond to opportunities to count and use their working hours in different ways.

NOTE

1. Quoted in David Ewing, *Freedom Inside the Organization* (New York: McGraw-Hill, Inc., 1977), p.12.

Case Study
AIDS in the Workplace:
Options and Responsibilities

A. R. Gini

"THE BARLYCORN RESTAURANT"

David Barry, the owner and general manager of the Barlycorn, a restaurant and bar catering to young, professional people in a midsized, eastern city, stared down at his desk. His two-year MBA degree from a local university hardly prepared him to confront the ethical dilemma he now faced. That morning, the former wife of one of his employees had come to him with confidential information about Tom Johnson, the twenty-four-year old cook that he had hired only nine months ago. Tom, she told him, had AIDS. David reflected on the fact that Tom had been an above-average employee in the restaurant. In attempting to decide what he should do, David wondered how news of the disease might affect the other thirteen of Tom's workers, some of whom had become close friends with Tom. He also wondered how news of AIDS might affect his customers and business.

What action, if any, should David Barry take? (Thomas Donaldson)

CASE NOTES

Although medical journals as early as 1977 carried articles reporting on a pneumonialike illness that affected mostly homosexual and bisexual males and IV drug users, little national press attention was paid to it. Even in 1981, when the Centers for Disease Control officially diagnosed the first case of AIDS in America, the story was only accorded back-page coverage. According to Randy Shilts in his best-seller *And the Band Played On*, until 1985 AIDS was seen as a comfortably distant threat that limited itself to rather distinct classes of outcasts and social pariahs. But when Rock Hudson was diagnosed and subsequently died from the disease in October of 1985, it was almost impossible to pick up a newspaper or a magazine without seeing a front-page story about the AIDS epidemic. Seemingly overnight, researchers began to generate new evidence that indicated that although the disease was found primarily in the homosexual population, 2 to 4 percent of all AIDS victims were heterosexuals. "Suddenly," said Shilts, "the AIDS epidemic became palpable and the threat loomed everywhere . . ." Indeed, on the day Rock Hudson died, some 12,000 American were already dead and dying of AIDS, and hundreds of thousands more were infected with the virus that causes the disease (Shilts, 1987, pp. xxi–xxiii).

By the summer of 1988, the meeting of the *Fourth International Conference on AIDS* in Stockholm reported that the World Health Organization had documented 96,000 cases of AIDS in 136 countries. However, Dr. Jonathon Mann, World Health Organization AIDS director, believes that this is a conservative figure. He estimates that probably only half of all worldwide cases are officially reported. The actual number of AIDS cases is probably closer to 200,000. Mann also estimates that another 5 to 10 million persons are infected with the AIDS virus (Monmaney et al., 1988).

International observers feel that the lessons to be learned from the Stockholm meeting are few and rather grim:

A. There is no longer any place on earth immune from the specter of AIDS.
B. The disease itself is more complex and more virulent than initially imagined.
C. No vaccine is available or foreseeable in this century.
D. No treatment, let alone a cure, is yet effective.
E. Whatever its etiology and initial "community of infection," the disease has spread across all lines of sexual preference and practice.

Scientists now believe that no one is safe from AIDS. AIDS is no longer the disease of a small fringe segment of society. It is now a disease that can touch us in our personal, family, and professional lives. AIDS is, as columnist Ellen Goodman has suggested, an "equal opportunity infector" that does not discriminate on the basis of race, age, sex, or sexual orientation (Fields, 1986).

Although statistics indicate that while most of us will probably not experience AIDS in our private or family lives a significant number of us will be forced to grapple with AIDS in the workplace. This paper is an attempt to examine the business community's response to AIDS, and the possible options and strategies that especially larger corporations might use in responding to the medical, legal, and ethical dimensions of the disease. According to Nancy L. Merritt, vice-president and director of equal opportunity at Bank of America, AIDS raises at least three fundamental issues in the workplace: How do you handle an employee with AIDS? How do you educate and ensure the safety and morale of your other employees? How do you balance the needs of business with the human ethical considerations raised by the disease? Such questions, Merritt maintains, will become more and more pressing as the AIDS epidemic continues to spread (Merritt, 1988).

AIDS—WHAT IS IT?

Surgeon General C. Everett Koop has likened AIDS to the Black Death of the fourteen century, which exterminated an estimated one-third to one-half of the European population in just four years. The major difference is that not everyone infected with the bubonic plague bacillus, known as *yeesinia-pestis*, necessarily died from it. AIDS, however, is always fatal.

AIDS stands for Acquired Immune Deficiency Syndrome. AIDS is caused by a virus commonly known as HIV (Human Immunodeficiency Virus) or HTLV-III (Human T-Lymphotropic Virus Type III) or LAV (Lymphadenopathy Associated Virus). The AIDS virus infects and destroys T-helper lymphocytes, a type of white blood cell that maintains a person's immune system. Without a properly functioning immune system, a person becomes vulnerable to a variety of opportunistic infections and malignancies, the most common of which are *Pneumocystic carini* pneumonia, a parasitic lung infection; and Kaposi's Sarcoma, a rare and virulent form of skin cancer. People don't die of AIDS, per se. They die of the opportunistic diseases and infections that their system cannot fight off.

Once a person has been exposed to the HIV virus, there is a period of incubation estimated to last between three months and ten years, when the infected person can transmit the disease but remains entirely asymptomatic. Part of the public's fear of AIDS and its real public health danger lie in its prolonged period of infection, during which an apparently healthy individual can unknowingly spread the disease.

As the illness progresses, some or all of the following persistent symptoms develop: high fevers, including severe night sweats; rapid weight loss for no apparent reason; swollen lymph glands in the neck, underarm and groin area; constant fatigue, unexplained diarrhea; white spots or blemishes in the mouth. In the later stages, the immune system of persons with AIDS becomes severely weakened and essentially collapses, turning normally mild, harmless infections into potentially fatal conditions. Once clinical symptoms appear, the illness can run a short, aggressive course lasting for weeks, many months or, in a few cases, years.

According to the Federal Centers for Disease Control, 30 percent of those individuals exposed to the HIV virus will develop AIDS. Another 25 to 50 percent of those exposed to the HIV virus will develop ARC, AIDS-Related Complex, which essentially is a less severe form of AIDS in which fewer of the symptoms and opportunistic infections are present. However, as many as 50 percent of those who contract ARC will, in five- to ten-year period, develop AIDS (Koop, 1986).

HOW IS AIDS TRANSMITTED?

Most researchers agree that AIDS is transmitted through sexual contact and exposure to infected blood or blood components and perinatal from mother to neonate. The HIV virus has been isolated from blood, semen, vaginal secretions, saliva, tears, breast milk, cerebrospinal fluid, amniotic fluid, and urine and is likely to be isolated from other body fluids, secretions, and excretions. However, epidemiologic evidence has implicated only blood, semen, vaginal secretions, and possibly breast milk in transmission (Centers for Disease Control, 1987).

AIDS TESTING

Current available testing for evidence of HIV exposure involves tests that demonstrate the presence of antibodies in the bloodstream that have been produced to ward off the HIV virus. The presence of the antibodies, however, determines only whether an individual has been exposed to the AIDS virus. It does not reveal conclusively that a person who has the disease will ever develop the disease or is even contagious.

There are two principal tests for AIDS antibodies: the ELISA test (enzyme-linked immuno absorbent assay) and the Western Blot test. Neither test is perfectly reliable because they often produce false positives. (The most legitimate use of these tests has been to screen blood donors for the nation's blood supply. A positive result automatically disqualifies the donated blood.) When an individual is tested positive for AIDS, most health care services administer a second ELISA test and then a Western Blot test to help guarantee the accuracy of their diagnosis (O'Keefe, 1988).

PRESENT/EPIDEMIOLOGICAL STATISTICS

The Centers for Disease Control reports that percentages of adult and adolescent cases of AIDS by source of infection are divided into the following groups (Centers for Disease Control, 1988):

Homosexual/Bisexual Males	64.1%
Heterosexual Intravenous Drug Abusers	18.4%
Homosexual Male and Intravenous Drug Abusers	7.3%
Heterosexuals	3.9%
Undetermined	2.8%
Transfusion/Blood Components	2.5%
Hemophilia/Coagulation Disorders	1.0%

According to press reports from the *Fourth International Conference on AIDS* the United States has the dubious distinction of having the greatest number of AIDS cases—65,000—which represents 64 percent of the reported total worldwide AIDS population (National Public Radio, 1988). It is also estimated that the death toll from AIDS in America has passed the 30,000 mark (Kazman, 1988).

Although AIDS has spread into all 50 states it is primarily concentrated in urban areas, with New York and San Francisco having 39 percent of all reported cases (Siwolop et al, 1987). Surgeon General Koop claims that approximately 1.5 to 2 million people have been exposed to the HIV virus and that of these, a new clinically certifiable AIDS case is being reported every fourteen minutes. He believes that by the end of 1991 the United States will have experienced 270,000 AIDS cases resulting in 179,000 deaths. He further claims that in 1991 we will have 145,000 patients living with AIDS who will need health and supportive services at a total cost of between 4.5 and 16 billion dollars (Koop, 1986, p. 6, Gorner, 1988).

According to the Centers for Disease Control and the *Journal of the American Medical Association,* although many AIDS patients do not require long-term hospitalization, the medical costs involved are not insignificant, approximately $147,000 per patient. If this figure is correct, in 1991 the total cost for the maintenance and care of 145,000 AIDS patients will be $21,315,000,000. The burden of these costs will not be easily met, whether it is done by means of government subsidy, private research funding, insurance carriers, personal saving, or a combination of all four (Hary et al., 1986).

A recent study sponsored by Allstate Insurance Company and *Fortune* magazine found that although a majority of U. S. corporate executives believe that AIDS is one of the major problems facing the country, most companies lack direction in dealing with the problem in their workplaces. Only 29 percent of the executives in the 623 nationwide companies polled said that their companies have or are planning to formulate a written or unwritten policy on AIDS (Kittrell, 1988, p. 3). The *Fourth International Conference on AIDS* reported that only 8 percent of U. S. *Fortune* 500 firms and 25 percent of Canadian *Fortune* 500 firms have developed formal policies on AIDS (National Public Radio, 1988). Seemingly, most companies are unwilling, unable, and unprepared to handle the problem and teeter between denial and procrastination. Why?

One common answer given is their concern for the number of employees affected and the costs involved in either long-term disability payments or health care coverage. However, while such a response may have some validity for smaller organizations, does it also apply to larger corporations?

According to Cheryl Russell, editor-in-chief of *American Demographics,* of the 2 million Americans who died in 1987, AIDS victims accounted for only 14,000 of these deaths or less than 1 percent of the total morbidity rate. In contrast, heart disease killed 800,000 and cancer another 500,000. Pneumonia, suicide, and cirrhosis of the liver were also far more important causes of death than AIDS. In numbers of deaths, AIDS ranks with emphysema, kidney failure, and murder. Russell went on to state that even if the projections for AIDS deaths in 1991 are correct—54,000—this figure will account for less than 3 percent of all deaths that year.

By 1991, AIDS will have killed about 180,000 Americans during its ten-year existence in the United States. During those same ten years, more than 20 million Americans will have died. For the nation as a whole, AIDS is an insignificant disease in absolute numbers of deaths—a mere blip in our mortality statistics (Russell, 1987).

When these figures are broken down and applied to the workplace, what it means is that in any given company only a relative handful of employees will be affected by AIDS. For example, Control Data Corporation conducted a self-study which predicts that, at most, 104 of its 34,000 employees will die of AIDS in the next five years—fewer than will die of other major killer diseases (Siwolop, et al., 1987).

So the question remains: Why the hesitancy of so many corporations to formulate policies and procedures in regard to AIDS? A big part of the answer at both the human and corporate level is fear. Fueled by irresponsible headlines and controversies in the press, no disease in modern times has generated so much fear and anxiety. Much of this fear is, in some sense, understandable, because AIDS touches on many of the basic taboos of human experience: sex, homosexuality, illness, suffering, and death. As Reverend Ann Showalter, a Mennonite minister and director of the Chicago-based *AIDS Pastoral Care Network,* has said, "There are really two epidemics—one of the disease and one of fear. And the fear is much more readily transmitted than the disease" ("Aids: Lending a Hand," 1987, p. 23). What corporations and individuals alike fear as much as the costs and suffering involved in the disease is the social stigma associated with the disease as well as the unknowns and the intangibles in regard to contagion and cure.

Many social commentators believe that this fear factor, no matter how exaggerated or misplaced, has immobilized the corporate sector and thereby diminished its possible effectiveness in the handling of a crisis that will not go away.

The issues raised by the AIDS epidemic are many and varied:

Human rights—The denial of any correlation between sexual identity or sexual orientation and the essential quality and worth of any human person.

Civil Rights—The right to personal and physical privacy which includes the presumption of confidentiality and nongovernment involvement, without a specific need to know in regard to health records, financial accounts, and job evaluations or performance records.

The right to work which includes the right not to be discriminated against in matters of hiring, firing, compensation and terms, conditions, and privileges of employment on the basis of race, color, religion, sex, or national origin.

Public health—The obligation of government to protect the public health in regard to infectious and communicable diseases, and, by extension, the obligation of government to protect employees in the workplace from disease and unnecessary physical hazards.

Social ethics—A commitment to the general notion of fair treatment and justice for all members of society, especially in regard to political minorities, the young, the aged, the mentally disabled and the physically handicapped.

While each of these issues deserves to be addressed in detail, perhaps the only practical way to approach AIDS in the workplace is as a human relations or employee management problem. That is, given the presence of AIDS in our society, workplace policies must at one and the same time protect the welfare of those employees who do not have AIDS as well as the civil liberties of those who are infected with the disease. The two most pressing questions that must be answered are: Is AIDS readily contagious? Should AIDS victims be categorized as medically handicapped employees?

Unlike most transmissible diseases (e.g., colds, flu, measles), AIDS is not transmitted through sneezing, coughing, eating, or drinking from common utensils or from merely being around an infected person. All scientific evidence thus far indicates that transmission is not possible through casual personal contact and activities that occur at the workplace. Indeed, there is overwhelming medical consensus on the difficulty of transmitting the AIDS virus. Its transmission is limited to four very specific high-risk activities:

Sexual intercourse,
The sharing of needles to inject drugs,
The exchange of blood,
Infected mothers to their unborn children through a contaminated blood supply.

Because of its difficulty of transmission, AIDS is far and away an avoidable disease. Risk of contagion is proportional to high risk behavior. Except for health care workers engaged in invasive procedures that bring them into contact with blood and other bodily fluids, under normal working conditions employees or patients afflicted with AIDS do not present a health risk to their fellow employees (Centers for Disease Control, 1987). You have about as much chance of catching AIDS in the workplace as you do of catching cancer or multiple sclerosis. Corporations will have to realize that, although AIDS is a health issue, as well as a legal and moral issue, it is not a contagion issue. And they should not allow fear and ignorance to disrupt the workplace and all those on the workforce (Merritt, 1987).

From an employee's point of view, there is only one thing worse than having AIDS—loosing one's job because of it. Prior to 1987, although a patchwork of federal, state, and municipal laws existed that spoke either to the problem of AIDS or to the employer's responsibility to handicapped or disabled employees, AIDS victims had few legal rights or unambiguous remedies in regard to their status in the workplace.

Until recently, the doctrine of "employment at will" permitted employers almost unlimited discretion to fire individuals for any reason or for no reason whatsoever. Only union contracts and specific legislative provisions limited this plenary authority (Werhane, 1985, pp. 80–93). In effect, many employers solved the problem of AIDS in their workplaces by firing those with the disease and sometimes even firing those they feared might have or get the disease. As recently as June 1986, a United States Justice Department memorandum specified that "fear alone" was legitimate grounds for dismissal. The opinion stated in part, "Acting on an irrational fear of contagion is not prohibited by law and thus not discriminatory" (Ward, 1987). This led to a surge of firings, particularly in smaller companies.

Many employers also dismissed employees with AIDS or simply suspected of having AIDS because they feared the threat of reprisals from other workers more than they feared the disease itself. For years, protests and strikes over health and safety issues have been sanctioned by the law. Under Section 7 of the National Labor Relations Act, employees have the right to engage in "concerted activity" for their "mutual aid and protection." This means that two or more employees have a right to withhold services to protest issues affecting their wages, hours, terms, and conditions of employment. In addition, Section 502 of the Labor Management Relations Act specifically protects employees' rights to stop working because of "a good faith belief" that abnormally dangerous conditions exist in the workplace. Thus, employers feared that if a group of employees refused to work with a person who had or was suspected of having AIDS because of health concerns, the action of the group could be viewed by the National Labor Relations Board as a valid protest strike over a health and safety issue (Schachter and Seeburg, 1986, p. 23).

Since 1987, the pendulum of law and court decisions has swung to the side of AIDS victims, and employers must now deal with a new central legal proposition: Employees with AIDS *may* now be covered by state and federal laws and regulations that protect handicapped people against discrimination. Although it is not yet official law, many labor law attorneys believe that the March 3, 1987, Supreme Court ruling in *School Board of Nassau County* v. *Arline* (No. 85-1277) effectively preempts the plenary authority of "employment at will," negates the Justice Department's opinion on fear of contagion, and overrides any possible ruling by the National Labor Relations Board in regard to the unwillingness of fellow employees to work with a colleague suffering from AIDS.

Gene A. Arline, a Florida schoolteacher, suffered from recurring bouts of tuberculosis but claimed she was not contagious. She argued that her firing by the school district violated Section 504 of the Federal Rehabilitation Act of 1973, which imposes a duty upon the federal government, employers with federal contracts, and employers who are recipients of federal assistance, not to discriminate against handicapped persons. The Act defines a handicap as "a physical or mental impairment or infirmity which substantially limits one or more of a person's major life activities . . ." and expressly extends coverage to those not only presently disabled, but who have a "record of such impairment" or are "regarded as having such an impairment."

Until this ruling, appellate courts have applied section 504 only to conditions such as heart disease, cancer, blindness, epilepsy, multiple sclerosis, diabetes, and dyslexia. The question of whether contagious diseases were covered had never been addressed. When the high court agreed with Arline and ordered her reinstatement, its decision effectively extended the Act's protection to those with transmittable diseases (Goldberg, 1987, pp. 55–57). Persons suffering from AIDS would now appear to be covered because the ability to fight off infection and preserve health is a "major life function" (Schacter and Seeburg, 1986, pp. 40, 41).

It is important to note, however, that although labor law scholars believe that the Supreme Court's decision protects symptomatic AIDS victims from "discrimination on the basis of a handicap," its ruling does not resolve the question of whether an asymptomatic carrier of a contagious disease such as AIDS qualifies for protection as a handicapped person under the 1973 Federal Act.

> The United States argues that it is possible for a person to be simply a carrier of a disease, that is, to be capable of spreading a disease without having a "physical impairment" or suffering from any other symptoms associated with the disease. The United States contents that this is true in the case of some carriers of the Acquired Immune Deficiency Syndrome (AIDS) virus. From this premise the United States concludes that discrimination solely on the basis of contagiousness is never discrimination on the basis of a handicap. The argument is misplaced in this case, because the handicap here, tuberculosis, gave rise both to a physical impairment *and* to contagiousness. This case does not present, and we therefore do not reach, the questions whether a carrier of a contagious disease such as AIDS could be considered to have a physical impairment, or whether such a person could be considered, solely on the basis of contagiousness, a handicapped person as defined by the Act (No. 85-1277, note 7).

Nevertheless, even with this critical distinction left unresolved, the court's ruling, in effect, now classifies all life-disabling, life-threatening, and contagious illnesses under the general heading of "handicapped" and that all "handicapped" employees must be "protected against discrimination" in the workplace. With this decision, the door to the summary dismissal of AIDS patient-workers has begun to close because it both implies and mandates what an employer cannot do.

A. An employee may not be terminated or otherwise discriminated against solely because of a handicap that does not interfere with the performance of the employee's job. A handicapped AIDS employee may be terminated only if and when the condition substantially interferes with his or her job performance.

B. While no company is legally obligated to hire workers with AIDS, a business cannot refuse to hire individuals because of their disease. The only acceptable criterion for hiring or firing is that employees (or perspective employees) must be able to intellectually and physically perform the job without presenting a clear and direct danger to themselves or others.

C. An employer must make reasonable accommodations for all handicapped individuals. The exact accommodations that will be necessary will depend on several factors, such as the nature of the work, the size of the organization, and the costs involved. In general, no radical changes are necessary. Accommodations might include offering flexible hours, parttime work, or transfer to a less taxing position.

D. In the face of overwhelming evidence that AIDS is not transmitted from person to person in the workplace, the 1987 Supreme Court ruling implies that employers have no demonstrable interest that would justify using blood tests to screen for exposure to the AIDS virus. If the employee or applicant is currently capable of performing the job, the results of the test cannot be used in making employment decisions. Any adverse action premised on the results of the test would be unlawful (Waks, Meyers, 1987, p. 985).

E. An indirect benefit coming out of this ruling is that insurance companies may now be prohibited from requiring or using HIV testing, preexisting conditions, or any consideration of sexual orientations as an excuse for denying coverage (Brostoff, 1988). Moreover, this decision may have the added effect of prohibiting insurance companies from denying health care coverage to any employee of any customer company. Since most American workers are protected against health care liabilities through employment-based insurance policy plans, the possible far-ranging implications of this decision are not only actuarial and economic but social and moral as well (Bayer and Oppenheimer, 1986).

Given *Nassau County* v. *Arline* what can and ought companies and business do? Three possible options exist.

The first option, while abiding by the letter of the law, does not necessarily conform to its spirit, and its precise legality remains to be adjudicated. Numerous firms are still unwilling to deal with the personnel problems involved with an AIDS-infected staff member. They argue that no matter what experts might say, retaining an employee with AIDS, whether on the shop floor or in the executive offices, creates feelings of anxiety and unrest among a significant portion of their other employees, suppliers, and customers as well. To meet this problem and yet address the needs of an afflicted employee, some firms are electing to continue to pay the employee's full salary and medical and retirement benefits on the stipulation that the employee does not return to work.

As one vice-president for personnel management of a *Fortune* 500 firm related in a private conversation:

> Who are we hurting? For the guy who's got it—we're helping him pay his bills, keep his house and get first-rate medical attention through our group coverage for as long as he needs it. And from the point of view of the people he worked with, well—I'm sure they're glad he's taken care of and I know they're relieved by his absence. Look, don't kid yourself. Even if it isn't contagious, it's just not the same thing as working next to someone who has cancer or a heart condition. As far as I'm concerned, this is just as much a morale issue as it is a moral one.

When pressed on the legality of such a policy and the possibility of civil litigation, the vice-president's answer was equally forthright:

> Why would they sue? We haven't fired anyone. We don't even list them as being on leave, and we never put them on disability. They will still be getting full pay without losing any benefits. We'll even give them their annual raises when it comes up. So what could they sue us for—loss of meaningful work? That would be a tough one to win. And even if they did win, it could prove to be a hollow victory if it took longer than forty-eight months to get it through the courts.
>
> I just don't see it happening. It's just not worth the effort and grief involved.

The second option seems to be the option of choice for most American corporations and businesses. Many companies feel that it is not advisable for them to adopt specific policies that deal solely with AIDS because (1) they don't want to draw attention to the problem and unnecessarily alarm their employees; (2) current company policy on life-threatening illnesses probably covers the situation and therefore there is no reason to treat AIDS any differently from any other illness; and (3) a specific AIDS policy may prove too restrictive, since flexibility is needed as changes in scientific knowledge and the law rapidly occur (Waks and Meyers, 1987, p. 986).

The key element in this approach is *flexibility,* because the companies involved believe that each AIDS case is different and must be handled on an individual ad hoc basis. IBM is one of the companies that uses its basic policy on catastrophic illness to deal with "the handful" of AIDS patients among its 400,000 employees. If they're fit, they can work. If they want counseling, they can get it. If the co-workers want counseling, IBM will offer that, too. But essentially the same rules apply to all workers whether they have AIDS or cancer or have suffered a heart attack (Pave, 1985).

The third option is the development, publication, and implementation of a specific policy on AIDS. So far, only a few major concerns, including Syntex, Bank America, AT&T, Transamerica, Levis Strauss, Wells Fargo, and Pacific Telesis, have adopted specialized personnel policies to handle the problems that AIDS poses in the workplace (Younger and Harris, N.D., N.P.), (see Appendix A).

All such AIDS policies are formulated around a commitment to six underlying principles:

(1.) AIDS is a bloodborne virus that cannot be transmitted through causal social or workplace contact (see Appendix B).

(2.) All human beings gain much of their self-identify and self-esteem from their work. Moreover, good health is often enhanced by working at one's regular job, no matter what the diagnosis. Because of this, all workers should be allowed to determine for themselves, within the limits of safety and physical ability, how long and/or if they want to continue to work (Gini and Sullivan, 1987, pp. 249–60).

(3.) All companies have an absolute obligation to provide a safe working environment for all employees and customers. Every precaution must be taken to ensure that an employee does not present a health or safety threat through loss of physical or mental abilities to other employees and customers. However, as long as medical evidence indicates that persons with life-threatening illnesses do not represent threats to themselves or others, managers should be sensitive to their conditions and ensure that they are treated consistently with other employees.

(4.) The basic posture of every AIDS policy in the workplace must be educational, because while AIDS is a disease that cannot be cured, it *can* be stopped. Information, training, and counseling are the cornerstones to any company's response to AIDS in regard to its victims and to their fellow workers.

Several companies have been quite progressive in educating themselves and their employees concerning AIDS. Taking the lead in this area is the Business Leadership Task Force, which consists of fifteen major employers based in northern California. These companies have pooled their resources to provide a comprehensive AIDS-education program for their employees and their families. The basic message of the Task Force is a simple one: They want to encourage all employers to address the issues of AIDS in the workplace to avoid hysteria and mistrust. Levi Strauss, for example, a leading member of the Task Force, has developed programs that include lectures for managers by experts on AIDS; resource and support classes for persons with AIDS as well as anyone who knows or is related to a person with AIDS; a video presentation that can be checked out for home viewing; and regular updates on AIDS in the company newsletter. Pacific Bell, another Task Force member, provides AIDS seminars and publishes information on topics not normally covered in a company vehicle, such as sexual activity and sexuality. All of the Task Force members also discuss AIDS in regard to their existing employee benefits programs. This provides them with the opportunity to remind their employees of the protection being provided for them and to reassure them of continued protection (Younger, Harris, N.D., N.P.).

(5.) Special care must be taken with all issues of confidentiality. Management's best course of action is a simple one: Except when required by law to do so, never reveal any part of an employee's confidential medical record without that employee's written consent (see Appendix C).

(6.) Any employee refusing to work with an AIDS-afflicted fellow worker is, after appropriate counseling and formal warnings, subject to discharge.

The real import of a carefully rendered AIDS policy is that it communicates a company's concern to provide a safe, healthy, and efficient work environment. It also demonstrates to workers, suppliers, and customers alike, that management cares about the continued success of its business and also about the well-being of its employees and the people they serve. Sadly, however, as *Business Week* commentator Irene Pave (1985) has stated:

> Most companies . . . have yet to come to grips with AIDS. But . . . no responsible employer can continue to duck the issue. The peace of mind of future AIDS patients and the stability of a company's work force depend on setting a fair policy without delay. (p. 126).

ENDNOTES

"AIDS: Lending a hand" (1987). *Company: A Magazine of the American Jesuits,* Winter 1987, pp. 22–24.

BAYER, RONALD, AND GERALD OPPENHEIMER (1986). "AIDS in the Workplace: The Ethical Ramifications," *Business and Health,* January/February, pp. 30–34.

BROSTAFF, STEVEN (1988). "Feds Study Insurer AIDS Treatment," *National Underwriter,* February 29, pp. 56, 57.

CENTERS FOR DISEASE CONTROL (1987). "Recommendations for prevention of HIV Transmission in Health-Care Settings," MMWR, 36, 2S, pp. 35, 38.

CENTERS FOR DISEASE CONTROL (1988). "Update: AIDS and HIV Infection Among Health-Care Workers," MMWR, 37, No. 15, p. 230.

COLLIN, DOROTHY (1988). "Senate Passed Bill for Assault on AIDS," *Chicago Tribune,* April 29, sect. 1, p. 1.

FIELDS, SUZANNE (1988). "AIDS Is Not a Serious Problem for All." In Hall, Lynn and Thomas Modl (eds.), *AIDS,* p. 27, St. Paul: Greenhaven Press.

GINI, A. R. AND T. SULLIVAN (1987). "Work: The Process and the Person," *Journal of Business Ethics,* 6, pp. 249–260.

GOLDBERG, STEPHANIE BENSON (1987). "The Meaning of 'Handicapped'," *ABA Journal,* March 1, pp. 56–61.

GORNER, PETER (1988). "Koop Sounds Cautionary Note," *Chicago Tribune,* June 14, sect. 1, p. 9.

HARY, A. M., K. RAUCH, D. ECHENBERG, W. M. MORGAN, J. W. CURRAN, (1986). "The Economic Impact of the First 10,000 Cases of AIDS in the United States," *Journal of the American Medical Association,* January 10, vol. 255, No. 20, p. 209.

KAZMAN, SAM (1988). "A Reform of the FDA Could Give Hope to AIDS Victims," *Chicago Tribune,* April 14, sect. 1, p. 23.

KITTRELL, ALLISON (1988). "Employers Lack AIDS Strategy: Study," *Business Insurance,* February 1, pp. 3, 4.

KOOP, C. EVERETT (1986). *Surgeon General's Report on Acquired Immune Deficiency Syndrome.* U.S. Department of Health and Human Services, pp. 1–36.

MERRITT, NANCY (1987). "Bank of America's Blueprint for a Policy on AIDS," *Business Week,* March 23, p. 127.

MONMANEY, T., M. HAGER, AND R. MARSHALL (1988). "More Facts, Less Hope," *Newsweek,* June 27, pp. 46, 47.

NATIONAL PUBLIC RADIO (1988). "All Things Considered," Wednesday, June 15.

O'KEEFE, PAUL (1988). "The Medical Perspective." In Bensinger, Gad, and Cyprian Rowe (eds.), *Law Enforcement and AIDS.* Chicago: Loyola University Press, pp. 10–16.

PAVE, IRENE (1985). "Fear and Loathing in the Workplace: What Managers Can Do About AIDS," *Business Week,* November 25, p. 126.

RUSSELL, CHERYL (1987). "Fear of AIDS May Re-create the Virtuous '50's." In Hall, Lynn, and Thomas Modl, (eds.), *AIDS.* St. Paul: Greenhaven Press, p. 199.

SCHACTER, VICTOR AND SUSAN SEEBURG (1986). *AIDS: A Manager's Guide.* New York: Executive Enterprises Co., Inc.

SHILTS, RANDY (1987). *And The Band Played On.* New York: St. Martin's Press.

SIWOLOP, S., S. TICER, R. RHEIN, L. TERRIEN, C. EKLUND, D. HUNTER, AND M. MAREMONT, (1987). "The AIDS Epidemic and Business." *Business Week,* March 23, p. 123.

WAKS, JAY AND LORI MEYERS (1987). "An Introduction to AIDS Coverage Under Corporate Policies on Infectious Diseases and Life-Threatening Illnesses, *Business Laws, Inc. (CPS),* pp. 985–989.

WARD, GARY (1987) "What a Manager Should Know About AIDS in the Workplace," Chicago: The Darnell Corporation, p. 4.

WERHANE, PATRICIA (1985). *Persons, Rights and Corporations.* Eaglewood Cliffs, NJ: Prentice-Hall, Inc.

YOUNGER, ELIZABETH AND LINDA HARRIS, (N.D.). "AIDS: Employer's Rights, Responsibilities and Opportunities, *Washington Business Group on Health,* 229½ Pennsylvania Avenue, S.E., Washington, D.C. 20003, N.P.

QUESTIONS FOR DISCUSSION

1. Do you believe that there is sufficient scientific evidence to comfortably claim that AIDS is primarily a "bloodborne" disease and is not easily communicated to others?

2. How would you feel if a classmate or fellow worker announced that he or she was HIV-positive or began to show various symptoms of AIDS?

3. Why do you think there is an almost xenophobic reaction against AIDS victims?

4. If AIDS affects only "a relative handful of any company's workforce," why do so many corporations hesitate to develop formal policies in its regard? What do they fear most: the disease; the costs involved; reprisals by other workers; or the social stigma associated with the disease?

5. Should AIDS victims be categorized as medically handicapped employees?
6. Is AIDS in the workplace a matter of civil liberties or of public health?

APPENDIX A

PERSONAL
POLICIES & PRACTICES
XYZ Corporation (Name withheld upon request)
(*Fortune* 500, Chicago-based firm)

TITLE: Life-Threatening Illness

APPLICATION: All Employees

DATE ISSUED   9/1/87

SUMMARY STATEMENT

The Company recognizes that employees with life-threatening illnesses, including, but not limited to cancer, heart disease, and AIDS, may wish to continue to work. As long as medical evidence indicates that their condition is not a threat to themselves or others, and their job performance is acceptable, the Company will ensure that they are treated consistently with other employees.

Should the Company have a reasonable basis to believe that employees with life-threatening illnesses are unable to perform their job or are a threat to others, the Company reserves the right to require an examination by a medical doctor appointed by the Company to determine whether the employee should be placed on medical disability.

Life-threatening illnesses may be considered protected handicaps. In conjunction with our Equal Employment Opportunity and Affirmative Action Policies, the Company will not discriminate against individuals with life-threatening illnesses.

PURPOSE

To ensure that the Company deals with life-threatening illnesses consistently, equitably, and in the best interest of the Company and its employees.

PROCEDURES

Consistent with the Company's concern for employees with life-threatening illnesses, the Company will make resources available through the respective Corporate/Subsidiary Human Resources/Employee Relations

Department. When dealing with situations involving employees with life-threatening illnesses, managers should:

1. Remember that an employee's health condition is personal and confidential, and reasonable precautions should be taken to protect information regarding an employee's health condition. Confidentiality shall be maintained until such a time as the respective Corporate/Subsidiary Human Resources/Employee Relations Department deems it necessary to divulge this information.

2. Contact the respective Corporate/Subsidiary Human Resources/Employee Relations Department if you believe that you or other employees need information about terminal illness, or a specific life-threatening illness, or if you need further guidance in managing a situation that involves an employee with a life-threatening illness.

3. Contact the respective Corporate/Subsidiary Human Resources/Employee Relations Department if you have any concern about the possible contagious nature of an employee's illness.

4. Contact the respective Corporate/Subsidiary Human Resources/Employee Relations Department to determine if a statement should be obtained from the employee's attending physician that continued presence at work will pose no threat to the employee or co-workers.

5. If warranted, make reasonable accommodation for employees with life-threatening illnesses consistent with the business needs of the subsidiary/department.

6. Make a reasonable attempt to transfer employees with life-threatening illnesses who request a transfer as a result of undue emotional stress. Transfer shall be contingent upon available openings at the facility where the employees are located as well as the employee's possessing the necessary qualifications for such openings.

7. Be sensitive and responsive to co-workers' concerns, and emphasize employee education available through the respective Corporate/Subsidiary Human Resources/Employee Relations Department.

8. Do not give special consideration beyond normal transfer requests for employees who feel threatened by a co-workers's life-threatening illness.

9. Be sensitive to the fact that continued employment for an employee with a life-threatening illness may sometimes be therapeutically important in the remission or recovery process, or may help to prolong that employee's life.

10. Encourage employees to seek assistance from established community support groups for medical treatment and counseling services. Information on these can be requested through the respective Corporate/Subsidiary Human Resources/Employee Relations Department.

APPENDIX B

SUMMARY OF CENTER FOR DISEASE CONTROL GUIDELINES ON AIDS IN THE WORKPLACE (NOVEMBER 1985)

1. The basic recommendation is that an employee with AIDS need not be restricted from work in any area unless they have evidence of other infections or illnesses for which any employee in that area of work should also be restricted.

2. Personal service workers whose services require needles or other instruments that penetrate the skin are urged to follow infection control recommendations that have been issued for health care workers. Instruments that penetrate the skin, e.g., tattooing and acupuncture needles or ear piercing devices, should be used once and disposed of or be thoroughly cleaned and sterilized. Instruments not intended to penetrate the skin, but which may become contaminated with blood (e.g., razors) should be used for only one client and disposed of or thoroughly cleaned and disinfected.

3. No special precautions are required for personal service workers whose services do not involve a risk of blood contamination.

4. The CDC does not recommend a prohibition on employment of a person with AIDS working in food services. No evidence exists of transmission of either the AIDS virus or hepatitis B virus during the preparation or serving of food or beverages.

5. Workers with AIDS in a setting such as an office, school, factory or construction site have no known risk of transmitting the infection to co-workers, clients or consumers.

6. The CDC finds the greatest risk of transmission of HTLV-III/LAV in the health care work place, especially those health care workers who take part in invasive procedures, such as surgery. It is the CDC's position that even health care workers who are known to be infected with HTLV-III/LAV, but who do not perform invasive procedures, "*need not* be restricted from work unless they have evidence of other infection or illness for which any (health care worker) should be restricted." The CDC intends to issue further guidelines on health care workers who perform invasive procedures.

APPENDIX C

DOCTORS, ON AIDS PRIVACY
The New York Times: July 1, 1988
CHICAGO, June 30—The American Medical Association House of Delegates adopted the following amendment, offered by New York doctors, on how physicians should warn their patients' sexual partners if the patients are carrying the AIDS virus. It read, in part:

> Ideally, a physician should attempt to persuade the infected party to cease endangering the third party; if persuasion fails, the authorities should be notified; and if the authorities take no action, the physician should notify and counsel the endangered third party.
>
> In some states, strict confidentiality laws may limit the exercise of this duty by reason of severe penalties for any breach of confidentiality, especially HIV-related information. Special legislation is needed in these states in order to grant a physician legal immunity to act in the following ways; the legal right to notify directly; or the option of notifying public authorities, or the choice of not acting at all if, in the physician's judgment, the danger to the third party is seen to fall short of substantial risk.

(This appendix has been included to indicate that the issue of confidentiality in regard to AIDS is by no means solved or settled.)

Court Decision
Palmateer v. International
Harvester Company

(Illinois Supreme Court, 1981)*

In 1981, the Supreme Court of the State of Illinois made what should prove to be a monumental decision. It said that an employee of International Harvester Corporation, Ray Palmateer, was wrongly fired for supplying information to local police about employee theft at International Harvester. The company tried to justify its firing of Palmateer on the basis of a doctrine called Employment at Will. Under this common law principle, unless specified by law or by contract, an employer has the right to hire, demote, promote, or fire "at will" whom and when it wishes. The Palmateer decision is a landmark decision because it reverses the longstanding tradition that employer wishes always take precedence over employee rights in the workplace. For employees working under a terminable "at will" employment contract, Illinois has now given hope to those workers who regard their loyalty to the general public as more important than their loyalty to their employer or their own job.

Mr. Justice Simon delivered the opinion of the court:

The Plaintiff, Ray Palmateer, complains of his discharge by International Harvester Company (IH). He had worked for IH for 16 years, rising from a unionized job at an hourly rate to a managerial position on a fixed salary. Following his discharge, Palmateer filed a four-count complaint against IH alleging in count II that he had suffered a retaliatory discharge. According to the complaint, Palmateer was fired both for supplying information to local law-enforcement authorities that an IH employee might be involved in a violation of the Criminal Code of 1961 and for agreeing to assist the investigation and trial of the employee if requested. The circuit court of Rock Island County ruled the complaint failed to state a cause of action and dismissed it; the appellate court affirmed in a divided opinion. We granted Palmateer leave to appeal to determine the contours of the tort of retaliatory discharge approved in *Kelsay v. Motorola, Inc.* (1978), 74 Ill. 2d 172.

In *Kelsay,* the plaintiff was discharged in retaliation for filing a worker's compensation claim. The court noted that public policy strongly favored the exercise of worker's compensation rights; if employees could be fired for filing compensation claims, that public policy would be frus-

* (85 Illinois 2d, 124)

trated. Despite a dissent urging that the creation of a new tort should be left to the legislature, the court said, "We are convinced that to uphold and implement this public policy a cause of action should exist for retaliatory discharge." The court then considered the claim for damages and decided that punitive damages would be allowed in retaliatory discharge cases, but only in the future . . .

With *Kelsay*, Illinois joined the growing number of states recognizing the tort of retaliatory discharge. The tort is an exception to the general rule that an "at-will" employment is terminable at any time for any or no cause. This general rule is a harsh outgrowth of the notion of reciprocal rights and obligations in employment relationships—that if the employee can end his employment at any time under any condition, then the employer should have the same right. As one nineteenth-century court put it:

> May I not refuse to trade with any one? May I not forbid my family to trade with any one? May I not dismiss my domestic servant for dealing, or even visiting, where I forbid? And if my domestic, why not my farm-hand, or my mechanic, or teamster . . . ?
> . . . All may dismiss their employees at will, be they many or few, for good cause, for no cause or even for cause morally wrong, without being thereby guilty of legal wrong. *Payne* v. *Western & Atlantic B.B. Co. (1884), 81 Tenn. 507, 518–20.*

Recent analysis has pointed out the shortcomings of the mutuality theory. With a rise of large corporations conducting specialized operations and employing relatively immobile workers who often have no place to market their skills, recognition that the employer and employee do not stand on equal footing is realistic. In addition, unchecked employer power, like unchecked employee power, has been seen to present a distinct threat to the public policy carefully considered and adopted by society as a whole. As a result, it is now recognized that proper balance must be maintained among the employer's interest in operating a business efficiently and profitably, the employee's interest in earning a livelihood, and society's interest in seeing its public policies carried out.

By recognizing the tort or retaliatory discharge, *Kelsay* acknowledged the common law principle that parties to a contract may not incorporate in it rights and obligations which are clearly injurious to the public. This principle is expressed forcefully in cases which insist that any employer is in contempt for discharging an employee who exercises the civic right and duty of serving on a jury. But the Achilles heel of the principle lies in the definition of public policy. When a discharge contravenes public policy in any way, the employer retains the right to fire workers at will in cases "where no clear mandate of public policy is involved." But what constitutes clearly mandated public policy?

There is no precise definition of the term. In general, it can be said that public policy concerns what is right and just and what affects the citizens of the State collectively. It is to be found in the State's constitution and statutes and, when they are silent, in its judicial decisions. Although there is no precise line of demarcation dividing matters that are the subject of public policies from matters purely personal, a survey of cases in other states involving retaliatory discharges shows that a matter must strike at the heart of a citizen's social rights, duties, and responsibilities before the tort will be allowed. Thus, actions for retaliatory discharge have been allowed where the employee was fired for refusing to violate a statute. Examples are: for refusing to commit perjury: for refusing to engage in price-fixing: for refusing to violate a consumer credit code. It has also been allowed where the employee was fired for refusing to evade jury duty.

The action has not been allowed where the worker was discharged in a dispute over a company's internal management system, where the worker took too much sick leave, where the worker refused to be examined by a psychological-stress evaluator, where the worker was attending night school, or where the worker improperly used the employers' Christmas fund.

The cause of action is allowed where the public policy is clear, but is denied where it is equally clear that only private interests are at stake. Where the nature of the interest at stake is muddled, the courts have given conflicting answers as to whether the protection of the tort action is available. Compare the inconsistent results where the discharge was for opposition to sexual discrimination or harassment (*McCluney* v. *Jos. Schlitz Brewing Co.* (E.D. Wis. 1980), 489 B. Supp. 24, and *Monge* v. *Beebe Rubber Co.* (1974), 114 N. H. 130, 316 A.2d 549), for refusal to falsify official reports (*Hinrichs* v. *Tranquilaire Hospital* (Ala. 1977), 352 So.2d 1130, and *Trombette* v. *Detroit, Toledo & Ironton R. R. Co.* (1973), 81 Mich. App. 489. 265 N.W. 2d 385), and over internal company disputes regarding product safety *Geary* v. *United States Steel Corp.* (1974), 45b Pa. 171, 319 a.2d 174, and *Pierce* v. *Ortno Pharmaceutical Corp.* (1979), 166 N.J. Super. 335, 339 A.2d 1023).

It is clear that Palmateer has here alleged that he was fired in violation of an established public policy. The claim is that he was discharged for supplying information to a local law-enforcement agency that an IH employee might be violating the Criminal Code, for agreeing to gather further evidence implicating the employee, and for intending to testify at the employee's trial, if it came to that. There is no public policy more basic, nothing more explicit in the concept of ordered liberty than the enforcement of a state's criminal code. There is no public policy more important or more fundamental than the one favoring the effective protection of the lives and property of citizens.

No specific constitutional or statutory provision requires a citizen to take an active part in the ferreting out and prosecution of crime, but public policy nevertheless favors citizen crime-fighters. "Public policy favors the exposure of crime, and the cooperation of citizens possessing knowledge thereof is essential to effective implementation of that policy. Persons acting in good faith who have probable cause to believe crimes have been committed should not be deterred from reporting them by the fear of unfounded suits by those accused." (*Joiner* v. *Benton Community Bank* (1980), 82 Ill. 2d 40,44.) Although *Joiner* involved actions for malicious prosecution, the same can be said for the citizen employee who fears discharge. Public policy favors Palmateer's conduct in volunteering information to the law-enforcement agency. Once the possibility of crime was reported, Palmateer was under a statutory duty to further assist officials when requested to do so. Public policy thus also favors Palmateer's agreement to assist in the investigation and prosecution of the suspected crime.

The foundation of the tort of retaliatory discharge lies in the protection of public policy, and there is a clear public policy favoring investigation and prosecution of criminal offenses. Palmateer has stated a cause of action for retaliatory discharge.

IH contends that even if there is a public policy discouraging violations of the Criminal Code, that public policy has too wide a sweep. IH points out that the crime here might be nothing more than the theft of a $2 screwdriver. It feels that in the exercise of its sound business judgment it ought to be able to properly fire a managerial employee who recklessly and precipitously resorts to the criminal justice system to handle such a personnel problem. But this response misses the point. The magnitude of the crime is not the issue here. It was the General Assembly, the People's representatives, who decided that the theft of a $2 screwdriver was a problem that should be resolved by resort to the criminal justice system. IH's business judgment, no matter how sound, cannot override that decision, "[T]he employer is not so absolute a sovereign of the job that there are not limits to his prerogative." (*Tameny* v. *Atlantic Richfield Co.* (1980), 27 Cal.3d 167, 178, 610 P.2d 1330, 1336, 164 Cal. Rptr. 839,845.) The law is feeble indeed if it permits IH to take matters into its own hands by retaliating against its employees who cooperate in enforcing the law.

IH also decries the lack of specificity of Palmateer's complaint. Because the precise crime suspected was not set forth, no one beyond Palmateer, the unnamed employee, and the local law-enforcement agency yet knows the particulars of the investigation. It is understandable that, in view of the novelty of the type of complaint that was filed, Palmateer refrained from identifying his fellow employee through the complaint. IH did not move for a more definite statement, as was its right under section 45 of the Civil Practice Act. Instead it merely moved to dismiss the complaint for failing to state a cause of action. "No pleading is bad in substance which contains such information as reasonably informs the opposite party of the nature or the claim or defense which he is called upon to meet." (Ill. Rev. Stat. 1979, ch. 110, par. 42[2]). This complaint is less specific than it could be but it informed IH of the crux of the claim and stated a cause of action. If IH desires, on remand there are ample procedures under the Civil Practice Act and the rules of this court to put any needed meat on the bones of the complaint.

Finally, IH contends that *Kelsay* requires there be an adversarial relationship before the cause of action for retaliatory discharge is allowed. Even under this theory, it seems that whenever a claim is filed by a former employee, the former employment relationship has already degenerated into an adversarial relationship, at least in the broad sense of the term. But more importantly, *Kelsay* put no such requirement on the cause of action, and we see no rationale for limitation. All that is required is that the employer discharge the employee in retaliation for the employee's activities, and that the discharge be in contravention of a clearly mandated public policy. . . .

Case Study
Whistle Blower:
Dan Gellert, Airline Pilot

Dan Gellert

I had been a pilot for over twenty-five years, the last ten of them with Eastern Airlines, when in 1972 I blew the whistle on a serious defect in the new Lockheed 1011 aircraft. At the time I was in middle management, involved in flight training and engineering safety. Eastern had sent me to the Air Force Safety School, the Army Crash Survival Investigators Course, and Aerospace Systems Safety, a training course given at the University of Southern California. You might say that they created their own monster because, through my safety training, I was able to spot a serious design problem in their 1011 aircraft, first coming into service at that time. But my warnings were ignored and the design problem resulted in a crash killing 103 people. Now, five years, two lawsuits, and a $1,600,000 judgment later, I am still with Eastern and still effecting flight safety.

It all started in the summer of 1972 when I was going through flight training school for the 1011. My roommate was in a simulator when the auto pilot and flight engineer instrumentation disengaged, crashing the flight simulator on a practice landing approach. Even though you don't get hurt when a simulator crashes, he reported this to Eastern's flight operations people. They ignored him.

When Lockheed designed and manufactured the 1011, they failed to recognize a serious safety hazard in the auto-pilot mechanism. The problem was much more insidious than an engine fire or a wing coming off, which most people recognize as a safety hazard. Instead, the defect involved the complex interaction between the crew and the auto pilot and related instrumentation which they relied upon to conduct a safe approach to a runway when landing the aircraft. About ninety seconds before reaching ground level—or about two thousand feet above the ground—the auto pilot would disengage without any warning. In essence, the instruments would lie to the pilot at the critical part of the approach, telling him that he was maintaining elevation when, in fact, he was not. If the weather was bad

Dan Gellert, "Whistle Blower: Dan Gellert, Airline Pilot," *The Civil Liberties Review*, September–October, 1978. Reprinted with permission.

or there were other visual obstructions to ground level, or there was some other distraction, the crew could easily fail to recognize their situation and a crash could result.

In September of 1972 I was flying a 1011 and I noticed that the auto pilot tripped off a number of times without any warning or triggering an alert light on the instrumentation panel. I made a verbal report to a management official who said, "We'll look into it." I replied, "You'd better before we kill a bunch of people." And that's exactly what happened barely four months later.

On December 29, 1972, an Eastern Airlines 1011 crashed, killing 103 people. After learning of the accident, I immediately wrote to the top three people in the company—Frank Borman, vice president of operations; Floyd Hall, chairman of the Board; and Samuel Higgenbottom, president of operations—sending them a two-page evaluation of the 1011 auto-pilot system. Then I just sat back and waited. It wasn't until February that Borman replied with a letter, pointing out that it was pure folly to say that any one safety procedure could prevent all accidents. I realized that I had to do something else.

I then sent my two-page evaluation to the Airline Pilots Association and to the National Transportation Safety Board (NTSB) which was about to conduct a hearing into the crash. At this point my main concern was not the crash, but the horrors that potentially lay in store for Eastern Airlines: more crashes, deaths, destruction of property, and punitive damages assessed against the company.

Immediately after receiving my letter the NTSB called me to discuss the situation. They agreed that the auto pilot was a cause of concern, and they sent me a subpoena. A number of "friends" at Eastern suggested I ignore the subpoena and not testify. Instead, I ignored my so-called friends.

At the NTSB hearing, I stressed the problem with the auto pilot. All the other witnesses, however, blamed the crash on pilot error; after all, its the pilot's responsibility to monitor the flight instruments. Nevertheless, since the time available for the crew to catch the malfunction was minimal—especially during any sort of stress situation—a safe landing under the circumstances would be difficult at best. In June 1973 the NTSB released their "probable cause" results—pilot error. This, of course, took the pressure off Eastern and Lockheed. Instead of having to pay punitive damages to the relatives of the people killed in the December crash, they only had to pay compensatory damages.

Through all these months I had little idea of the collusion between Eastern and NTSB, a government agency, in their attempts to cover up the real cause of the crash and the fact that Eastern had been warned of it in time to have prevented a disaster. The day after the crash in December, the head of 1011 flight training, Thad Royall (who was promoted to a management position after he had caused a fiery crash of two airliners on a runway while serving as a pilot), and Mr. Turner of the NTSB went into the flight simulator and flew the same flight pattern as the crashed aircraft. They did exactly what the original crew did and crashed the simulator at almost exactly the same spot where the aircraft actually crashed. Royall, who was later removed from flight training and put into another management position, was one of the people I had notified when I first recognized the problem with the auto pilot. He and Turner decided to keep the incident quiet. Then in March 1973 there was a meeting attended by Borman, Royall, and other Eastern executives, where Borman decided not to change the design of the 1011 because "the FAA had approved it." It wasn't until July, after the NTSB released its findings, that they decided to quietly modify the auto-pilot design.

After the NTSB findings, I tried to just forget the whole incident. But in December 1973, I was flying in a 1011 when the auto pilot tripped off twice. The second time it happened the plane broke out of the clouds about 200 feet over houses, when our instruments said we should have been at 500 feet. The crew had to put on take-off power in order to make the runway. I knew it was time to take action.

I wrote a twelve-page petition to the NTSB explaining the situation (I didn't know that the design was being modified at this time) and requesting modification of the "probable cause" findings. I sent a copy of this petition to Borman. I still considered myself a loyal Eastern employee and thought it was possible that Borman just wasn't fully informed of the situation. I realized that I might be getting myself into trouble, but I just didn't see any other way I could deal with the situation in good conscience; after all, lives were at stake.

The next thing I knew, Eastern demoted me to co-pilot. Twice a year pilots bid on a base, a position, or a particular airline. Eastern, in a letter addressed to "Dear Occupant," said that I returned a blank bid sheet so they had no choice but to give me a co-pilot slot. Since I had not returned a blank bid sheet at all, I soon realized that I was being penalized for my petition to the NTSB. I then wrote a letter of protest to Borman.

Before receiving Borman's reply, I decided that perhaps I should leave Eastern for a while, if not for good (I was permitted to take a three-year leave of absence). The FBI was recruiting agents at that time who had a knowledge of Eastern Europe. Since I had grown up in Hungary, I decided to apply. I had passed the interview and was all set to work for them when I received Borman's reply to my letter—I was grounded.

In grounding me, Eastern sent me an astonishing letter that questioned my ability to fly an aircraft since, they said, I had written to many letters concerning safety. In my quarter of a century as a pilot, I had never had a passenger complaint or a crew complaint. I had never so much as blown a tire. Not only was I furious, but I started wondering what Eastern was going to do to me next. Rather than leave Eastern and join the FBI—which I felt would make it appear that Borman had justification for grounding me—I decided to remain with Eastern and salvage my reputation. I decided the only way to protect myself from further action was to file suit against them.

It took seven months of going through grievance procedures before I was allowed to fly again in the second half of 1974. In 1975 my attorney filed suit against Eastern charging them with "intentional affliction of mental stress." Then on May 27, 1977, four months before my case was finally tried, I was grounded again. Apparently, Eastern thought that by grounding me they would prove to the Florida jury that I was incompetent. But this attempt at influencing the jury backfired on them and, in fact, helped me to win the case when it reached the courts in September. I had asked for $1,500,000 in damages, but the judge awarded me $1,600,000—the extra $100,000 was just to show Eastern how really angry the judge was at Eastern's blatant attempt to discredit me.

After the ruling Eastern grounded me once again in an effort to "starve me out." They knew that I couldn't find work at any other airline because they had blackballed me. (They told me that not only would they not recommend me, but they wouldn't even answer letters of reference that were sent to them by prospective employers.) They wanted me to sign a letter that they had written which said that I relieved them of any liability involved with the case. In other words, in exchange for my job, I would not make them pay me the $1,600,000. I realized that my only alternative was to file a second suit.

In June 1978 I filed a $12 million lawsuit charging Frank Borman, Tim Button, vice president of flight operations, and Bill Bell, Eastern's attorney, with "civil conspiracy to force me out of employment." I expect the case to reach the courts by spring of 1979, if it gets that far. After losing the first case (which they are appealing now), Eastern has no defense; I expect them to try to settle with me out of court. Since June when I filed the second suit I have been put back on salary, although I'm still not flying. I do hope to be flying by this September though.

As the events of the past five years seem to be drawing to some sort of conclusion, I find it odd to note the change in my "image." I began as a conservative Republican, firmly entrenched in the middle management echelon of big business. And now I am labeled a "whistle blower." The whole nightmare of these years is that I never wanted to be a whistle blower, but my professional ideals and my conscience would allow me to be nothing else. We airline captains have a responsibility to our passengers, our fellow crew members, and our aircraft that supersedes the balance sheets or the income statements of our corporations. And if more of us would speak up instead of protecting our jobs by remaining silent about safety hazards like the one in the 1011, who knows how many accidents could be averted and lives saved.

QUESTIONS FOR DISCUSSION

1. How should Eastern Airlines have responded to Gellert's original letter to Frank Borman?
2. Were there better ways for Dan Gellert to get his point across to Eastern officials? Discuss them.
3. What steps, if any, might Eastern Airlines take to avoid similar problems in the future?

Court Decision
Weber v. *Kaiser*
Aluminum and United Steelworkers

*(U.S. Supreme Court, 1979)**

Decision: Corporation's voluntary affirmative action plan, granting preference to black employees over more senior white employees in admission to in-plant craft training programs, held not violative of 42 USCS §§ 2000e-2(a), (d). [Title VII]

SUMMARY

A union and a corporation entered into a master collective bargaining agreement covering terms and conditions of employment at several of the corporation's plants. Among other things, the agreement contained an affirmative action plan designed to eliminate conspicuous racial imbalances in the corporation's almost exclusively white craft work force. After setting black craft hiring goals for each plant equal to the percentage of blacks in the respective local labor forces, the plan established on-the-job training programs to teach unskilled production workers the skills necessary to become craft workers. At one particular plant, where the craft work force was less than 2% black even though the local work force was 39% black, the corporation established a training program and selected trainees on the basis of seniority, with the proviso that at least 50% of the new trainees were to be black until the percentage of black skilled craft workers in the plant approximated the percentage of blacks in the local labor force. During the plan's first year of operation, the most junior black trainee selected had less seniority than several white production workers whose bids for admission to the program were rejected. One such white worker instituted a class action in the United States District Court for the Eastern District of Louisiana alleging that the manner of filling craft trainee positions discriminated against him and other similarly situated white employees in violation of §§ 703(a) and 703(d) of Title VII of the Civil Rights Act of 1964 (42 USCS §§ 2000e-2(a), (d)). The District Court held that the plan violated Title VII, entered a judgment in favor of the class of white employees, and granted a permanent injunction prohibiting the corporation and the union from denying members of the class access to on-the-job training programs on the basis of race. . . . The United States Court of Appeals for the Fifth Circuit affirmed, holding that all employment preferences based upon race, including those preferences incidental to bona fide affirmative action

*443 U.S. 193 (1979).

plans, violated Title VII's prohibition against racial discrimination in employment. . . .

On certiorari, the United States Supreme Court reversed. In an opinion, by BRENNAN, J., joined by STEWART, WHITE, MARSHALL, and BLACKMUN, JJ., it was held that (1) the prohibition in §§ 703(a) and 703(d) of Title VII against racial discrimination does not condemn all private, voluntary, race-conscious affirmative action plans, since any contrary interpretation of §§ 703(a) and 703(d) would bring about an end completely at variance with the purpose of the statute, the inference that Congress did not wish to ban all voluntary, race-conscious affirmative action being further supported by its use only of the word "require," rather than the phrase "require or permit," in § 703(j) of Title VII . . . which provides that nothing in Title VII shall be interpreted to "require" any employer to grant preferential treatment to any group, because of that group's race, on account of a de facto racial imbalance in the employer's work force, and (2) the affirmative action plan under consideration, which was designed to eliminate traditional patterns of conspicuous racial segregation, was permissible under Title VII, especially in light of the fact that it did not require the discharge of white workers and their replacement with new black hirees, did not create an absolute bar to the advancement of white employees, and was a temporary measure not intended to maintain racial balance but simply to eliminate a manifest racial imbalance.

BLACKMUN, J., concurring, expressed the view that while it would have been preferable to uphold the corporation's craft training program as a "reasonable response" to an "arguable violation" of Title VII, the court's reading of Title VII, permitting affirmative action by an employer whenever the job category in question is "traditionally segregated," was an acceptable one.

BURGER, CH. J., dissenting, expressed the view that the quota embodied in the collective-bargaining agreement discriminated on the basis of race against individual employees seeking admission to on-the-job training programs, such discrimination being an "unlawful employment practice" under the plain language of 42 USCS § 2000e-2(d) [i.e., Title VII].

REHNQUIST, J., joined by BURGER, CH. J., dissenting, expressed the view that the corporation's racially discriminatory admission quota was flatly prohibited by the plain language of Title VII, and furthermore was sanctioned by neither the Act's legislative history nor its "spirit."

POWELL and STEVENS, JJ., did not participate.

OPINION OF THE COURT

Mr. Justice Brennan delivered the opinion of the Court.

[1a] Challenged here is the legality of an affirmative action plan—collectively bargained by an employer and a union—that reserves for black employees 50% of the openings in an in-plant craft training program until the percentage of black craft workers in the plant is commensurate with the

percentage of blacks in the local labor force. The question for decision is whether Congress, in Title VII of the Civil Rights Act of 1964 as amended, . . . left employers and unions in the private sector free to take such race-conscious steps to eliminate manifest racial imbalances in traditionally segregated job categories. We hold that Title VII does not prohibit such race-conscious affirmative action plans.

In 1974 petitioner United Steelworkers of America (USWA) and petitioner Kaiser Aluminum & Chemical Corporation (Kaiser) entered into a master collective-bargaining agreement covering terms and conditions of employment at 15 Kaiser plants. The agreement contained, inter alia, an affirmative action plan designed to eliminate conspicuous racial imbalances in Kaiser's then almost exclusively white craft work forces. Black craft hiring goals were set for each Kaiser plant equal to the percentage of blacks in the respective local labor forces. To enable plants to meet these goals, on-the-job training programs were established to teach unskilled production workers—black and white—the skills necessary to become craft workers. The plan reserved for black employees 50% of the openings in these newly created in-plant training programs.

[2a] This case arose from the operation of the plan at Kaiser's plant in Gramercy, La. Until 1974 Kaiser hired as craft workers for that plant only persons who had had prior craft experience. Because blacks had long been excluded from craft unions, few were able to present such credentials. As a consequence, prior to 1974 only 1.83% (five out of 273) of the skilled craft workers at the Gramercy plant were black, even though the work force in the Gramercy area was approximately 39% black.

Pursuant to the national agreement, Kaiser altered its craft hiring practice in the Gramercy plant. Rather than hiring already trained outsiders, Kaiser established a training program to train its production workers to fill craft openings. Selection of craft trainees was made on the basis of seniority, with the proviso that at least 50% of the new trainees were to be black until the percentage of black skilled craft workers in the Gramercy plant approximated the percentage of blacks in the local labor force. . . .

During 1974, the first year of the operation of the Kaiser-USWA affirmative action plan, 13 craft trainees were selected from Gramercy's production work force. Of these, 7 were black and 6 white. The most junior black selected into the program had less seniority than several white production workers whose bids for admission were rejected. Therefore one of those white production workers, respondent Brian Weber, instituted this class action in the United States District Court for the Eastern District of Louisiana.

The complaint alleged that the filling of craft trainee positions at the Gramercy plant pursuant to the affirmative action program had resulted in junior black employees receiving training in preference to more senior white employees, thus discriminating against respondent and other similarly situated white employees in violation of §§ 703(a) and (d) of Title VII. The District Court held that the plan violated Title VII, entered a judgment in favor of the plaintiff class, and granted a permanent injunction prohibiting Kaiser and the USWA "from denying plaintiffs, Brian W. Weber and all other members of the class, access to on-the-job training programs on the basis of race." A divided panel of the Court of Appeals for the Fifth Circuit affirmed, holding that all employment preferences based upon race, including those preferences incidental to bona fide affirmative action plans, violated Title VII's prohibition against racial discrimination in employment. . . . We reverse.

We emphasize at the outset the narrowness of our inquiry. Since the Kaiser-USWA plan does not involve state action, this case does not present an alleged violation of the Equal Protection Clause of the Constitution. Further, since the Kaiser-USWA plan was adopted voluntarily, we are not concerned with what Title VII requires or with what a court might order to remedy a past proven violation of the Act. The only question before us is the narrow statutory issue of whether Title VII forbids private employers and unions from voluntarily agreeing upon bona fide affirmative action plans that accord racial preferences in the manner and for the purpose provided in the Kaiser-USWA plan. That question was expressly left open in *McDonald* v. *Santa Fe Trail Trans. Co.,* . . . (1976) which held, in a case not involving affirmative action, that Title VII protects whites as well as blacks from certain forms of racial discrimination.

Respondent argues that Congress intended in Title VII to prohibit all race-conscious affirmative action plans. Respondent's argument rests upon a literal interpretation of §§ 703(a) and (d) of the Act. Those sections make it unlawful to "discriminate . . . because of . . . race" in hiring and in the selection of apprentices for training programs. Since, the argument runs, *McDonald* v. *Santa Fe Trans. Co.,* . . . settled that Title VII *forbids* discrimination against whites as well as blacks, and since the Kaiser-USWA affirmative action plan operates to discriminate against white employees solely because they are white, it follows that the Kaiser-USWA plan violates Title VII.

[1b, 2] Respondent's argument is not without force. But it overlooks the significance of the fact that the Kaiser-USWA plan is an affirmative action plan voluntarily adopted by private parties to eliminate traditional patterns of racial segregation. In this context respondent's reliance upon a literal construction of §§ 703(a) and (d) and upon McDonald is misplaced. . . . It is a "familiar rule, that a thing may be within the letter of the statute and yet not within the statute, because not within its spirit, nor within the intention of its makers." *Holy Trinity Church* v. *United States* . . . (1892). The prohibition against racial discrimination in §§ 703(a) and (d) of Title VII must therefore be read against the background of the legislative history of Title VII and the historical context from which the Act arose. . . . Examination of those sources makes clear that an interpretation of the sections that forbade all race-conscious affirmative action would "bring about an end completely at variance with the purpose of the statute" and must be rejected. . . .

Congress' primary concern in enacting the prohibition against racial discrimination in Title VII of the Civil Rights Act of 1964 was with "the plight of the Negro in our economy." 110 Cong Rec 6548 (remarks of Sen. Humphrey). Before 1964, blacks were largely relegated to "unskilled and semi-skilled jobs. . . ." at 6548 (remarks of Sen. Humphrey). Because of automation the number of such jobs was rapidly decreasing. As a consequence "the relative position of the Negro worker [was] steadily worsening. In 1947 the non-white unemployment rate was only 64 percent higher than the white rate; in 1962 it was 124 percent higher." (remarks of Sen. Humphrey). See also id., at 7204 (remarks of Sen. Clark). Congress considered this a serious social problem. As Senator Clark told the Senate:

> The rate of Negro unemployment has gone up consistently as compared with white unemployment for the past 15 years. This is a social malaise and a social situation which we should not tolerate. This is one of the principal reasons why this bill should pass.

Congress feared that the goals of the Civil Rights Act—the integration of blacks into the mainstream of American society—could not be achieved unless this trend were reversed. And Congress recognized that that would not be possible unless blacks were able to secure jobs "which have a future." As Senator Humphrey explained to the Senate:

> What good does it do a Negro to be able to eat in a fine restaurant if he cannot afford to pay the bill? What good does it do him to be accepted in a hotel that is too expensive for his modest income? How can a Negro child be motivated to take full advantage of integrated educational facilities if he has no hope of getting a job where he can use that education?
> Without a job, one cannot afford public convenience and accommodations. Income from employment may be necessary to further a man's education, or that of his children. If his children have no hope of getting a good job, what will motivate them to take advantage of educational opportunities?

These remarks echoed President Kennedy's original message to Congress upon the introduction of the Civil Rights Act in 1963.

> There is little value in a Negro's obtaining the right to be admitted to hotels and restaurants if he has no cash in his pocket and no job.

Accordingly, it was clear to Congress that "the crux of the problem [was] to open employment opportunities for Negroes in occupations which have been traditionally closed to them," (remarks of Sen. Humphrey), and it was to this problem that Title VII's prohibition against racial discrimination in employment was primarily addressed.

It plainly appears from the House Report accompanying the Civil Rights Act that Congress did not intend wholly to prohibit private and voluntary affirmative action efforts as one method of solving this problem. The Report provides:

> No bill can or should lay claim to eliminating all of the causes and consequences of racial and other types of discrimination against minorities. There is reason to believe, however, that national leadership provided by the enactment of Federal legislation dealing with the most troublesome problems *will*

create an atmosphere conducive to voluntary or local resolution of other forms of discrimination. 88th Cong, 1st Sess (1963) (emphasis supplied.) . . .

[1c] Our conclusion is further reinforced by examination of the language and legislative history of § 703(j) of Title VII. Opponents of Title VII raised two related arguments against the bill. First, they argued that the Act would be interpreted to *require* employers with racially imbalanced work forces to grant preferential treatment to racial minorities in order to integrate. Second, they argued that employers with racially imbalanced work forces would grant preferential treatment to racial minorities, even if not required to do so by the Act. See 110 Cong Rec (remarks of Sen. Sparkman). Had Congress meant to prohibit all race-conscious affirmative action, as respondent urges, it easily could have answered both objections by providing that Title VII would not require or *permit* racially preferential integration efforts. But Congress did not choose such a course. Rather, Congress added § 703(j) which addresses only the first objection. The section provides that nothing contained in Title VII "shall be interpreted to *require* any employer . . . to grant preferential treatment . . . to any group because of the race . . . of such . . . group on account of" a de facto racial imbalance in the employer's work force. The section does *not* state that "nothing in Title VII shall be interpreted to *permit*" voluntary affirmative efforts to correct racial imbalances. The natural inference is that Congress chose not to forbid all voluntary race-conscious affirmative action.

The reasons for this choice are evident from the legislative record. Title VII could not have been enacted into law without substantial support from legislators in both Houses who traditionally resisted federal regulation of private business. Those legislators demanded as a price for their support that "management prerogatives and union freedoms . . . be left undisturbed to the greatest extent possible. . . ." Section 703(j) was proposed by Senator Dirksen to allay any fears that the Act might be interpreted in such a way as to upset this compromise. The section was designed to prevent § 703 of Title VII from being interpreted in such a way as to lead to undue "Federal Government interference with private businesses because of some Federal employee's ideas about racial balance or imbalance." 110 Cong Rec, (remarks of Sen. Miller). . . . Clearly, a prohibition against all voluntary, race-conscious, affirmative action efforts would disserve these ends. Such a prohibition would augment the powers of the Federal Government and diminish traditional management prerogatives while at the same time impeding attainment of the ultimate statutory goals. In view of this legislative history and in view of Congress' desire to avoid undue federal regulation of private businesses, use of the word "require" rather than the phrase "require or permit" in § 703(j) fortifies the conclusion that Congress did not intend to limit traditional business freedom to such a degree as to prohibit all voluntary, race-conscious affirmative action.

[1d] We therefore hold that Title VII's prohibition in §§ 703(a) and (d) against racial discrimination does not condemn all private, voluntary race-conscious affirmative action plans.

We need not today define in detail the line of demarcation between permissible and impermissible affirmative action plans. It suffices to hold that the challenged Kaiser-USWA affirmative action plan falls on the permissible side of the line. The purposes of the plan mirror those of the statute. Both were designed to break down old patterns of racial segregation and hierarchy. Both were structured to "open employment opportunities for Negroes in occupations which have been traditionally closed to them." 110 Cong Rec (remarks of Sen. Humphrey).

[1e] At the same time the plan does not unnecessarily trammel the interests of the white employees. The plan does not require the discharge of white workers and their replacement with new black hires. Cf. *McDonald* v. *Santa Fe Trail Trans. Co.,* supra. Nor does the plan create an absolute bar to the advancement of white employees; half of those trained in the program will be white. Moreover, the plan is a temporary measure; it is not intended to maintain racial balance, but simply to eliminate a manifest racial imbalance. Preferential selection of craft trainees at the Gramercy plant will end as soon as the percentage of black skilled craft workers in the Gramercy plant approximates the percentage of blacks in the local labor force. . . .

We conclude, therefore, that the adoption of the Kaiser-USWA plan for the Gramercy plant falls within the area of discretion left by Title VII to the private sector to voluntarily adopt affirmative action plans designed to eliminate conspicuous racial imbalance in traditionally segregated job categories. Accordingly, the judgment of the Court of Appeals for the Fifth Circuit is reversed.

Mr. Justice Powell and Mr. Justice Stevens took no part in the consideration or decision of this case. . . .

Mr. Chief Justice Burger, dissenting.

The Court reaches a result I would be inclined to vote for were I a Member of Congress considering a proposed amendment of Title VII. I cannot join the Court's judgment, however, because it is contrary to the explicit language of the statute and arrived at by means wholly incompatible with long-established principles of separation of powers. Under the guise of statutory "construction," the Court effectively rewrites Title VII to achieve what it regards as a desirable result. It "amends" the statute to do precisely what both its sponsors and its opponents agreed the statute was not intended to do.

When Congress enacted Title VII after long study and searching debate, it produced a statute of extraordinary clarity, which speaks directly to the issue we consider in this case. In § 703(d) Congress provided:

> It shall be an unlawful employment practice for any employer, labor organization, or joint labor-management committee controlling apprenticeship or other training or retraining, including on-the-job training programs, to discriminate against any individual because of his race, color, religion, sex, or national origin in admission to, or employment in, any program established to provide apprenticeship or other training.

Often we have difficulty interpreting statutes either because of imprecise drafting or because legislative compromises have produced genuine ambiguities. But here there is no lack of clarity, no ambiguity. The quota embodied in the collective-bargaining agreement between Kaiser and the Steelworkers unquestionably discriminates on the basis of race against individual employees seeking admission to on-the-job training programs. And, under the plain language of § 703(d), that is "an unlawful employment practice."

Oddly, the Court seizes upon the very clarity of the statute almost as a justification for evading the unavoidable impact of its language. The Court blandly tells us that Congress could not really have meant what it said, for a "literal construction" would defeat the "purpose" of the statute—at least the congressional "purpose" as five Justices divine it today. But how are judges supposed to ascertain the purpose of a statute except through the words Congress used and the legislative history of the statute's evolution? One need not even resort to the legislative history to recognize what is apparent from the face of Title VII—that it is specious to suggest that § 703(j) contains a negative pregnant that permits employers to do what §§ 703(a) and (d) unambiguously and unequivocally forbid employers from doing. Moreover, as Mr. Justice Rehnquist's opinion—which I join—conclusively demonstrates, the legislative history makes equally clear that the supporters and opponents of Title VII reached an agreement about the statute's intended effect. That agreement, expressed so clearly in the language of the statute that no one should doubt its meaning, forecloses the reading which the Court gives the statute today.

Arguably, Congress may not have gone far enough in correcting the effects of past discrimination when it enacted Title VII. The gross discrimination against minorities to which the Court adverts—particularly against Negroes in the building trades and craft unions—is one of the dark chapters in the otherwise great history of the American labor movement. And I do not question the importance of encouraging voluntary compliance with the purposes and policies of Title VII. But that statute was conceived and enacted to make discrimination against *any* individual illegal, and I fail to see how "voluntary compliance" with the nondiscrimination principle that is the heart and soul of Title VII as currently written will be achieved by permitting employers to discriminate against some individuals to give preferential treatment to others.

Until today, I had thought the Court was of the unanimous view that "discriminatory preference for any group, minority or majority, is precisely and only what Congress has proscribed" in Title VII. *Griggs* v. *Duke Power Co.* . . . (1971). Had Congress intended otherwise, it very easily could have drafted language allowing what the Court permits today. Far from doing so, Congress expressly prohibited in §§ 703(a) and (d) the discrimination against Brian Weber the Court approves now. If "affirmative action" programs such as the one presented in this case are to be permitted, it is for Congress, not this Court, to so direct.

It is often observed that hard cases make bad law. I suspect there is some truth to that adage, for the "hard" cases always tempt judges to exceed the limits of their authority, as the Court does today by totally rewriting a crucial part of Title VII to reach a desirable result. Cardozo no doubt had this type of case in mind when he wrote:

> The judge, even when he is free, is still not wholly free. He is not to innovate at pleasure. He is not a knight-errant, roaming at will in pursuit of his own ideal of beauty or of goodness. He is to draw his inspiration from consecrated principles. He is not to yield to spasmodic sentiment, to vague and unregulated benevolence. He is to exercise a discretion informed by tradition, methodized by analogy, disciplined by system, and subordinated to 'the primordial necessity of order in the social life.' Wide enough in all conscience is the field of discretion that remains. B. Cardozo, *The Nature of the Judicial Process* 141 (1921).

What Cardozo tells us is beware the "good result" achieved by judicially authorized or intellectually dishonest means on the appealing notion that the desirable ends justify the improper judicial means. For there is always the danger that the seeds of precedent sown by good men for the best of motives will yield a rich harvest of unprincipled acts of others also aiming at "good ends."

Mr. Justice Rehnquist, with whom The Chief Justice joins, dissenting.

In a very real sense, the Court's opinion is ahead of its time; it could more appropriately have been handed down five years from now, in 1984, a year coinciding with the title of a book from which the Court's opinion borrows, perhaps subconsciously, at least one idea. Orwell describes in his book a governmental official of Oceania, one of the three great world powers, denouncing the current enemy, Eurasia, to an assembled crowd:

> It was almost impossible to listen to him without being first convinced and then maddened. . . .
> The speech had been proceeding for perhaps twenty minutes when a messenger hurried onto the platform and a scrap of paper was slipped into the speaker's hand. He unrolled and read it without pausing in his speech. Nothing altered in his voice or manner, or in the content of what he was saying, but suddenly the names were different. Without words said, a wave of understanding rippled through the crowd. Oceania was at war with Eastasia! . . .
> The banners and posters with which the square was decorated were all wrong! . . .
> [T]he speaker had switched from one line to the other actually in midsentence, not only without a pause, but without even breaking the syntax. G. Orwell, *Nineteen Eighty-Four*, 182–83 (1949).

Today's decision represents an equally dramatic and equally unremarked switch in this Court's interpretation of Title VII.

The operative sections of Title VII prohibit racial discrimination in employment simpliciter. Taken in its normal meaning, and as understood by all Members of Congress who spoke to the issue during the legislative debates . . . this language prohibits a covered employer from considering race when making an employment decision, whether the race be black or white. Several years ago, however, a United States District Court held that "the dismissal of white employees charged with misappropriating company property while not dismissing a similarly charged Negro employee does not raise a claim upon which Title VII relief may be granted." *McDonald* v. *Santa Fe Trail Transp. Co.* . . . (1976). This Court unanimously reversed, concluding from the "uncontradicted legislative history" that "Title VII prohibits racial discrimination against the white petitioners in this case upon the same standards as would be applicable were they Negroes. . . ."

We have never wavered in our understanding that Title VII "prohibits *all* racial discrimination in employment, without exception for any particular employees." . . . In *Griggs* v. *Duke Power Co.* . . . (1971), our first occasion to interpret Title VII, a unanimous court observed that "[d]iscriminatory preference, for any group, minority or majority, is precisely and only what Congress has proscribed." And in our most recent discussion of the issue, we uttered words seemingly dispositive of this case: "It is clear beyond cavil that the obligation imposed by Title VII is to provide an equal opportunity for *each* applicant regardless of race, without regard to whether members of the applicant's race are already proportionately represented in the work force." *Furnco Construction Corp.* v. *Waters* . . . (1978) (emphasis in original).

Today, however, the Court behaves much like the Orwellian speaker earlier described, as if it had been handed a note indicating that Title VII would lead to a result unacceptable to the Court if interpreted here as it was in our prior decisions. Accordingly, without even a break in syntax, the Court rejects "a literal construction of § 703(a)" in favor of newly discovered "legislative history," which leads it to a conclusion directly contrary to that compelled by the "uncontradicted legislative history" unearthed in McDonald and our other prior decisions. Now we are told that the legislative history of Title VII shows that employers are free to discriminate on the basis of race: an employer may, in the Court's words, "trammel the interests of white employees" in favor of black employees in order to eliminate "racial imbalance." . . . Our earlier interpretations of Title VII, like the banners and posters decorating the square in Oceania, were all wrong.

As if this were not enough to make a reasonable observer question this Court's adherence to the oftstated principle that our duty is to construe rather than rewrite legislation, *United States* v. *Rutherford,* . . . (1979), the Court also seizes upon § 703(j) of Title VII as an independent, or at least partially independent, basis for its holding. Totally ignoring the wording of that section, which is obviously addressed to those charged with the responsibility of interpreting the law rather than those who are subject to its proscriptions, and totally ignoring the months of legislative debates preceding the section's introduction and passage, which demonstrate clearly that it was enacted to prevent precisely what occurred in this case, the Court infers from § 703(j) that "Congress chose not to forbid all voluntary race-conscious affirmative action."

Thus, by a tour de force reminiscent not of jurists such as Hale, Holmes, and Hughes, but of escape artists such as Houdini, the Court eludes clear statutory language, "uncontradicted" legislative history, and uniform precedent in concluding that employers are, after all, permitted to consider race in making employment decisions. It may be that one or more of the principal sponsors of Title VII would have preferred to see a provision allowing preferential treatment of minorities written into the bill. Such a provision, however, would have to have been expressly or impliedly excepted from Title VII's explicit prohibition on all racial discrimination in employment. There is no such exception in the Act. And a reading of the legislative debates concerning Title VII, in which proponents and opponents alike uniformly denounced discrimination in favor of, as well as discrimination against, Negroes, demonstrates clearly that any legislator harboring an unspoken desire for such a provision could not possibly have succeeded in enacting it into law.

Case Study
Small Plant Lay-Off

Harold Oaklander

The Mountainside plant can be approached from the east, driving by orchards and farms. In the flat valley that gives way to the Appalachian Mountain range lie two main buildings, surrounded by open fields and dominated by a huge water tower. The factory is flanked by orderly rows of bare truck chassis, seats exposed and steering columns pointed skyward.

Each chassis is moved into the plant to receive careful grafts of panel upon panel, accessory upon accessory, until the particular delivery vehicle has been completed some 120 working hours later. The General Motors or Ford chassis is thus made complete with a Mountainside body. It will then be serviced in preparation for its delivery to one of the regional bread companies or motor express companies, or some other familiar company whose trade name is colorfully displayed on the finished vehicles.

THE DELIVERY-VEHICLE OPERATION IN THE OVERALL ENTERPRISE

The Mountainside name is used locally, but the full name of the operation is Orion-Mountainside. It is the oldest of five body plants that comprise one division of Orion-Diversified Industries Incorporated, a subsidiary of the Orion General Corporation. A new type of mass transportation vehicle is being produced by another division of the Orion-Diversified subsidiary. The Annual Report attributes a 10.5 percent decline in earnings to a multimillion dollar pretax loss from "start-up problems in the production" of the new vehicle.

Orion General's reputation lies with the aircraft it produces, referred to by its Chief Executive Officer as "those unmatched flying systems." Thousands of these consistent profit makers have been produced by the company's aerospace subsidiary over its long history, primarily for the United States and other governments. According to a recent annual report the company overall had 28,000 employees, a shareholder's equity of $220 million, sales of $1.49 billion and a net income of $19.5 million.

The 14 officers of Orion-Diversified from Chairman of the Board to Comptroller are identified in the annual report. Vice-Presidents of several of its different lines of business are indicated. No officer is identified with the vehicle body business, nor are financial figures broken down to that level of operation. The report does mention that the demand for delivery vehicles continues strong, that rising fuel costs also stimulate the market for light weight, durable aluminum bodies, and that the company sold a record number during the year for $63 million.

Vehicle body production has been an expanding enterprise for the company ever since it began some 30 years ago. Operations were shifted to Rhone in the mid-1950s and over the years four additional plants were established to cater to regional markets as far away as the west coast. Headquarters for the five plants are centrally located 150 miles away from Rhone, and the marketing and purchasing functions are performed there. Design engineering is carried out at the largest of the plants.

The Plant Manager of the Rhone works, Mr. David Cannon, had come to the plant some seventeen years before my visit. He had had previous experience in varied aspects of production control with Westinghouse and a university degree in economics.

Early in July of 1980, Mr. Cannon called his staff together to discuss a threatening development, the possibility of having to lay off a number of workers because of looming production and marketing problems affecting all five plants of the vehicle body division. This was not the first time in the history of the plant that such deliberations were held. This episode and the consequences to follow will be better understood if the production and marketing processes particular to Orion-Mountainside are examined first.

THE PRODUCTION SYSTEM

Vehicles supplied by Mountainside are made to order, incorporating company designs and often the user's own specifications. Occasionally orders are received from major truck dealers who put the finished delivery vehicles into their stock and thus are able to provide immediate delivery to their own customers. When a user orders a number of vehicles directly from the company, the requisite number of chassis must first be ordered from Detroit. Each chassis must then be modified to receive a particular body. The body is constructed in panels, riveted, then bolted to the chassis.

From the time a chassis is fed from the storage yard into the assembly building, some 110 to 175 working hours, depending upon the options, will elapse. The finished unit is moved to a separate area for road preparation and delivery. The average production cycle is 2½ to 3 weeks per vehicle. Aluminum for this assembly process is housed in the metal storage and layout building. Here a multimillion-dollar inventory of aluminum sheet, extruded shapes and standard structural members is received, stored, cut and the pieces grouped for transport to the assembly building.

The almost exclusive use of aluminum distinguishes Mountainside bodies from those of its major competitor who uses mostly steel in its custom bodies. The majority of light trucks in the United States are of standard design and made of steel. The big three automobile manufacturers turn them out in great numbers. Yet business for aluminum bodies has been favorable in recent years. This is because weight reduction means fuel economy, also because of the corporation's tradition of precision work with light metals in its aircraft subsidiary. The fabrication of aluminum vehicle bodies also requires special expertise. With rising prices buyers feel, according to company officials, that they are getting more quality for their money.

BUSINESS FACTORS TRIGGERING THE LAY-OFF DELIBERATIONS

By July 1980, orders had indeed slackened off, but not critically. Consideration was given to anticipating future orders so that more work could be provided. However, a more ominous threat to the maintenance of full work schedules loomed as the month passed—a drop in the supply of chassis.

The supply situation which the general manager and his staff worried about was influenced by events in Detroit. The major automobile and truck manufacturers who supplied their chassis had suffered severely in 1980 and many auto workers had been laid off. Under normal business circumstances vehicle production lines* in Detroit are shut down for model changes for the traditional one or two week period. That year the interruption might be longer.

This spelled trouble for the Rhone plant. Ways of circumventing a lay-off were considered during the entire month of July. Mr. Cannon, who has considerable latitude to make locally important decisions such as the decision to lay-off, touched bases frequently with division headquarters.

When the plant shut-downs in Detroit started on July 20th, Mountainside was informed that chassis production would not resume until September 8th. Even if this date were kept it would still mean that chassis would not begin to arrive for another three weeks at the earliest. An overall delay of at least ten weeks loomed.

The situation would worsen if, by September 8th, the automobile companies had not accumulated sufficient orders for their own standard

---

*Truck chassis are built on the same assembly line as automobiles, light trucks, and other vehicles.

trucks and automobiles to be able to start *uninterrupted* production. All truck body plants of the division would suffer from the want of their small share of Detroit's truck chassis output.

HISTORY OF PREVIOUS LAY-OFFS

Twice before the management of the Mountainside plant had been threatened in this way and had found it necessary to resort to lay-off. Approximately 75 workers from the Rhone area were laid off when the company ceased its marine engine operations in a nearby plant and at the same time a strike at General Motors cut off the flow of chassis for the truck body plant. No lay-off was experienced during the subsequent 1970–71 recession. In January of 1975, the combination of the energy crisis and the severe recession precipitated the dismissal of 50 employees, some 28 percent of the work force. Half of the laid off workers were recalled that July, with the balance returning to work by February of the following year. Some 20 to 25 percent of those dismissed did not respond to recall. They had found other work or had other reasons for not returning.

Mr. Cannon spoke of several close calls which had nearly led to layoffs when material or chassis shortages had slowed production. Each time, dismissals were avoided by scheduling special work. He explained that Orion-General "gives special consideration to its employee relations." Were events to lead to a close call or to a lay-off in July of 1980?

THE FINAL DELIBERATIONS AND THE EVENTS THAT FOLLOWED

Mr. Cannon and his staff of managers discussed the evolving situation many times during the month of July. The problem was not discussed with the workers who are not represented by a union. As the month drew to a close with no improvement in Detroit, management came to feel that a layoff would have to be put into effect. A procedure was then agreed upon.

On the last Friday morning of the month, the production manager called all foremen into his office. He told them for the first time that a layoff involving seventeen workers would be implemented that afternoon and provided them with the procedure worked out by the plant management. Who was to be laid off was decided strictly by seniority: it was deemed the only fair way. In an effort to give the same picture to every one the following message was prepared:

> Due to general economic conditions and questionable chassis production start-up of 1981 models, it has become necessary for the plant to have a reduction of employees for an indefinite period. When business conditions so warrant, employees will be recalled as required.

That afternoon the plant manager and his personnel manager called into his office the fifteen workers who were present, out of the total of seventeen surplus workers. Mr. Cannon estimated that the meeting took some five minutes. It was intentionally kept short and was based on the prepared message. The employees were then invited to remain and ask questions. None did so.

Meanwhile, foremen out in the plant were telling the remaining workers of the lay-off. They used the prepared message given to them earlier in the day. The message was posted on the plant bulletin boards. The lay-off was to take effect immediately.

While instructing the supervisors in preparation for this meeting, questions were anticipated from workers not scheduled for lay-off. Some might speculate that they would be next because of their low seniority. Supervisors were instructed to respond that no new lay-offs were presently being planned, but that this was not a guarantee against future lay-offs.

WHY THE LAY-OFF WAS IMPLEMENTED AS IT WAS

The personnel manager explained, weeks later, that no advance notice was given because it wouldn't do to have workers around the plant after they had been notified. He felt that their attitude towards their work would change.

This was the personnel manager's first experience with a lay-off. He was relatively new at the job and had previously been a partner in a small business. His professional education had been in accounting. He was described as one who was interested in taking care of the employees. He expressed his helplessness in this situation with the comments, "We don't have control over the economy," and "We are responsible to the stockholders." His son was among the seventeen workers dismissed.

In response to my inquiry as to whether any form of work force adjustment other than lay-off was considered—for example, work sharing—Mr. Cannon responded that work sharing had been considered. It was not a new concept for the company. His predecessor had used work sharing in the 1960s but had come to feel that it didn't work. It was resented by the older workers who felt that they had been around long enough to be entitled to job security. For them, job security meant the full pay checks necessary for full bags of groceries on a regular basis. In July 1980, according to Mr. Cannon, there was little talk among the workers about work sharing as an option for avoiding dismissal in the recent lay-off.

The plant manager had considered discussing the lay-off with the local office of the state labor department prior to its occurrence. Even though this might have expedited the payment of benefits, he did not do so because "It might have given away the lay-off plans." He did not want to alarm the workers unnecessarily in case the lay-off were to be called off at the last minute. Even with all these precautions some of the more experienced workers might have suspected an impending lay-off, since there was an obvious reduction in the number of chassis in the storage yard.

WHAT OF THOSE LAID OFF?

All of the laid off workers had been hired by Mountainside after September 4th, 1979. At most they had accumulated 11 months of experience. Their ages ranged from 19 to 49, with an average age of 24. One woman (from a female work force of 15 to 20 percent of the total) and two black workers (of five on the payroll) were among the dismissed.

Some of the workers lived near the plant, the furthest lived 15 miles away. The group was fairly evenly divided among married and single individuals. The dependent children numbered eight. The average hourly pay at time of lay-off was $4.35.

The laid off workers were the most junior in terms of experience as well as seniority. They would probably still be classified as unskilled by their next employer because of the shortness of their service and because Mountainside had hired them as unskilled.

In fact they had learned a lot during their tenure at the body works. All had survived the close scrutiny of a ninety-day probationary period. While a formal system of job classification was not used in the plant, all new employees, and senior employees as well, were encouraged to acquire new skills. They might even be switched to different jobs if they expressed an interest in doing so. They were not entrusted with highly skilled jobs, such as sheet metal layout and maintenance of equipment; these high status jobs were relative to semi-skilled jobs and were held by employees with long service. Thus, the skills built up by those laid off were not yet adequate to establish them as skilled workers. One can surmise that, while workers lucky enough to be called back will continue to build up skills, those who are not will have to start again as unskilled workers in a new job.

It became obvious to the writer during the tour of the plant that the plant manager knew all of the employees by their first names and he was accustomed to spending time in the work areas. He had asked the personnel manger to keep track of how the discharged workers were making out. "We lost some good people and we want them back after the chassis come in." Six weeks after the lay-off, the personnel manager reported that all the dismissed workers were still unemployed. This information was obtained from state unemployment insurance records. Mr. Cannon mentioned that even though he knew of the one week waiting period before the start of benefits, he was surprised and dismayed when he discovered that it took three weeks for unemployment checks to reach those entitled to them. He added: "Laying off employees was an extremely unpleasant thing to have to do."

On September 17th, seven weeks after the lay-off, Mr. Cannon brought me up to date on the chassis problem. While General Motors had started producing 1981 model chassis, he did not know whether any of the first ones produced would be earmarked for Mountainside Rhone. "It is difficult to get information from them. Sometimes we receive chassis before we receive notice that they have been shipped. We were able to avoid a lay-off in mid July when some chassis came in unexpectedly."

BENEFITS AND SERVICES FOR THOSE LAID OFF

There are several potential sources of assistance for laid off workers. The company itself is closest to the worker, but various government agencies offer a wider range of services.

I asked the plant manager what benefits and services the seventeen displaced workers had received from the company. All had been paid for vacation accrued but not taken; because of their short tenure this amounted to a few days at best. Severance pay is not a fringe benefit in Orion-Mountainside. Even if severance pay were provided, the short service of those dismissed would have entitled them to very little. All other fringe benefits, including group health and other protective benefits, cease with termination of employment. There is a 31 day grace period during which the company group health policy may be transferred to other health insurance. None of those laid off had worked long enough to win vested rights in the pension plan. Even if they had, they would not have realized them until retirement age. Mr. Cannon pointed out that, in general, senior workers received more benefits than junior workers, except for health insurance.

The seventeen dismissed workers also missed benefitting from a profit sharing plan by falling short of its one-year waiting period. The plan pays two ways: Half of the profit sharing bonus is paid in cash at the end of each year, and half is deferred until the employee leaves the company. The deferred portion is partially vested, with the employee entitled to 10 percent after one year of membership and 100 percent after ten years of service. This plan benefits all types of employees. Similar plans are installed in most other divisions of the corporation.

The unemployed worker's ultimate concern is to find another job. He needs all the help he can get, especially in recessionary times. Like practically all other American companies, with the recent exception of the Goodyear Tire Company, Orion-Diversified provides no formal outplacement counseling (systematic placement and search assistance) for blue collar workers.

Company policy calls for exit interviews of workers who resign, in order to try to obtain information that may help improve working conditions. Mr. Cannon mentioned that he was able to provide placement counseling to some resigning workers during exit interviews. There was no opportunity to give exit interviews to any of the 17 laid-off workers.

To determine what services and benefits are provided to laid-off workers by agencies outside the company, I consulted the local office that distributes unemployment insurance benefits, the county CETA bureau (Comprehensive Education and Training Act) concerned with the hard-to-employ, and the local office of the state employment service that helps unemployed workers find new jobs.

Situated in a small town some five miles from the plant, the local unemployment service office processed the claims of the dismissed Mountainside workers. While a routine form reporting the lay-off to the state was completed, the purpose of such reports is merely informational. The local office takes no special action when groups of individuals are involved in a lay-off. Records are kept only by individuals' social security numbers.

How much do benefit checks amount to in the state? It depends upon how long the applicants were employed, how large a premium their employer paid for them (based on a percentage of their weekly wages), and whether or not they had previously received unemployment benefits. No benefits are paid unless an unemployed worker has accumulated twenty or more weeks of service with previous employers. The average full-week payment to unemployed workers was $79.47 in August of 1980, according to state published statistics. The maximum weekly benefit that can be paid, according to current regulations, is $125.00. Specific information on the unemployment insurance benefits received by the dismissed workers was not locally obtainable. These records are kept by the company at division headquarters. Nevertheless, the average unemployment insurance benefit paid to the dismissed workers was estimated to come closer to the state average.

Normally, benefits are paid weekly, up to a maximum of 26 weeks. Under the federal Extended Benefits program thirteen additional weeks of benefits can be paid when unemployment rises to high levels in the nation or within particular states. Mountainside was located in one of seventeen states paying extended benefits in August of 1980. Unemployment levels for that month were 7.6 percent nationally, 7.7 percent in the state, and 6.8 percent in the county, down from an average county level of 10.9 percent for the first four months of the year.

The county CETA office was aware of the Mountainside lay-off. CETA deals with employers through its Private Industry Council (PIC). PIC's primary activity is to assist members of "targeted groups" (those identified by the federal government as the hard-to-employ) to obtain job training and employment. The Mountainside plant is not a member of PIC. As a matter of fact, only a small minority of the private industry in the county is active with this voluntary group.

Mr. Cannon expressed the policy of his company towards CETA when he commented that the company provides training to new employees "on its own initiative." He described the many hours spent in attempting to recruit minority group members who could pass the probationary period. He had achieved limited success and was disturbed that two black workers were among those laid off.

The local CETA office indicated that it does not get involved with unemployed workers unless they have been unemployed for at least fifteen weeks and come from disadvantaged families. Also, CETA is not staffed to handle lay-offs. Only 10 percent of its training budget is earmarked for private sector activities. CETA's placements in the county are, of necessity, mostly in the public sector.

The local state employment service office provided insights into other difficulties that the dismissed workers from the Rhone plant faced in getting new jobs. This information applied to all local workers since no specific information about the laid-off workers could be obtained from any institutional source.

"We don't get involved in lay-offs" was the gist of the information provided by the employment service. For one thing, advance notice of a lay-off is rarely received. For another, many of the lay-offs in the county are seasonal and therefore routine. They involve vacation resorts and farming activities when the summer months are over, and ski resorts and associated businesses when the winter season is over.

Many industrial employers are afraid to tell their displaced workers that a lay-off is permanent. One of their reasons, according to the local office of the employment service, is that they don't want the community to know that things are bad. As a result, many displaced workers tell the unemployment insurance office that their lay-off is temporary. Ordinarily, in order to qualify for unemployment benefits, laid off workers must go to the employment office and, by seeking assistance in locating another job, demonstrate that they are ready, willing and able to work. The unemployment insurance office does not require workers on temporary lay-off to go to the employment office until it becomes apparent that they may not be returning to their previous job soon, if at all. Mr. Cannon designated the lay-off as "indefinite," lest his workers be deceived by the label "temporary" into assuming they did not need the services of the employment office, and, of course, because of the uncertainty regarding the delivery of chassis.

Local job-seekers were portrayed by the employment office as falling into two categories: (1) those who possess skills, really want to work, and are willing to commute if necessary, to the tri-city area, some 25 miles north, where higher pay is offered; (2) those who are less anxious to work or who are unwilling to commute to the higher wage area and settle for the lower local wage. When the less ambitious are unemployed they are inclined to avoid work for as long as the unemployment insurance benefits hold out; then they will accept local employment at local wages. There is no great difference between take home wages in this area and the amount of the untaxed unemployment insurance benefits, according to a local employment service expert.

Employers in the area often downgrade the classification of the jobs they post with the employment service. They want to pay only slightly more than the prevailing minimum wage of $3.10 per hour. Since Mountainside has the reputation of paying higher than average wages, these other jobs may not attract laid off Mountainside workers whose wage averaged $4.35, especially if they do not perceive their indefinite lay-off as permanent.

In 1980 one had to look beyond the local scene to find comprehensive services to assist the job hunt of workers rendered unemployed by lay-offs. In each of the regional offices of the United States Department of Labor a bureau administers the employee assistance provisions of the Trade Act of 1974. A lay-off qualified under the provisions of the Act can attract extended unemployment benefits, as well as financial assistance for training for another line of work. Financial assistance is also provided for job search in distant locations as well as for the cost of relocating.

To qualify for such assistance the employer must have been hurt by foreign imports, a claim made by Chrysler in its appeal for federal assistance. One cannot make a case for foreign imports being responsible for the lay-off in Rhone. The appeal for comprehensive worker assistance is usually made by a local union. The Mountainside plant is not unionized.

THE LAY-OFF IN RETROSPECT

The interviews required to prepare this case gave the management of Mountainside many opportunities to reflect on the events attendant on the lay-off. When asked whether a cost-benefits analysis of the lay-off had been or might be made, their response was no.* Had they contemplated such an analysis they would have had to plan it in advance of the lay-off. Line supervisors would have had to gather much of the information, part of it before a lay-off that management wanted to keep secret.

The lay-off appeared to have gone smoothly. As a result of the company's encouragement of skill development and internal job mobility, intraplant transfers were made as soon as the lay-off was implemented. There was no discernible worker resistance. The plant did not experience disruptions, such as the interdepartment "bumping," which is more likely to occur in unionized plants than in nonunion plants, when plant-wide seniority is applied to a lay-off.

Mr. Cannon compared the two lay-offs he had implemented. In 1975, the Mountainside workers were told the lay-off was to be "temporary"; in 1980, those dismissed were informed it was for an "indefinite" period. In 1975, but not in 1980, telephone contact was maintained with many of the dismissed workers. Because the work force reduction was designated temporary, the plant management felt committed to keeping track of their past, and hopefully, future employees. They kept abreast of the employees' welfare and were able to inform them of changing business conditions and of when they might expect to return to work. These contacts also gave management some idea of who might not be returning or who had taken another job.

Mr. Cannon recalled that in 1975 a small but unanticipated number of workers had expressed bitterness when they were recalled to work. This bitterness persisted for some time. He could not determine whether it was the result of certain individuals having been included among those laid off—some had had long service, as much as ten years—or whether it was a result of the suffering and demoralization of a lengthy period of unemployment—five months for some and almost a year for others.

Workers laid off in 1980 had had shorter service and were not as well known to management. They were also younger. Still, the plant manager knew that some of these workers had families and would experience hardship during unemployment. The welfare of the newly dismissed workers was monitored informally through casual information around the plant, and through unemployment insurance reports to the company. No direct

---

*The overall cost to manufacture vehicles at Mountainside was allocated to materials (60%), direct labor (15%), and overhead (25%).

contact was attempted because management feared it would give the workers false hope that recall was imminent. The plant manager did not want to get involved in situations where he could do nothing to benefit the worker.

As late as three months after the lay-off there was no sign that the company would be able to invite workers to return. Five of the seventeen dismissed had found new jobs. After months of reflection over the causes, implementation, and consequences of the lay-off Mr. Cannon was beginning to formulate ideas which he felt might be put into effect to mitigate future work force reductions.

QUESTIONS FOR DISCUSSION*

1. Should employees have certain rights concerning the conditions and procedures of layoffs? If so, what are those rights?
2. Was Mr. Cannon correct in thinking that economic considerations justified the layoff? If so, did the same considerations justify his action of waiting until the last moment to notify employees? Why or why not?
3. What do you think Mr. Cannon *should* have done?

Case Study
Harman International:
A Workplace Democracy

Daniel Zwerdling

You'll find Harman International Industries on the edge of the sleepy town of Bolivar, Tennessee, population 7,000. Bolivar still has a monument to the confederacy, only one movie theater, one radio station, two restaurants and no bars. Aside from the old-time southern courthouse, the biggest buildings in town are the agricultural supply stores where farmers pull up in their coveralls and pickups and chat about the crops and the weather.

Harman Industries, which makes most of the auto rearview mirrors in the U.S., is a crucial force in Bolivar and surrounding Hardeman County, for it is the second largest employer in the region next to the state mental hospital. But Harman has another distinction which gives it a more important niche in United States labor history: Harman is home for what was the first and perhaps most important management-union experiment in worker participation in the nation. The experiment—launched in 1972 by the United Auto Workers, the Harman management, and consultants from the Harvard Project on Technology, Work and Character—has involved virtually every worker in the factory.

The working core of the Work Improvement Program is a network of more than 30 shopfloor committees, in which employees initiate changes from painting the walls to redesigning an assembly line. Some changes have been unusual: workers who achieve their production quota in less than the normal eight hours can leave their job and go home if they like. But the most significant feature of the project isn't so much the specific changes that have taken place inside the factory—it's the fact that unlike other workplace participation projects, none of the changes have been imposed by top union officials or management. The shopfloor employees have initiated virtually all the changes on their own. . . .

The organizers of the Work Improvement Program have deliberately attempted to make the Harman-UAW experiment a living model for corporations and unions across the nation. "The goal of the Bolivar project," writes former project director Michael Maccoby, "is to create an American model of industrial democracy: a model that is acceptable to unions and that might stimulate further union efforts. The project is based on the view that a national movement to improve the quality of work is unlikely to succeed without union support."

INAUSPICIOUS ORIGINS

The Work Improvement Program did not come to Harman Industries in Bolivar because it was a comfortable, model plant. Far from it: The approximately 1,000 workers were housed in three huge Quonset huts left over from World War II. When the project was getting underway, one of the consultants, Robert Duckles, wrote this candid account:

> The production floor is dirty and disorderly, compared to many large factories belonging to richer companies. Like most engaged in this kind of work, it is noisy. A shortage of storage space and the pace of production which overworks the luggers and towmotor operators result in parts and materials being pushed into every available corner and sometimes strewing out into the aisles. No time is allowed for anyone to keep his work area clean and orderly. Many machines are kept in poor repair due to lack of replacement parts and a lot of ad hoc repairs with wire and roughly cut pieces of metal.
> "The atmosphere is stuffy and irritating to some because of fumes from die cast, plating and paint, and the towmotors, even though efforts have been made to blow away the most noxious fumes. There are holes in the roof and pools of water on the floor. In winter there is inadequate heating; in the summer no air conditioning. Comfort and sometimes safety have been ignored in the all-out effort to maximize production and profits. Only recently has management started to improve the physical conditions of the plant . . .
> The offices of the managers, engineers and clerical workers are in the front of the building, sealed off from the production area. They are cleaner, quieter and air-conditioned.

The Harman factory had been built in the Bolivar region because there were few unions and labor was cheap. The United Auto Workers didn't organize the plant until 1969. Historically, management and union officials agreed, labor relations had been strained.

"At the start of the project . . . the spirit was one of hostility, resistance and open conflict between management and workers," Maccoby writes. "The economics of the auto parts industry, fierce competition, price squeezing by the four customers, and fluctuating demand for cars, intensified insecurity and the dehumanizing conditions of work which fed this spirit." Workers, Maccoby says, were treated as a "standardized replaceable part of the process," which bred "anger, hostility, depression and stifled creativity. . . ."

As Michael Maccoby remembers, the Work Improvement Project began when UAW vice president Irving Bluestone, a longtime advocate of industrial democracy, met then company president and owner Sidney Harman at a conference on workplace democracy. Like most union officials, Bluestone had strongly opposed workplace participation projects controlled unilaterally by management; unlike many union officials, he was eager to experiment with shopfloor democracy projects controlled jointly by management and the union. Harman had earned a reputation as a progressive businessman who insisted management "must have the courage to run risks." Before taking over Harman Industries, he had been president of the experimental Friends World College on Long Island. Harman had a "sense of mission," as Maccoby told the press. Harman and Bluestone agreed to launch the first management-union workplace participation project in the nation.

The project began during the summer of 1973. The management, union and their consultants—a third party team led by Maccoby, who insisted the consultants would remain neutral—decided to take the experiment one step at a time, making sure they had a strong base before moving on to the next development. The first step was to gather accurate information about employee attitudes, so that researchers conducting future studies would have base data to which they could compare. The study, conducted with the help of the W.E. Upjohn Institute for Employment Research, was based on in-depth, four-hour interviews with 60 workers, plus shorter interviews with about 300 more employees and 50 managers.

WHAT WORKERS SAID

The results confirmed in detail what most people already knew: the employees were intensely dissatisfied with their work. As the researchers reported, "most workers don't trust the company": 55 percent disagreed that "when management says something, you can really believe it is true." Most workers felt management ignored them: 77 percent agreed, "it is hard to get people higher up in the organization to listen to people at my level." And the majority of the workers, 77 percent, asserted that, "This company cares more about money and machines than people."

It was a factory where workers did their jobs silently—"don't speak unless spoken to"—and where almost half the employees had ideas for improving work which they never told anyone. The majority complained that their share of the company's earnings was not fair, and many blacks and women, who accounted for 40 percent and 30 percent of the workplace, respectively, charged there was widespread discrimination.

Workers at Harman were so hostile toward management, in fact, that many went out of their way to be destructive: 57 percent said they or fellow workers had occasionally performed work "badly, slowly or incorrectly on purpose" to strike back at management. Employees seemed so turned off to the company, in fact, that when the consultants held some seminars to discuss the results of their study with any workers who wanted to attend, only three or four out of 1,000 workers showed up.

The next step in the experiment was to set up a management-union structure which would screen and approve all project developments. First, the project organizers created a top-level management-union "advisory" committee, including the corporation executives, members of the UAW International, and nationally known experts in the quality of work field. In the fall of 1973, the Working Committee was born, comprised of five representatives from the union and five from local management. One of the key strategies of the project structure, Maccoby stressed, was never to bypass the conventional management-union structures but to strengthen them, to "respect the existing authorities and try to improve them." If any part of the experiment, no matter how small, was initiated without the management and union playing an equal role, Maccoby emphasized, it would be sure to generate "opposition"—and the project would collapse.

Next the management and union agreed to pursue a common set of principles. "The purpose of the joint management-labor Work Improvement Program is to make work better and more satisfying for all employees, salaried and hourly, while maintaining the necessary productivity for job security," the agreement began. But while many worker participation projects in the U.S. have aimed at boosting productivity, the Harman project declared pointedly, "The purpose is *not* to increase productivity." Project participants worried that if they increased plant production, especially given the stagnant economic climate, the management might lay off workers, ensuring the project's collapse.

STEPS TOWARD CHANGE

The project's goals were "ambitious" as Maccoby has described them. While many previous worker participation programs have been motivated by management desires to reduce absenteeism, turnover, sabotage, and other symptoms of workers malaise, the Harman-UAW Work Improvement Program set out "to reorganize the way the company itself operates." The union and management officials pledged to pursue four specific goals:

1. *Security*—creating conditions which free workers from the fear of losing their jobs, and which maximize their financial income;

2. *Equity*—guaranteeing fairness in hiring, promotions and pay; an end to discrimination against women and minorities, and profit sharing if productivity increases;

3. *Individuation*—understanding that each worker is different. Individuation, as the participants define it, means that changes in the workplace should be structured to allow each worker to satisfy her or his individual development. The employee must not be forced to participate in a prescribed way that executives and social scientists have deemed is "satisfying" for them. Changes in the workplace should accommodate everyone as much as possible, and permit workers to get the job done at their own pace;

4. *Democracy*—making free speech, due process, and workers' participation in decisions which directly affect them a way of life in the corporation.

Once the management and union participants had agreed on the four principles, they began to solve actual problems in the workplace. At first they concentrated on issues which the workers themselves had identified, in the survey interviews, as the most pressing—environmental problems such as the temperature extremes in the plant, the irritating air pollution, and traffic jams in the parking lots. . . .

FIRST EFFORTS

Despite the early tensions and anxieties, participants recall, the first meetings were productive. Workers soon began to propose, and then carry out, some small but effective changes. For instance, they decided to equip the production line with a backup screwdriver so the line wouldn't have to stop, as it normally did, every time the bit in the main screwdriver broke. They decided to teach the woman who operated the screwdriver to change bits herself so she wouldn't have to wait for another worker, who specialized in changing the bits, to be called from another part of the plant. . . .

After two months, the experimental group in the assembly department devised an even more ambitious plan: if the workers could achieve the production quota before quitting time on any given day, they would continue working anyway—and accumulate the extra hours as "bonus" hours, which they could take off some day in the future. Before, workers would sit idly around their machines and knit and chat whenever they reached production in less than eight hours; they were bored and it didn't do the company any good. Now, workers who finished their quota early could go home a couple hours before quitting time or save up their bonus hours over a few weeks and then take a couple days off.

As the assembly department project was getting underway, other experimental groups were struggling to start in other parts of the plant. A group of six workers in the polish and buff department collapsed when an employee grievance generated management-worker tensions—"worker members of the group informed us they did not have enough trust in management to continue with the experiment," Duckles and Lyle wrote.

Undaunted, the Working Committee circulated a memo to workers describing the purpose of the experiment in detail, assuaging some of the employees' fears, and seven workers volunteered to join the experiment. After a few meetings, they decided to experiment with some workplace changes: the members of the group would decide work assignments as a team, rather than merely obey the directives of a foreman; workers who finished their jobs early would help out teammates who took more time; and the worker team would keep its own records of parts produced, efficiency, and the number of bonus hours the team members were accumulating.

A third experimental group was born spontaneously when women on the pre-assembly line, where the mirror shell is bracketed and screwed to its base, asked their foreman if they could join the project. The foreman passed their request to the Working Committee, which agreed, and the women began to organize their own meetings. They hammered out eight goals, including: helping each other achieve production quotas; gaining free time to learn new skills, and go home early; making their workplace more attractive; improving the quality of their work; reducing "downtime," and installing better tools and fixtures at their work stations.

Within a few months the women had increased their production speed so much that they began accumulating substantial chunks of bonus time. One week they threw a party during work hours while another week they used their bonus hours to tour the factory—something few employees had ever done before. A week later, the women chose to use their bonus hours to go home a few hours before quitting time. The project began to nurture cooperation among the workers, cooperation they said had never existed before. When one of the women on the line offered to quit because she couldn't work as fast as the others, and "held them back," for instance, the team "told her not to worry about it as they were all in this to help each other," according to Duckles and Lyle. The workers began tagging their work so they could be held accountable, and recognized, for its quality. Within two weeks, Duckles and Lyle report, the value of wasted, carelessly stripped screws plunged from almost $40 a day to zero. . . .

Consultants Robert and Margaret Duckles have stressed that "the functioning of the core groups has not always been as smooth" as it might seem. . . . In some cases, according to Duckles, core group members have worked smoothly together and with their fellow workers, while the meetings in other core groups have "been difficult and at times tempestuous."

But one important sign that the project is altering the way employees perceive their work, consultants say, is that the roles of the core groups and behaviors of the employees are continually changing. Early in the project, for instance, core group meetings "had to be initiated by the staff almost entirely," the Duckles report. "Now meetings are initiated by the core groups themselves" most often.

These changing roles and behaviors, consultants say, are the most important achievements of the experiment. Since the Work Improvement Program was first launched, the consultants and the Working Committee have agreed that the specific changes carried out in the factory are not as important as the *way* those changes were initiated and carried out. For the most part, the changes have been initiated and carried out by the workers.

"The *way* in which we do things is as important as what we do," Duckles and Lyle wrote. "This program of work improvement is not one which is designed by concerned managers, with the help of social scientists, and imposed on the plant, but a program that is owned by everything that it affects from the beginning . . . This process is quite different from job enrichment, in which experts may enlarge a job for workers. The workers at Harman may decide to make changes similar to job enrichment . . . but *they* have made the changes and reserve the right to modify them. The goal is to institute a *process* of democratic decision-making and evaluation rather than any specific changes in tasks."

LIVE-IN CONSULTANTS

One of the most important—and unusual—features of the Harman program has been the work of the third party consultants. From the beginning of the program, the consultants have seen their roles not as experts who impose or even propose projects for the workers to follow, but as instructors who teach the Harman workers to analyze their jobs and job environments and make changes on their own. The consultants have tried to maintain complete neutrality since the project began, and most workers and managers say they have succeeded and earned their complete trust.

Unlike consultants at any other work participation project in the nation, the Harman consultants live in the community and work fulltime in the Harman plant. They have become a crucial resource for both shopfloor workers and managers in the factory, asking some of the tough questions which workers or managers are afraid to ask, proposing possible solutions (without advocating one more than the other) which workers and managers don't think to suggest, prodding workers and managers alike to speak freely and honestly at core group and working committee meetings. Unlike the consultants at most projects, who visit the factory once or twice a week, or less, the Harman consultants have become intimately familiar with the plant, the business and the personalities—which encourages workers and managers alike to trust their judgments and advice.

Most of the work participation projects in the United States have been limited to changes in the way work is performed on the factory floor. But the Bolivar Work Improvement Program has attempted to go beyond these projects by attempting to bridge the gap which separates most workers' lives inside the factory from their lives outside the gates. Perhaps the most unusual innovation is the in-plant school. Workers, their families, and even residents in the community can attend a rich variety of classes, which are held before the shift, after the shift, sometimes even during the shift, at lunch. "Improvement in the workplace and education go hand in hand," as one worker told the Third International Conference on Self-Management.

The school began early in 1975 when the experimental core groups began discussing different ways they could use earned idle time. Many employees said they would like to use their bonus hours not just for going home early—although that is an important benefit for workers with families and workers with part-time farms—and not just for socializing. Instead, many said they wanted the chance to learn new work skills or drafts which had always intrigued them. Others had never finished high school and wanted to get a degree. So a management-union committee was formed to draft an educational program for the working committee.

Today, more than 40 classes have been formed, with well over two hundred students. Teachers are paid by the union-management project fund, although some teachers are funded by the county under its vocational education budget. It's a little like the "free schools" which have sprouted in a college towns across the country, except the Harman school is housed in a mirror factory. . . .

NOW THE FLAWS

The achievements of the Work Improvement Project do not mean that the project is without its critics and faults. Some workers have charged that the changes in the "quality of work life" in the factory have actually been meager. "We cannot get a fan. We cannot get anything but a patchup job done on our dust system," a 12-year veteran of the plant told a local newspaper. "The program is in reality nothing but a scheme to get more work out of the employees, but it's done nothing to improve the quality of life for most of us in the plant." Some employees charge that they have little or no power, despite the core groups; "everything that works out seems to be the company's idea," one told the local press.

Part of the discontent seems to result from the gap between inflated worker expectations and the reality of what the project has delivered. Some workers expected the core groups and working committee to give the employees decision-making powers. But as project consultant Michael Maccoby has stressed, the project was nothing of the kind.

> The principle of democracy was interpreted as establishing the right of each individual to have a say in decisions directly affecting him. In fact, the factory was and is in many ways not democratic. Managerial authority is handed from the top down and workers have no say over who will be their supervisors, much less who runs the company. Decisions about investments and pricing are not usually discussed (although the company did consult with the union about pricing in order to save jobs). What the program has done is to create new areas of democracy and participation in analysis and decision-making which can grow as participants develop greater understanding about the business.

Other problems stem from the resistance among some managerial-level employees to the Work Improvement Program. When middle-line managers, such as foremen and supervisors, have endorsed the program, the core groups have often worked well. But when middle-level managers have resented the program, employees have confronted major obstacles to carry out changes in their workplace. Some managers at Harman say the foremen are the most neglected employees in the plant.

"The foremen at our company don't know what the hell to do. They feel like no one's supporting them," a middle-level manager says. "We haven't had any training for them, and they don't really know what the program's supposed to be about or how far they can go with it. The workers want one thing from them but they aren't sure whether they have the authority to give it. And some of them are scared, they feel like they're being squeezed out of a job if the shopfloor employees and core groups get too much influence. How do we make the program a growth experience for them too?"

Still another problem which weakens the Work Improvement Program, according to some employees, is that many workers don't participate actively enough. "We sometimes get irritated and frustrated at griping without initiative," write the Duckles, who say that many employees complain about the way things are at Harman, without actively trying to create some alternatives. But they add, "When we get impatient in this way we are usually forgetting that the American industrial tradition is one in which energetic managers determine what needs to be done . . . The tradition is *not* to listen to employees and join with them in the search for alternatives . . . The Bolivar employee, like most others, is thoroughly socialized to expect this as 'the way things are done.'"

In late 1977, Sidney Harman sold the company to the Beatrice Corporation, a $5 billion multinational conglomerate. Beatrice has maintained that it supports the Work Improvement Program and will encourage the project to continue. And while there have been no major new initiatives, the WIP does seem to be going strong. Core groups are meeting, and workers are initiating occasional changes on the shopfloor; the Harvard consultants have been replaced by an in-house staff; old courses at the factory school are coming to an end and new courses are taking their place.

Employees, observers say, have learned much about analyzing problems and proposing solutions on their own initiative, and making decisions in groups—and they have learned that changes are possible. These skills, more than any single change, are perhaps the main accomplishments of the Harman management-union experiment.

QUESTIONS FOR DISCUSSION

1. Is worker participation or industrial democracy an obligation or a workplace option?

2. Beyond decent pay and safe working conditions, is there such a thing as an employee's "right to meaningful work?"

3. What should worker participation include and what can it exclude?

4. What are the responsibilities of the employees to the employer in a program of worker participation?

5. Why would some critics of worker participation see it as "nothing but a scheme to get more work out of the employees"?

Case Study
Management Dilemma

Fred E. Schuster

Stan Fritzhill, Manager of the Data Analysis Department of Aerostar, Inc., a small research firm, pondered how he should utilize a salary increase budget of $18,700 (10% of total payroll) to reward the five semi-professional employees in his unit. He knew that he did not have to spend the full budget, but under no circumstances could he exceed it. In his opinion, all of these individuals were properly paid in relation to their relative performance and seniority one year (12 months) ago, when he last adjusted their compensation. The rate of inflation last year was 7%.

Fritzhill had assembled a summary of his performance appraisals (see Appendix 1 on page 156) and other pertinent data to assist in determining his recommendations, which he knew were needed immediately.

QUESTIONS FOR DISCUSSION*

1. Is the information provided in the column titled "personal circumstances" relevant to Mr. Fritzhill's decision? Why or why not?

2. Is the information provided in the column titled "years in department" relevant to Mr. Fritzhill's decision? Why or why not?

3. If it appears that an employee has been unfairly denied raises in the past, should special "make-up" raises be given? Are there any employees in this case who appear to have been unfairly treated?

4. How should Fritzhill distribute the money? What role, if any, should inflation play in his deliberations?

This case was prepared by Professor Fred E. Schuster of Florida Atlantic University as a basis for class discussion rather than to illustrate either effective or ineffective handling of an administrative situation. All names have been disguised. Salary amounts in the case have been adjusted upward to reflect more recent salary scales. Copyright © 1978 by Fred E. Schuster. Reprinted with permission.

NAME	PRESENT SALARY	TITLE	SALARY GRADE	YEARS IN DEPT.	PERFORMANCE	PERSONAL CIRCUMSTANCES
John Mason	$42,000	Analyst	6	5	Acceptable quality; several important deadlines have been missed but may not be his fault.	Married. Large family dependent on him as sole support.
G. W. Jones	$36,000	Analyst	6	2	Outstanding. Sometimes a bit "pushy" in making requests and suggestions about the department.	Single. No dependents. Has no pressing need for money. Reported to lead a rather "wild" life outside the office.
Jane Boston	$34,000	Junior Analyst	5	8	Consistently an excellent performer, though not assigned to the full range of duties of an analyst. Dependable. Often initiates improvements in work methods.	Married. Husband is a successful architect. Children in high school.
Ralph Schmidt	$43,000	Senior Analyst	7	15	Acceptable, but not outstanding. Few original contributions recently. Seems to be a "plodder." Content to get by with minimum performance and participation.	Married. Financially pressed because he has 2 children in college (one plans to go on to Med. School).
Hillary Johnson	$32,000	Junior Analyst	5	6	Acceptable volume of performance, but continues to make costly mistakes. Has repeatedly been warned about this over the last years.	Single. Has a dependent mother who is chronically ill.

Case Study
Vital Information at Complex

Thomas Donaldson

Martha Van Hussen, Regional Director of Sales at Complex Corporation, was feeling vaguely uneasy as she sipped her morning coffee and glanced again at the latest memo from corporate headquarters. The memo stressed once more the need to block absolutely any information leaks to competitors both about changes in Complex's rapidly evolving line of computer software products and about its latest marketing strategies. Complex found itself in the middle of one of the hottest and most competitive markets in the world. The software it handled was sold primarily to banks, savings and loans, and brokerage firms, and although in the beginning Complex had been virtually alone in the market, in recent years a number of increasingly aggressive competitors had slowly whittled away at Complex's market share. The difference between a sale and a lost sale was frequently only the difference between being able to boast or not of a minor software innovation. Martha reminded herself as she looked at the memo that great hopes were being attached to the company's new "Data-File" line of products to be publicly announced in three months. Already salespeople in the division had been briefed on the new line in behind-closed-doors sessions to prepare them for selling the new products effectively.

What worried her was not so much that one of her salespeople would *intentionally* provide information to competitors, as that someone might allow an *unintentional* leak. It was true, she confessed to herself, two members of her twenty member sales force had been disgruntled over recent salary decisions and had threatened to quit. But she doubted they would actually commit an act of outright sabotage. More problematic was the fact that one of her salespersons, Frank Wright, was married to an employee of one of Complex's major competitors. Because Frank's wife, Hillary, was a software designer, Martha knew that she could interpret any relevant information, even off-hand information offered in casual remarks, decisively.

Of course, Martha had no reason to question the conduct either of Frank or Hillary. Both seemed to be good, down-to-earth types, and she had especially enjoyed chatting with them at a recent dinner party. Frank, furthermore, had done well during his first three years with the company. To further complicate the overall problem, two other members of her staff had relatives working for competing firms. In one case the relative was an uncle, and in the other it was a cousin. She also knew that her sales staff met infrequently with other salespersons from rival firms at conferences and exhibits.

Martha reminded herself that she had already called her people together to emphasize the need to protect vital corporate information. She had also sent each employee a copy of a recent memo from corporate headquarters, and had reminded them of the item in the company's Code of Conduct that stipulated that disclosure of vital information was a cause for dismissal.

The question nagging her now was: Is there something more I should do? Should I take specific actions in specific cases? If so, what? Was it fair to penalize a person simply because he or she had the misfortune to be related to a competitor's employee? As she pondered these issues, one fact stared her in the face with perfect clarity: any leaks, either now or in the future, could seriously jeopardize the company's well-being; and moreover, if any leaks were tracked to her division, *she* would be held responsible.

Two days later, Martha received a phone call from the Vice President in charge of her Division, Mr. John Sears. Mr. Sears informed her that evidence had emerged indicating that crucial product information had been leaked by a member of her department. Two things were known for certain: (1) that Complex information had been obtained by a major competitor, and (2) that some of the information leaked had been circulated only to Van Hussen's staff. Mr. Sears was reluctant to divulge more, but he did remark that he was doubtful that more information would be forthcoming to use in tracing the leak to a specific member of Van Hussen's department. He concluded the phone call by saying, "I want you to do whatever is necessary to stop this problem."

QUESTIONS FOR DISCUSSION

1. Should employees have the right not to be discriminated against on the basis of outside personal activities (for instance, by being denied the same access to information as their fellow workers)?
2. How should Martha Van Hussen respond to the problem of information leaks?

Case Study
Sexual Discrimination
at Eastern Airlines?

A. R. Gini

On December 28, 1983, a federal judge ordered Eastern Airlines to reinstate a pilot who had been fired following a sex-change operation in 1980.
The pilot, who flew for the airline for 12 years as Kenneth Ulane, is now
known as Karen Ulane. Before joining Eastern in 1968, Ulane had previously been an Army pilot and was decorated for valor in connection with
missions flown in Vietnam.[1]

In 1979, following years of psychiatric consultation, Ulane took a
leave of absence and underwent a sex-change operation in April 1980.
When she returned to work, the airline would not reinstate her as a pilot.
After refusing to accept other administrative positions, Eastern fired her
on April 24, 1981. Ulane charged that her dismissal was a direct result of
her sex-change operation and filed a sex-discrimination suit. "In terms of
sexual discrimination," said one of her lawyers, "Karen Ulane was kind of a
perfect control group. As a male pilot, Eastern's own witnesses acknowledge that she was one of their better pilots. When she changed her sex, she
was all of a sudden not acceptable. Eastern was willing to retain one sex in
their employ, but not willing to retain the other."[2] At the time, only two of
Eastern's 4,200 pilots were women.

In an emotionally charged two-hour oral opinion, Judge John Grady
found in favor of Ulane and berated Eastern for their "ostrich-like and
contemptuous attitude toward transsexuals."[3] Grady based his decision on
Title VII of the Civil Rights Act of 1964. This statute provides that

> It shall be an unlawful employment practice for an employer to fail or refuse
> to hire or to discharge any individual or otherwise to discriminate against any
> individual with respect to his compensation, terms, conditions or privileges of
> employment because of such individual's race, color, religion, sex, or national
> origin.

The specific question before the court, Judge Grady suggested, is whether
the phrase "because of the individual's sex" encompasses a person such as
the plaintiff who alleges that she is a transsexual or, alternatively, that
having gone through sex-reassignment surgery, she is now no longer a
man but a woman. In other words, is a person's sexual identity a protected
category under the Civil Rights Act?[4]

Judge Grady pointed out that this section of the Civil Rights Act had originally prohibited discrimination on the basis of race but not sex. An amendment introducing sex into the statute was offered by a southern senator who hoped that by this gambit he would prevent the bill's passage. His ploy obviously did not work, but neither was there much discussion at that time concerning the scope of the term *sex*. Grady therefore set himself the task of defining *sex* in the context of Title VII. He first distinguished between our understanding of the terms *homosexual* and *transvestite* on the one hand, and *transsexual* on the other. The latter group, he argued, has problems relative to their sexual identities as men or women, while the former do not. He indicated that, while the statute in question cannot reasonably be extended to matters of sexual preference it is an altogether different matter as to whether the matter of sexual identity is included in our general understanding of the term *sex*.[5]

In his ruling, Grady interpreted the word *sex* to reasonably include the question of sexual identity. He said that, prior to his participation in this case, he would have had no doubt that the question of gender was straightforward. But after hearing the testimony, he realized that there is no settled definition in the medical community as to what we mean by *sex*. He argued that sex is defined by something more than the biological. It is also defined by society, because the way an individual is perceived by society plays a crucial role in a persons sense of sexual identity.[6]

Having concluded that the term *sex* in Title VII reasonably includes the question of sexual identity, Grady then considered whether Ulane was indeed a transsexual. The defendants argued that Ulane is really a transvestite and hence is not protected by the statute. Grady contended that both the Gender Identity Board of the University of Chicago Medical School and her own doctor had found Ulane to be a transsexual. The defense countered that the plaintiff had only managed to persuade these medical practitioners—through some retrospective distortion—that she is transsexual. Grady dismissed this claim, saying that Ulane knew as much as most psychiatrists about her condition and the possible risks of her operation, and that she could hardly have any ulterior motive in undergoing such a radical procedure. He contended that the fact of Ulane's operation argues for her being a true transsexual, since she must have been aware that transvestites have very poor prognosis after sex-reassignment surgery.[7]

Grady then considered the question of whether Ulane had been discharged because of her sex. The evidence presented at the trial indicated that Eastern began to develop their brief leading to Ulane's discharge just after her surgery. Prior to that time, Eastern had no complaints about her performance as a pilot.[8] Eastern's legal department drafted two separate discharge letters which contained seven essential arguments, each of which they felt represented independent "nondiscriminatory" reasons for dismissal.[9]

(1.) Eastern alleged that because of Ulane's "underlying psychological problem" her presence in the cockpit represented an unjustifiable safety hazard to passengers and crew. Grady argued that Eastern was prejudiced from the start and had invented all sorts of dangers that inhered in the so-called "underlying psychological problem." Furthermore, Eastern never gave Ulane a fair hearing on this issue or the opportunity to show that they were wrong or at least had no reason for concern in her particular situation.[10]

(2.) Eastern charged that Ulane's medical certification was not unconditional after her surgery. Here, Grady compared her case to that of alcoholic pilots, whose certificates are also conditional. The FAA had, in fact, indicated that Ulane was fit to fly, and had ordered her to undergo periodic counseling only in order to help her deal with any problems created by unfriendly co-workers.[11]

(3.) Eastern complained that sex-reassignment surgery does not solve the underlying psychological problem. Grady indicated that there was no evidence of change in the plaintiff's psychological adjustment profile. Ulane, therefore, would be no more dangerous in the cockpit than before her surgery. Moreover, the judge cited evidence that such surgery actually decreases the patient's anxieties and makes them more stable in regard to their own sense of self-esteem. Grady concluded that the fact of transsexuality does not in itself constitute a safety problem, any more than does, say, left-handedness.[12]

(4.) Eastern claimed that Ulane's presence in the cockpit would counteract its efforts to assure the public that airline travel is safe. Grady drew a parallel here between Eastern and those who at one time believed that black salesclerks or waiters would drive customers away. The American public, said Grady, is a lot smarter than Eastern gives it credit for, and rejected their contention as prejudicial.[13]

(5.) Eastern alleged that, by virtue of her operation, Ulane was no longer the same person they had hired, and that, knowing what they do now, they would not have hired her in the first place. According to Grady, Eastern reacted to the situation as a public-relations problem: "A transsexual in the cockpit? The public wouldn't accept it! We will be the laughing stock of the airline industry! We have got to do something about it!" Grady ruled that this line of argumentation was a virtual admission of discrimination based on sex.[14]

(6.) Eastern alleged that Ulane had failed to disclose to the company the medication and medical and psychiatric treatments she had received over the years for her condition. Grady pointed out that the drugs Ulane had taken were approved by the FAA as not being dangerous. Therefore, he concluded that her flying ability was not impaired by the medication she was taking. He again drew a parallel between Ulane and male pilots who were alcoholics. Alcoholic pilots rarely, if ever, disclose their problems to the company, but they are not fired for that, even though the dangers of alcohol are well known. Female hormones, on the other hand, have no known effects on flying ability. Grady contended that Eastern had not followed its normal procedure in this case as a result of its initial prejudice against Ulane. If one employee is fired for failure to disclose, all should be treated alike.[15]

(7.) Eastern alleged that Ulane had instigated publicity damaging to Eastern Airlines. Grady countered that the company must have known that this case would inevitably draw publicity even as it drew up its letters of discharge. Besides, Eastern had raised no similar fuss when some of its female employees were featured nude in *Playboy* magazine.[16]

Grady dismissed all of Eastern's justifications for firing Ulane as mere pretexts. He concluded that, but for her being a transsexual, Ulane would not have been discharged.

> I am satisfied from this evidence that while some transsexuals, just as some tall people and some left-handers, some fat people, and some Irishmen would not be safe airline pilots, it is true that some transsexuals would not be safe airline pilots. But it cannot be said with any rationality that all transsexuals are unsafe airline pilots. Neither can it be said with any rationality that it is impossible to make this determination of whether or not a safety hazard is really involved on an individualized basis.[17]

Grady ordered Ulane reinstated with back pay and seniority. The amount of the award was not set during the hearing, but was estimated at about $142,000. Ulane had been receiving an annual salary of $50,000 at the time of her dismissal in 1981.[18]

Eastern said it would appeal what it calls Judge Grady's "novel view of the law" and stated that "Eastern remains confident that its position in this case is correct under the law."[19] Grady indicated that if the U.S. Court of Appeals rules that transsexuals are not protected under Title VII, he will reconsider the question of whether Ulane could claim discrimination because she is a woman. Ulane had originally contended that she was fired because she is a transsexual and a woman. Grady said he was unsure if he could rule that Ulane is a woman. "I don't think I can find the plaintiff is both a transsexual and a woman," he said. "She's either one or the other. . . ."[20]

In the end, Judge Grady saw Eastern's dismissal of Ulane as an attempt by the company to maintain its image at the expense of a good employee's career. But, according to labor-relations attorney Gerald Skoning, the basic premise behind Grady's decision—that sexual identity is defined by something more than the number of X and Y chromosomes present at birth—could have far more extensive implications.[21] Until now the courts have generally refused to grant employment protection for homosexuals under Title VII, saying that although it prohibits discrimination based on sex, it was not intended to prohibit discrimination based on "sexual preference." Many legal scholars believe, however, that if Grady's ruling is upheld on appeal, the decision may be used to try to win protection for homosexuals. Although other scholars are not sure Grady's decision can be extended that far, the ruling, if upheld, not only protects reassigned transsexuals, but all men who feel like a woman but have not undergone surgery.[22]

UPDATE

"Transsexual Pilot Loses Job Appeal"
Adrienne Drell
Chicago Sun Times
August 3, 1984

A federal appeals court ruled yesterday that Karen Ulane, a former Eastern Airlines pilot fired after undergoing a sex-change operation, is not entitled to regain her job.

The 7th Circuit Court of Appeals reversed a Dec. 28 decision by U.S. District Judge John F. Grady that Eastern had violated federal sex discrimination laws.

The 12-page opinion by a three-judge panel, written by Harlington Woods Jr., said *the law does not cover transsexuals or anyone with a "sexual identity disorder. . . ."*

The appellate court said federal law "implies that it is unlawful to discriminate against women because they are women and against men because they are men. . . . A prohibition against discrimination based on an individual's sex is not synonymous with a prohibition against discrimination based on an individual's sexual identity disorder or discontent with the sex into which they were born."

Ulane is entitled to any "personal belief about her sexual identity she desires," the opinion notes. "But even if one believes that a woman can be so easily created from what remains of a man, that does not decide this case."

NOTES

1. *New York Times,* December 29, 1983, p. 18.

2. *Ibid.*

3. *Chicago Tribune,* January 1, 1984.

4. *Karen Frances Ulane* v. *Eastern Airlines, Inc., et al.,* No. 81 C 4411, U.S. District Court, Northeastern Illinois.

5. *Ibid.,* p. 5.

6. *Ibid.,* p. 6.

7. *Ibid.,* pp. 15, 16, 17.

8. *Ibid.,* p. 19.

9. *Ibid.,* p. 33.

10. *Ibid.,* p. 22.

11. *Ibid.,* p. 27.

12. *Ibid.,* p. 30.

13. *Ibid.,* p. 32.

14. *Ibid.,* p. 14.

15. *Ibid.,* p. 15.

16. *Ibid.,* p. 16.

17. *Chicago Tribune,* January 11, 1984, sec. 2, p. 8.

18. *Ulane* v. *Eastern Airlines*, p. 47.
19. *New York Times*, December 29, 1983, p. 18.
20. *Chicago Tribune*, January 11, 1984, sect. 2, p. 8.
21. *Chicago Tribune*, January 8, 1984, p. 1.
22. *Ibid.*, p. 10.

QUESTIONS FOR DISCUSSION

1. Do you believe that a person should be penalized or discriminated against because of his or her sexual preference or sense of sexual identity?
2. Was Eastern, in effect, saying that they were unwilling to hire and retain women as pilots or simply that they were unwilling to hire and retain transsexuals as pilots?
3. Given Ulane's prior outstanding performance as a pilot, if she had not undergone the reassignment surgery but rather had suffered a psychological breakdown or succumbed to a severe bout of alcoholism, do you think that Eastern would have been so eager to demote or fire her?
4. Was Eastern's decision based on fact or fear of public perception and reaction?
5. Does an employer's right to fire (employment at will) include the right to dismiss an employee because of his or her private or personal life-style decisions?

Case Study
Walter Stanton: Employee Responsibility and the Use of Time

Clinton L. Oaks

Walter Stanton, in discussing the responsibility of an employee to his or her employer with a group of MBA students at a southwestern business school, was surprised at the number of questions he received and the diversity of opinion he found among his students regarding the use of time on and off the job. In order to give some focus to the discussion, he asked each student to write up a short incident describing a specific situation in his own experience in which this question had arisen. The following are a few of the incidents reported by the students.

JERRY DONALDSON

"Last summer I was employed in a service station in my home town in Idaho. Besides selling petroleum products, this station had a Big O Tire and Honda motorcycle franchise. My responsibilities included pumping gas, fixing tires, greasing cars, making minor motorcycle repairs, and assembling new motorcycles which came in crates from Japan. I also assisted the mechanic and the manager whenever they needed me.

"Early in the summer, the manager decided that it would be profitable to stay open 24 hours a day. Many tourists traveled through our town during the summer months and they had no place to purchase gas after 10:00 p.m. The manager also thought that the night man could clean up the station, do the necessary motorcycle repairs and assemble at least two motorcycles each night shift.

"Although I was reluctant to work the 10:00 p.m. to 7:00 a.m. shift, I finally agreed to rotate every other week with another of the employees.

"During my first week of working night shifts, I went over the detailed list of duties for the night man to perform and planned out how much time I had to accomplish each assigned job. I tried to use all of the time allotted to each job even if it meant doing the job very slowly. This method allowed me to be busy the whole night and made the time go faster. I also found that if I wasn't busy all the time, I became very bored and drowsy. Therefore I always tried to stay busy.

"About the third week of working night shifts, however, I started to see how fast I could finish all of the assigned tasks. I worked out a whole series of short-cuts for cleaning the station and found that I could do it in an hour less than it had taken me previously. I also found that I could up my efficiency in working motorcycle repairs and in assembling new Hondas. I made a game out of pushing myself and found that I could do all of the jobs and still have at least two hours left after they were all completed. At first I did not know what to do during the two hours, and they went by very slowly. I have always enjoyed tinkering with my car, however, so I decided that during this spare time I would wash and wax it, work on the tune-up, and make all of the little repairs that it needed. I always felt a little guilty working on my car while I was getting paid, but since I was doing a good job of finishing all the assigned tasks, I felt I was justified in using any spare time on my own projects.

"My boss evidently was pleased with my work because he frequently commended me on doing my job well. Several times I heard him 'chewing out' the other employee for not doing a good job. I never told him that I worked on my car, but since I had him get some parts for me I was pretty sure he knew what I was doing. He never said anything to me about it.

"Towards the end of the summer, my boss announced that the corporation that owned this station had decided that it would be beneficial to the company if every employee in the company received a polygraph test at least once a year. They had all of their employees sign a statement that they agreed to take the test.

"Early one Saturday morning when I arrived at work, I discovered that the test administrator was at our station and that I was to take the test that morning. I was not alarmed since I had been honest in putting all money that I had received in the till and making a proper receipt out after each sale.

"After putting all of the equipment on me and turning on his tape recorder, the man began asking me some general questions regarding my honesty. I felt very comfortable telling him I had never stolen any money from the till and that I always accomplished tasks that were assigned to me. Towards the end of the test he asked, 'Do you make good use of all of your time at work?' Suddenly, I felt very uncomfortable and could feel my heart start to beat a lot faster."

ALLEN KNIGHT

"After I finished my undergraduate work in mathematics and computer science, my wife persuaded me to take a job for a couple of years so that we could pay off some of our bills and get ahead a little before I started on my MBA. She was also concerned that I wasn't spending enough time with my two young sons. Between the demands of my course work and a part-time job, I usually left early in the morning and often was not home until after they had been put to bed.

"One of my undergraduate professors was instrumental in getting me a job with Nelson Data Processing. I understood before I started that they were a hard-driving firm with a reputation for high quality work. Once aboard, I found that the company had a large backlog and that management was encouraging everyone to put in overtime, for which they paid a generous hourly rate on top of the employee's salary.

"We needed the money and the work was interesting. Before long, I found myself working late almost every night. Barbara, my wife, didn't say much at first, but I could tell she wasn't happy with the way things were working out. Finally one day she said, 'Allen, you were spending more time at home when you were in school than you are now.' I mumbled something about 'trying to cut it down a little' and dropped the subject.

"The next day at noon when another employee and I were on our way out to grab a sandwich, I mentioned that my wife was unhappy about all the time I was spending away from home. He said, 'Look, Allen, you don't have to punch a time clock on those extra hours. A lot of the guys just take their work home with them. Keep track of your time and turn it in just like you do now. I'm not sure what the company policy is, but I have been doing this every so often for several months now, and nobody has ever said anything about it.'

"The more I thought about the idea of doing my overtime at home, the better I liked it. I could spend the early evening with the family and then, after the boys were to bed, I could really get some work done. As I had expected, Barbara was elated when I explained to her what I was going to do.

"The first few nights I found it hard to get up to speed again after letting down for dinner and roughhousing with the kids. As I got into the swing of it, however, I found that since there were no distractions, as there often were at the office, I could do a lot more at home in an hour than I was doing at work. Whenever I needed someone to help with the checking or sorting, Barbara was always available and seemed to enjoy working with me. I found that there were some things she could do faster and more accurately than I could. One night after we had finished a particularly long and involved task in about half the time it would ordinarily have taken me, I said, 'Barbara, there ought to be some way to put you on the payroll.' She laughed and said, 'Why don't you just increase the number of hours put in for yourself to cover it?'"

WELDON GATES

"I had been working for Patterson Engineering for nearly a year when I decided to come back and get my MBA. About three weeks before school was to start, I gave my superior, Jim, who was really a great boss, my two-week notice. Since he and I had talked a number of times about my going on to school as a preparation for a move into management, he was not at all surprised. He asked me to come in his office for a few minutes later that morning to make plans for my departure. I thought he might be concerned about several things I was working on that would be hard to turn over to anyone until I completed my present segment. I wasn't too concerned, however, because I had worked out a careful schedule and I figured I would just have time to do it all in those last two weeks.

"When I entered my supervisor's office, he said, 'Weldon, you have done a great job for us, and when you finish your education, we want you to keep us in mind. You said that school started right after the first of next month?' I nodded, and he went on to say, 'I imagine that you have a lot of work to do to get packed and moved, don't you?' I replied, 'Boy, I'll say! Moving is always such a hassle. We want to get out of our apartment by the fifteenth so that we can get our deposit back. I would like to have allowed myself a few more days, but when we figured out what we would need for school this year, we found that the money from these last two weeks was really crucial.'

"My supervisor smiled and leaned back in his chair. 'Yes,' he said, 'I remember how it was. I think, though, that I can help you out. According to my records, you have accumulated about 12 days' sick leave. Is that right?' 'Yes,' I answered. 'Well, as you know, the firm doesn't pay any sick leave unless you are actually sick. In your case, though, you are going to be sick—sick of moving. I want you to spend this afternoon acquainting Tom with where you are on each one of your projects. Then each morning for the next two weeks I want you to call in sick. If there is any question about it, I'll cover for you.'

"That night I thought a lot about what Jim had said—but I just didn't feel good about it. Tom was a good man, but it would take someone else at least twice as long to finish the things I was working on as it would take me. One of the projects was the kind that someone new would almost have to start over. The executives at Patterson had really been good to me in terms of the kinds of assignments they had given me—and I had been given a pay raise every six months instead of every year as was typical with new employees.

"I went in early the next morning and was right in the middle of my most important project when Jim came by. He frowned when he saw me at my desk. 'I thought I told you to take these two weeks off. I don't want to see you in here after today!' "

LORRAINE ADAMS

"When I was an undergraduate, I worked summers on an electronic composer for Brown Publishing. This is a typewriter with a memory which enables it to type course material in columns and justified (flushed right) margins. Because it is difficult to determine how long it takes to type material into memory and play it back, I often went for four hours without taking the fifteen-minute break we were supposed to have both morning and afternoon. Some of the other girls, who had the same problem, kept track of the breaks they didn't take and then used them as justification for leaving a half hour early or arriving a half hour late, recording their time as if they had left or arrived at the normal time. One girl even saved hers for two weeks and then took an afternoon off to do some shopping. I am sure that this was contrary to company policy, but our supervisor was a very relaxed and friendly woman who never seemed to notice when someone was gone.

"Another problem I had with breaks is 'What can constitute a break?' If a friend, who wasn't an employee of the company, dropped in for a few minutes, I always thought of that as a break. But what if some other employee who is tired, bored, or worried comes by and spends a few minutes talking about her work, her plans for the weekend, her current boy friend or some personal problem? Should you count that as a break? One morning our supervisor talked to me for twenty minutes about job opportunities for women with MBAs. Was that a break?

"Accounting for my time has always been a problem for me. Last summer, I worked as a department manager in a branch of a larger department store in Los Angeles. A number of the department managers would arrive at 8:00, as we were supposed to do, and then take off across the mall to a coffee shop 'to make plans for the day.' They usually got back just before the store opened at 9:30. I went with them a couple of times and found that if they discussed anything related to their work in the store, it was only an incidental part of their conversation. A couple of these guys would also regularly take up to an hour and a half for lunch and then check out right after five. Since we didn't have to check in and out for breaks or for lunch, their time card would show an eight-hour day. When I said something to one of them about it one day, he answered, 'Listen, Lorraine, summer is a slack time around here. You ought to be here during the

Christmas rush. We work a lot of hours then that we don't get paid for. The store owes us a chance to relax a little when the heat is off.' "

ROBERT JEFFRIES

"Before I came back to school, I worked for two years for a branch of Jefferson Sporting Goods. Jefferson had five larger stores located in different metropolitan areas in the state and did a large volume in men's and women's sports clothes. Our branch wasn't the largest in the chain but would have been second or third.

"The store manager, Rand Walker, had been manager since the store was opened. He had previously had soft goods experience with several other stores and really knew that part of the business.

"We got along really well. Not long after I came to work, Rand put me in charge of the shoe department. Later he made me manager of the men's clothing department, and, a year later, he made me assistant manager. He always saw that I got a substantial raise after each six-month review. He seemed to have a lot of trust in me. I noticed, for example, that even before I had been there for a year, he shared a lot of confidential figures with me that he didn't show to any of the other managers.

"One day Rand called me into his office. He had me shut the door so that no one else would hear our conversation. 'Bob,' he said, 'I've got a chance to buy the Blue Hills Pant Depot and I want to know what you think about it.' Blue Hills was in a suburb about ten miles north of our store. Rand proceeded to tell me the details of the offer. 'It looks like a good deal as far as I can tell,' I said, 'but would it be as profitable for you as Jefferson's has been?' (I was assuming he would quit when he bought the store.) 'Oh,' he said, 'I'm not going to quit unless Elliot Jefferson, the owner, tells me to.' I was surprised because it looked to me like a clear case of conflict of interest. I knew that Rand had been looking at some outside investments since he had done very well at Jefferson's, but I hadn't thought he would consider buying another clothing store.

"I didn't say much after that, trying not to get too involved with what was happening. Many times Rand would come to me to ask my opinion on certain clothing lines. He asked me to give him a list of the top five pant vendors and their salesmen's names and addresses, which I did.

"Several weeks later, I asked Rand if he had made a decision on the store. He said he had gone ahead and bought it. He said he put it under his wife's name, and that she was going to run it; that way he felt he could justify continuing his work at Jefferson's.

"After that, I noticed that Rand spent a lot more time in his office and less time out on the floor. Occasionally, I would drop into his office to see him and find him paying invoices and doing book work for his pant store. I never asked anything about it and, in fact, tried to keep our conversations on problems that needed attention at Jefferson's.

"This situation remained unchanged for several months. I concentrated my attention on doing my job and kept my thoughts to myself. Many of the other employees kept asking me about the Pant Depot. They wanted to know, for example, who really owned it, Rand or his wife. I would just tell them I didn't know.

"In October, Rand came to me again and said that he was planning on acquiring a second pant store in another suburb about fifteen miles south of our store. A clothing store in that town was going out of business, and he had a chance to rent the building. This really surprised me. I kiddingly asked if he was planning to open a whole chain. He replied that he would like to open several stores similar to the one he had already and that all he needed was to find good locations where he could rent store space cheaply.

"On November 1, Rand opened his second store. It immediately became a success, almost equalling the volume of the first.

"After that, I seldom saw Rand on the floor. He was either in his office or gone. I found myself trying to cover for him when he would get calls from the home office. This situation made me very uncomfortable. When he did come in, he seemed a lot more absent-minded about things in our store.

"I wondered how much Elliot Jefferson knew (or suspected) about Rand's involvement in these other stores. I wondered, too, if I should tell the home office why our reports were slow and why our sales had stopped increasing as rapidly as they had when Rand spent full time managing the store."

QUESTIONS FOR DISCUSSION*

Jerry Donaldson

1. How should Jerry Donaldson respond to the polygraph operator's final question?

Allen Knight

1. Is it morally permissible for Allen Knight to count Barbara's hours on his own time report?

Weldon Gates

1. How should Weldon Gates respond to his supervisor's request? Compare this case with the Jerry Donaldson case.

Lorraine Adams

1. Compare and contrast the troublesome situations described by Lorraine Adams concerning employee use of time. What principles should govern "fair" use of time by an employee?

Robert Jeffries

1. Should Robert Jeffries report the problem with Rand Walker to his superiors? To other employees? How does the issue in this case involving questionable practices by a supervisor compare with that in the earlier case of Weldon Gates?

5

Obligations
to Stakeholders:
Employees, Customers,
Community and Stockholders

History reveals marked differences in the ways that cultures treat business obligations to consumers. The Code of Hammurabi, almost 4,000 years old, holds merchants to certain standards of fair dealing and product safety. Seventeenth-century France under the rule of Louis XIV maintained a complex set of regulations and procedures governing product quality. Yet with the dawn of the Industrial Revolution and the influence of laissez-faire economic theorists such as Adam Smith, there came a dramatic loosening of government restraints. Smith and others argued that efficiency is significantly impaired when government tries to guarantee consumer satisfaction and safety; in turn the doctrine of "caveat emptor," or "buyer beware," dominated the economic scene during the first chapter of U.S. history.

Since the mid-nineteenth century, however, there has occurred a gradual shift in product liability law away from caveat emptor and in favor of caveat venditor, or "seller beware." In 1850 U.S. law decreed that only those who could prove fraud or breach of warranty could collect damages in the event they were harmed by a defective product. Not only did consumers find it extremely difficult to satisfy the courts' strict concepts of "fraud" and "breach of contract" but they were also required to sue only those with whom they existed in a relationship of "privity." "Privity" referred to a direct commercial relationship; thus a consumer who purchased a toxic bottle of aspirin from a drugstore could only sue the owner of the drugstore (with whom he or she had privity), and *not* the maker of the aspirin. This was true even when it was the maker of the aspirin who through negligence had mislabeled the toxic substance.

By the turn of the century, courts had struck down the doctrine of privity and were forcing companies to compensate injured consumers in a variety of instances. And by the mid-twentieth century, courts were holding corporations liable according to a doctrine of "strict liability," a doctrine under which consumers can collect damages even when it is impossible to prove corporate negligence. This means that so long as the product is defective and causes damage (barring dramatic consumer negligence), the producer is liable for damages—even when the producer took all possible safety precautions in the production of the product. Thus, if a can of hair spray explodes in a consumer's hands, the manufacturer of the spray is liable regardless of safety precautions taken.

Judges have justified strict liability using some of the following reasons:

1. The burden for consumer damage is best shouldered by corporations, who have "deep pockets," or in other words, more substantial financial reserves than do individual consumers. Since producers will necessarily raise prices somewhat to cover the most of anticipated liability, it will be consumers, not corporations, who will shoulder the ultimate financial burden for liability protection. But it is more efficient to protect the general public in this way than to rely on individual consumers to purchase a complex package of individual insurance for hair spray liability, jet engine liability, cosmetic liability, and so on.

2. Producers hold themselves to be "experts" and hence offer an "implied warranty" that their products will perform their intended functions without damaging the user. That is to say, few of us could be expected to know about the combination of steel and stress in the design of a lawnmower; yet we assume that the manufacturer does, and moreover that the lawnmower will mow grass without throwing its blade dangerously through the mower housing. If and when it throws its blade, then we can claim the violation of an implied warranty, and we can claim it even when unable to prove that the manufacturer was, in fact, negligent.

3. Finally, a policy of strict liability is seen as a deterrent to dangerous practices. If a manufacturer knows that any attempt to hide behind excuses will fail in court, then the manufacturer may well be prompted to take special precautions to insure that nothing goes wrong.

One must clearly distinguish, however, *legal liability* from either *criminal* or *moral responsibility*. Legal liability, for example, can occur when there is no criminal or moral responsibility. If a small child throws a rock through a neighbor's window, the parents may be legally liable; that is, they may be required to compensate the injured party financially. And yet the parents may not be morally or criminally responsible at all (unless, say, they were morally guilty by failing to raise the child properly or criminally responsible through ordering the child to throw the rock). Similarly, a corporation may be found financially liable for compensating an injured consumer without criminal or moral blame being attached.

The "Ford Pinto" case found in this section is a good example of this distinction. In a long series of trials, Ford was found financially liable time after time. It was required in turn to compensate the victims and relatives of victims of the Pinto's exploding gas tank. Thus in a short time the issue of whether Ford was liable was settled: Ford *was* financially liable. But the questions of criminal and moral responsibility remained. In the version of the Pinto case in this section, the emphasis is on the question of criminal and moral responsibility. It centers on the celebrated trial in which Ford Motor Company was charged with criminal homicide. No company in the United States, interestingly enough, had ever been found guilty of homicide. The "Dalkon Shield" case not only examines A. H. Robins's legal liability but also deals with the question of its criminal and moral responsibility. The fact is, Robins produced a product that caused injury and harm to many women. The question is, did Robins conspire to misinform its customers about the health factors involved in the use of the Dalkon Shield?

The other five pieces in this section deal with problems that do not involve direct physical harm. The essay "Stocks, Bonds and Insider Trading" deals with the financial harm that can occur when individuals legally or illegally conspire to acquire stocks by means of "insider information." "Leveraged Buyouts: America Pays the Price" is an essay that argues that America has had enough mammoth takeovers, insider trading scandals, and leveraged buyouts. "Even by the cynical standards of the 1980's Wall Street is giving greed a bad name." The counterpoint essay, "The Case for Takeovers," is a baldfaced defense of takeover acquisitions by the reputed dean of corporate raiders, Carl Icahn. The case "Oklahoma Meets Wall Street" deals with the moral issues that arise in a completely legal takeover. What responsibilities, if any, does the new ownership have in regard to the acquired company's employees, customers, and the general community in which the company is located? In the final series of cases under the heading of "Roger Hixon," we confront the moral issue of exactly how much information a seller must reveal to a potential buyer. In other words, what obligation, if any, does a seller have to point out the flaws or defects of a product they wish to sell?

Case Study
The Ford Pinto

W. Michael Hoffman

I

On August 10, 1978 a tragic automobile accident occurred on U.S. Highway 33 near Goshen, Indiana. Sisters Judy and Lynn Ulrich (ages 18 and 16, respectively) and their cousin Donna Ulrich (age 18) were struck from the rear in their 1973 Ford Pinto by a van. The gas tank of the Pinto ruptured, the car burst into flames and the three teen-agers were burned to death.

Subsequently an Elkhart County grand jury returned a criminal homicide charge against Ford, the first ever against an American corporation. During the following 20-week trial, Judge Harold R. Staffeldt advised the jury that Ford should be convicted of reckless homicide if it were shown that the company had engaged in "plain, conscious and unjustifiable disregard of harm that might result (from its actions) and the disregard involves a substantial deviation from acceptable standards of conduct."[1] The key phrase around which the trial hinged, of course, is "acceptable standards." Did Ford knowingly and recklessly choose profit over safety in the design and placement of the Pinto's gas tank? Elkhart County prosecutor Michael A. Cosentino and chief Ford attorney James F. Neal battled dramatically over this issue in a rural Indiana courthouse. Meanwhile, American business anxiously awaited the verdict which could send warning ripples through board rooms across the nation concerning corporate responsibility and product liability.

II

As a background to this trial some discussion of the Pinto controversy is necessary. In 1977 the magazine *Mother Jones* broke a story by Mark Dowie, general manager of *Mother Jones* business operations, accusing Ford of knowingly putting on the road an unsafe car—the Pinto—in which hundreds of people have needlessly suffered burn deaths and even more have been scarred and disfigured due to burns. In his article "Pinto Madness" Dowie charges that:

> Fighting strong competition from Volkswagen for the lucrative small-car market, the Ford Motor Company rushed the Pinto into production in much less than the usual time.

> Ford engineers discovered in pre-production crash tests that rear-end collisions would rupture the Pinto's fuel system extremely easily.
>
> Because assembly-line machinery was already tooled when engineers found this defect, top Ford officials decided to manufacture the car anyway—exploding gas tank and all—even though Ford owned the patent on a much safer gas tank.
>
> For more than eight years afterwards, Ford successfully lobbied, with extraordinary vigor and some blatant lies, against a key government safety standard that would have forced the company to change the Pinto's fire-prone gas tank.

By conservative estimates Pinto crashes have caused 500 burn deaths to people who would not have been seriously injured if the car had not burst into flames. The figure could be as high as 900. Burning Pintos have become such an embarrassment to Ford that its advertising agency, J. Walter Thompson, dropped a line from the ending of a radio spot that read "Pinto leaves you with that warm feeling."

Ford knows that the Pinto is a firetrap, yet it has paid out millions to settle damage suits out of court, and it is prepared to spend millions more lobbying against safety standards. With a half million cars rolling off the assembly lines each year, Pinto is the biggest-selling subcompact in America, and the company's operating profit on the car is fantastic. Finally, in 1977, new Pinto models have incorporated a few minor alterations necessary to meet that federal standard Ford managed to hold off for eight years. Why did the company delay so long in making these minimal, inexpensive improvements?

> Ford waited eight years because its internal "cost-benefit analysis," which places a dollar value on human life, said it wasn't profitable to make the changes sooner.[2]

Several weeks after Dowie's press conference on the article, which had the support of Ralph Nader and auto safety expert Byron Bloch, Ford issued a news release attributed to Herbert T. Misch, vice president of Environmental and Safety Engineering at Ford, countering points made in the *Mother Jones* article. Their statistical studies significantly conflicted with each other. For example, Dowie states that more than 3000 people were burning to death yearly in auto fires; he claims that, according to a National Highway Traffic Safety Administration (NHTSA) consultant, although Ford makes 24 percent of the cars on American roads, these cars account for 42 percent of the collision-ruptured fuel tanks.[3] Ford, on the other hand, uses statistics from the Fatality Analysis Reporting System (FARS) maintained by the government's NHTSA to defend itself, claiming that in 1975 there were 848 deaths related to fire-associated passenger-car accidents and only 13 of these involved Pintos; in 1976, Pintos accounted for only 22 out of 943. These statistics imply that Pintos were involved in only 1.9 percent of such accidents, and Pintos constitute about 1.9 percent of the total registered passenger cars. Furthermore, fewer than half of those Pintos cited in the FARS study were struck in the rear.[4] Ford concludes from this and other studies that the Pinto was never an unsafe car and has not been involved in some 70 burn deaths annually as *Mother Jones* claims.

Ford admits that early model Pintos did not meet rear-impact tests at 20 mph but denies that this implies that they were unsafe compared to other cars of that type and era. In fact, its tests were conducted, according to Ford, some with experimental rubber "bladders" to protect the gas tank, in order to determine how best to have their future cars meet a 20 mph rear-collision standard which Ford itself set as an internal performance goal. The government at that time had no such standard. Ford also points out that in every model year the Pinto met or surpassed the government's own standards, and

> it simply is unreasonable and unfair to contend that a car is somehow unsafe if it does not meet standards proposed for future years or embody the technological improvements that are introduced in later model years.[5]

Mother Jones, on the other hand, presents a different view of the situation. If Ford was so concerned about rear-impact safety, why did it delay the federal government's attempts to impose standards? Dowie gives the following answer:

> The particular regulation involved here was Federal Motor Vehicle Safety Standard 301. Ford picked portions of Standard 301 for strong opposition way back in 1968 when the Pinto was still in the blueprint stage. The intent of 301, and the 300 series that followed it, was to protect drivers and passengers after a crash occurs. Without question the worst post-crash hazard is fire. So Standard 301 originally proposed that all cars should be able to withstand a fixed barrier impact of 20 mph (that is, running into a wall at that speed) without losing fuel.
>   When the standard was proposed, Ford engineers pulled their crash-test results out of their files. The front ends of most cars were no problem—with minor alterations they could stand the impact without losing fuel. "We were already working on the front end," Ford engineer Dick Kimble admitted. "We knew we could meet the test on the front end." But with the Pinto particularly, a 20 mph rear-end standard meant redesigning the entire rear end of the car. With the Pinto scheduled for production in August of 1970, and with $200 million worth of tools in place, adoption of this standard would have created a minor financial disaster. So Standard 301 was targeted for delay, and with some assistance from its industry associates, Ford succeeded beyond its wildest expectations: the standard was not adopted until the 1977 model year.[6]

Ford's tactics were successful, according to Dowie, not only due to their extremely clever lobbying, which became the envy of lobbyists all over Washington, but also because of the pro-industry stance of NHTSA itself.

Furthermore, it is not at all clear that the Pinto was as safe as other comparable cars with regard to the positioning of its gas tank. Unlike the gas tank in the Capri which rode over the rear axle, a "saddle-type" fuel tank on which Ford owned the patent, the Pinto tank was placed just behind the rear bumper. According to Dowie,

> Dr. Leslie Ball, the retired safety chief for the NASA manned space program and a founder of the International Society of Reliability Engineers, recently

made a careful study of the Pinto. "The release to production of the Pinto was the most reprehensible decision in the history of American engineering," he said. Ball can name more than 40 European and Japanese models in the Pinto price and weight range with safer gas-tank positioning.

Los Angeles auto safety expert Byron Bloch has made an indepth study of the Pinto fuel system. "It's a catastrophic blunder," he says. "Ford made an extremely irresponsible decision when they placed such a weak tank in such a ridiculous location in such a soft rear end. It's almost designed to blow up—premeditated."[7]

Although other points could be brought out in the debate between *Mother Jones* and Ford, perhaps the most intriguing and controversial is the cost-benefit analysis study that Ford did entitled "Fatalities Associated with Crash-Induced Fuel Leakage and Fires" released by J. C. Echold, Director of Automotive Safety for Ford. This study apparently convinced Ford and was intended to convince the federal government that a technological improvement costing $11 per car which would have prevented gas tanks from rupturing so easily was not cost-effective for society. The costs and benefits are broken down in the following way:

BENEFITS

Savings:	180 burn deaths, 180 serious burn injuries, 2,100 burned vehicles
Unit Cost:	$200,000 per death, $67,000 per injury, $700 per vehicle
Total Benefit:	180 × ($200,000) + 180 × ($67,000) + 2,100 × ($700) = $49.5 million.

COSTS

Sales:	11 million cars, 1.5 million light trucks
Unit Cost:	$11 per car, $11 per truck
Total Cost:	11,000,000 × ($11) + 1,500,000 × ($11) = $137 million

And where did Ford come up with the $200,000 figure as the cost per death? This came from a NHTSA study which broke down the estimated social costs of a death as follows:

COMPONENT	1971 COSTS
Future Productivity Losses	
Direct	$ 132,000
Indirect	41,300
Medical Costs	
Hospital	700
Other	425
Property Damage	1,500
Insurance Administration	4,700
Legal and Court	3,000
Employer Losses	1,000

Victim's Pain and Suffering	10,000
Funeral	900
Assets (Lost Consumption)	5,000
Miscellaneous	200
TOTAL PER FATALITY	$ 200,725

(Although this analysis was on all Ford vehicles, a breakout of just the Pinto could be done.) *Mother Jones* reports it could not find anybody who could explain how the $10,000 figure for "pain and suffering" had been arrived at.[8]

Although Ford does not mention this point in its News Release defense, it might have replied that it was the federal government, not Ford, that set the figure for a burn death. Ford simply carried out a cost-benefit analysis based on that figure. *Mother Jones,* however, in addition to insinuating that there was industry-agency (NHTSA) collusion, argues that the $200,000 figure was arrived at under intense pressure from the auto industry to use cost-benefit analysis in determining regulations. *Mother Jones* also questions Ford's estimate of burn injuries: "All independent experts estimate that for each person who dies by an auto fire, many more are left with charred hands, faces and limbs." Referring to the Northern California Burn Center which estimates the ratio of burn injuries to deaths at ten to one instead of one to one, Dowie states that "the true ratio obviously throws the company's calculations way off."[9] Finally, *Mother Jones* claims to have obtained "confidential" Ford documents which Ford did not send to Washington, showing that crash fires could be largely prevented by installing a rubber bladder inside the gas tank for only $5.08 per car, considerably less than the $11 per car Ford originally claimed was required to improve crash-worthiness.[10]

Instead of making the $11 improvement, installing the $5.08 bladder, or even giving the consumer the right to choose the additional cost for added safety, Ford continued, according to *Mother Jones,* to delay the federal government for eight years in establishing mandatory rear-impact standards. In the meantime, Dowie argues, thousands of people were burning to death and tens of thousands more were being badly burned and disfigured for life, tragedies many of which could have been prevented for only a slight cost per vehicle. Furthermore, the delay also meant that millions of new unsafe vehicles went on the road, "vehicles that will be crashing, leaking fuel and incinerating people well into the 1980s."[11]

In concluding this article Dowie broadens his attack beyond just Ford and the Pinto.

> Unfortunately, the Pinto is not an isolated case of corporate malpractice in the auto industry. Neither is Ford a lone sinner. There probably isn't a car on the road without a safety hazard known to its manufacturer . . .
> Furthermore, cost-valuing human life is not used by Ford alone. Ford was just the only company careless enough to let such an embarrassing calculation slip into public records. The process of willfully trading lives for profits is built into corporate capitalism. Commodore Vanderbilt publicly scorned

George Westinghouse and his "foolish" air brakes while people died by the hundreds in accidents on Vanderbilt's railroads.[12]

Ford has paid millions of dollars in Pinto jury trials and out-of-court settlements, especially the latter. *Mother Jones* quotes Al Slechter in Ford's Washington office as saying: "We'll never go to a jury again. Not in a fire case. Juries are just too sentimental. They see those charred remains and forget the evidence. No sir, we'll settle."[13] But apparently Ford thought such settlements would be less costly than the safety improvements. Dowie wonders if Ford would continue to make the same decisions "were Henry Ford II and Lee Iacocca serving 20-year terms in Leavenworth for consumer homicide."[14]

III

On March 13, 1980, the Elkhart County jury found Ford not guilty of criminal homicide in the Ulrich case. Ford attorney Neal summarized several points in his closing argument before the jury. Ford could have stayed out of the small car market which would have been the "easiest way," since Ford would have made more profit by sticking to bigger cars. Instead Ford built the Pinto "to take on the imports, to save jobs for Americans and to make a profit for its stockholders."[15] The Pinto met every fuel-system standard of any federal, state or local government, and was comparable to other 1973 subcompacts. The engineers who designed the car thought it was a good, safe car and bought it for themselves and their families. Ford did everything possible quickly to recall the Pinto after NHTSA ordered it to do so. Finally, and more specifically to the case at hand, Highway 33 was a badly designed highway, and the girls were fully stopped when a 4,000-pound van rammed into the rear of their Pinto at at least 50 miles an hour. Given the same circumstances, Neal stated, any car would have suffered the same consequences as the Ulrich's Pinto.[16] As reported in the *New York Times* and *Time,* the verdict brought a "loud cheer" from Ford's Board of Directors and undoubtedly at least a sigh of relief from other corporations around the nation.

Many thought this case was a David against a Goliath because of the small amount of money and volunteer legal help Prosecutor Cosentino had in contrast to the huge resources Ford poured into the trial. In addition, it should be pointed out that Cosentino's case suffered from a ruling by Judge Staffeldt that Ford's own test results on pre-1973 Pinto's were inadmissible. These documents confirmed that Ford knew as early as 1971 that the gas tank of the Pinto ruptured at impacts of 20 mph and that the company was aware, because of tests with the Capri, that the over-the-axle position of the gas tank was much safer than mounting it behind the axle. Ford decided to mount it behind the axle in the Pinto to provide more trunk space and to save money. The restrictions of Cosentino's evidence to testimony relating specifically to the 1973 Pinto severely undercut the strength of the prosecutor's case.[17]

Whether this evidence would have changed the minds of the jury will never be known. Some, however, such as business ethicist Richard De George, feel that this evidence shows grounds for charges of recklessness against Ford. Although it is true that there were no federal safety standards in 1973 to which Ford legally had to conform and although Neal seems to have proved that all subcompacts were unsafe when hit at 50 mph by a 4,000-pound van, the fact that the NHTSA ordered a recall of the Pinto and not other subcompacts is, according to De George, "*prima facie* evidence that Ford's Pinto gas tank mounting was substandard."[18] De George argues that these grounds for recklessness are made even stronger by the fact that Ford did not give the consumer a choice to make the Pinto gas tank safer by installing a rubber bladder for a rather modest fee.[19] Giving the consumer such a choice, of course, would have made the Pinto gas tank problem known and therefore probably would have been bad for sales.

Richard A. Epstein, professor of law at the University of Chicago Law School, questions whether Ford should have been brought up on criminal charges of reckless homicide at all. He also points out an interesting historical fact. Before 1966 an injured party in Indiana could not even bring civil charges against an automobile manufacturer solely because of the alleged "uncrashworthiness" of a car; one would have to seek legal relief from the other party involved in the accident, not from the manufacturer. But after *Larson v. General Motors Corp.* in 1968, a new era of crashworthiness suits against automobile manufacturers began. "Reasonable" precautions must now be taken by manufacturers to minimize personal harm in crashes.[20] How to apply criteria of reasonableness in such cases marks the whole nebulous ethical and legal arena of product liability.

If such a civil suit had been brought against Ford, Epstein believes, the corporation might have argued, as they did to a large extent in the criminal suit, that the Pinto conformed to all current applicable safety standards and with common industry practice. (Epstein cites that well over 90% of U.S. standard production cars had their gas tanks in the same position as the Pinto.) But in a civil trial the adequacy of industry standards is ultimately up to the jury, and had civil charges been brought against Ford in this case the plaintiffs might have had a better chance of winning.[21] Epstein feels that a criminal suit, on the other hand, had no chance from the very outset, because the prosecutor would have had to establish criminal intent on the part of Ford. To use an analogy, if a hunter shoots at a deer and wounds an unseen person, he may be held civilly responsible but not criminally responsible because he did not intend to harm. And even though it may be more difficult to determine the mental state of a corporation (or its principal agents), it seems clear to Epstein that the facts of this case do not prove any such criminal intent even though Ford may have known that some burn deaths/injuries could have been avoided by a different placement of its Pinto gas tank and that Ford consciously decided not to spend more money to save lives.[22] Everyone recognizes that there are trade-offs between safety and costs. Ford could have built a "tank" instead of a Pinto, thereby considerably reducing risks, but it would have been relatively unaffordable for most and probably unattractive to all potential consumers.

To have established Ford's reckless homicide it would have been necessary to establish the same of Ford's agents since a corporation can only act through its agents. Undoubtedly, continues Epstein, the reason why the prosecutor did not try to subject Ford's officers and engineers to fines and imprisonment for their design choices is because of "the good faith character of their judgment, which was necessarily decisive in Ford's behalf as well."[23] For example, Harold C. MacDonald, Ford's chief engineer on the Pinto, testified that he felt it was important to keep the gas tank as far from the passenger compartment as possible, as it was in the Pinto. And other Ford engineers testified that they used the car for their own families. This is relevant information in a criminal case which must be concerned about the intent of the agents.

Furthermore, even if civil charges had been made in this case, it seems unfair and irrelevant to Epstein to accuse Ford of trading cost for safety. Ford's use of cost-benefit formulas, which must assign monetary values to human life and suffering, is precisely what the law demands in assessing civil liability suits. The court may disagree with the decision, but to blame industry for using such a method would violate the very rules of civil liability. Federal automobile officials (NHTSA) had to make the same calculations in order to discharge their statutory duties. In allowing the Pinto design, are not they too (and in turn their employer, the United States) just as guilty as Ford's agents?[24]

IV

The case of the Ford Pinto raises many questions of ethical importance. Some people conclude that Ford was definitely wrong in designing and marketing the Pinto. The specific accident involving the Ulrich girls, because of the circumstances, was simply not the right one to have attacked Ford on. Other people believe that Ford was neither criminally nor civilly guilty of anything and acted completely responsibily in producing the Pinto. Many others find the case morally perplexing, too complex to make sweeping claims of guilt or innocence.

Was Ford irresponsible in rushing the production of the Pinto? Even though Ford violated no federal safety standards or laws, should it have made the Pinto safer in terms of rear-end collisions, especially regarding the placement of the gas tank? Should Ford have used cost-benefit analysis to make decisions relating to safety, specifically placing dollar values on human life and suffering? Knowing that the Pinto's gas tank could have been made safer by installing a protective bladder for a relatively small cost per consumer, perhaps Ford should have made that option available to the public. If Ford did use heavy lobbying efforts to delay and/or influence federal safety standards, was this ethically proper for a corporation to do? One might ask, if Ford was guilty, whether the engineers, the managers, or both are to blame. If Ford had been found guilt of criminal homicide, was the proposed penalty stiff enough ($10,000 maximum fine for each of the three counts = $30,000 maximum), or should agents of the corporation such as MacDonald, Iacocca, and Henry Ford II be fined and possibly jailed?

A number of questions concerning safety standards are also relevant to the ethical issues at stake in the Ford trial. Is it just to blame a corporation for not abiding by "acceptable standards" when such standards are not yet determined by society? Should corporations like Ford play a role in setting such standards? Should individual juries be determining such standards state by state, incident by incident? If Ford should be setting safety standards, how does it decide how safe to make its product and still make it affordable and desirable to the public without using cost-benefit analysis? For that matter, how does anyone decide? Perhaps it is putting Ford, or any corporation, in a catch-22 position to ask it both to set safety standards and to competitively make a profit for its stockholders.

Regardless of how the reader answers these and other questions it is clear that the Pinto case raises fundamental issues concerning the responsibilities of corporations, how corporations should structure themselves in order to make ethical decisions, and how industry, government, and society in general ought to interrelate to form a framework within which such decisions can properly be made in the future.

NOTES

1. *Indianapolis Star,* March 9, 1980, sec. 3, p. 2.

2. Mark Dowie, "Pinto Madness," *Mother Jones,* Sept/Oct, 1977, pp. 18 and 20. Subsequently Mike Wallace for "Sixty Minutes" and Sylvia Chase for "20-20" came out with similar exposés.

3. Ibid., p. 30.

4. Ford News Release (Sept. 9, 1977), pp. 1–3.

5. Ibid., p. 5.

6. Dowie, "Pinto Madness," p. 29.

7. Ibid., pp. 22–23.

8. Ibid., pp. 24 and 28. Although this analysis was on all Ford vehicles a breakout of just the Pinto could be done.

9. Ibid., p. 28.

10. Ibid., pp. 28–29.

11. Ibid., p. 30.

12. Ibid., p. 32. Dowie might have cited another example which emerged in the private correspondence which transpired almost a half century ago between Lammot du Pont and Alfred P. Sloan, Jr., then president of GM. Du Pont was trying to convince Sloan to equip GM's lowest-priced cars, Chevrolets, with safety glass. Sloan replied by saying: "It is not my responsibility to sell safety glass. . . . You can say, perhaps, that I am selfish, but business is selfish. We are not a charitable institution—we are trying to make a profit for our stockholders." Quoted in Morton Mintz and Jerry S. Cohen, *Power, Inc.* (New York: The Viking Press, 1976), p. 110.

13. Ibid., p. 31.

14. Ibid. p. 32.

15. Transcript of report of proceedings in *State of Indiana* v. *Ford Motor Company,* Case No. 11-431, Monday, March 10, 1980, pp. 6202-3. How Neal reconciled his "easiest way" point with his "making more profit for stockholders" point is not clear to this writer.

16. Ibid., pp. 6207–9.

17. *Chicago Tribune,* October 13, 1979, p. 1, and sec. 2, p. 12; *New York Times,* October 14, 1979, p. 26; *Atlanta Constitution,* February 7, 1980.

18. Richard De George, "Ethical Responsibilities of Engineers in Large Organizations: The Pinto Case," *Business and Professional Ethics Journal,* vol. 1, no. 1 (Fall 1981), p. 4. *New York Times,* October 26, 1978, p. 103, also points out that during 1976 and 1977 there were 13 fiery fatal rear-end collisions involving Pintos, more than double that of other U.S. comparable cars, with VW Rabbits and Toyota Corollas having none.

19. Ibid., p. 5.

20. Richard A. Epstein, "Is Pinto a Criminal?" *Regulation,* March/April, 1980, pp. 16–17.

21. A California jury awarded damages of $127.8 million (reduced later to $6.3 million on appeal) in a Pinto crash where a youth was burned over 95% of his body. See *New York Times,* February 8, 1978, p. 8.

22. Epstein, p. 19.

23. Ibid., pp. 20–21.

24. Ibid., pp. 19–21.

QUESTIONS FOR DISCUSSION*

1. Evaluate from a moral perspective the "cost-benefit" analysis conducted by Ford.

2. Did Ford "knowingly and recklessly choose profit over safety in the design and placement of the Pinto's gas tank"?

3. How might Fort alter its policies to avoid a similar disaster in the future?

Case Study
A. H. Robins:
The Dalkon Shield

A. R. Gini
T. Sullivan

On August 21, 1985, A. R. Robins of Richmond, Virginia—the seventeenth largest pharmaceutical house in America and corporately rated as number 392 in the Fortune 500—filed for reorganization under Chapter 11 of the 1978 Federal Bankruptcy Code. On the surface, Robins seemed to be a thriving company. Its popular products, including Robitussin cough syrup, Chap Stick lip balm, and Sergeant's flea and tick collars for cats and dogs, generated record sales in 1985 of $706 million with a net income in excess of $75 million. Robins' petition for protection under Chapter 11 stems directly from the "blitz of litigation" over a product it has not produced since 1974, the Dalkon Shield intrauterine birth control device. At the time it filed for bankruptcy Robins had been deluged with more than 12,000 personal injury lawsuits charging that the Dalkon Shield was responsible for countless serious illnesses and at least 20 deaths among the women who used it.

In many ways this bankruptcy petition mimes and mirrors (Johns-) Manville's unprecedented request for reorganization in 1982. Manville, the nation's, if not the world's, largest producer of asbestos, claimed that it was succumbing to a "blitz of toxic torts" and therefore could not carry on with business as usual. In August 1982 Manville was facing 16,500 suits on behalf of people who claimed to have contracted cancer and other diseases caused by asbestos and the asbestos-related products that the company produced.

Like Manville, A. H. Robins is defending and explaining its actions by claiming that it simply cannot go on and fulfill its immediate and potential obligations to its stockholders, customers, employees, and litigants (claimants) unless it takes dramatic financial action. In filing for Chapter 11 Robins has won at least temporary respite from its legal woes. Although the company will continue operating during the reorganization, all suits now pending are frozen and no new suits can be filed. While the company develops a plan to handle its liabilities, it is up to the bankruptcy courts to deal with all present claims as well as to establish guidelines for the handling of any future claims.[1] Whatever the final results, the Dalkon Shield case may well turn out to be the worst product liability nightmare that a U.S. drugmaker or major corporation has ever suffered.[2]

The A. H. Robins Company is essentially a family owned and operated organization. The original company was founded by Albert Hartley Robins, a registered pharmacist, in 1866 in Richmond, Virginia. His grandson, E. Claiborne Robins, built and directed the company into a multinational conglomerate which was able to obtain Fortune 500 status by the middle of the twentieth century. While E. Claiborne Robins remains Chairman of the Board, E. Claiborne Junior is now the firm's president and CEO. Both the family and the company are much liked and respected in their home state. Generations of employees have repeatedly claimed that E. Claiborne Senior was at his worst a "benevolent despot" and at his best a kind and gentle man sincerely interested in quality control as well as his employees' well being. By all reports E. Claiborne Junior seems to be following in his father's footsteps. Moreover, the family's kindness has not been limited to its employees. In 1969 E. Claiborne Senior personally donated over $50 million to the University of Richmond. Since then the Robins family has given at least $50 million more to the university, and additional millions to other universities and to diverse other causes. In

December 1983 *Town and Country* magazine listed Claiborne Senior among the top five of "The Most Generous Americans."

Both the family and the company take pride in having "always gone by the book" and always giving their customers a good product at a fair price. In its 120 years of operation the company had done business without having a single product-liability lawsuit filed against it. Critics now claim that Robins has been involved in a directly ordered, prolonged institutional cover-up of the short- and long-term effects of the use of the Dalkon Shield. Moreover, many critics claim that, more than just stonewalling the possible side effects of the Shield, Robins is guilty of marketing a product they knew to be relatively untested, undependable, and therefore potentially dangerous. Robins is accused of having deceived doctors, lied to women, perjured itself to federal judges, and falsified documentation to the FDA. According to Morton Mintz, Robins' most outspoken critic, thousands, probably tens of thousands, of women who trusted the doctors who trusted A. H. Robins paid a ghastly price for the use of the Dalkon Shield: chronic pelvic infections, impairment or loss of childbearing capacity, children with multiple birth defects, unwanted abortions, recurring health problems, and chronic pain.

IUDs are among the most ancient forms of contraception, known for more than two thousand years. Exactly how an IUD prevents conception is not known. It may interfere with the fertilization of the eggs, but most experts believe that when inserted into the uterus it prevents pregnancy by making it difficult for a fertilized egg to attach itself to the wall of the uterus. Over the centuries the materials used in the fabrication of IUDs included ebony, glass, gold, ivory, pewter, wood, wool, diamond-studded platinum, copper, and plastic.[3] The Dalkon Shield was developed by Dr. Hugh J. Davis, a former professor of obstetrics and gynecology at the Johns Hopkins University, and Irwin Lerner, an electrical engineer. In 1970 they sold their rights to the Shield to Robins, who agreed to pay royalties on future sales and $750,000 in cash. Between 1971 and 1974 Robins sold 4.5 million Dalkon Shields around the world, including 2.85 million in the United States.

By the late 1960s large numbers of women had become concerned about the safety of the Pill. These women formed an ever-growing potential market for an alternative means of birth control. Many of these women switched to "barrier" methods of birth control, particularly the diaphragm, which, when used with spermicidal creams or jellies, can be highly effective, though inconvenient. Others turned to IUDs, which, although convenient, previously had been considered unsafe—causing pelvic infections, irregular bleeding, uterine cramps, and accidental expulsion. Robins leapt at an opportunity to develop a new market with their product. The company's task was to convince physicians that the Shield was as effective as oral contraceptives in preventing pregnancies and that it was safer, better designed, and afforded greater resistance to inadvertent expulsion from the uterus than other IUDs.[4]

In January 1971 Robins began to sell the Dalkon Shield, promoting it

as the "modern, superior," "second generation" and—most importantly—
"safe" intrauterine device for birth control. The Shield itself is a nickel-
sized plastic device that literally looks like a badge or a shield with spikes
around the edges and a thread-sized "nylon tail string," which allowed both
the wearer and the physician a means to guarantee that the device had not
been expelled. The Shield was relatively inexpensive. The device itself sold
for between $3.00 and $4.50 (its production costs were an incredibly low
figure of $.25 a Shield). The only other cost associated with the Shield was
the doctor's office fee for insertion and a recommended yearly pelvic examination. Dr. Hugh Davis claimed that the Dalkon Shield was the safest
and most effective IUD because it is "the only IUD which is truly anatom-
ically engineered for optimum uterine placement, fit, tolerance, and reten-
tion."[5] Davis was able to persuade a large number of physicians of the
effectiveness of the Shield in an article he published in the "Current Investigation" section of the *American Journal of Obstetrics and Gynecology* in February 1970. The article described a study conducted at the Johns Hopkins
Family Planning Clinic involving 640 women who had worn the Shield for
one year. His analysis was based on 3,549 women-months of experience.
Davis cited five pregnancies, ten expulsions, nine removals for medical
reasons, and three removals for personal reasons. His startling results:
tolerance rate (non-expulsion), 96 percent; pregnancy rate, 1.1 percent.
The A. H. Robins Company reprinted no fewer than 199,000 copies of the
Davis article for distribution to physicians.[6]

    While various executives strongly recommended that other studies be
commissioned to validate Davis's results, in January 1971 Robins began to
market and sell the Shield on the basis of Davis's limited analysis. Robins'
decision to produce and sell the Shield based on Davis's statistics may not
coincide with the highest standards of scientific research, but it did not
violate any FDA statutes and was therefore perfectly legal. At the time
Robins produced the Shield, FDA had no regulatory policies in force regarding IUDs of any kind. While FDA had the authority to regulate the
production, testing, and sales of all new prescriptions, it could only
recommend testing on new medical devices. It could not monitor, investigate,
or police a device unless charges of lack of effectiveness, injury, or abuse
were formally leveled against the device or the producer.

    In December 1970 Robins commissioned a major long-term study to
reinforce Davis's results. The study concentrated on ten clinics, seven in the
United States and one each in Canada, Nova Scotia, and British Columbia.
Between December 1970 and December 1974 (six months after Robins
suspended domestic sales) 2,391 women were fitted with the Shield. The
first results came out in November 1972, and only about half of the women
enrolled in the study. The statistics showed a sixteen month pregnancy rate
of 1.6 percent. The Robins home office was more than pleased and immediately communicated this information to its sales staff. Thirteen months
later, with all the women now participating in the program, less happy
figures began to show up. The pregnancy rate after six months was 2.1
percent; after twelve months, 3.2 percent; after eighteen months, 3.5 percent; and after twenty-three months, 4.1 percent. In a final report pub-

lished as a confidential internal document in August 1975 the final figures and results were even more devastating. The pregnancy rate after six months was 2.6 percent; after twelve months, 4.2 percent; after eighteen months, 4.9 percent; and after twenty-four months, 5.7 percent. Two of the scientists involved in this project submitted a minority report claiming that the Shield was even less effective than these already damaging figures indicated. They claimed that the pregnancy rate during the first year was much higher: after six months, 3.3 percent; and after twelve months, 5.5 percent. This twelve-month pregnancy rate is exactly five times *higher than* the rate Robins advertised and promoted—1.1 percent—to catapult the Shield to leadership in the IUD business.[7] This minority report was never disclosed to the medical community by Robins. Nor did Robins communicate these results to its own sales force. It did report some of these findings to FDA in July 1974, but only after the company had suspended domestic sales earlier that June.

Soon after the Shield entered the marketplace, independent research results began to appear in both national and foreign journals of medicine. In 1970 and 1971 Dr. Mary O. Gabrielson, working out of clinics in San Francisco and Oakland, did an eighteen-month study on 937 women with results that Robins would not want to advertise. The rate of medical removals was 26.4 percent; the pregnancy rate, 5.1 percent. In 1973 the *British Medical Journal* published a study showing a 4.7 percent pregnancy rate in Shield users.[8] Again because there was no law requiring disclosure of this new research information, Robins did not rush to inform the general public, the medical community, or the FDA.

At the same time that the Robins Company was receiving research results pointing to poor statistical effectiveness of the Shield, they also began to receive more and more "single physician experience" reports warning and complaining about some of the medical consequences from using the Shield. These physician's reports plus the statistics generated from controlled clinical reports began to portray the Shield as neither effective nor safe.

The primary cause of concern for Shield users proved to be a much higher incidence of uterine/pelvic bacterial infections. PID (pelvic inflammatory disease) is a highly virulent and very painful, difficult to cure, life-threatening infection, which more often than not impairs or destroys a woman's ability to bear children. Of those women who conceived with the Shield in place (approximately 110,000 in the United States), an estimated 60 percent of them miscarried after suffering severe bacterial infections (PID). In 1974 FDA reported that over 245 women in their fourth to sixth month of pregnancy suffered the relatively rare bacterially-induced miscarriage called septic spontaneous abortion. For fifteen women, these septic abortions were fatal.[9] Moreover, hundreds of women throughout the world who had conceived while wearing the Shield gave birth prematurely to children with grave congenital defects, including blindness, cerebral palsy, and mental retardation.[10]

Scientists now believe that the systemic cause for these virulent forms of bacterial infection is the nylon tail of the Shield itself. The Dalkon Shield tail string runs between the vagina, where bacteria are always present, and the uterus, which is germ free. It then passes through the cervix, where cervical mucus is the body's natural defense against bacterial invasion of the uterus. Robins claimed that cervical mucus would stop all germs from entering and infecting the uterus. To the naked eye, the Dalkon Shield tail string is an impervious monofilament, meaning that bacteria on it could not get into it. Actually, however, it is a cylindrical sheath encasing 200 to 450 round monofilaments separated by spaces. While the string was knotted at both ends, neither end was actually sealed. Therefore, any bacteria that got into the spaces between the filaments would be insulated from the body's natural antibacterial action while being drawn into the uterus by "wicking," a phenomenon similar to that by which a string draws the melting wax of a candle to the flame. Scientists believe that the longer the Shield and its string/tail is in place, the greater the chances for its deterioration and infiltration, thereby inducing infection in the uterus. Scientists now also contend that the "syndrome of spontaneous septic abortions" that occurred to women who had the Shield in place in the early second trimester of their pregnancy was caused by the tail string. That is, radical and sudden infection occurred when the uterus expanded to the point where it tended to pull the tail string into itself thereby bringing on instant, often lethal, contamination.[11]

In the summer of 1983 the Centers for Disease Control in Atlanta and the FDA recommended that all women still using the Shield should contact their physicians and have it immediately removed. The Agencies found that women using the Shield had a fivefold increase in risk for contracting PID as compared to women using other types of IUDs. No change in contraceptive practice was recommended for women using any other type of IUD.[12] In April 1985 two studies funded by the National Institute of Health announced yet another dire warning. These studies showed that childless IUD wearers who have had PID run a higher risk of infertility if their devices were Shields than if they were other makes.[13]

Throughout all of this, A. H. Robins officials appeared to be unaware of, or at best indifferent to, the issues, facts, and effects of their product. The company assumed the position of complete denial of any intentional wrongdoing or any malicious intent to evade full public disclosure of pertinent medical information about the safety and effectiveness of the Shield. On numerous separate occasions both in public forums and under oath, E. Claiborne Robins, Senior, has claimed near ignorance of Robins' sixteen-year involvement with the Dalkon Shield. At a series of depositions taken in 1984 Robins Senior swore that he was unable to recall ever having discussed the Shield with his son, the company's chief executive officer and president. When asked, "You certainly knew, when you started marketing this device, that PID was a life-threatening disease, did you not?" Robins testified: "I don't know that. I never thought of it as life-threatening." Did he know it could destroy fertility? "Maybe I should, but I don't know that. I have heard that, but I am not sure where." Carl Lunsford, senior vice-president for research and development, swore he could recall no "expression of concern" by any company official about PID, and he didn't remember having "personally wondered" about the toll it was taking. He had not tried to find out how many users had died. He had not "personally reviewed" *any* studies on the Shield's safety or effectiveness. When asked if he had "any curiosity" regarding the millions of dollars the company had been paying out in punitive damages to settle lawsuits, his answer was, "No."[14] The case of William Forrest, vice-president and general counsel of A. H. Robins, further strains belief. He has been described by E. Claiborne Junior as one of the company's "two most instrumental" persons in the Dalkon Shield situation. He was in effect in charge of all Shield matters and related legal issues for over a decade. In a trial proceeding, Forrest testified that his wife had worn a Shield until it was surgically removed. She had also had a hysterectomy. Although IUD removals and hysterectomies were frequently connected and simultaneous events for many infected Shield wearers, Forrest steadfastly denied any connection in his wife's case and gave vague and widely differing dates for the two events. He and his wife, he explained, did not discuss such matters in detail. Indeed, Forrest gave a series of confusing accounts of his wife's hysterectomy and its possible relationship to the Shield she had worn.

Q: Did her doctor advise her that her hysterectomy was in any way related to the Dalkon Shield?

A: Not that I know of, no, sir.

Q: Did you ever ask her that?

A: I don't recall. I may have asked her that. I don't recall the doctor telling her that. . . .

Q: . . . Are you telling the ladies and gentlemen of the jury that you and your wife have never had a discussion concerning whether or not the Dalkon Shield played a part in her hysterectomy?

A: Well, certainly, as I indicated to you, we had very general discussions. Now, if I asked her whether that played a part, I don't recall specifically if I did. If I did, to my knowledge, there was no indication that it did.[15]

The company's response to all claims of faulty product design and limited testing procedures has been counter assertions or counter claims regarding the faulty or improper use of the product by the user or the physician. The company has steadfastly maintained that there were no special dangers inherent in the device. In a report to FDA they stated: "Robins believes that serious scientific questions exist about whether the Dalkon Shield poses a significantly different risk of infection than other IUDs." Their continuous theme has been that doctors, not the device, have caused any infections associated with the Shield. The company was committed to the notion that pregnancy and removal rates could be kept extremely low by proper placement of the Shield. They also contended that user abuse played a part in the Shield's supposed malfunctioning. They defined user abuse as poor personal hygiene habits, sexual promiscuity or excessive sexual activity, or physical tampering with the device itself.

According to three different independent investigative reports,[16] the company's public face of calm denial and counterargument masked an internal conspiring to conceal information from the public, the court system, and the FDA. These reports (books) claim documented evidence of the multilevel cover-up. They claim that Robins quashed all documentation debating and contesting Dr. Hugh Davis's celebrated pregnancy rate of only 1.1 percent, and that Robins knew of the real significance and traumatic effect of the wicking process of the tail string but did nothing about it. Not only did the company know that the nylon cord used on the tail could degenerate and cause infection, but as early as the summer of 1972 the company was warned in writing by one of its chief consultants, Dr. Thad Earl, that pregnant women should have the Shield immediately removed to avoid "abortion and septic infection." These reports also contend that on at least three separate occasions executives and officials of Robins lost or destroyed company files and records specifically requested by the Federal Appellate Courts and the FDA.

By May 1974 Robins could no longer avoid the evidence presented to it by FDA implicating the Shield in numerous cases of spontaneous septic abortions and in the death of at least four women as a result. These findings were disclosed in a letter sent by the company to 120,000 doctors. In June 1974 Robins suspended the U.S. distribution and sale of the Shield. In January 1975 Robins called back and completely removed the Shield from the market. The company termed the action a "market withdrawal," not a recall, because it was undertaken voluntarily and not at the direct order of FDA. In September 1980 Robins again wrote the medical community suggesting as a purely precautionary measure that doctors remove the Shield from their patients. In October 1984 Robins initiated a $4 million television, newspaper, and magazine advertising campaign warning and recommending that all women still wearing the device have it removed at Robins's expense. In April 1985 Robins publicly set aside $615 million to settle legal claims from women who had used the Shield. This reserve is the largest provision of its kind to date in a product liability case. In May 1985 a jury in Wichita, Kansas, awarded nearly $9 million to a woman who had charged that the use of the Shield caused her to undergo a hysterectomy. The award was the largest ever made in the history of litigation involving the Shield. Officials of the Robins Company felt that adverse decisions of this magnitude could mean that their $615 million fund would prove to be inadequate. On August 21, 1985, Robins filed for Chapter 11 protection, citing litigation relating to the Shield as the main cause for its actions. Company spokesmen said that it hoped that the Federal Bankruptcy Court in Richmond would set up a payment schedule that would enable it to survive while insuring that victims "would be treated fairly." E. Claiborne Robins, Jr., called it "essential that we move to protect the company's economic viability against those who would destroy it for the benefit of a few."[17] The intriguing financial irony in all of this is that when Robins filed for Chapter 11 it had already spent, at a conservative estimate, $500 million in settlements, litigation losses, and legal fees for a product it had only manufactured for three years and from which it had only realized $500,000 in real profits![18]

In all candor it must be remembered that Robins's actions are not without danger. To the extent that Robins is using Chapter 11 as a shelter against the rush of product-liability litigation, the company is nevertheless taking a gamble. Robins must now operate under the eye of a federal bankruptcy judge, and as Lawrence King, Professor of Law at NYU, has said in regard to the Manville case, "Once you file, there is always a risk of liquidation."[19] For example, as part of their reorganization arrangement with the court, Robins agreed to a class action procedure in which they would begin a 91 nation advertisement campaign to announce to all former users their right to file a claim for compensation for any health problems that may have been caused by the Shield. All potential claimants are given a case number and sent a questionnaire to determine if they qualify for a financial settlement. As of June 1986 more than 300,000 claims have been filed against Robins![20] Numbers such as these may completely overwhelm the bankruptcy court's ability to reorganize and reestablish the company on a sound financial basis.

Given all of this data, perhaps there is only one thing we can say with certainty in regard to Robins's production of the Dalkon Shield: "In the pharmaceutical world, products that fail can cripple companies as well as people."[21]

AN UPDATE

Since filing for Chapter 11 in 1985 A. H. Robins has received at least three serious takeover bids. Two of these bids were made by the Rorer Group of Philadelphia and Sanofi the Paris-based pharmaceutical and cosmetics house. Both were rejected primarily because of their inability or unwillingness to guarantee the $2.475 billion escrow fund that the court has mandated be established for the payment of all possible liability and injury claims now pending against Robins.[22] On July 26, 1988, however, Judge Robert R. Merhige approved a plan for the acquisition of Robins by American Home Products of New York. Under this plan, American Home would pay Robins' shareholders about $700 million in American Home stock and provide for most of the Dalkon Shield trust fund with Aetna Life and Casualty Co. contributing $425 million. The judge decreed that since 94 percent of the Shield claiments and 99 percent of the Robins' stockholders approved of the plan, the reorganization, pending appeal, would become final on August 25, 1988.[23]

Yet even in an era of corporate raiders and mergers, why would so many major organizations want to take over a company bogged down in bankruptcy proceedings?

> The answer lies in such mundane but popular items as Robitussin and Dimetapp cold medicines, Chap Stick lip balm and Sergeant's flea-and-tick collars. These are among the products that make Robins one of the most profitable bankrupt companies in history. In the first three quarters of 1987,

Robins earned $60 million on sales of $621 million, compared with profits of $55 million on revenues of $579 million during the same period of 1986.[24]

Nevertheless, as Guerry Thorton Jr., a lawyer for the Dalkon Shield Victims Association, has pointed out, "the plans confirmation was a phenomenal success story. It has set a precedent by not allowing Robins to escape liability by filing for bankruptcy."[25]

NOTES

1. A. R. Gini, "Manville: The Ethics of Economic Efficiency?" *Journal of Business Ethics,* 3 (1984), p. 66.

2. *Time,* September 2, 1985, p. 32.

3. Morton Mintz, *At Any Cost* (New York: Pantheon Books, 1985), p. 25.

4. Ibid., p. 29.

5. Ibid., p. 82.

6. Ibid., pp. 29–31.

7. Ibid., pp. 86–88.

8. Ibid., pp. 81, 82.

9. *FDA Consumer,* May 1981, p. 32.

10. Morton Mintz, "At Any Cost," *The Progressive,* November 1985, p. 21.

11. *At Any Cost,* pp. 131–48 and 149–72.

12. *FDA Consumer,* July–August 1983, p. 2.

13. *Wall Street Journal,* April 11, 1985, p. 1.

14. Mintz, "At Any Cost," *The Progressive,* p. 24.

15. Mintz, *At Any Cost,* p. 111.

16. Mintz, *At Any Cost* (New York: Pantheon Books, 1985). Sheldon Engelmayer and Robert Wagman, *Lord's Justice* (New York: Anchor Press/Doubleday, 1985). Susan Perry and Jim Dawson, *Nightmare: Women and the Dalkon Shield* (New York: Macmillan Publishing, 1985).

17. *New York Times,* August 22, 1985, pp. 1, 6.

18. *Time,* November 26, 1984, p. 86.

19. Gini, "Manville: The Ethics of Economic Efficiency?" p. 68.

20. *Wall Street Journal,* June 26, 1986, p. 10.

21. *U.S. News and World Report,* September 2, 1985, p. 12.

22. *Time,* January 11, 1988, p. 59.

23. *New York Times—National Edition,* July 27, 1988, p. 32.

24. *Time,* January 11, 1988, p. 59.

25. *New York Times—National Edition,* July 27, 1988, p. 32.

QUESTIONS FOR DISCUSSION

1. Is A. H. Robins telling the truth about its knowledge of the health factors involved in the use of the Dalkon Shield? Is it true that they had no awareness of the connection between PID and spontaneous septic abortions and the nylon tail of the Shield? Or is it the case, as many of their critics contend, that they have conspired for more than sixteen years to both deny and cover up any knowledge of the short- and long-term effects of wearing the Shield?

2. Even if Robins is not guilty of conspiring to misinform its customers, why didn't simple prudence lead the company to go public immediately when "single physician experience" and the results of their own and outside testing procedures indicated from the beginning that there were serious drawbacks, limitations, and dangers inherent in the product? Moreover, after suspending production in 1974 because of FDA findings, why did Robins wait until 1984 to recommend that all women still wearing the Shield have it removed?

3. Is the 1978 Federal Bankruptcy code a proper valid means of seeking relief from immediate and possible future liability?

Essay
Stocks, Bonds,
and Insider Trading

Mark Schneider

I. INTRODUCTION:[1]

With the recent explosion in corporate takeover activity, an important set of moral issues is brought to the fore. Are corporate raiders and inside traders glowing examples of capitalist free marketeering at its best? Or, are they selfish criminals exploiting society and the economy for personal gain, with no regard for the effect on others? What are the moral implications of insider trading and corporate raiding?

Recent developments in and around Wall Street have left corporate management, investors in general, as well as the general public scared and shocked. We are living in an era of increased malfeasance in the stock market (or at least with an increased awareness of such activity) as well as an increase in corporate takeovers, mergers, and downsizing. While some of the *financial* effects of this activity are reasonably well known, there are many *moral* issues raised by this activity that are relatively less known. I will confine this discussion of insider trading to those transactions involving takeovers, even though this is by no means the only arena of insider trading.[2] The morality (or immorality) of insider trading can be divorced from the moral implications of takeovers in general, and this discussion will respect this distinction.

II. INSIDER TRADING

A. General Comments

Several years ago I attended a well-advertised public sale of a major luxury hotel's furnishings at what were alleged to be liquidation prices. The sale was part of the hotel's redecoration and refurnishing activity. Included in the sale were silverware, plates, crystal from the dining rooms, elaborate sconces, linens, etc. As it turned out, the sale drew much larger crowds than the hotel had anticipated; one had to wait in line for over an hour to enter the room where the sale merchandise was being displayed for sale. The sale was quite disappointing, as the hotel staff had been given first crack at the merchandise the evening before the sale was opened to the public. While there was certainly nothing illegal about this, it was quite disappointing to find that "all of the good stuff" was gone even before the sale had begun. The hotel's behavior smacked of unfairness, especially because interested buyers had had to wait in line so long. That is, many people would have behaved differently, had they known that the hotel employees had first crack at the sale merchandise. Many people might not have attended. In some sense, the sale really began before its publicized starting time.

Insider trading strikes most people as involving the same sort of unfairness as the hotel sale, although to a much greater degree. After all, the stock market is supposed to be fair. Insider trading—"exploiting advance knowledge of an important development to buy or sell stock before the public knows about it"[3]—is illegal and is almost universally thought to be immoral. However, the concept of insider trading itself, as well as the immorality of insider trading may be more difficult to explain than is generally thought.

On the one hand, playing the stock market involves decisions under uncertainty. Clearly, the more relevant information one possesses about one's impending stock transactions in particular, and prevailing market conditions in general, the more likely one is to achieve the desired result— profit (or at least minimizing one's losses). That is, when faced with a decision under uncertainty, it is rational to try to minimize the amount of uncertainty. So a rational stock speculator should try to obtain as much information about the market as possible, either directly or by employing a competent broker. But the law appears to tell us that too much of a good thing is bad.

On the other hand, the stock market depends on the assumption that all information relevant to potential investors is *public*. The stock market is supposed to be a fair market, one in which everyone potentially has equal access to all information. It is claimed that the general public's faith in the stock market would be undermined if there was a general belief among investors that the stock market is rigged, or at least the plaything of a privileged few insiders. Such a belief can be the result of evidence of widespread insider trading, or stock manipulation.[4] Recent publicity of various cases of insider trading have already had such an effect; the average person is participating less and less in the stock market. This leaves the stock market in a position of being a private club for large institutional investors, and insiders. This is because small, private investors believe that the market is outside their control, in short, that they are at the whim of the "big boys." But, the insiders maintain their advantage in the stock market precisely because they can and do exert control over the market via inside information and stock manipulation.[5]

No one wants to gamble when the game is fixed to their disadvantage. Thus, at least one presumption against insider trading is that frequent insider trading will undermine confidence in the market, thereby undermining the market itself. Is there anything about insider trading that makes it immoral, over and above the fact that it can limit the general public's participation in the stock market?

Insider trading is generally conceived of as involving stock transactions based on privileged information gained by someone with a fiduciary responsibility to the company and its stockholders. But it is not always clear whether a particular stock transaction should be considered an instance of insider trading. To examine insider trading from a moral perspective, it is important to get as clear an understanding as possible of what exactly constitutes insider trading. Only then can we assess the moral issues raised by this sort of behavior.

B. How Insider Trading in Takeovers Works

Takeovers can involve many individuals outside both companies involved in the takeover process, among them lawyers, accountants, and investment bankers. This is because the potential purchaser does not always have all of the resources required to execute the takeover all by itself. The price of the stock of a company rumored to be "in play", that is, facing takeover activity, usually goes up, often dramatically. Thus, it is clearly profitable to buy such stock prior to the general public being made aware of the takeover intentions of the buying company. Consequently it is also important to maintain the secrecy of takeover intentions. In fact, anticipating takeovers, or even mere rumors of takeovers, is so lucrative that there is even a specialized category of investment professionals called arbitragers. Arbitragers specialize in speculation involving stocks of companies potentially involved in takeover or merger activity. Clearly it is in the best interest of these "arbs," as they are known in the investment community, to have as much knowledge as possible concerning takeovers. Where, however, is the line to be drawn between good research activity—which is both moral and legal—and inside information—which is illegal and generally believed to be immoral? There are several borderline types of cases. For example, suppose that stockholding managers in a company buy more stock in their own company based merely on the belief that the new CEO is far superior to the one that has just been replaced? Or, suppose that an investment banking house passes information from its loan department (where investors go to borrow money for takeover attempts) to its investment department (which buys stocks with company funds)? Even the law is relatively vague about this matter.[6] Consider the following examples:

Case 1. A printer prepares sensitive financial reports for company A concerning their takeover plans for company B, then buys shares in company B.

Case 2. A bartender at a Wall Street bar buys and sells stocks based on conversations that he overhears from his clients, all knowledgeable professional members of the investment community.

Case 3. An investment banker who has agreed to help finance the takeover of company B by company A, invests in a block of company B's stock.

Case 4. A noted Wall Street columnist, R. Foster Winans, whose job involves writing about stock trends (in a column called "Heard on the Street"), including recommending particular stocks, sells information from his column prior to its publication.

Case 5. Ivan Boesky receives information from consultants hired by company A to investigate the financial worthiness of acquiring company B. Ivan Boesky then buys a large block of shares in company B prior to any public knowledge of company A's intentions. For example, *The New York Times*[7] reported on the following four transactions from which Ivan Boesky allegedly profited by having conspired with Martin Siegel, then an investment banker with Kidder, Peobody & Co.

1. Boesky bought stock in Carnation, the subject of a tender offer by Nestle. Siegel was a financial adviser to Carnation. Boesky made $28.3 million buying and selling Carnation stock.
2. Siegel advised Diamond Shamrock about their tender offer to Natomas. Boesky made $4.8 million on Natomas stock.
3. Siegel acted as investment banker to Martin Marietta regarding their tender offer to Bendix. Boesky made $120 thousand on Bendix stock.
4. Boesky made $220 thousand on Getty stock, while Siegel was an adviser to Getty, regarding matters of internal control of Getty.

Boesky was also being fed information from an investment banker named Dennis Levine. Boesky's conspiratorial activity allegedly involved sharing his profits with his sources of information. What seems questionable in these cases is the exchange of information between Boesky and his confederates. Should we conceive of these examples as conspiratorial insider trading? Or, can it be argued that Boesky's activity was simply careful consultation with experts; and/or the paying of consulting fees to those experts? Did Boesky have a right to that information in advance of its disclosure to the general public? Were Siegel and Levine under any obligation to *not* disclose that information?

C. Moral Investigation

Some people claim that "gleaning a good tip, over hors d'oeuvres or from the dentist, is precisely what playing the market is all about."[8] In fact, the SEC has suffered setbacks involving regulating insider trading when the U.S. Supreme Court, in cases 1 and 2 above, claimed that the individuals involved did not have any duty to refrain from using what they had learned.[9] The court appears to be suggesting that these cases are more like the doctor or stockbroker who gives free advice to family members or who acts according to special information he or she possesses in virtue of being a trained professional.

On the other hand, some argue that even these cases involve misappropriation of information—a form of stealing. It is frequently argued, under the rubric of a view known as the "agent-principal thesis," that employees or outside consultants are implicitly or explicitly obligated to maintain the privacy and secrecy of information gleaned while on the job. That is, accepting employment or consulting work involves promising that secrecy and privacy will be maintained, and that inside information gleaned via consultancy and/or employment will neither be used for personal gain nor disclosed to members of the general public. This doctrine is analogous to the privileged status of relationships between doctor and patient, lawyer and client, and other professional-client relationships. Acting on inside information gleaned as an employee or outside consultant can tip off market analysts about impending transactions. In general, having trade secrets fall into the hands of competitors or the general public can harm the company to whom those secrets belong. In particular, given that takeover rumors boost stock prices, a definite harm to the acquiring company can result from inside information being prematurely used or leaked. However, it is far from clear whether and when any individual is morally or legally obligated to refrain from using legally obtained information for personal gain.

Another problem with assessing both the legality and morality of insider trading involves the seeming lack of a victim as a result of insider trading. This involves the idea that the criminality of an act should, at least in part, derive from that act harming someone, its putative victim. One might argue that the seller, unaware of the takeover rumor, is selling himself short and is therefore a victim. But, it seems clear that not all voluntary sales, under imperfect information, are immoral. If you sell me "that old piece of junk" and don't know (but I do) that it is worth slightly more than you thought, I am under no moral or legal obligation to inform you of its real value. Thus it is far from clear whether a person who sells stock unwittingly to an insider trader is the victim of an immoral transaction. Neither is it clear whether the alleged criminality or immorality of insider trading depends on there being a clearly specifiable victim of such activity.

According to Daniel Fischel, a teacher of corporate law at the University of Chicago,

> The idea that the stock market should be a level playing field, with everyone having equal access to information and an equal chance to profit, is rubbish. Obviously a market professional who spends all his time analyzing stocks is going to have an advantage over the casual investor, and there's nothing illegal about that.[10]

While it is abundantly clear that stockbrokers know more about the market than the average individual, their knowledge is accessible to the interested public. The point is not *whether* you knew, but whether you *could have* known! That is, when I am ill, I might consult a doctor. The doctor has specialized knowledge about illnesses and their cures. Many of my friends do not possess this knowledge. But, as it is contained in libraries and available from college courses, my friends and I could come to possess this specialized medical knowledge. That is, the expert knowledge may be hard earned, but it is not secret.

Nonetheless, according to Henry Manne, Dean of the George Mason University Law School,

> Almost all insider trading should be legal. . . . allowing people with pertinent information to trade on it would help the market reflect actual stock values more quickly and accurately. It would also prevent the abrupt price jumps that now occur when a major development is eventually announced. And . . . wire fraud and mail fraud statutes can readily take care of instances where confidential information is stolen or used in a clearly wrongful way.[11]

NOTES

1. I would like to thank Thomas Donaldson, A. R. Gini, Benjamin Schneider, and Marland O. Webb for their helpful comments on earlier versions of this case study.

2. Others include announcements of new technology, climate and conditions relevant to agriculture.

3. *The New York Times*, February 14, 1987, p. 23.

4. In fact, *mere belief* in such improprieties, rather than actual misconduct, causes a lack of faith in the stock market on the part of the general public.

5. Large investors also have access to computers that allow them to respond to market information much faster than the average investor.

6. My concern here, however, is not with the law, per se.

7. February 14, 1987, p. 21.

8. *The New York Times*, 7/21/86, p. 23.

9. As mentioned in *The New York Times*, 7/21/87, p. 23.

10. Ibid.

11. Ibid.

QUESTIONS

1. Under what circumstances would exploiting inside information be moral or immoral?

2. Should there be specific limits placed on the use of insider information?

Essay
Leveraged Buyouts:
America Pays the Price

Robert B. Reich

> When the capital development of a country
> becomes a byproduct of the activities of a
> casino, the job is likely to be ill-done. The
> measure of success attained by Wall
> Street . . . cannot be claimed as one of the
> outstanding triumphs of laissez-faire
> capitalism.
> JOHN MAYNARD KEYNES, *"The General Theory of
> Employment, Interest and Money" (1936)*

First came the mammoth takeovers. Then the insider-trading scandals. Then the stock-market crash of October 1987. Then the giant leveraged buyouts, culminating in the $24.88 billion takeover of RJR Nabisco Inc. Then Drexel Burnham's guilty plea to criminal fraud.

America has had enough. Even by the cynical standards of the 1980's, Wall Street is giving greed a bad name.

In a typical takeover, the raider buys enough stock to gain control of a company; in a leveraged buyout, a company's own executives are often among the buyers. A popular way to finance these deals is through "junk" bonds—I.O.U.'s paying hefty interest, reflecting their higher-than-normal risks.

Only a portion of the money involved in these activities is actually used up in the takeover and buyout process. Most of its circulates among investment bankers, arbitragers, portfolio managers, brokers and other financial intermediaries, as they trade shares of stock in companies about to be taken over, or about to be disassembled, or they make bets on whether other financial intermediaries will expect such companies to be taken over or disassembled, and so on, in an almost infinite regression of trades and takeover bets, and bets on takeover bets, and trades on bets on takeover bets.

Defenders of such antics argue that they are justified by "economic fundamentals." Corporate executives speak of wondrous gains from "synergy"—the dynamic effects of combining managerial talent, research laboratories and production facilities, making the whole greater than the sum of the parts. They then wax with equal enthusiasm over the gains to be had

Source: Robert B. Reich, *Leveraged Buyouts: America Pays the Price, New York Times Sunday Magazine,* January 19, 1989 pp. 32, 36, 40. Copyright © 1989 by The New York Times Company. Reprinted by permission.

from disassembling and selling off piecemeal such parts, thus making the sum of the parts (at least in dollar terms) greater than the whole.

Through it all, they exhibit faith—endless, indomitable faith—in the hidden, *potential* value of the companies being purchased, relative to the price they could currently fetch on the stock market. In other words, the prices listed on the stock exchange understate what the companies are potentially worth.

Most of this is nonsense, or worse. The record of the 1970's and 80's is dismally clear on this point. There is little evidence to suggest that mergers have on the average enhanced the profitability or productivity of merging enterprises. The subsequent rush to dismember suggests, in fact, the reverse.

In 1985, R. J. Reynolds, the giant tobacco corporation, merged with Nabisco, the giant food-processing company. At the time, the merger was hailed as a brilliant strategy, through which the tobacco company would diversify into foods. Just three years later, the newly merged company became the object of a mammoth contest between armies of investment bankers pledging billions of dollars for the privilege of breaking it up once again.

Although takeover defenders claim that mergers and acquisitions are not a speculative game but a means by which the financial market insures that money is available for new investment, close examination belies this view. Wall Street's dynamism has little to do with the financing of new commercial ventures. During the 1980's, new issues of common stock averaged only about 1 percent of the total stock outstanding; the action was in the 99 percent of shares already in circulation.

The American economy as a whole has not benefited demonstrably from all this activity. Since the mid-1970's, when most of this began, productivity gains have slowed. Adjusted for inflation, average wages have stagnated, corporate profits have been lackluster and the Dow Jones industrial average has yet to regain the peak it achieved in January 1973. And only the public-relations office of the United States Chamber of Commerce would contend that American companies have stayed competitive with those of Japan, West Germany, South Korea and other places around the globe where, incidentally, hostile takeovers and leveraged buyouts rarely, if ever, occur.

If there is little economic justification, why does the wheeling and dealing continue?

Let us go back to 1974. That year, the International Nickel Company decided to buy up enough shares in the Electric Storage Battery Company to give International Nickel control over the board of directors of Electric Storage, and thus allow International Nickel to run the company. International Nickel argued that its nickel powder used in rechargeable batteries made Electric Storage a perfect complement. But Electric Storage did not want to be taken over and thus regarded International Nickel's act as hostile. International Nickel won.

Before International Nickel made its takeover bid, Wall Street had viewed such aggression as unseemly, if not unethical. One didn't just take over a company. A company was its managers and employees, its trademark and reputation. These attributes could not be purchased against its will—or so it was assumed.

Then Wall Street's other shoe fell. In 1975, the Securities and Exchange Commission decreed that commissions paid on stock transactions were no longer to be based on fixed rates, but were to be negotiable. Henceforth, brokers' commissions were to be subject to the free market. Within two years, revenues on Wall Street plunged $600 million. This was no time for niceties. The Street had to forage for new sources of earnings, and hostile takeovers looked like just the place to start.

Of mergers and acquisitions each costing $1 million or more, there were just 10 in 1970; in 1980, there were 94; in 1986, there were 346. A third of such deals in the 1980's were hostile. The 1980's also saw a wave of giant leveraged buyouts. Mergers, acquisitions and L.B.O.'s, which had accounted for less than 5 percent of the profits of Wall Street brokerage houses in 1978, ballooned into an estimated 50 percent of profits by 1988. And profitable it has been. Last year, Wall Street firms earned about $2.2 billion before taxes, compared with $1.1 billion in 1987.

Deal-making has proved particularly lucrative because every time industrial assets are rearranged, the paper entrepreneurs earn money. The larger and more complex the escapade, the more money they earn. And here is the critical point: paper entrepreneurs not only do the deals, but also advise their clients (corporate directors, chief executives, pension-fund managers) about when and whether such deals should be made.

The RJR Nabisco deal generated almost $1 billion in fees, including an estimated $153 million in advisory fees; $294 million in financing fees for investment banks, and $325 million in commercial-bank fees. Lawyers' fees, which are usually not disclosed, are estimated to have run in the millions.

Should the economy collapse, paper entrepreneurs are prepared. Investment banks already have amassed funds for "deleveraged buyouts," which will do the reverse of what was done during boom times: buy back the I.O.U.'s of the bankrupt companies at a small fraction of their face value and issue new shares of stock to the remaining creditors. Then sell the newly reorganized companies—now free of debt—for a fat profit.

Through all this, the historical relationship between product and paper has been turned upside down. Investment bankers no longer think of themselves as working for the corporations with which they do business. These days, corporations seem to exist for the investment bankers.

Whole departments of investment banks now scan corporate America for businesses ripe for the plucking. It is as if doctors or auto mechanics went from house to house, instructing the occupants on what they must do to avoid death or breakdown, and then ripping them or their cars apart to make the prescribed repairs.

In fact, investment banks are replacing the publicly held industrial corporations as the largest and most powerful economic institutions in America. Twenty-five years ago, most investment banks were small partnerships. Today, many are giants. In 1987, Drexel Burnham Lambert posted earnings estimated at $500 million, putting it right up there with Xerox, Monsanto and Kraft.

A quarter-century ago, the titans of American industry were chief executive officers of major industrial corporations. Today, as in the late 19th century, they are investment bankers. Henry R. Kravis and George R. Roberts, two principal partners of Kohlberg, Kravis, Roberts & Company, each earn about $70 million a year. The firm is the majority owner of some 20 companies, including Owens-Illinois and Safeway and (as soon as the paperwork is completed) RJR Nabisco as well. Rarely have so few earned so much for doing so little. Never have so few exercised such power over how the slices of the American pie are rearranged.

I do not want to suggest that all efforts directed at rearranging corporate assets are necessarily wasteful. To the extent that they allocate capital more efficiently to where it can be most productive, they make our economy perform better. But given the recent record of rampant speculation and finagling, one must ask whether these benefits are worth what we are paying for them, in terms of both direct costs and future productivity.

The current obsessions with asset-rearranging harms productivity in four related ways:

Myopia. Research aimed at developing fundamentally new technologies is apt to go slowly, yielding little or no profit for many years. Even many service businesses require years of steady investment in quality controls and personnel training. All this demands a willingness to invest now for returns in a distant future.

But fear of a takeover, or the necessity of paying off a large loan, forces managers to focus on the short term—and cut back on long-term investments. General Electric's costly acquisition of RCA, for example, resulted in less research for both. In 1987, G.E. cut its research spending by $300 million; under new management, RCA's famed David Sarnoff Research Center—for decades an incubator of television technology—slashed its staff by 25 percent. A survey last year by the National Science Foundation determined that takeovers and leveraged buyouts were to blame for a marked slowdown in corporate research-and-development spending.

The changing pattern of stock ownership has encouraged mergers and acquisitions, contributing to the emphasis on immediate gains. Not long ago, the majority of stocks were owned by individuals and many of them held on to their shares for years. It was not unusual for such an investor to take a mildly proprietary interest in how his or her company was doing, and what it was planning to do. Today, 70 percent of the volume of stock trading is done by institutions, mainly mutual funds, pension funds and insurance companies—which are under pressure to produce the short-term earnings that clients demand.

On the management side, the motivation is similar. The frenetic movement of corporate assets engenders a similar shifting of managerial talent. Top executives are dismissed, or they are lured to another newly rearranged corporation. They feel no loyalty to their present company, which, after all, is regarded by its directors and stockholders as little more than a collection of financial assets. Thus, the average term of office for today's chief executive officers is only five to six years.

If you compare those industries in which our competitive position continues to decline—semiconductors, consumer electronics, machine tools—with those in Japan, South Korea and West Germany, you will find the same myopic pattern. The American companies have lower research-and-development budgets and older plant and equipment.

Wasted Talent. Asset-rearranging also harms productivity by using up the energies of some of our most talented citizens. Paper entrepreneurs are responsible for the nation's most innovative economic strategies. The result is a "brain drain" from product to paper.

Today's corporate executives spend an increasing portion of their days fending off takeovers, finding companies to acquire or responding to depositions in lawsuits instead of worrying about the quality of their products and how they can be distributed more efficiently. More of our top corporate executives are trained in law and finance than in any other field—in contrast to the case three decades ago when most were trained in marketing, engineering and sales.

Meanwhile, our best minds are increasingly drawn to the pie-dividing professions of law and finance, and away from pie-enlarging professions like engineering and science. (My most talented students continue to march to Wall Street where they are promised starting salaries and bonuses of $100,000 or more.) Although graduate programs in law and finance are booming, those in engineering and science and foundering—again in contrast to other industrialized nations.

In 1987, the majority of students graduating from American universities with doctorates in engineering were foreign nationals, most of whom, presumably, will return to their home countries. Out of every 10,000 citizens in Japan, only 1 is a lawyer and 3 are accountants; in the United States, 20 are lawyers and 40 are accountants. Out of the same group in Japan, 400 are engineers; in the United States, only 70 are engineers.

There is a basic distortion here. The bankers and lawyers who helped RJR Nabisco move out of equities and into debt late last year earned about $1 billion for their efforts. This sum exceeded the total amount devoted by the United States in all of 1988 to the search for a cure for AIDS.

Debt. Typically, the money required to rearrange industrial assets—to mount hostile takeovers, to defend against hostile takeovers, to return a company to private ownership by repurchasing the publicly owned shares of stock—is borrowed. High leverage creates extraordinary opportunities for profit, but it also creates substantial danger, should the economy sputter and interest payments be missed. This was the lesson we were supposed to have learned in the 1920's, when Americans last went on a speculative spree with borrowed money.

Corporate debt in the 1980's has reached alarming proportions. Twenty-five years ago, the average American corporation paid 16 cents of every dollar of pre-tax earnings in interest on its debt. In the 1970's, it was 33 cents. Since 1980, it has been more than 50 cents. Few highly leveraged corporations have yet succumbed to bankruptcy, but most of their debt has been accumulated since 1983, during an economic expansion.

Economic history suggests that recessions do occur periodically. The Brookings Institution, not known for its alarmist rhetoric, undertook to examine the effects on corporate America of a recession similar in severity to that which rocked the nation in 1974 and 1975. The Brookings computer simulation revealed that, with the levels of debt prevailing in the late 1980's, 1 in 10 American companies would succumb to bankruptcy.

Distrust. An economy based on asset-rearranging has a final disadvantage. It invites zero-sum games, in which one group's gain is another's loss. As those engaged in rearranging the slices of the pie become more numerous and far more wealthy than those dedicated to enlarging the pie, trust declines. Without trust, people won't dedicate themselves to common goals. They will turn their energies instead to defending their own interests. In a corporation, this means declining productivity.

There are signs that a vicious spiral has begun, as each corporate player seeks to improve its standard of living at the expense of another's.

Corporate raiders transfer to themselves, and other shareholders, part of the income of employees by forcing the latter to agree to lower wages. (T.W.A.'s stock price rose after Carl Icahn took over, largely because T.W.A. employees were forced to accept reduced wages.)

Corporate borrowers utilizing high-yield "junk" bonds make off with the gains anticipated by regular bondholders and other creditors, who never bargained for the kind of risk to which the enterprise is now exposed. (After the mammoth deal was announced, regular RJR Nabisco bondholders suddenly discovered that their bonds were worth far less than before because of the new debt load.)

Executives deprive stockholders of their gains by paying greenmail—exorbitant payoffs—to would-be acquirers or by undertaking a leveraged buyout and then reselling the company at a higher price.

And then there are the investors who rob other investors of potential market gains by illegally trading on inside information.

The catch is that these groups seeking to grab assets from one another are often the very groups whose collaboration is necessary for real growth to occur. The surest path to greater productivity is through collaboration—blue collar and white collar, investors and managers, creditors and stockholders, investors and employees.

How are we to break out of the downward spiral of asset rearranging? Defenders of free-market orthodoxy argue that nothing should be done, on the principle that less government intervention is always preferable to more. What they fail to comprehend (or to admit) is that the Government already motivates paper entrepreneurs through tax and securities laws.

The choice is not between more or less intervention, but between different laws designed to motivate different behavior. On occasion, when the motive has been to increase productivity, takeovers and leveraged buyouts have been beneficial. To reduce the incentive to speculate, the Government could start by taking these steps:

First, make debt less attractive. Many deals are done because junk bonds have all the benefits and risks of equity, but the tax advantages of debt. For the corporation, interest payments are deductible; dividends are, in fact, taxed twice—as income to the corporation and then as income to the investor. Rather than engage in a fruitless debate about the what's debt and what's equity, Congress should allow the deductibility of all such payments, regardless of whether they are called dividends or interest—but only up to a certain ceiling. Above the ceiling (say, the Federal funds rate plus 2 percent), the payments are assumed to be dividends, and are thus taxed as income.

Alternatively, bar corporate raiders or leveraged-buyout moguls from deducting interest payments on very large borrowings (exceeding some fixed percentage of a company's assets) used to purchase corporate stock. If a prospective takeover or leveraged buyout promises new efficiencies, the deal should be sufficiently attractive to survive without the extra sweetener of a tax incentive. (Caution: with the tax laws of many foreign countries allowing interest deductions on takeover loans, foreigners would have an edge in taking over American companies—unless we levied a special tax on foreign takeovers.)

To discourage dangerous levels of indebtedness, the Federal Reserve Board should establish guidelines discouraging banks from providing easy credit for excessively leveraged deals. (Commercial banks, still coping with precarious third-world debtors, have been funding more than half of leveraged buyouts.)

To encourage the long view, stockholders who invest for the long haul should be rewarded; speculators, penalized. On assets held for five months or less, the capital-gains tax rate should be high (say, 50 percent); on assets held for five years or more, low (10 percent). This "five and five" plan should result in no overall diminution of tax revenues, just a more beneficent allocation of incentives.

Or put a small sales tax on stocks. A one-half of 1 percent tax on every stock transaction would dampen the speculative urge and also raise about $10 billion a year for the Treasury.

Amend the securities laws to bar the more egregious forms of paper shuffling—golden parachutes (princely severance payments to departing top executives) and greenmail. Without these innovations, speculative deals would be less attractive.

Finally, enforce the antitrust laws. The Philip Morris Companies, owner of General Foods, recently acquired Kraft. The deal probably would not have withstood antitrust scrutiny a decade ago, when the antitrust division of the Justice Department and the Federal Trade Commission were more intent on antitrust enforcement.

What's the possibility of any of this being done? Washington's solicitude toward Wall Street should never be underestimated. The House Ways and Means Committee briefly considered removing interest deductions on takeover loans in 1987, but quickly scotched the proposal after Wall Street blamed it for having helped precipitate the crash. Moreover, in recent years, the denizens of Wall Street have been particularly generous in financing election campaigns.

Yet there are signs that the Street may finally have overreached. Reform is in the air. Last November, Senate minority leader Robert Dole raised the possibility of revising the tax code to curb acquisitions financed largely with borrowed funds. Alan Greenspan, chairman of the Federal Reserve Board, recently suggested curbs on bank lending for such escapades. Treasury Secretary Nicholas F. Brady also is interested in curbing Wall Street's excesses. Leading Democrats are sounding the alarm. Last week, the Senate Finance Committee began hearings on setting limits to mammoth takeovers and leveraged buyouts, and other Senate and House panels will be following suit.

Indeed, even top Wall Street bankers are saying enough is enough. They understand that without prudent reform now, politicians may overreact in the future and ban all giant takeovers and leveraged buyouts. Unless the reckless driving is soon curbed, Wall Street may be turned into a pedestrian mall.

Essay
The Case for Takeovers

Carl C. Icahn

The takeover boom is a treatment for a disease that is destroying American productivity: gross and widespread incompetent management. Takeovers are part of a free-market response, working to unseat corporate bureaucracies, control runaway costs and make America competitive again.

A most interesting, yet often ignored, fact about takeovers is that in all bids for control—hostile or friendly—a price much higher than current market value is paid for the company. This is generally referred to as a "premium for control." But, generally, what the acquirer is really saying when he or she pays this premium is that the company is actually worth more if the ability to remove top management exists.

In almost every takeover, the purchaser has been able to make the assets of the company more profitable and productive than the previous, entrenched management could. The corollary is that current management is not doing the proper job.

Top management in this country is mediocre, yet we do very little about it. Corporate executives are judged by their peers not on how profitable their departments are, but on how many people report to them. The

Source: Carl C. Icahn, *The Case for Takeovers, New York Times Sunday Magazine,* January 19, 1989, p. 34. Copyright © by The New York Times Company. Reprinted by permission.

chief executive officer's compensation is often based on the size of the company rather than on the company's profitability.

With a number of notable exceptions, American C.E.O.'s, while not the best and the brightest, are politically astute and possess finely honed survival instincts, which may explain why they generally select seconds-in-command who are not quite as bright as they are; smarter ones would constitute a threat. When the C.E.O. retires, however, that second-in-command takes the reins. We clearly have an anti-Darwinian principle working in our executive suite: the survival of the unfittest. At the same time, companies are burdened by layers of vice presidents who not only don't produce, but are often counterproductive.

We have, therefore, created a corporate welfare state.

The astounding and tragic thing is that nothing of significance is being done to correct the problem. We give lip service to "corporate democracy" and "accountability" but in reality they don't exist.

After World War II, we were unquestionably the greatest power in the world. We were the only country left with great productive machinery and a willing and healthy work force. Today, we are fast becoming a second-rate power with huge budget and trade deficits. Were the incompetent, inbred managements of many of our major corporations replaced by strong and capable leadership, we might still be able to save our economy from decline.

I've had some opportunities to test my thesis. In 1983, I took a major position in ACF Industries, a Fortune 500 company in the railcar manufacturing and leasing industry. Although I knew nothing about the railcar business when I took over, I have been able to increase the earnings of the basic operating company to $35 million from $4.5 million.

In 1986, I took control of T.W.A., which was on the brink of bankruptcy, having lost about $200 million in the previous year. I managed to eliminate more than $300 million a year in waste and bureaucracy; an additional $200 million a year in savings was provided by union concessions. I accomplished this without sacrificing revenue, and, in fact, improved the quality of service. Today, far from being in the red, we are setting earnings records; net earnings for 1988 were about $300 million.

Critics of takeovers say that we bust up companies. If this means that we sell off divisions that don't fit in with the main business and whose assets can be used more productively at another company, I proudly plead guilty. More of that is exactly what America needs to compete.

Another criticism is that "raiders" put people out of work. On a percentage basis, I have put far fewer people out of work at ACF and T.W.A. than have A.T.&T. and G.M. or, for that matter, other Fortune 500 companies in their restructurings. The difference is that I and other "raiders" usually eliminate the people who are most responsible for the mess—the "Top Brass."

In the last 20 years, Japan's total average percentage change in the rate of manufacturing productivity (as measured by output per hour) has been more than four times greater than America's. I believe that a major reason for this discrepancy is our lack of managerial talent and the strangling bureaucracy that exists in most of corporate America.

The productive engine of our country will simply not be able to support the war babies, who will begin to retire in the first part of the next century. Today, there are 3.4 workers per Social Security beneficiary. The ratio of workers per beneficiary may fall early in the next century to under 2, and shortly thereafter to just over 1. If we fail to make managements accountable and corporations more productive, the result will be economic chaos and rampant inflation.

A criticism often heard against trying to make poor management more accountable is that insistence on better performance might force management to concentrate on short-term goals rather than on research and long-term planning. This criticism is nonsense. It is analogous to saying, "Don't reprimand your 16-year-old for getting poor grades in high school because he or she may punish you by not planning for college." Moreover, if this were true, we would have witnessed intensive takeover activity in research-driven industries, such as pharmaceuticals, aerospace and high technology. That has not happened. Instead, the stocks of these companies are generally given a high value by analysts, which discourages takeover bids.

Most of the approximately 2,000 takeovers and leveraged buyouts since 1981 have been characterized by a redeployment of assets to create greater competitive and economic gains. The fact is that this decade has seen the highest business investment, as a proportion of gross national product, since World War II and has, in addition, brought greater research and development spending than we saw in the 1970's. The real problem is not that we are failing to do enough research and long-term planning, but that we are not productive enough to compete in world markets.

Since true corporate elections are a rarity, by far the most effective way to remove ineffective management and enhance productivity is through a takeover and/or a leveraged buyout.

The reason there is so much capital available for L.B.O.'s and takeovers is that tremendous amounts of capital are dammed up in pension funds. These funds must generate a certain return in order to support future retirees. Therefore, pension managers lend money for L.B.O.'s. The fund is taking most of the risk with little of the reward and admittedly, in some L.B.O.'s today there is too much debt and too much risk.

It would be far better for the economy if pension funds invested directly in a takeover rather than merely being lenders. This way, the pension plans would stand to profit much more from the success of the takeover, taking for themselves some of the huge profits now reaped by L.B.O. fund managers. Additionally, with pension funds as equity investors, much of the problem of debt overburdening now appearing in certain L.B.O.'s would disappear.

Perhaps more importantly, if pension plans were willing to invest in hostile takeovers, the mere knowledge of this fact would cause many managements to become more interested in enhancing shareholder value and by so doing, make their companies more productive.

A simple way to help clear the way for true accountability would involve passing a law to provide that, should a merger offer for any and all the stock of a company be made by a credible purchaser, the company would have to allow the shareholders to vote on the offer, and management would have to abide by the vote. Of course, during the time preceding the vote, managements would be permitted to campaign against the offer and/or find a higher offer. This would do away with unnecessary shark repellents, litigation and like deterrents, and open the way for responsible bids.

The assets of our country are mired in the quicksand of waste. If we do nothing to redeem our corporations, future historians will marvel at why, when we could have so easily. However, it is still not too late, and takeovers are an essential part of the solution.

Case Study
Oklahoma
Meets Wall Street

Paul Hirsch

> "We're still in business," said spokesman Steve Milburn. He said despite the fact that the company has shut down its famous oil well on the state capital grounds in Oklahoma City, along with its historic Burbank Field wells in Osage county, Phillips still has 8,000 producing wells in the U.S.[1] *Bartlesville Examiner-Enterprise August 1986*

Phillips Petroleum was on the ropes. The giant oil company dropped nearly 10,000 people between 1985 and 1987, close to 25 percent of its work force worldwide. Bartlesville, Oklahoma, its affluent, largely white-collar headquarters city of 38,000, was especially hard hit.

"Anyone with the brains God gave a grasshopper is not buying a house in Bartlesville," said one Phillips manager in summer 1986.[2] Two of the only retailers with something to smile about were the local U-Haul and Ryder trunk renters, whose volume always goes up "as people pack up to move on . . . 'If you wanted a truck today, you couldn't get one,'" said

Paul Hirsch, *Pack Your Own Parachute,* © 1987, Addison-Wesley Publishing Co., Inc., Reading, Massachusetts. Pages 1–13. Reprinted with permission.

Gordon Brown, owner of Bartlesville Auto Supply.[3] Social workers noticed a different kind of increase—in the amount of anxiety and tension among Phillips employees as they saw their job prospects dwindling. Even before the waves of layoffs and early retirements, Jerry Poppenhouse, art director at Phillips, told a reporter, "The mood now is, 'Who's going to be next?' "[4] Another manager and Bartlesville resident added, "Outsiders don't understand that even if you aren't laid off, or your co-workers aren't, you still go to church or scouts or soccer with someone who is."[5]

Phillips Petroleum, the nation's seventeenth largest industrial corporation and eighth biggest oil producer, was cash poor. Deeply in debt, it had to raise vast sums of money very quickly. Asked which of the company's far-flung operations might be for sale in 1985, Chairman and Chief Executive Officer William Douce said, "All of them—and that's no joke."[6] This included oil fields in Africa, Alaska, the Gulf of Mexico, and the North Sea around Holland—where Phillips had been the first to discover oil that helped Europe become less dependent on supplies from the Middle East. All or parts of these were soon sold, along with coal and geothermal facilities in Texas, Utah, Nevada, and California. In addition to selling off petroleum reserves and other properties, Phillips axed or delayed some big research and exploration projects.

Cutting back its work force and payroll was another policy Phillips adopted to raise cash. Nearly every employee was offered incentives to quit voluntarily before the company moved on to layoffs and terminations. People fifty-five or older were promised a larger pension if they signed up for early retirement immediately. A majority of long-service managers at all levels took the offer. Some were ready and welcomed the opportunity. But others felt rejected, helpless, and all alone.

"Some simply have resigned themselves to resigning," said one. "I mean to retiring without knowing if they would be able to get another job and if they will need one . . . Many would rather still be working, and not only just for the money."[7] Another recent retiree added:

> The ones I feel sorry for are those still in their middle fifties. Fifty-five is early to retire. There's no other work here right now, though if you want to go to California or New York you can probably start over. But it's not just a matter of getting in your car and going. Say you're a homeowner. If you were transferred the company would take it off your hands. But you're retired now. You have this real estate you can't dispose of. Right now I don't think you can even rent out many of the houses for sale. It's a tough situation.[8]

In spite of these hardships, Phillips employees and Bartlesville residents still considered themselves "lucky." Only seventeen months earlier, Phillips had won a crucial victory for them. It succeeded, against strong odds, in keeping the company independent and in Oklahoma. In an extraordinary four-month period etched in the memory of Bartlesville's small population, corporate raiders T. Boone Pickens and Carl Icahn each attempted to purchase Phillips Petroleum from its shareholders. "How would you feel," asked one Bartlesville citizen, "if Godzilla and Frankenstein both stomped through your town?"[9]

To beat them back, Phillips had repurchased much of its own stock and taken on billions of dollars in new debt to pay for it. Both current and former employees knew why the company had to raise so much cash. They knew their pain stemmed from the bills falling due for this victory. If employment was down here, many said, look at what happened to people at the other companies that tangled with T. Boone Pickens or blew themselves up to avoid him.

"Look at Gulf and its white knight, Chevron," exclaimed one Phillips staffer. "I have a good friend at Chevron. In another year or two they'll be operating both companies with the same number of employees Chevron had when they took Gulf over. That's 50 percent fewer people working than when the two companies were running separately."[10] Before driving Gulf into Chevron's embrace, Pickens had made profitable runs on Cities Service (in neighboring Tulsa), Superior Oil, Supron Energy, and General American Oil (which chose to be acquired by Phillips in 1983, rather than be taken over by Pickens's Mesa Petroleum Company). None of these companies exists independently any longer. "The other companies all lost their identities, and we feared that," commented another Phillips veteran. "Everybody's pleased Phillips was able to retain it. We're grateful the company is still intact."[11]

Soon after Phillips repulsed its invaders, one of its computer engineers, A. J. Lafaro, received an unusual request from Los Angeles, home of Unocal ("76") Oil. Pickens had selected Unocal as his next takeover target, and some of its employees remembered a "Boonebuster" T-shirt worn all over Bartlesville during the time Phillips was fighting the same battle. Lafaro had designed it at about the same time that the movie *Ghostbusters* was a big success. He superimposed the international symbol for "No" over a picture of Mr. Pickens, who also purchased some to give as Christmas presents. Unocal employees now wanted them for their impending struggle. Said one Phillips official, "Believe me, if they're going through anything like what we went through, they could use [them]!"[12]

The "Boonebuster" shirt is only one example of the enthusiasm and commitment Bartlesville citizens showed for Phillips during its bitter fights to stay independent. The community was shocked, angered, and scared at the possibility of losing any or all of the company to a corporate takeover. Here was the largest employer in the state brought to its knees, with its fate hinging on maneuvers in far-away boardrooms on Wall Street. "I get the feeling that a bunch of strangers are out there playing Russian roulette with the future of this community—this state, really—and I don't like it," said Josef Derryberry, a jeweler in Bartlesville.[13]

At a crisis forum of 8,000 residents, speakers discussing what the loss of Phillips would mean to the community and nation included the area's school superintendent, the director of the National Institute for Petroleum and Energy Research, the Sears manager at a newly built shopping mall, a former vice president of what had been the Cities Service Oil Company, student officers from the local high school, and the Osage Indian chief on whose nearby land Frank Phillips had originally struck oil. Rudy Taylor, a newspaper publisher in neighboring Caney, Kansas, received a standing ovation when he said:

> Without Phillips, we'd just be Mayberry R.F.D., and with Phillips we have a lot of confidence in our future and we have a world of ideas on how we can improve our little corner of the world . . . Our chief industry in Caney, Kansas, is Phillips Petroleum Company; it's been that way for over a half century and . . . because of their influence our community is a progressive one. We feel the Phillips influence in our schools, and in our places of business and in our churches and our lodges . . . We're in this fight with you and we're in it to win. Let's do it!"[14]

Looking back on the community's outpouring of support, a Phillips manager later commented:

> Farming and oil are the lifeblood of this part of the country. And farming was already in bad shape. Bartlesville has no other appreciable industry that I am aware of. It's pretty much Phillips, and if Phillips goes or starts trimming down, everything turns down. The impact on the community if Phillips were to go is that others would just vanish. Bartlesville would be a ghost town. But as long as there is some nucleus of Phillips here, there will be the Phillips people and there will be these other people from the supporting communities in surrounding areas who will come to Bartlesville.[15]

Christmas in Bartlesville, 1984, turned out to be a happy one. On Christmas eve, just three weeks after Pickens launched his takeover bid, he and Phillips announced a settlement. "We were very pleased Phillips maintained its identity," recalls one retiree, "but at the same time I think people resented Mr. Pickens making the profit he did."[16] In financial terms, Phillips agreed to repurchase the 8.9 million shares in the company Pickens had accumulated, for $10 a share more than they had cost him. This yielded a gross profit of $89 million for Pickens on shares he had held for roughly six weeks. Phillips would also pay Pickens and his group $25 million more to cover expenses they ran up in making their run on the company.

But this was only the beginning. The settlement also required Phillips to present an expensive plan at its next annual meeting designed to raise its shares' value for other investors as well. The company would propose to buy back 38 percent of all its stock. (Pickens had only owned about 6 percent, or less than one-sixth of the additional amount the company agreed to repurchase.) To remove Pickens's takeover threat and satisfy his demands, Phillips had spent $57 million in three weeks and was now committed to borrowing nearly $3 *billion* to cover its proposed stock buyback program.

As the dust settled from one battle and the new year got under way, Phillips next heard from Carl Icahn, perhaps Wall Street's most feared financier and corporate raider. Icahn was buying big blocks of the company's stock and demanding Phillips pay more for the shares it proposed to buy back. He had substantial support from what *New York Times* writer Daniel Cuff called "those cold and distant institutions that own 47 percent of Phillips [stock] and hold the key to its future."[17] On February 5, 1985, Icahn offered to buy Phillips from its shareholders for a higher price. Now in its second battle in two months, there was little doubt at Phillips or in Bartlesville this time about the company's fate if it lost this ownership contest. Pickens at least said he would move to Bartlesville and run the company if he gained control. Financial analyst George Sneed's chilling interpretation of Icahn's intentions made Pickens sound like a long-lost friend:

> Icahn and his backers have no interest in buying Phillips Petroleum Company to operate it. They would liquidate the company if they get control of it. They are trying to force the price up and if they can get Phillips merged or bought out at a higher price, that is what they want . . . There is an awful lot of stock in the hands of short-term speculators and they absolutely do not care what happens to Bartlesville.[18]

While local residents disliked both corporate raiders, Icahn was generally deemed even less trustworthy and more dangerous than Pickens. Jeweler Josef Derryberry again spoke for many when he said he could not trust Icahn's remarks about his plans for Phillips: "One moment you'll keep Phillips in Bartlesville and the next moment you say you'll sell it to the highest bidder. There's only one business I know of that you can sell and keep it too," he said.[19] Asked to compare people's reactions to Icahn and Pickens, a Phillips manager recalled:

> Pickens wasn't too well liked, but Icahn, well we really had to campaign against him . . . Pickens was a petroleum man. But Icahn, and there were several with him, had made quite a reputation and a lot of money just moving parts of companies around. They were both looked at in a different way. I think in Bartlesville they both were considered SOB's, but Boone at least was Mr. SOB.[20]

Not everyone agrees. As one retail merchant, whose business has still not recovered, sees it, "We put Icahn and Pickens in the same classification. One was an easterner, one a southwesterner. You know, it doesn't make any difference whether you got shit on your boots or wear a bow tie. If you're a corporate raider looking for a quick profit, who cares who he is?"[21]

On March 5, 1985, Phillips assured its independence for the foreseeable future by meeting Icahn's terms. It "sharply improved the terms" of its offer to repurchase much of the company's stock from its shareholders.[22] To pay for it, the company took on more debt. Published estimates of Mr. Icahn's gross profit from his roughly six-week investment in Phillips stock range from $30 million to $75 million. The company also paid an additional $25 million of Icahn's expenses from their takeover fight. These included payments to "a consortium of private and institutional investors, including such active raiders as the Canadian Belzberg family, Saul Steinberg, and the Leucadia National Corporation, [which, for holding aside] $1.5 billion for about two weeks [to loan Icahn if he had needed it], received $5,625,000 in fees and never had to put up a nickel."[23] In return, Phillips got agreements from Carl Icahn and his main Wall Street backer, Drexel Burnham Lambert, Inc., to stop trying to buy the company. Phillips' outlay, for the three months of legal and financial services it bought itself and its raiders, exceeded $200 million. Irwin Jacobs, one of Icahn's best-known allies in the just-finished battle, summed it up very well: "Phillips has bought its independence, and the town of Bartlesville can rest easy tonight."[24]

Once again, Phillips employees and Bartlesville were relieved the company stayed independent and intact. The city had recently been in the news for mailing heart-shaped Valentine's Day cookies with the Phillips 66 shield on them to Icahn and large shareholders during the latest battle. But the mood was less joyful and more subdued than when the contest with Pickens ended. Now, Bartlesville heaved "a collective sigh of relief. 'Conservative optimism' is how the editor of the local paper describes the mood," reported the *Christian Science Monitor*.[25] A Phillips manager recalls:

> After a while people had just sort of gotten used to it. A little jaded, probably more fatalistic. Yeah, we might be taken over. Another one just showed up with more threats, so they'll fight it out. Much of the outrage and shock was probably used up in the struggle with Pickens. Everyone was still upset, but people just got on with other things as the fights dragged on.[26]

Six weeks after Phillips settled with Icahn, David Oakley, owner of the city's Pontiac-Buick dealership, reported that car sales were improving. "People are convinced now that there is going to be a community, although they're not sure if they're going to have a job," he said.[27]

To remain independent and keep raiders at bay, Phillips had taken a very high stakes gamble. This was that its oil and gas, combined with the sale of assets, would keep generating enough cash to cover payments due on the billions it borrowed to buy back 50 percent of its stock.

In less than a year, the company's debt had tripled from $2.8 to $8.6 billion. Its credit rating had been lowered. Phillips's interest payments for 1985 zoomed to $846 million, more than double its earnings. Company officials, and some oil industry experts, downplayed the seriousness of the situation. Phillips planned to reduce its debt quickly by selling at least $2 billion in assets. "They've got salable stuff coming out their ears . . . [and] could get rid of $2 billion without blinking," said one industry analyst.[28] Company Chairman William Douce acknowledged that "it's a pretty good debt load for a while, but we have a strong cash flow and that's really the name of the game."[29] After leading his company through the two brutal takeover wars, Douce referred to himself as a "born-again debtor."[30] "We can remain strong and vital, no question," he said.[31]

Others were less optimistic about the firm's chances for a quick comeback. "Phillips has mortgaged its future. The price of independence is a mountain of debt," said Sanford Margoshes, senior oil analyst at Shearson/American Express.[32] He believed that "this is a company where some of the glow has been extinguished."[33] Many observers called Phillips's debt, now between 75 and 80 percent of its total capital, "staggering." They predicted management's energy would be absorbed more by cutting debt and expenses than by competing hard for new oil fields and customers. Phillips is "definitely a weaker competitor," said Lawrence Funkhauser, Chevron's vice president for exploration and production.

"They've got a period of four or five years to get back to where they were before Pickens attacked them."[34] Amoco's chief economist, Ted Eck, also commented, "It's hard to see how you could be a superaggressive exploration company when you've got 75 percent debt."[35]

The most critical wild card in Phillips's high-stakes gamble would be the price of oil. The cash flow it needed to pay off its huge debt required a minimum price of $20 per barrel. After the big stock buyback, the *Washington Post* reported:

> About the only thing analysts believe could put Phillips' rebuilding efforts out of kilter would be an unexpected drop in the price of oil. In setting up its restructuring, Phillips has assumed an average oil price for the next few years of about $27 a barrel, and a worst-case scenario of about $20 a barrel.[36]

"If the price of oil goes down, Phillips is going to be in trouble," said oil analyst Fred Leuffer.[37] Another analyst, who asked not to be identified, added, "If oil prices went down to $20 a barrel, Phillips faced financial peril."[38] The experts' consensus tied Phillips's recovery to these magic numbers. If they fell below $20, that would mean lower prices for the assets Phillips needed to sell, and less cash from the sale of its own oil and gasoline. Since the company had to repay its steep loans, no matter what, the missing balance would have to come from elsewhere if oil prices did drop.

Within five months of Phillips's successful fights to stay independent, oil prices started a plunge toward $10 a barrel. The company's strategy of "borrow now, pay later" began to unravel. Its high debt and cash-poor position left it without any of the "rainy day" money companies need to tide themselves over during hard times. Phillips was more vulnerable to falling prices than any other oil company (except Unocal, which had followed Phillips's example by also going into deep debt to fight off another bid by T. Boone Pickens). Two *Wall Street Journal** reports show how precarious the company's financial position became by the summers of 1985 and 1986:

> Bob Crawford raises his voice to be heard over a thumping oil pump he has just lubricated in the Phillips Petroleum Co. oil field here [in Shidler, Oklahoma]. "If oil prices drop farther, Phillips will have to liquidate this field and me with it," he says. For Phillips and several other major oil companies, "the crunch" came mainly from taking on massive increases in debt at a time

when oil prices were slumping. The result is a double-edged sword that threatens to seriously reduce both revenue and profit in the industry.

The heavy debt, low-price bug has made no big oil company sicker than Phillips. Just last year, Phillips was weathering the energy slump quite nicely. Its profit rose 12%, and its debt load was one of the lightest around. But the company's bitter takeover battles with Messrs. Pickens and Icahn earlier this year changed all that. To fend them off, Phillips borrowed $4.5 billion, raising its debt-to-equity ratio to a staggering 80%. That's easily the highest among the majors, and analysts are worried, particularly in light of falling prices.

"They're over my danger line," says Kurt Wulff, a Donaldson, Lufkin & Jenrette analyst . . . Living on the edge is proving painful for the nation's eighth biggest oil company.[39]

(August 9, 1985)

Most energy-related companies have been forced to cut costs sharply because of the oil price plunge, but Unocal and Phillips are in especially difficult positions . . . "they're hanging on with bloody fingers at this point," says [analyst] Alan Edgar . . .

For its part, Phillips has taken drastic steps in light of lower oil prices. Its work force has been cut by 3,400 employees, to 21,900, since the first of the year.[40]

(July 28, 1986)

In Bartlesville, Phillips acknowledged that by summer 1985, it was using up oil reserves faster than it was replacing them. "If we continued that way, it would make us self-liquidating," said Bill Thompson, vice president for planning and development. "It's like having a house that takes four gallons of paint and you've got only three—the house will look like hell."[41] A common feeling managers expressed was that budget reductions were cutting into the bone of their operations. For example:

Staffing and operations have been cut back to a point where I can no longer function smoothly. This happened just as markets became chaotic because of falling oil prices. So now we are missing business we should be getting because we just can't handle it. And it's not because people are lazy or stupid, people are working very hard at nights and on weekends. I work feverishly all day and then bring a briefcase full of work home and work until 10:30 or so every night, and still can't keep up. If things stay like this, Phillips has a serious problem, because we can't continue as we are.[42]

Referring back to the takeover battles, the same manager says, "We've done the equivalent of somebody who was threatened by a mugger, sitting there slashing your wrist so you scare them off with all the blood. We don't have the strength to go out and lift weights anymore. We've had to pull back our operations and try to conserve cash as much as possible."[43]

Mr. Pickens was not convinced the company's operations had been streamlined far enough. His recommendations in both summer 1985 and 1986 reportedly suggested that Phillips should continue "slimming the . . . payroll"[44] and "cut their costs and trim exploration budgets before cutting dividends further."[45]

Phillips Petroleum has retained its independence, but the price of victory was very high for the company, its employees, and the people of Bartlesville. Many jobs were lost, and for those remaining the company is a much leaner "home away from home." The takeover battles also left scars on the community at large. One of the city's leading retailers believes the experience "destroyed a part of" its spirit.[46] John Norell, president of a Phillips research subsidiary, wrote in a letter to the U.S. House Energy and Commerce Committee, "There is something fundamentally wrong in America that a $16 billion company who is financially strong and interested in long-range developments for itself, the country, and humanity on one day can then on the next day, after a run on it by Mr. T. Boone Pickens, be reduced to a debt-ridden, short term, and cost-cutting entity."[47]

Oil industry analyst Sanford Margoshes spoke for many when he said, "As a member of the planet I would say one should not be pleased with a proliferation of this type of development."[48]

NOTES

Abbreviations:

BW = Business Week
WSJ = Wall Street Journal
NYT = New York Times

All unattributed quotes in this case come from interviews arranged and conducted by Dr. Dennis Wheaton, a native of Whizbang, Oklahoma, an abandoned boomtown located fifty miles west of Bartlesville in the Burbank Field of Osage County.

1. "Wells in the U.S." Tim Hartley, "Conflicting Signals: Phillips Reductions Complete but Home Sales Continue Strong," *Bartlesville Examiner-Enterprise* (8/4/86), p. 2.

2. "House in Bartlesville." Personal interview (7/86).

3. "Couldn't Get One." Tim Hartley, op. cit., p. 1.

4. "To Be Next?" David Clark Scott, "Although raid at Phillips is over, the company is the poorer," *Christian Science Monitor* (3/12/85), p. 21.

5. "Someone Who Is." In Sallie Turcott, "Phillips Workers Wait for Bad News," *Tulsa World* (4/4/86), p. D-1.

6. "That's No Joke." John Williams and Charles McCoy, "Phillips, Icahn Set Pact to Halt Takeover Effort," *WSJ* (3/5/85), p. 20.

7. "For the Money." Personal interview (7/86).

8. "A Tough Situation." Personal interview (7/86).

9. "Through Your Town?" Personal interview (7/86).

10. "Were Running Separately." Personal interview (10/86).

11. "Is Still Intact." Personal interview (10/86).

12. "Could Use [Them!]." "Odds & Ends," *WSJ* (4/11/85), Section 2, p. 1.

13. "Don't Like It." "Bartlesville Is Wary," *NYT* (2/6/85), p. 29.

14. "Let's Do It!" *Bartlesville Constitution: Extra* (12/14/84), p. 3.

15. "Come to Bartlesville." Personal interview (10/86).

16. "Profit He Did." Personal interview (10/86).

17. "To Its Future." Daniel Cuff, "Hometown Fights for Phillips," *NYT* (2/11/85), p. D1.

18. "Happens to Bartlesville." In "Icahn Moves to Block Phillips Plan," *Bartlesville Constitution* (2/6/85), p. 1.

19. "Too,' He Said." Scott Andrews, "Douce: Phillips has other options," *Bartlesville Examiner-Enterprise* (2/28/85), p. 1.

20. "Was Mr. SOB." Personal interview (7/86).

21. "Who He Is?" Personal interview (7/86).

22. "Improved the Terms." Robert J. Cole, "Icahn Ends Offer for Phillips; All Shareholders to Get More," *NYT* (3/5/85), p. 1.

23. "Put Up a Nickel." Moira Johnston, *Takeover: The New Wall Street Warriors*. New York: Arbor House (1986), p. 151.

24. "Rest Easy Tonight." Robert J. Cole, op. cit., p. D9.

25. "Describes the Mood," David Clark Scott, op. cit.

26. "Fights Dragged On." Personal interview (7/86).

27. "Have a Job." David Clark Scott, "How Citizens and Businesses Rally Round when a Takeover Threat Strides into Town," *Christian Science Monitor* (4/22/85), p. 14.

28. "$2 Billion Without Blinking." John Williams and Charles McCoy, "Phillips Is Expected to Retain Its Current Shape Even After Planned Sale of $2 Billion in Assets," *WSJ* (3/6/85), p. 2.

29. "Name of the Game." Daniel Cuff, "Phillips Sees Benefits in Fight; Others Unsure," *NYT* (3/6/85), p. D1.

30. "Born-Again Debtor." Mark Potts, "Phillips Offers Blueprint for Industry Change," *Washington Post* (3/17/85), p. D8.

31. "Vital, No Question." John Williams and Charles McCoy, op. cit.

32. "Mountain of Debt." David Clark Scott, op. cit.

33. "Glow Has Been Extinguished." Daniel Cuff, op. cit.

34. "Pickens Attacked Them." In "Shifting Strategies: Surge in Restructuring is Profoundly Altering Much of U.S. Industry" (Special Report), *WSJ* (8/12/85), p. 12.

35. "75 Percent Debt," Mark Potts, "Does Another Oil Shock Lie Ahead?", *Washington Post* (5/5/85), p. F20.

36. "$20 a Barrel." Mark Potts, "Phillips Offers Blueprint For Industry Change," *Washington Post*, op. cit., p. D1.

37. "Be in Trouble." David C. Scott, op. cit.

38. Faced Financial Peril." Daniel Cuff, "Phillips Sees Benefits in Fight; Others Unsure," op. cit.

39. "Biggest Oil Company." Laurie Cohen and Johnathan Dahl, "Phillips Is Pressured by Debt, Oil-Pride Slide," *WSJ* (8/9/85), p. 6.

40. "First of the Year." Frederick Rose and Karen Blumenthal, "Heavy Debts Weigh on Unocal, Phillips," *WSJ* (7/28/86), p. 6.

41. "Look Like Hell." Laurie Cohen and Johnathan Dahl, op. cit.

42. "Continue As We Are." Personal interview (10/86).

43. "Much as Possible." Personal interview (7/86).

44. "Slimming the . . . Payroll." In "Shifting Strategies: Surge in Restructuring. . . ," op. cit.

45. "Cutting Dividends Further." Frederick Rose and Karen Blumenthal, op. cit.

46. "Destroyed a Part of." Personal interview (10/86).

47. "Cutting Entity." David Clark Scott, "How Citizens and Businesses Rally Round when Takeover Threat Strides into Town," op. cit.

48. "Type of Development." Daniel Cuff, "Phillips Sees Benefits in Fight; Others Unsure," op. cit.

QUESTIONS FOR DISCUSSION

1. Are there moral differences between a takeover for the purpose of corporate consolidation and growth, a takeover for the purpose of forcing a "buyback program," and a takeover done for the explicit purpose of selling off the newly acquired company, piecemeal, in order to increase the profits of the parent takeover company?

2. In any form of takeover, what are the rights of the long-term employees, customers and suppliers of the newly acquired firm?

3. What can happen to a company town when the company in town is taken over by another company that doesn't care about the town?

4. What is likely to happen to a company when it "mortgages its future" and acquires a "mountain of debt" in order to avoid a takeover so as to save their independence and identity?

Case Study
Roger Hixon:
Let the Buyer Beware

Clinton L. Oaks

What obligation, if any, does a vendor have to point out to a prospective buyer the flaws or defects in his product? Roger Hixon, a former executive with a national firm and now a teacher of business policy at a western college, raised this question with respect to the remarks of a guest speaker in a previous class period. The speaker had talked about various levels of business ethics among the salesmen for companies with whom he dealt regularly. He had concluded that while some companies had a very strict policy calling for honesty and complete disclosure, many did not.

During the ensuing discussion, one student commented, "I hear all these platitudes being mouthed about how 'complete disclosure is always good business practice.' How many of you practice complete disclosure in your personal business dealings? I am sure I don't." At this point, just as the discussion was beginning to get a little heated, the instructor noted that the class period was nearly over. He invited several of those who were participating most actively in the discussion to write up a specific incident for discussion the next time the class met.

JOAN STULLARD

"My parents, who live in a small college town in the northern part of the state, decided a year ago last spring to try to sell their home and move into a condominium. Since my father is pretty close to retirement, they tried to sell the place themselves rather than going through a real estate agent. The real estate market up there, unlike that in many urban areas, was quite slow. By late August, they had only had one potential buyer who had shown enough interest to come back several times.

"One of the nicest features of our home was its large backyard. A huge cottonwood tree standing in one corner of the yard provided the entire house and yard with shade against the late afternoon sun. The tree was very large—its trunk had a circumference of nearly fifteen feet. The only problem with it was that it was dying. While it looked healthy and green from our house, our neighbors behind the tree could see many dead and potentially dangerous branches. A violent storm would often litter their yards and prompt them to call us and demand that we cut down the tree.

"The prospective buyer who had shown the greatest interest in the place was standing on the patio one afternoon with my father. 'That sure is a nice, big tree,' he said. I was standing at the door, and overheard his remark. His comment wasn't one that required an answer. I found myself wondering what, if anything, my father would say."

MARK BASCOM

"My brother is working as a used car salesman at Clark Motors. He tells me that the manager of the used car lot keeps a folder on every car in stock. Everything that is known about the car is recorded in the folder. This would include information about the previous owner, any major body or engine repairs, the mechanic's evaluation at the time the car came on the lot, etc.

"Before school started, my brother got permission to borrow a Buick Estate Wagon for several days to take a short vacation. He said he and his wife really enjoyed the car but they were appalled at the gas mileage—less than eight miles per gallon on the open road. When he returned the car, he made a note of this in the car's folder. He also talked to one of the mechanics about it. 'I'm not surprised,' the mechanic commented. 'As you know, we clean the carburetor, put in new plugs and points, adjust the timing and so forth whenever we get a car—but that particular model always was a gas hog.'

"A few days later, a young couple who were looking at cars on the lot expressed a great deal of interest in this car. They asked my brother a lot of questions and he, having had some personal experience with the car, was able to answer them in greater detail than was normally the case. He was also able to point out some of the features of the car that might have otherwise been overlooked. The longer they talked, the more enthusiastic the couple became. Almost the only question they didn't ask was about the car's mileage. They had to leave at 4:30 to pick up their child at the babysitter's but made an appointment to come back at 9:30 the next morning to work out the details of the sale.

"That night my brother came over to talk about a deal we were working on together. While he was there he told me about what had happened and said, 'As you know, things have been really tight for Jean and me since we took that trip, and the commission on this sale would really help us right now. I have always tried, as a matter of policy, to answer honestly any question that a prospective buyer raises. If I were to tell this couple about the gas mileage on that car, however, I'm pretty sure they would back out of the sale. I don't intend to try to deceive them, but do I have any obligation to tell them about it if they don't ask?'"

JEFF MOYER

"My wife and I live approximately thirty-five miles away from the university. She teaches school in a district that is also about thirty miles from where we live, but in the opposite direction. As you can imagine, transportation is a big item in our budget. Neither of us has been successful in finding a car pool. Fortunately, my wife's parents have graciously allowed us to continue to use the car my wife drove before we were married. We own an older car, and with the two cars we have been able to get by up to now.

"When my wife accepted the teaching position we knew the travel involved would be both time consuming and expensive. However, our projections on costs were painfully underestimated. Not only have gas and oil prices increased sharply, but we hadn't realized that both cars would need new tires. Because we drive as far as we do, we have had to have tune-ups on both cars more frequently than anticipated. In addition to all this, we have had to have work done on our own car's distributor, muffler and lights—all of which has cost us well over two hundred dollars. Just recently we had more trouble requiring a mechanic's examination. His diagnosis was 'You need a valve job.'

"While I was trying to figure out where I could borrow the projected $240 for the valve job, the mechanic said, 'The engine block is pitted and needs to be ground down. If you are going to do that you might as well overhaul the whole engine.'

"'How much will that be over the $240,' I asked, bracing for the shock.

"'About $360,' the mechanic replied.

"Fighting the churning feeling in my stomach, I asked what would happen if he didn't grind down the block. I was told that the engine head and block might not seal when put back together after the work was done on the valves. 'Just try to get it to seal,' I told him knowing our budget was already dripping with red ink.

"The mechanic put the engine back together and I crossed my fingers. Evidently it sealed because the car is running now. I suspect that with all the miles that it travels weekly it may need the overhaul before long. I can't begin to afford that. Both my father and father-in-law have given me the same advice. 'Get rid of the car while it is still running.'

"I checked on the Blue book value of this model and it ranged from $1600 to $2300. I was pretty sure that if I were to tell the buyer about the engine block, I would have more difficulty in selling it and I would probably have to knock $400 to $800 off the going price.

"I try to think of myself as an honest person, and I don't think I could lie about it if someone asked me whether or not the car engine needed an overhaul. But suppose they didn't ask? Am I obligated to tell them anyway?

"Suppose I were to trade in the car on another car at an auto dealership. A dealer will almost always have a mechanic check out the car before he makes you an offer. Do I need to say anything in a situation like that? If I said anything I am sure it would lower the offer the dealer would make to me, but I am not at all sure, based upon my past experience, that the dealer would pass this information and a lower price on to another customer. In such a transaction isn't there almost a mutual understanding that everyone is governed by the old merchant's law of 'Let the buyer beware'?

"Having decided not to keep the car, I felt my choices were: (1) tell whoever buys the car about the engine; (2) tell whoever buys the car about the engine only if he or she asks if I know of any mechanical flaws; (3) tell about the engine only if I sell the car myself instead of trading it in; and (4) don't tell anyone about the engine even if asked. What should I have done?"

DON CASE

"Just after I turned sixteen, I spent a summer working with my best friend on his dad's used car lot. Our job was to 'clean-up' and 'recondition' cars before they were put on the sales lot. We were to make them presentable so they could be shown to prospective buyers.

"Some of the things we had to do were what you might expect. We washed and waxed the body, scrubbed the seats and door interiors and shampooed the rugs. We also tightened any loose screws and repositioned the carpet, tightening down the carpet edges.

"My friend's dad taught us how to do a lot of other things as well. We were to use a powerful grease cutting detergent to wash the engine and eliminate the dirt, oil and grease that had accumulated on it. 'A buyer is always impressed with a clean engine,' he told us, 'and besides he won't be alarmed by any evidence that oil is leaking from the engine.' We were also shown how to use a spray shellac on all the rubber hoses so that they would look like they were new.

If the car was burning any oil, we were to add a can of STP. If the blue smoke coming out of the back end was heavy we would add two cans and sometimes three.

"Rust had often eaten through the steel from the wheel well and would show around the fenders. With the help of a steel brush and can of spray paint this was easily hidden and the rust would not show through the paint again for at least a month.

"Sometimes the carpets were too stained with grease and dirt to be cleaned. A coat of dark spray coloring hid the stains and would make the carpets look nice for at least a week or two after the car was purchased.

"I was young enough at the time and grateful enough to have a job that I don't ever remember even questioning the rightness or wrongness of the things we did. My friend's dad's conscience must have troubled him a little, however, because he was always telling us that there wasn't anything wrong or illegal about what we were doing. He told us that every used car lot did the same thing and he had to do it to remain competitive. 'We never turn back an odometer,' he said. "That is illegal. The buyer expects that a used car lot will do everything possible to make a used car look good—and part of his job as a buyer is to check out anything that might be wrong.'

"Two or three years later, I had a used car of my own to sell. Without thinking much about it, I gave it some treatment we used to give cars on the lot, including the addition of two cans of STP. I put a "For Sale" sign in the window and parked it on our curb. The next night, a girl about my age who evidently didn't know much about cars, came by to ask me how much I was asking for it. After I told her, she asked, 'Is the car in good condition? Do you know of any problems that I am likely to have with it?' What should I have said?"

NED OBORNE

"At the end of last spring semester, one of my roommates transferred to a school down in Texas. Before he left, he turned over to me two pairs of skis, both virtually new. He said, 'There isn't any market for these right now but they should be easy to sell in the fall. Why don't you keep them for me until then?'

"Knowing that he wasn't much of a skier, I asked him, 'Where did you get them? He replied, 'One of the guys I run around with gave them to me. I don't know for sure, but I wouldn't be surprised if he picked them up off an unlocked ski rack on a car parked in front of the motel where he used to work. At any event there aren't any identifying marks on them. I checked in the local ski shops around here and both pairs retail for around $300. Sell them for whatever you can get and you keep half of it.' Before I had any chance to protest, he took off.

"Those skis stood in my closet for nearly six months. late in the fall, we got a little cramped for room and I decided I had better do something with them. I was half tempted to just turn them over to campus security and tell them that they had been left in my apartment and I didn't know whose they were.

"One day when I was trying to rearrange some of the things in the closet, I had both pairs of skis out on my bed. A friend of another roommate saw them and said, 'You wouldn't like to sell a pair of skis, would you? I am really in the market and they look just like what I have been looking for.'

"Without stopping to think about it, I asked, 'What will you give me?' He said, 'I'll give you $150.00 for the pair on the right.'

"What should I have done? My textbooks that fall had cost me about twice what I had estimated and I was really strapped for cash. I hadn't stolen the skis—in fact I didn't know for sure they had been stolen. I could truthfully say that a roommate had left them with me to sell and let it go at that. Was I obligated to tell a prospective purchaser that they might have been stolen? I can imagine what effect that might have had on the reputation of those of us living in the apartment.

"If the skis were stolen, it was extremely unlikely that the rightful owners could ever be located. In view of this, what difference did it make whether or not they had been stolen? If I turned them over to campus security, they would probably just keep them for a while and then sell them at an auction. If the end result would be the same—that is, that the skis would end up with some third party who didn't know who the original owner was and who could care less—why shouldn't I pick up a few dollars to cover my 'costs of handling' "?

QUESTIONS FOR DISCUSSION*

Joan Stullard

1. Should Joan's father disclose to prospective buyers the status of the cotton-wood tree?

Mark Bascom

1. How should Mark respond to his brother?

Jeff Moyer

1. Which of Jeff's four strategies should he adopt?

Don Case

1. How should Don respond? Does the fact that an action is a customary industry practice make a moral difference?

Ned Oborne

1. Should Ned sell the skis?

6

Multinationals

Global corporations are leading actors in the increasingly complex drama of international trade and development. Also called "transnationals," "extranationals," and "cosmocorps," these giants refuse to be subsumed under traditional categories. They are called *multi*national, but in fact they are *uni* national: Although they do business in a variety of countries they are chartered in a single, home country. Most are chartered in the United States, Japan, West Germany, or one of the other developed Western nations. And while they are subject not only to the conditions of their charter but also to the laws prevailing in the countries they inhabit, they frequently have the capacity to influence laws by using organizational skills and economic clout.

We would do well to distinguish the power a global corporation exercises directly through political or financial strength from the power it manifests as a possessor of technology and as a representative of the prevailing market ideology. Today, the first kind of power is seldom employed through direct military intervention. Gone is the time when the East India Company could raise the largest standing army in Asia, and gone also is the time when multinationals could push home governments to intervene militarily. Multinationals can still depend, however, on a sympathetic hearing from most government officials of their home countries, with the result that government representatives to international financial organizations, such as the International Monetary Fund and the World Bank, tend to support the interests of their home multinationals. Since international financial organizations tend to be dominated by the industrialized countries, and since most multinationals are based in these countries, the interests of multinationals are well represented in such organizations. Multinationals also receive indirect government support. It is probably not accidental that shortly after U.S. government agencies helped to advise groups undertaking military coups in Indonesia, Greece, Chile, and Brazil, the new governments opened their doors to U.S. investment under favorable conditions

In addition to straightforward political and financial power, multinationals also wield indirect power related to technological prowess, organizational know-how, and their status as representatives of the dominant market ideology. It was the organizational know-how of the multinational that made U.S. businessmen in Brazil the leading sponsors of the Businessmen's Council Brazil-U.S., a council that is said to be the principal representative of the total Brazilian private sector. Today it is the accounting know-how of the multinational which allows it to maintain complex and sophisticated record-keeping procedures that sometimes baffle even government tax experts. And it is the access to legal know-how on the part of the multinational which makes it a force sometimes even in the drafting of national laws pertaining to itself.

As the representative of a successful commercial ideology, the multinational is also frequently an exporter of dreams. The underdeveloped country sometimes views the multinational as the legitimate example of life as it should be lived at its best. During the 1970s the United States' two leading advertising agencies were earning over 50 percent of their profits overseas. Richard Barnet tells of how shoeshine boys in Beirut save their piasters in order to buy Coca-Cola, the "real thing," instead of off-brand colas that sell for half the price.

Multinationals are not bad because they have power. Power in itself is neither good nor bad; it depends on how it is used. Opinions vary greatly about whether multinationals use their power wisely. Some people, of course, see multinationals as engines of global injustice, allowing the rich nations to enslave the poor nations with wondrous, though regrettable, efficiency. Others, however, see multinationals as the last hope for world peace, and as the only means to correct the blindness of nationalism. Given the sorry record of political programs in curing human misery, they note, multinationals have the advantage of relying not on unstable political emotions, but on the proven propensity for human trade. The Third World desperately needs information and skills from developed countries, and the most efficient means of communicating these, say defenders, is the multinational.

The moral analysis of multinationals is especially important since they, unlike national entities, exist under diverse legal systems with conflicting demands. The law cannot be relied upon to set the final moral parameters for the simple reason that many of the laws themselves are in conflict. If the law in the United States prevents the sale of "tris-treated" infant sleepwear on the grounds that the fire retardant contained in the clothing is carcinogenic, yet the law in an underdeveloped country permits the clothing's sale (an actual case that occurred in the 1970s), a company must make its own decision about the morality of selling the product abroad. Or, to take the case of "Dresser Industries and South Africa," which appears in this section, Dresser Industries cannot rely on the law in its decision about whether to discriminate against blacks in South Africa, since U.S. law prohibits such discrimination, while South African law *requires* it.

The remaining cases in this section examine the morality of specific overseas business practices. The "Project Jari" case deals with the issue of the environmental and economic exploitation of a Third World country. Even when invited in, does any multinational ever have the right to use the resources of a host country in a way that could do permanent damage to that country's overall ecosystem? Although multinationals have a right to make a profit on their investment, are they not also obligated to enhance the general socioeconomic stability of the country they are doing business in? In the "Abbot Laboratories" case, the emphasis is on the much-discussed issue of the sale of infant formula to developing countries. Should companies ever restrict their marketing behavior even in the absence of legal restraints? If so, what form should the restrictions take?

Case Study
Dresser Industries and South Africa

Patricia Mintz
Kirk O. Hanson

At its 1980 shareholders annual meeting, Dresser Industries had successfully opposed and defeated an activist shareholder resolution demanding that the company sign what had come to be popularly known as the Sullivan Principles. However, due to the aggressiveness of the groups promoting the resolution, Dresser's management faced the likelihood that they would again have to contend with the resolution in 1981. The 1980 resolution had received 11.2% of the shareholder votes cast, and under Securities and Exchange Commission (SEC) regulations, any resolution receiving a vote of more than 3% the first time it was proposed qualified for reintroduction the following year.

The Sullivan Principles—a set of norms for U.S. corporate operations in racially-divided South Africa—were first articulated by the Reverend Leon Sullivan, a black Philadelphia minister and the first minority member

Reprinted from *Stanford Business Cases 1980* with permission of the publishers, Stanford University Graduate School of business, © 1980 by the Board of Trustees of the Leland Stanford Junior University. The case was prepared by Patricia Mintz, MBA, under supervision of Kirk O. Hanson, Lecturer in Business Administration.

of General Motors' Board of Directors. By 1980, 135 corporations, representing 85% of U.S. investment in South Africa, had signed the Principles. Dresser, whose fully-owned subsidiary, Dresser South Africa (Pty.) Ltd., employed 1,100 workers, had not signed, nor had 163 other U.S. companies operating there.

DRESSER INDUSTRIES

Headquartered in Dallas, Texas, Dresser Industries was, in 1980, one of the world's leading diversified suppliers of technology, products, and services to industries involved in the development of energy and natural resources. The company had been founded in 1880 by Solomon R. Dresser in the oil boomtown of Bradford, Pennsylvania. Dresser had started as an oil prospector in Western Pennsylvania and had developed and patented a rubber "packer" cap—a device that separated oil from other elements in newly struck oil wells. By the turn of the century, Dresser had diversified into the natural gas industry, and by the 1930s into a wide spectrum of energy-related businesses. After 1933, the company's growth had been fueled by over 30 acquisitions.

By 1944, with the purchase of International Stacey Corporation, Dresser's operations began developing abroad. Following World War II, Dresser continued to diversify into new, energy-related businesses and to expand the scope of its international operations.[1]

In 1979, Dresser's revenues were $3.46 billion, a 13% increase over the prior year. Its net earnings for 1979 were $228 million, up 12% over 1978. In 1979, Dresser was ranked 98th in sales and 73rd in total profit among the Fortune 500 industrial firms.

Dresser operated in five major industry segments: (1) petroleum operations; (2) energy processing and conversion; (3) refractories and minerals; (4) construction and mining equipment; and (5) industrial specialty products, ranging from drilling bits to environmental control systems. The company's overseas sales in 1979 were $1.2 billion, an 11% increase over 1978 foreign sales of $1.08 billion. These sales represented approximately 35% of Dresser's total 1979 revenues. Dresser operated a total of 80 plants throughout the world and employed 55,200 people—13,200 of whom worked outside the U.S.[2]

DRESSER'S OPERATIONS IN SOUTH AFRICA[3]

South Africa provided a unique operating environment for Dresser and other multinational firms. The Republic of South Africa, situated at the southern tip of the African continent, was rich in natural resources; the country in 1979 controlled 65% of the world's gold reserves, 50% of its diamonds and manganese, and 25% of its uranium. South Africa's 1979 GNP of $57.7 billion represented a quarter of the African continent's gross output.[4]

Dresser's first significant involvement in South Africa began in 1974 when the firm acquired Jeffrey-Galion, an Ohio manufacturing firm which produced heavy roadbuilding and mining equipment and operated a South African subsidiary. Dresser incorporated Jeffrey-Galion's South African operation as a wholly-owned subsidiary, Dresser South Africa (Pty.) Ltd. Subsequent acquisitions of other firms with South African branches, such as the 1977 purchase of Marion Power Shovel Company, increased the scale of Dresser's South African operations. As of 1980, Dresser South Africa's principal products included: Galion roadbuilding machinery and hydraulic cranes; Jeffrey underground mining equipment, ore crushers and materials handling equipment; Marion power shovels and drag lines; and Lodge-Cottrell pollution abatement devices. The majority of Dresser South Africa's sales, according to company officials, was made to South African government-owned corporations.

In 1979, Dresser South Africa reported revenues of $45.8 million, an increase of 23% over 1978 sales of $37.1 million, and had total assets of $39.1 million. The South African subsidiary employed 1,110 workers: 360 blacks, 100 coloreds (South Africans of mixed racial origin) and 650 whites. Thus, Dresser's South African workers composed only two percent of its total work force and approximately nine percent of all its workers outside the U.S.

SOUTH AFRICA AND APARTHEID

South Africa was first populated by Europeans during the 17th and 18th century as a colony controlled by the Dutch East India Company. During the 1700s, German immigrants and French Huguenots sought religious freedom there. These immigrants, who became known as Afrikaners or Boers, had been excluded from government, education and politics by the British who had seized South Africa in 1795. The principal reason for this exclusion was that the Afrikaners did not speak English. During the 1830s the Afrikaners migrated to the interior of South Africa where sporadic warfare broke out between them and black natives who migrated throughout the interior in search of grazing land. The discovery of gold in the interior in 1886 led to a large influx of English-speaking settlers, and constant conflict between Afrikaners and the British finally culminated in the Anglo-Boer War of 1899–1902 and the defeat of the Afrikaners.

Eight years later, in 1910, the previously separate Afrikaner (or Boer) and English-speaking states were combined to establish an independent country, the Union of South Africa. Still bitter at their defeat in the Anglo-Boer war, the Africaners—after independence was won—maintained their own language, culture, and religion and worked to seize political power in the country. They finally gained control of the government in 1948, as the Nationalist Party.

The British had withdrawn the rights of all nonwhites to sit in parliament in 1909. When the Africaner government came to power, legislation formalizing a policy of apartheid (separation of the races) was expanded.

Between 1948 and 1979, the South African Parliament had adopted 300 pieces of legislation on apartheid.

The premise underlying the apartheid laws was that South Africa's racially heterogeneous population of 26 million people—18.6 million blacks, 4.3 million whites, 2.4 million "coloreds" (people of mixed race) and 740,000 Asians—could not and should not be integrated. Rather, the country should evolve as a commonwealth of separate states, nine African and one white.

There were three main components to the Nationalist government's apartheid policy: petty apartheid; the homelands (Bantustan) policy of separate development; and influx control restrictions on black movement and employment in white areas.[5]

Petty apartheid referred to the physical segregation of blacks and whites in all public places such as buses, restaurants, beaches, theaters, and sports events. Likened to segregation in the U.S. South prior to the 1960s, it remained fixed in law in 1980. However, under Nationalist Prime Minister P. W. Botha, who was appointed in 1979, petty apartheid was being partially re-examined. In a series of statements, the Prime Minister had called for an end to "unnecessary, discriminatory measures" and had suggested that certain laws forbidding intermixing of the races be reviewed.

Homelands Policy. Under the Homelands Citizenship Act of 1970, the government had proclaimed that all blacks living in South Africa henceforth were citizens of one of nine tribal "homelands" or Bantustans and hence were aliens in the white Republic of South Africa. Blacks living in South Africa were assigned to one of these homelands according to their tribal ancestry. The homelands comprised approximately 13% of the total land area of South Africa. Three of the nine—Transkei, Bophuthatswana, and Venda—had been declared independent by 1980, with the others slated to follow shortly.

Also under the separate development policies, all government programs, including those for education, health and social welfare, industrial development, and agriculture, were administered separately for each racial group.

Through the earlier Group Areas Act of 1940, each race living within or around one of South Africa's urban centers was assigned to a certain living zone or township in the area. Africans living in Johannesburg, the capital city, were assigned to live in Soweto, a township of about 1.5 million people located 10 miles outside the center of the city. Within each such township, housing areas were further assigned by tribal group. The government reserved the right to declare any area for another racial group and to relocate all people living in that area. Between 1950 and 1980, approximately 500,000 people were relocated under this policy.

Influx Control. Beginning in 1921, the government had passed a series of laws to control the number of blacks living or working outside their assigned homeland, particularly near the urban areas. The most significant was the Bantu Consolidation Act of 1945 which provided that an African could not visit a white urban area for longer than 72 hours without first obtaining a special permit, and could not reside there unless he or she had lived there continuously since birth, had worked continuously for 10 years with a single employer, or was the spouse or minor of someone who had received the legal right to live there. To facilitate monitoring of blacks in white areas, the government required all blacks over the age of 16 to carry passbooks for identification whenever they were travelling in white areas.

In addition to the pass laws, it had been government policy to restrict training of blacks for skilled jobs to the homelands. In 1975, the government agreed for the first time to establish 16 industrial training centers for blacks in white areas to train approximately 1,500 blacks a year for semi-skilled jobs in such areas as welding, metal work, and keypunch operation.

RECENT DEVELOPMENTS IN APARTHEID POLICY

While reaffirming the policy of separate development and the need for homelands, Botha's government by 1980 was considering easing the restrictions of petty apartheid. Additionally, it had adopted the recommendations of two "blue ribbon" South African commissions that called for eased restrictions on training and job advancement for Africans, desegregation of facilities, rights for Africans to join trade unions, and liberalization of the pass laws for Africans already living legally in white areas.

Simultaneously, racial tensions in the country appeared to be increasing. The black township of Soweto had been the scene of several days of rioting in 1975 and 1976. The dissension centered on black working and living conditions and the use of the Afrikaans language in black schools. Additional outbreaks of violence in 1977 followed the death while in prison of Steve Biko, a leader of the black consciousness movement. Most recently, in the Spring of 1980, Capetown had been the site of a school boycott by 100,000 colored students who were protesting the uneven government contribution toward education between whites and non-whites. *Per capita* expenditures on education were estimated to be $900 for each white student, $280 for each colored student, and $70 for each black student enrolled in the three school systems. Finally, government leaders were expressing concern that the recent election of a Marxist black leader, Robert Mugabe, in neighboring Zimbabwe (formerly the white-dominated country of Rhodesia) might incite further outbreaks of violence among South African non-whites.

Despite continuing racial pressures, South Africa was recovering strongly in 1980 from the effects of a severe economic recession which had taken hold from 1975 to 1978. Largely due to the high price of gold and other scarce minerals, the country's GNP rose from $50.6 to $57.7 million between 1978 and 1979, and the need for outside capital to stimulate economic growth was reduced.

U.S. CORPORATE ACTIVITY IN SOUTH AFRICA[6]

U.S. Corporate investment in the Republic of South Africa began shortly after World War II when the country began a major industrial expansion effort. Aggregate U.S. private investment grew to $286 million by 1960, to

$964 million by 1970, and to $1.99 billion by 1978. In that year, 350 of the best known companies in the U.S., including 55 of the *Fortune* top 100 companies, had subsidiaries operating in South Africa. Six thousand more did business indirectly through sales agents and distributors. The total value of U.S. direct investment in South Africa by 1978 was approximately 1.2% of total U.S. direct investment abroad. For most American companies, their investment in South Africa represented less than one percent of their total assets.

Within the South African economy, the U.S. firms provided 16.4% of total foreign direct investment which constituted, in turn, 24% of all private investment in South Africa. American companies controlled about 40% of the petroleum market, 23% of auto sales, and 65% of computer sales. Investment had tended to concentrate in these fast-growing sectors of the South African economy.

U.S.-owned firms employed approximately 100,000 people out of a labor force of eight million. Of these 100,000 workers, 70,000 were black, and composed approximately 1% of the country's black labor pool. Twenty-one American firms had more than 1,000 employees and seventy-two employed more than 250.

U.S. POLICY TOWARD SOUTH AFRICA[7]

Since the early 1970s, the U.S. government's stated policy had been to encourage South Africans to work for a "society in which there could be full rights, justice, and political participation for all people." At the same time, the government had not actively discouraged U.S. investment in South Africa. Implementation of this policy had moved along two paths: support for the Sullivan Principles as a "voluntary" corporate-sponsored effort to improve labor practices and, beginning in February 1978, imposition of Commerce Department restrictions that barred the sales of U.S. products and technology to the South African police and military. Additionally, Congress had passed a bill in 1978 that prohibited the Export-Import Bank from extending credit for any export that would contribute to the maintenance of apartheid by the South African government. The legislation curtailed Ex-Im bank credits to South Africa. U.S. policy toward South Africa was characterized in 1980 as advocating gradual change through direct and indirect economic pressures, but not major confrontation.

THE SOUTH AFRICAN ISSUE[8]

Beginning in the early 1970s concern over U.S. corporate involvement in South Africa began to mount. There were two main sources of the dissent: church groups, led primarily by the Interfaith Center on Corporate Responsibility (ICCR), an affiliate of the National Council of Churches, and university groups on a number of major campuses, including Harvard, Yale, Stanford, Princeton and the University of Michigan.

Founded in 1972, the ICCR was a coalition of seventeen Protestant denominations and 170 Catholic orders and dioceses. Since its inception, its focus had been on introducing corporate shareholder resolutions on a wide range of social issues. The issues included corporate activity in South Africa, infant formula marketing practices, and nuclear power. In 1979, ICCR-related church groups filed eighty-two resolutions, including thirty on South Africa, addressed to sixty-one U.S. corporations. In addition to sponsoring shareholder resolutions on South Africa, ICCR-affiliated church groups had with increased frequency met directly with corporate leaders, requesting clarification of their corporate policies in South Africa.

Simultaneously, student activism against universities' investments in firms with operations in South Africa had created campus advocacy groups such as the Harvard-Radcliffe Solidarity Committee, the (Yale) Anti-Apartheid Coalition, and the (Stanford) Committee Against Apartheid to lobby for university divestiture of such stocks. In 1977, Wesleyan students had occupied their president's office for three days in protest of Wesleyan's portfolio on investment securities, including South African associated companies; at Stanford in the same year, 234 students were arrested after demonstrating against a Board of Trustees decision not to support a shareholder resolution asking Ford Motor Company to withdraw from South Africa.

In partial response to student pressures, many universities had established committees of students, faculty and alumni to formally review and recommend how the university should vote its proxies on shareholder resolutions and when to consider divestiture of a particular stock. It was estimated that educational institutions (including private and public universities and preparatory schools) collectively owned common stock valued at approximately ten billion dollars, of which an estimated 15% was held in companies with South African operations.

THE SULLIVAN PRINCIPLES[9]

The Sullivan Principles had become one of the focal points of the controversy surrounding U.S. corporate involvement in South Africa. The Principles had been developed by Reverend Leon H. Sullivan, a black minister and employment activist from Philadelphia. Appointed to General Motors' Board of Directors in January 1971, Sullivan attracted national attention at his first annual meeting as a GM director by voting for a shareholder resolution—the first of its kind—that called for General Motors to withdraw from South Africa.

Subsequent trips to that country and meetings with white and black South African and U.S. leaders convinced Sullivan that there might be a more effective alternative than advocating complete corporate withdrawal from South Africa. He commented in 1975:

What I sensed all the people who came to me were saying was, 'You say you want to help us. Well, why don't you try to make American companies operating here real agents of change.' I'm not sure yet whether it was the right thing to do but I came home determined to get American companies there to change their policies and practices.[10]

In January 1976, Sullivan, together with Thomas A. Murphy, chief executive of General Motors, and Frank Cary, chief executive of IBM, presided over a meeting with representatives from fifteen major U.S. corporations with South African interests to discuss how they could become constructive agents for change in South Africa. The participants agreed that the most effective tactic would be to draft a statement of principles governing corporate conduct in South Africa and then to get as many corporations as possible to sign.

On May 1, 1977, Sullivan released a statement of six principles to which 12 of the 15 companies had agreed. These Sullivan Principles covered such areas as non-segregation of all facilities; equal pay for equal work; equal employment practices; initiation of training programs for non-white workers; increased numbers of non-whites in managerial positions; and improved quality of life for employees outside of work in areas such as housing, education, and health. Exhibit 1 gives the text of the six Principles.

In preparing the six Principles, Sullivan, accompanied by Murphy and Carey, called on the South African Ambassador in Washington, D.C. The ambassador said he found the Principles "acceptable" but asked that accompanying language pledging the companies to seek changes in "existing South African laws and customs" be softened. Others in South Africa were clearly not as sanguine; the Johannesburg *Citizen* grumbled: "There is nothing in the South African scheme of things which prevents any company from carrying out such a programme. What sticks in our gullet is that the code of conduct is being forced on American firms here by civil rights campaigners in the U.S., . . . as if it were an extension of their campaign in the U.S. Why not campaign to end tokenism in America—where the token black is advanced as a sop to the Negro community?"

Sullivan and his corporate allies kept closely in touch with American diplomatic officials. Secretary of State Cyrus Vance appeared at a Sullivan dinner in October 1977 and said, "You can count on us in the government to support you in every way for this private effort. . . . And at any time that we can do anything to help you in this most important effort, we are there, and just call us."

By June 1978, 105 companies had signed the Principles. Companies obviously had different reasons for signing. Some felt under direct shareholder pressure; twenty-three of forty signatories in one period would have faced shareholder resolutions demanding that they sign the Principles, if they had not done so voluntarily. Other company executives expressed the desire to be a force for social change in South Africa, if they were to remain in the country. Paul R. Gibson, an executive vice president for international operations at Envirotech, one of the early signatory companies, commented:

> . . . in order to remain in South Africa—and we do want to remain—we must establish a continuing and expanding program for disregarding South Africa laws, regulations, and customs that discriminate against our employees because of their color. . . . The primary vehicle we have chosen to work with for direction and guidance of our human rights program is the Reverend Leon Sullivan and his ever-expanding Statement of Principles on human rights.[11]

In July 1978, Sullivan's group enlarged its focus to increase the emphasis on implementation of the Principles. For the first time, it initiated a reporting procedure for signatory companies whereby each firm reported on its progress semi-annually in each of the six areas. Exhibit 2 identifies the criteria used to rate the companies' compliance with the Principles. Arthur D. Little, a management consulting firm, was hired to analyze these reports and to publish the results.

By the time the Sullivan group's Third Report was published in October 1979, the progress reports included a system for ranking each of the 135 signatory companies into three major categories: "making good progress," "making acceptable progress," and "need to become more active." By 1979 the signatory companies represented over 85% of U.S. investment and over 90% of U.S. employees in South Africa.

Additionally, the reports included for the first time a listing of the 164 U.S. companies which had subsidiaries in South Africa but had not signed the Principles.

In addition to initiating a reporting and rating system of signatory companies, the Sullivan group began expanding the Principles themselves. In July 1978 and again in May 1979, Reverend Sullivan had amplified the Principles by requiring signatory companies to:

acknowledge the rights of blacks to form or join trade unions

assist in developing black and non-white enterprises

lobby for the abolition of South African laws that reserved higher paying skilled jobs for whites and that restricted black and non-white apprenticeship programs

support change in the influx control laws that prohibited the families of black workers from living in South Africa with the employee.

It was expected that companies which had signed the Principles would accept and work to implement these and future amplifications articulated by Reverend Sullivan. He also had organized seven Task Forces—composed of U.S. corporate representatives, their South African managers, and South African blacks—to oversee the implementation and potential future refinements of each Principle. The seventh Task Force studied the format of the progress reports with the goal of reducing the reporting burden to the company.

Beginning in 1979, Sullivan had also begun to send on-site monitors to South Africa to evaluate in person the progress of individual companies. While findings on these companies were not to be released, the results would be incorporated in future reports on aggregate corporate progress in implementing the Principles. Sullivan had indicated that the amount of monitoring by his organization would increase.

These additional demands on companies had provoked "some disagreements, but we haven't lost any companies," according to Dan Purnell, Executive Director of the Sullivan Principles organization.

Finally, in August of 1979, Reverend Sullivan intensified the pressure on the 164 non-signatory companies by personally writing to each one, strongly urging them to sign the Principles. This was followed by direct contact by the top management of signatory companies who further encouraged them to sign. Local church leaders and university representatives were also asked by the Sullivan Principles organization to meet with corporate leaders and urge them to comply with the Principles.

Sullivan and the corporate leaders found it difficult to evaluate the impact of their efforts. The campaign had not substantially changed South African policies. It was clear South African officials had chosen to overlook practices of American companies which violated existing laws and customs, but it was only in 1980 that the government finally announced its intention to desegregate toilets at company facilities or to permit any black workers to be fully represented by trade unions.

Despite his efforts in 1979 to stiffen the Principles and their enforcements, Sullivan himself was increasingly criticized by other activists in the United States and by black leaders in other parts of Africa. Some felt the Sullivan Principles had become a public relations tool which permitted American companies to continue to operate in South Africa.

DRESSER INDUSTRIES' RESPONSE TO THE SULLIVAN PRINCIPLES[12]

Dresser Industries was one of the non-signatories which faced growing pressure to sign the Principles. In 1978 university organizations and church groups affiliated with the Interfaith Committee on Corporate Responsibility had proposed to various companies 22 resolutions dealing with South Africa; by 1979 the number had grown to 34. Since many issues had been garnering three to nine percent of the votes cast, it was likely that the number of South Africa-related shareholder resolutions would increase—both because new companies would face resolutions and because resolutions raised in prior years with established firms would be re-introduced. According to SEC rules, a resolution could be reintroduced if it received three percent or more of shareholders' votes cast in the first year it was introduced, greater than six percent of the vote in the second year, and ten percent or more of the vote in subsequent years.

In August of 1979, Reverend Sullivan had written to the management of Dresser asking for a commitment to sign the Principles. The company's answer to Reverend Sullivan was an offer to sign, provided that they did not have to submit progress reports or permit on-site monitoring by a non-governmental authority. (See Exhibit 3 for Dresser Industries' letter.) According to Mr. Edward R. Luter, Dresser's Senior Vice President, Finance:

> . . . we had no problem with the Sullivan Principles as such. The Sullivan group, however, had added the requirement that signatory companies had to submit semi-annual progress reports and submit to periodic inspections. We could not agree to these latter requirements. The required reporting document was quite voluminous and we didn't feel like taking on voluntarily an additional reporting burden. We have enough of that with governmental bureaucracies that exist already. Additionally, we would not agree to let another organization inspect our premises.

Reverend Sullivan would not consent to these qualifications and Dresser's management elected not to sign the Principles. According to Mr. Luter,

> Reverend Sullivan understood our reservations about signing but could not agree to our desired qualifications. His organization was concerned that if we were allowed to waive the reporting and monitoring requirements, about one hundred and twenty-three other signatory companies would want the same waiver. . . . We parted on friendly terms.

In October of 1979, Dresser received a letter from the Executive Council of the Protestant Episcopal Church, which owned 21,300 shares of Dresser Stock. The letter informed Dresser that the church had submitted for SEC review a shareholder resolution that called on the company to sell its South African subsidiary if Dresser had not signed and complied with the Sullivan Principles by December 30, 1981. (See Exhibits 5, 6, and 7 for the text of the letter, the shareholder resolution, and the church's supporting statement for the resolution.)

The proponents cited three reasons for raising the resolution. First, they expressed concern over Dresser's statement that it intended to be a "good corporate citizen" in South Africa and "operate under the laws and customs of that country." They contended that such practices amounted to tacit endorsement of apartheid, since government laws and customs included wage and fringe benefit discrimination against non-whites, assignment of jobs by race, segregation of facilities, and prohibition against blacks occupying certain jobs or supervising whites.

Second, the proponents stated that they had selected the Sullivan Principles as the standard against which Dresser's labor practices should be measured because the Principles, which had already been widely adopted by American firms, represented "minimum desegregation and fair employment standards" and thus were the very least that a responsible company should be doing in South Africa.

Third, the proponents stated that many institutional investors adopted policies of selling stock "in companies which fail to subscribe to, or which violate, the Sullivan Principles."

Dresser's management responded to the church's letter a week later. (See Exhibit 8 for the text of this response.) In addition, Dresser's Board of Directors prepared a statement that detailed their opposition to the resolution. (See Exhibit 9 for Dresser's statement.) In accordance with SEC regulations, the shareholder resolution, the Church's supporting statement, and the company's opposing statement were all included in the proxy materials sent to all Dresser Industries' shareholders.

In arguing against the resolution, Dresser's management made four points. First, Dresser had already addressed the proponents' concern about its operations by adopting and implementing its own statement of equal opportunity principles (See Exhibit 4 for the statement.)

Secondly, the labor practices of American business in general, as well as those of Dresser itself, had benefited the black community in South Africa and "provided an example which should help influence a change in the social system in South Africa." Withdrawal of U.S. companies, management argued, would curtail this beneficial influence and would "contribute adversely to the economy of the country, which would have a disproportionately adverse effect upon the black community."

Thirdly, the company opposed the resolution "because it would subordinate business decisions to the foreign policy goals of particular shareholders." According to Edward Luter, the company believed the true purpose of the Dresser resolution, and similar resolutions to other companies, was to force the divestment of South African subsidiaries. He observed that:

> . . . no signatory company of the Sullivan Principles can be in full compliance with these Principles, since such compliance would require violation of South Africa's laws. Our position is to comply with the laws of the country. If you are a company doing business throughout the world, you can't go about flagrantly violating the laws of other countries.

Finally, the company believed divestment would harm not only the South African black community, but also Dresser shareholders who would suffer financial losses as the company attempted to sell its subsidiary "without regard to the effect on the company" in a "fire sale" atmosphere.

Soon after Dresser's top management learned of the upcoming shareholder resolution on the Sullivan Principles, they also began receiving concerned letters from twenty-five institutional investors. These institutional investors represented a broad spectrum of organizations and included insurance companies, banks, diversified corporations, non-profit foundations, state agencies, universities, and churches. Most of these investors requested that Dresser's management explain why it had not signed the Principles or more generally, that it clarify its policies for conducting business in South Africa.

One institutional investor had already taken stronger action the previous year to indicate its displeasure with Dresser's stand on the Sullivan Principles. On September 9, 1978, the Board of Regents of the University of Washington authorized the divestiture of all 4,000 shares of Dresser stock held in the University's endowment fund. The market value of the shares was $178,000 at the time of sale. The Regents had decided to divest after concluding that Dresser Industries did not conform to University standards of corporate responsibility in their business operations in South Africa. University policy called on all companies doing business in South Africa to adhere to the Sullivan Principles—or an equivalent code of conduct—as a minimum standard of corporate behavior.[13]

At Dresser's 1980 annual meeting, the resolution received 11.46% of the proxy votes cast. The vote represented the largest support for a shareholder resolution on the South African issue in the 1980 proxy season. The vote also made likely the prospect that the resolution would be brought up again before shareholders the following year.

The top management of Dresser Industries had to decide what action, if any, to take next.

NOTES

1. Background information on Dresser's early history is drawn from Darwin Payne, *Initiative in Energy: Dresser Industries* (Simon & Schuster, 1979).

2. All 1978–1979 financial and operating information is drawn from Dresser Industries' *1979 Report on Your Investment* (Annual Report).

3. Material in this section is drawn heavily from *Corporate Activity in South Africa: Dresser Industries, Inc.*, 1980 Analysis C, Supplement No. 2, February 28, 1980 (Investor Responsibility Research Center, Inc.).

4. *Prospectus for 1979*, South African Bureau for Economic Research (Johannesburg, 1979).

5. Information on apartheid policy is drawn heavily from *Corporate Activity in South Africa: Dresser Industries, Inc.*

6. Material in this section is drawn from E. J. Kahn, Jr., "Annals of International Trade: A Very Emotive Subject," *New Yorker*, May 14, 1979.

7. Material in this section is drawn heavily from *Corporate Activity in South Africa: Dresser Industries, Inc.*

8. Material in this section is drawn from "Annals of International Trade: A Very Emotive Subject."

9. Material in this section is drawn from "Annals of International Trade: A Very Emotive Subject," and from interviews with Mr. Dan Purnell, Executive Director and Mr. Warren Davis, Assistant to the Director of the Sullivan Principles Organization, the International Council for Equality of Opportunity Principles.

10. Reverend Sullivan is quoted in "Annals of International Trade: A Very Emotive Subject."

11. From Paul R. Gibson's speech before the Phoenix Committee on Foreign Relations, Phoenix, Arizona, July 27, 1979.

12. Material in this section is drawn from *Corporate Activity in South Africa: Dresser Industries, Inc.*, and from interviews with Mr. Edward R. Luter, Senior Vice President-Finance, Dresser Industries, Inc.

13. Interview with Dr. Steven Olswang, Assistant Provost for Academic Affairs, University of Washington.

AN UPDATE

Dresser's official position on its willingness to sign the Sullivan Principles while at the same time refusing to submit to yearly progress reports and on-site monitoring in South Africa ended in 1984. According to Herb

Ryan, Dresser's Director of Investor Relations, within months of J. J. Murphy being appointed CEO of Dresser, Murphy received a call from Secretary of State George Shultz inviting him to Washington for lunch with the president. At that luncheon, the president argued that his policy of avoiding "further federal sanctions against South Africa" would best be served if Dresser would be willing to "voluntarily" sign the Sullivan Principles and submit to "periodic reports on the progress that has been accomplished on the implementation of these principles."

Because of this conversation, said Mr. Ryan, Murphy decided to sign and comply with all aspects of the Sullivan Principles, and contracted the services of Arthur D. Little, Inc., Corporate Auditors and Consultants, to overview Dresser's progress in their regard. Since signing the accord, Dresser has received "favorable ratings" and has been certified by Arthur D. Little as being "full compliance" with the agreement.

Exhibit 1

DRESSER INDUSTRIES AND SOUTH AFRICA
TEXT OF THE SULLIVAN PRINCIPLES
(INCLUDING 1978 AND 1979 AMPLIFICATIONS)

Principle I   Non-segregation of the races in all eating, comfort and work facilities.

Each signator of the Statement of Principles will proceed immediately to:

Eliminate all vestiges of racial discrimination.

Remove all race designation signs.

Desegregate all eating, comfort and work facilities.

Principle II   Equal and fair employment practices for all employees.

Each signator of the Statement of Principles will proceed immediately to:

Implement equal and fair terms and conditions of employment.

Provide non-discriminatory eligibility for benefit plans.

Establish an appropriate comprehensive procedure for handling and resolving individual employee complaints.

Support the elimination of all industrial racial discriminatory laws which impede the implementation of equal and fair terms and conditions of employment, such as abolition of job reservations, job fragmentation, and apprenticeship restrictions for Blacks and other non-whites.

Support the elimination of discrimination against the rights of Blacks to form or belong to government registered unions, and acknowledge generally the right of Black workers to form their own union or be represented by trade unions where unions already exist.

Principle III   Equal pay for all employees doing equal or comparable work for the same period of time.

Each signator of the Statement of Principles will proceed immediately to:

Design and implement a wage and salary administration plan which is applied equally to all employees regardless of race who are performing equal or comparable work.

Ensure an equitable system of job classifications, including a review of the distinction between hourly and salaried classifications.

Determine whether upgrading of personnel and/or jobs in the lower echelons is needed, and if so, implement programs to accomplish this objective expeditiously.

Assign equitable wage and salary ranges, the minimum of these to be well above the appropriate local minimum economic living level.

Source: Amplified Guidelines to South African Statement of Principles, released by the International Council for Equality of Opportunity Principles, Inc.

Principle IV   Initiation of and development of training programs that will prepare, in substantial numbers, Blacks and other non-whites for supervisory, administrative, clerical and technical jobs.

Each signator of the Statement of Principles will proceed immediately to:

> Determine employee training needs and capabilities, and identify employees with potential for further advancement.
>
> Take advantage of existing outside training resources and activities, such as exchange programs, technical colleges, vocational schools, continuation classes, supervisory courses and similar institutions or programs.
>
> Support the development of outside training facilities individually or collectively, including technical centers, professional training exposure, correspondence and extension courses, as appropriate, for extensive training outreach.
>
> Initiate and expand inside training programs and facilities.

Principle V   Increasing the number of Blacks and other non-whites in management and supervisory positions.

Each signator of the Statement of Principles will proceed immediately to:

> Identify, actively recruit, train and develop a sufficient and significant number of Blacks and other non-whites to assure that as quickly as possible there will be appropriate representation of Blacks and other non-whites in the management group of each company at all levels of operations.
>
> Establish management development programs for Blacks and other non-whites, as appropriate, and improve existing programs and facilities for developing management skills of Blacks and other non-whites.
>
> Identify and channel high management potential Blacks and other non-white employees into management development programs.

Principle VI   Improving the quality of employees' lives outside the work environment in such areas as housing, transportation, schooling, recreation and health facilities.

Each signator of the Statement of Principles will proceed immediately to:

> Evaluate existing and/or develop programs, as appropriate, to address the specific needs of Black and other non-white employees in the areas of housing, health care, transportation and recreation.
>
> Evaluate methods for utilizing existing, expanded or newly established in-house medical facilities or other medical programs to improve medical care for all non-whites and their dependents.
>
> Participate in the development of programs that address the educational needs of employees, their dependents and the local community. Both individual and collective programs should be considered, including such activities as literacy education, business training, direct assistance to local schools, contributions and scholarships.
>
> Support changes in influx control laws to provide for the right of Black migrant workers to normal family life.

Increase utilization of and assist in the development of Black and nonwhite owned and operated business enterprises including distributors, suppliers of goods and services and manufacturers.

With all the foregoing in mind, it is the objective of the companies to involve and assist in the education and training of large and telling numbers of Blacks and other non-whites as quickly as possible. The ultimate impact of this effort is intended to be of massive proportion, reaching millions.

PERIODIC REPORTING

The signator companies of the Statement of Principles will proceed immediately to:

Utilize a standard format to report their progress to Dr. Sullivan through the independent administrative unit which he has established on a 6-month basis.

Ensure periodic reports on the progress that has been accomplished on the implementation of these principles.

Exhibit 2

DRESSER INDUSTRIES AND SOUTH AFRICA
RATING CRITERIA FOR SIGNATORY COMPANIES'
COMPLIANCE WITH THE SULLIVAN PRINCIPLES
JUNE 30, 1979

The use of this rating system will require a degree of judgment with respect to qualitative issues as well as adjustment for issues which may not be applicable to a particular reporting unit.

	PRINCIPLE 1	2	3
I	Full non-segregation	Full non-segregation schedule by 6/30/80	Segregated
II	IF UNIONS—all races have the same union, or if a white union is recognized, black union and unions for all races also recognized, or has posted a notice of willingness to recognize non-white unions, OR IF NO UNION(S)—uniform integrated grievance procedure	All races represented with non-integrated grievance procedures	Some races do not have grievance procedures
IIb	All benefits for non-whites equal to or better than for whites	All except one benefit are equal to or better than for whites	2 or more benefits for non-white are less than for whites
IIIa	Both equal pay & minimum entry level pay substantially above recognized local minimum economic living level	Both equal pay and minimum entry level pay at or above the recognized local minimum economic living level	Either unequal pay or minimum entry level pay below recognized local minimum economic living level
IIIb	Substantial effort	Advancement of blacks into higher job categories Fair effort	Little or no effect
IIIc	Quite considerable	Improvement in pay status of non-whites Fairly extensive	Little or none
IV	Active training for advancement and job skills	Active training for advancement OR job skills	Little or no training
V	Quite considerable	Advancement of non-whites Somewhat considerable	Slight or no advancement

| VI Considerable activity or significant improvement | Assisting outside the work environment Some activity or some improvement | Little or no assistance |

There are 9 issues which will be rated with each being given 1–3 points. The best rating a reporting unit could get would be a 9 by being judged to be entirely in the left-hand column above. A company which is described as being entirely in the second column would be rated 18. Other ratings would be determined by the addition of the 9 rating numbers and could lie anywhere from 9 to 27 inclusive. Reporting units would be grouped into the following categories:

I Making good progress   11 points (no 3's)
II Making acceptable progress   18 points or less
III Needs to become more active more than 18 points
IV Inadequate report
V Submitting first report

Exhibit 3

DRESSER INDUSTRIES AND SOUTH AFRICA LETTER TO REVEREND SULLIVAN

DRESSER INDUSTRIES, INC.
DRESSER BUILDING
ELM AT AKARD
DALLAS, TEXAS 75201

August 21, 1979

Reverend Leon H. Sullivan
Zion Baptist Church
N.W. Corner Broad & Venango Streets
Philadelphia, PA 19140

Dear Reverend Sullivan:

Thank you for your August 14 letter and attached information addressed to Mr. James. Let me first say that our previous decision not to formally adopt the Statement of Principles should not be construed as our opposing them or not supporting them. We have developed and implemented our own Statement of Principles, which we are monitoring to assure compliance. Attached is a copy of our Principles for your information. Our management has reviewed these principles with the Labor Attache of the U.S. Embassy in South Africa. The Labor Attache commented that our principles looked good, and he was impressed with our accomplishments to date. We are enthusiastic about the Statement of Principles which we have adopted and are confident they are in compliance with local laws.

If it would help your cause to identify Dresser with other U.S. companies fostering racial equality in South Africa, we would be willing to adopt such principles for this purpose. We are not willing to commit to the submission of progress reports or on-site monitoring in South Africa. Our reporting burden to governmental agencies is costing the company and its shareholders entirely too much already, and it is ever increasing. We participated in a study conducted by Arthur Andersen & Co. and found that in 1977 reporting requirements to only six federal agencies, i.e., EPA, OSHA, EEO, ERISA, FTC, and DOE, cost our company $10½ million. There is no telling what our total reporting and compliance costs are for all agencies worldwide.

If our formal adoption of your Statement of Principles, subject to the above conditions, will be of assistance to you, please let me know.

Sincerely,

Exhibit 4

ENCLOSURE WITH LETTER TO REVEREND SULLIVAN DRESSER SOUTH AFRICA (PTY) LIMITED STATEMENT OF PRINCIPLES

1. All Operations will provide equal employment opportunity to all employees and applicants for employment, regardless of race, color, religion, age, sex, or national origin. Such action will apply to all employment practices, including hiring, discharge, compensation, promotion, classification, training, apprenticeship, and terms, conditions and privileges of employment.
2. All Operations will provide equal pay for all employees doing equal or comparable work for the same period of time.
3. Dresser will promote and assist in providing training programs to assist Blacks to become literate, and those who have the capability of becoming administration clerks, artisans or supervisors. Where capabilities exist, Blacks will also be prepared for management positions.
4. Uniform pension schemes will be adopted for all employees, unanimously, and medical aid schemes for the Blacks and other Non-Whites will be provided as required.
5. Non-segregation of all races where the law permits.
6. All employees will respect one another's human dignity.

Source: Dresser Industries, Inc. literature (from Rev. Sullivan letter).

Exhibit 5

*DRESSER INDUSTRIES AND SOUTH AFRICA TEXT OF OCTOBER 1979 LETTER
TO DRESSER INDUSTRIES FROM THE EPISCOPAL CHURCH*

THE EPISCOPAL CHURCH CENTER
815 SECOND AVENUE
NEW YORK, NEW YORK 10017

October 31, 1979

President and Chief Executive Officer
Dresser Industries
Dresser Building
1505 Elm Street
Dallas, Texas 75221

On behalf of the Executive Council of the Protestant Episcopal
Church in the United States of America, *I submit herewith a shareholder resolution and supporting statement for inclusion in your proxy
statement for your 1980 annual meeting of shareholders.* The resolution
asks that Dresser Industries subscribe to the Sullivan Principles and
see that its South African affiliate complies with each of them.

It is our normal practice to discuss such a resolution with the
corporation to which it is to be submitted prior to its submission.
However, the untimely death of our staff person in this area,
combined with the relatively early filing date for your Company,
has not permitted this to occur. However, we are available to
discuss it with you at your early convenience. You can contact me
at:

35th Floor
400 Renaissance Center
Detroit, Michigan 48243
telephone: (313)568-6782

to make such arrangements.

Very truly yours,

John K. Cannon

/jkz

The Office of the Presiding Bishop and the
Executive Council of the General Convention

Exhibit 6

DRESSER INDUSTRIES AND SOUTH AFRICA TEXT OF SHAREHOLDER RESOLUTION TO DRESSER INDUSTRIES

Whereas, more than 115 major United States Corporations, including IBM, Exxon, General Motors, Ford, Mobil and General Electric have subscribed to the "Sullivan Principles";

Whereas, the six Sullivan Principles set forth the minimum desegregation and fair employment standards for American corporations operating in South Africa;

Whereas, these six principles provide for:

Nonsegregation of the races in all eating, comfort and work facilities;

Equal and fair employment practices for all employees (including non-discriminatory benefit plans);

Equal pay for all employees doing comparable work (including an equitable system of job classification);

Instituting training programs which will prepare substantial numbers of blacks for supervisory, administrative, clerical and technical jobs;

Increasing the number of blacks in management and supervisory positions;

Improving the quality of employees' lives outside the work place in areas such as housing, transportation, schooling, recreation and health facilities;

Whereas, Dresser has refused to subscribe to the Sullivan Principles, and has stated that it intends "to be a good corporate citizen" in South Africa and "operate under the laws and customs of [that] country";

Whereas, many institutional investors have stated that they will sell all their stock in companies which fail to subscribe to, or which violate, the Sullivan Principles;

Therefore, be it Resolved that the shareholders request the Board to establish the following as the policy of this corporation:

"That in the event that Dresser's South African affiliate has not complied, by December 31, 1981, in all respects with each of the six Sullivan Principles, the corporation shall take whatever steps are necessary to dispose promptly of its ownership interest in its South African affiliate."

Exhibit 7

DRESSER INDUSTRIES AND SOUTH AFRICA
STATEMENT OF THE EPISCOPAL CHURCH IN SUPPORT OF ITS DRESSER
INDUSTRIES SHAREHOLDER RESOLUTION

In 1977, the Senate Foreign Affairs Committee repeatedly requested Dresser to provide information on Dresser's South African employment practices in connection with Senate hearings on U.S. investment in South Africa. Dresser management refused to supply this data to Congress.

In 1977, 12 American corporations, including GM, Ford, IBM, Caltex and 3M, announced certain principles of fair employment practices for their South African operations. Subsequently, more than 100 additional U.S. corporations have signed these principles. Dresser has refused to sign. With approximately 1,000 employees and $60,000,000 of South African sales in 1977, Dresser is probably the largest American corporation operating in South Africa without signing these fair employment principles.

Instead, Dresser has publicly announced that it would follow the "customs" of South Africa. These customs include wage and fringe benefit discrimination against blacks, assignment of jobs by race, segregation of facilities, low wages and lack of advancement opportunities for blacks and prohibitions against blacks occupying certain jobs or supervising whites.

Much of what Dresser manufactures in South Africa with cheap black labor is exported.

We believe that Dresser should meet the minimum desegregation standards of the Sullivan Principles or, if it will not or cannot, it should withdraw from South Africa.

Exhibit 8

DRESSER INDUSTRIES AND SOUTH AFRICA TEXT OF DRESSER INDUSTRIES'
RESPONSE TO THE EPISCOPAL CHURCH

DRESSER INDUSTRIES, INC.
DRESSER BUILDING
ELM AT AKARD
DALLAS, TEXAS 75201

November 5, 1979

Mr. John K. Cannon
Executive Council of the Protestant Episcopal
   Church in the United States of America
35th Floor
400 Renaissance Center
Detroit, Michigan 48243

Dear Mr. Cannon:

This will acknowledge receipt of your letter of October 31, 1979, to
Mr. J. V. James, enclosing a shareholder resolution and supporting
statement for inclusion in the proxy statement of the 1980 Annual
Meeting of Shareholders of Dresser Industries, Inc. ("Dresser").

In considering what you wish to do, I would think you would have
an interest in knowing something about the communications between Dresser and Sullivan's organization. We received a letter
from Reverend Sullivan dated August 14, 1979, urging us to
support the Statement of Principles. In his letter, he said, "I am
prepared to work with you in overcoming obstacles that prevent
your company from making an affirmative response in this
regard."

Actually, Dresser had no problem with the six Sullivan Principles as
such. However, in early 1979 they issued a second amplification
requiring companies adopting the principles to make periodic (each
six months) reports on progress and to allow on-site monitoring of
their facilities. On August 21, I sent a letter to Reverend Sullivan
(copy attached) stating our willingness to adopt the Sullivan Principles but stating that we are not willing to commit to the submission
of progress reports or on-site monitoring because of our already
burdensome reporting requirements to many governmental agencies. In response, I received a phone call from Larry Wise, a
member of Sullivan's organization, stating that our adoption of the
principles would not be satisfactory unless we agreed to the report-

ing requirements and on-site inspection. He stated that they understood our reasoning for the position and hoped we would understand theirs.

We feel that we have been very reasonable and would still be willing to endorse the six principles but do not intend to make Dresser accountable to and place it under the scrutiny of a private organization with the resulting diversion of Dresser management's time and efforts.

We have reviewed the Dresser stockholders list and the Executive Council of the Protestant Episcopal Church of the United States of America, on whose behalf you state you are submitting the resolution, is not shown as a record owner of Dresser Common Stock. Therefore, we assume that it is a beneficial owner. We request that appropriate documentary support be submitted to Dresser for the claim that the Executive Council is a beneficial owner of Dresser Common Stock. As required by Rule 14a-8, the letter does not contain notification of intent to appear at the meeting to present the proposal.

Very truly yours,

cc. Mr. John J. Cannon
     The Episcopal Church Center
     815 Second Avenue
     New York, NY 10017

Registered Mail—Return Receipt Requested

Exhibit 9

DRESSER INDUSTRIES AND SOUTH AFRICA STATEMENT OF DRESSER INDUSTRIES' BOARD OF DIRECTORS AGAINST THE SHAREHOLDER RESOLUTION

Your Board of Directors recommends a vote AGAINST this proposal for the following reasons:

The Board of Directors believes in the elimination of segregation and the establishment of fair employment standards in the United States and throughout the world, including South Africa. The Company has taken appropriate action to further these objectives by adopting and implementing a Statement of Principles which provides in part that "all operations will provide equal employment opportunities to all employees and applicants for employment, regardless of race, color, religion, age, sex or national origin."

However, the Board of Directors is opposed to the adoption of the proponent's resolution because it would subordinate business decisions to the foreign policy goals of particular shareholders. In the opinion of management, to request the Directors of the Company to dispose of an ownership interest in an affiliate solely on the basis of one factor, without regard to the effect on the Company or even a determination as to whether the adequacy of the consideration received for such disposition is in the best interest of the Company or its South African employees, would not be in the best interest of all of the shareholders.

The proponent in support of its resolution has stated that the Company has refused to subscribe to the Sullivan Principles. On August 21, 1979, the Company advised the Reverend Leon H. Sullivan by letter: "If it would help your cause to identify Dresser with other U.S. companies fostering racial equality in South Africa, we would be willing to adopt such principles for this purpose. We are not willing to commit to the submission of progress reports or on-site monitoring in South Africa. Our reporting burden to governmental agencies is costing the Company and its shareholders entirely too much already, and it is ever increasing." In Reverend Sullivan's Amplified Guidelines to South African Statement of Principles, any adopting company is required to make semi-annual reports and submit to periodic on-site monitoring of facilities in South Africa. In response to the Company's letter to Reverend Sullivan, Larry Wise, who apparently is associated with the Sullivan organization, called and advised the Company that while they understood the Company's position, they could not accept the Company joining the cause with those reservations.

The Board of Directors has considered the effect of the Company's presence on the black majority population, as well as the presence of other American companies operating in South Africa. The Board of Directors has concluded that from an economic and social viewpoint, the black community in South Africa has benefited and is continuing to benefit from the presence of corporations like the Company's affiliate in South Africa. American sponsored business should remain in South Africa and by their practices provide an example which should help influence a change in the social system in South Africa. In the opinion of the Board of Directors the withdrawal of foreign investments from South Africa would curtail the influence of changes in the social and economic systems to eliminate the apartheid system and contribute adversely to the economy of the country, which would have a disproportionately adverse effect upon the black community.

In management's opinion the Company's South African operations are both a responsible and responsive corporate citizen to the concerns of all the people of South Africa.

Your Board of Directors recommends a vote "AGAINST" this proposal.

The affirmative vote of a majority of the shares represented at the meeting and voting on this proposal is required for the adoption of the shareholder proposal.

QUESTIONS FOR DISCUSSION*

1. Evaluate the claim by Edward Luter (Dresser's Vice-President) that the company must comply with the laws of South Africa.
2. Did Dresser Industries respond correctly to the most recent shareholder resolution? Why or why not?
3. If you were president of Dresser Industries, what would you do next?

Case Study
Project Jari:
Fiefdom or Commonwealth?

A. R. Gini

In January 1982 it was announced that Daniel K. Ludwig, American shipping executive and financier, planned to sell off the largest and most costly entrepreneurial effort ever made by one man, Project Jari, to a consortium of twenty-five Brazilian companies with the full support and guarantee of the Brazilian government. According to many critics and observers, the major reason for Ludwig's sale of his 4,000,000-acre Amazon complex—which combined forestry, mining, agriculture, and cattle raising—was quite simply that Jari had ceased to be a good financial prospect. What was once "Ludwig's passion" and "Brazil's pride" became too great a financial load for any one man or one company to bear. The story of Jari is a complex one. At its core it is the story of the problems involved in trying to industrialize and capitalize the untapped resources of a Third World nation, and at the same time it is a classic story of man's industrial might and money being pitted against the forces of nature.

For sheer immensity the Amazon is incomparable. Stretching some 4,000 miles from the Andes to the Atlantic, it possesses 1,100 tributaries, at least ten of which are longer than the 2,300-mile-long Mississippi. It spills across nine South American countries, and its volume exceeds the combined flow of the next eight largest rivers on earth. Rivaling the Nile in length, it is sixty times greater in volume of discharge at its mouth. At maximum flood, it pours eight trillion gallons into the ocean every day—enough to furnish two hundred times the municipal water requirements of the United States, or twenty times its total industrial, farming, and power needs. Moreover, the river is sufficiently broad and deep enough to accommodate oceangoing steamers as far as 2,300 miles inland. When first seeking a name to evoke the oceanic size of the Amazon's vast complex of waterways, the Portuguese explorers quite properly called it *O Rio Mar*, the River Sea.[1]

The Amazon River basin (Amazonia) is generally understood to be that region traversed by the Amazon and its various tributaries. The basin also includes the world's largest continuous tropical rain forest, which encompasses some three million square miles, an area larger than the continental United States. The so-called classic Amazon Basin makes up one-third of South America. Brazil's portion of the Amazon Basin is two million square miles, or 60 percent of Brazil's overall land mass. Yet with all of its size, the population density for the whole of the Amazon Basin only averages two persons per square mile.

Even statistics as wondrous as those that apply to the Amazon Basin do not begin to capture the size and complexity of the region. In size alone the basin would qualify to be the world's ninth-largest country were it a nation unto itself. Besides being the source of one-fifth of the world's fresh-water supply, the area has been called the "lungs of the world," insofar as the forests produce and replenish approximately 15 percent of the world's oxygen supply. The basin possesses seemingly unlimited reserves of fertile soil, wood supplies, mineral deposits, and precious metals. It also contains 20 percent of all known plant and animal species. As one local biologist has proudly stated: "The Amazon has over two million species of insects, over 100,000 species of plants, 2,000 species of fish, and 600 species of animals. What's most important is the diversity of species: In one hectare of forest, you find more species of plants and animals than you find in all of Europe."[2]

During the 1950s the Brazilian government began a national campaign to open up the interior of their country. As one commentator put it: "Brazilians are like crabs; they never leave the coast. The tragedy is that in embracing the sea they are ignorant of the riches and resources which could be the solution to their country's economic and political problems."[3] The government initially attempted to demonstrate its good faith in this project by starting construction on the "national dream" of an inland capital, which they hopefully christened Brasília—Gateway to the Interior. It was not until 1964, however, when the military seized power, that the nation made a concerted effort to seek out the material means, the finances, and the people to accomplish the exploration, colonization, and development of its hinterlands.

To further facilitate this goal, the government embarked on the construction of the 1,600-mile Trans-Amazon Highway. In conjunction with the construction of the highway, the government created a "homestead act," which promised 250 acres of land and a small house to every farmer willing to settle in the Amazon Basin. The government also began a liberal sales policy of kingdom-size land grants, none smaller than 125,000 acres, to large international corporations and some of Brazil's richest families for the purposes of export-oriented ranching and pulpwood production. Such well-known corporate dynasties as Goodyear, Volkswagen, Nestlé, Borden, and Mitsubishi began to buy "homesteads" on the banks of the Amazon. It was the government's hope that these companies with their vast capital resources and entrepreneurial know-how, could quickly and efficiently convert the virgin Amazonian forest into an agricultural and mining bonanza.

The generals had early on conceded the point that conservation was a luxury a developing nation could not afford. After a fifteen-month study of the Amazon Basin, even such an objective observer as Jacques Cousteau, the French oceanographer and film maker, concluded that its occupation was inevitable. "For anyone who lives in a developed country," he said, "it is very easy to say 'Don't do that,' or 'Don't touch this, don't cut down that tree, or save this.' But for people who are hungry, preservation and conservation can be just so many pretty words."[4] By the early 1970s, Brazil's foreign debt was conservatively estimated at $55 billion, and currently it is estimated at $95 billion and rising rapidly. Brazil therefore found itself hard-pressed to ignore the development possibilities of an area offering potentially inestimable land values, hardwood stocks valued at $1 trillion, minerals and precious metals estimated at $100 billion, and the potential production of 100 million kilowatts of hydroelectric power from the major tributaries of the Amazon.[5] Seemingly, with so much at stake and so much to be gained, the stage was set either for the entrance of a group of robber barons or philanthropic financiers.

Daniel Keith Ludwig does not fall into either of these categories. Rather, Ludwig is a hardworking, aggressive businessman whose eyes have always been on the future and who has always been willing to take a risk if he liked the odds and the dollar signs involved. At eighty-six he is considered to be America's wealthiest living individual, with a personal fortune worth perhaps as much as $3 billion.[6] Ludwig is America's biggest and probably the world's third-most-important shipping lord. His principal corporate vehicle, which he entirely owns, is National Bulk Carriers, Inc., whose fleet of ships includes forty-nine tankers. Ludwig's other interests include ranching in Venezuela, mining in Australia, salt production in

Mexico, savings and loan associations in California, and resort hotels in the Bahamas, Bermuda, and Acapulco.

Ludwig's fortune is based on foresight. After World II, Ludwig built the first supertanker in Japan and devised the means to finance ships through long-term charters. Recalls a former aide: "Often he just sits in his office and thinks three to twenty years down the road."[7] In the 1950s Ludwig began to ponder the world's increasing use and dwindling supplies of wood pulp and timber. He came to the conclusion that the world was outstripping its wood supplies and that by the 1980s the shortage would be acute. Never a man to plan on a small scale, in 1967 at the age of seventy, just when Brazil began to offer large tracts of land at giveaway prices, Ludwig bought four million acres of Amazonia at 75 cents per acre, or $3 million. So began an experiment that some have called "Capitalism's Finest Hour."

Project Jari is located at the confluence of the Amazon and Jari Rivers, some 200 miles from the sea. It encompasses approximately 6,000 square miles of dense rain forest and is larger in area than the states of Connecticut and Rhode Island combined. The primary purpose for Jari was to raise and harvest trees that would be suitable for the manufacture of furniture, for use in the housing industry, and for the production of wood pulp. But in order for this to occur Ludwig literally had to import or construct every piece of equipment and every facility necessary to convert Jari from a virgin rain forest into a working plantation.

Between 1967 and 1981 Ludwig expended over $1 billion, or an estimated $180,000 per day, of his private assets on his brainchild. In many ways, said Ludwig, "It was almost like developing a country."[8] By hiring the best and only buying the finest equipment Ludwig completely transformed the topography of his jungle kingdom. Monte Dourado (population 35,000) is the largest of four towns in Jari, and it possesses all the requirements of any modern community. It has schools, an eighty-five-bed hospital, modern houses, restaurants, a supermarket, a bakery, and even an ice-cream parlor. The plantation has 4,500 miles of access roads and trails that are well traveled by a fleet of more than 500 Jari cars and trucks. There are a half-dozen airstrips serviced by company planes. There is a thirty-seven-mile-long freight railway used to transport supplies from Monte Dourado's giant service depot, which regularly stores $6 million worth of spare parts and equipment. Jari also boasts its own fully operational deepwater port. Besides Jari's vast forestry project, Ludwig also experimented with other aspects of agriculture—both in the hopes of developing new markets and as a means of feeding his workers. The plantation has accommodated 4,700 head of cattle, 6,400 water buffalo, millions of chickens, and 86,500 acres of rice fields. But all of this is as of nothing in comparison to the "technological jewel" that sits on the edge of the Jari River some fifty miles upstream from the Amazon, a totally self-contained paper pulp mill and a power generating plant. The mill, which is able to produce 750 tons of pulp daily, and the generating plant, which can put out 55,000 kilowatts of power, measure seventeen stories high and three city blocks long. These plants were built in Japan at a cost of $269 million, put on floating platforms, and towed more than halfway around the world. Finally these factories were taken up the Amazon and Jari rivers, where they were hydraulically lifted onto 3,900 prearranged wooden pilings and soon thereafter made fully operational.

By 1967 Ludwig had established a beachhead and imported enough supplies and equipment to embark on the core of the project—wood and pulp production. His plan was both simple and direct. The problem was that the native forest of Amazonia contains literally hundreds if not thousands of species of trees. Because of their various textures, circumferences, heights, and growing characteristics, they are not well suited for commercial use. What is necessary is the ability to "plant trees like rows of corn," and this requires a single and uniform species of tree.[9] After a long and extensive search, Ludwig's agents found a tree that fit the bill. The *Gmelina arborea* (pronounced "ma*li*na ar*bor*ea"), is a hardwood native of Burma and India that grows to fifteen inches in diameter in five years and thirty inches in twelve, or roughly twice as fast as the southern pine, a major source of American pulp. Besides pulp the *Gmelina* is suitable for furniture, veneer, matches, and construction.

Initially, gargantuan thirty-five-ton Caterpillar D-9 Tractors were brought in to clear away the jungle. These tractors, mounted with angle plows weighing 2,500 pounds each, started bulldozing the forest at the rate of 2,700 yards an hour, uprooting everything in sight. In some areas the job called for two D-9s with a heavy chain between them rolling a hollow steel ball eight feet in diameter and weighing 6,000 pounds. As the tractors moved forward, the chain jerked out the trees, destroying the extensive matted root system and exposing the thin tropical soil.[10] When this procedure proved to be excessively destructive to the delicate soil covering, Ludwig began to clear the forest of the unwanted trees by means of the age-old slash-and-burn technique. Two years after the initial plantings, Jari's forestry experts found that the *Gmelina* could not grow properly on the parts of the plantation that contained sandy soil. So Caribbean pine (a fast-growing pine that can be harvested in nineteen years) was brought in and planted in those areas where the soil was predominantly sandy.[11] By 1978 some 270,000 acres of neatly manicured, lightly cultivated forests were in place, with plans already on the drawing boards for a second forest of the same size. Ludwig's timetable was geared to meet his prophesied mid-1980s paper and wood shortage. By 1979 Jari was to be producing woodstuffs on a limited basis; by 1983–84 it was to be fully operational; and by 1989 it was to have increased its yearly output by one-half.

Many factors contributed to Jari's demise. To begin with, Ludwig's long-predicted pulp shortage failed to occur on schedule; in fact the price of wood pulp remained relatively low. The general state of the worldwide recession in the 1970s and the ever-increasing indebtedness of all of South America in no way helped Ludwig's position. Moreover, the cost overruns for Jari, which Ludwig paid for out of his own pocket, exceeded 350 percent. Other contributing factors were Ludwig's temperamental management style—which resulted in more than thirty changes of project directors in fourteen years—as well as his passion for secrecy, which gave rise to widely circulated false rumors, a poor public relations image, and a great deal of bad press. However, the two most important issues that led to the failure of this minutely planned, financially well-endowed and self-contained jungle empire were Ludwig's and Jari's enmeshment in the ecological debates over the human occupation of Amazonia, and the emergence of "economic nationalism" as a part of Brazil's internal and diplomatic policy over the past decade.[12]

At the time Ludwig laid plans for his tree-farming experiment, he (like the vast majority of scientists and horticulturalists) believed that rain forests possessed unlimited fertility and growth potential. Because of the lushness of rain forests, it had been assumed that the soil on which they grew would support flourishing grain crops and provide perfect grazing land for cattle farms. However, in the last ten years scientists have learned that there is only one to three inches of fertile topsoil on the forest floor. They have also learned that the nutrient cycle of a tropical rain forest—unlike that of Kansas wheat fields, for example, which get most of their nourishment from the soil—depends on the foliage of the vegetation for an estimated 70 percent of its nourishment. In a temperate forest, leaves decay relatively slowly, thereby creating an ever-deeper accumulation of nutrient-rich topsoil. In a tropical forest, the heat and humidity promote the rapid decomposition of vegetation. A leaf that may take eighteen months to fully decompose in Kansas could be broken down in a matter of hours in the Amazon. Given such rapid decay, the organic matter is directly assimilated into new plant life. Tropical plant life is virtually a closed cycle of growth and decay. The minute fraction that escapes this cycle becomes a nutrient-poor topsoil that acts more as a mechanical support for plant life than as a source of nutrients.[13]

What ecologists are now claiming is that the Amazon is really a "counterfeit paradise," and that if the umbrellalike rain forest canopy is stripped away, the torrential rains—sometimes dumping six to eight inches in a single day—will wash away the unshielded topsoil, and the equatorial sun will bake what remains into a bricklike wasteland.[14] One ecologist has described the Amazon as "a desert covered with trees." Writing in *Bioscience Magazine*, Susan Walton said, "We know of no sustainable use for the land after the tropical moist forests have been destroyed."[15] Many scientists have concluded that no new planting of crops, trees, or grasses can forestall the eventual destruction of the fragile topsoil.

Although Ludwig and his forestry experts disputed most of these findings, because of issues like these, Ludwig has sometimes been portrayed by Brazilian press as a vile American billionaire, raping the Amazon ecosystem. Ludwig claimed that he was somewhat puzzled by the charges that he was wrecking the environment. In a rare interview granted to *National Geographic Magazine*, Ludwig expressed real anger over a slogan that had caught on in Brazil, "Save the Amazon, Save the World." He stated that "only numbskulls would censure our use of .03% of the Amazon Basin to provide food and fiber for the future." He also disagreed with the phrase "surprisingly fragile eco-system," which is now being used to describe the Amazonian rain forest. He always believed the old saying, "While you're clearing the jungle from your door, it's coming in the windows." "Hell's bells," he said, "I spend five million dollars a year just to whack down the wild growth that springs up among our planted trees."[16] It was Ludwig's contention that the world will lose its present appetite for wood long before it consumes even an infinitesimal fraction of the Amazon forest.

Although it is a fact that Daniel K. Ludwig was openly courted by members of the Brazilian cabinet to locate his agribusiness project in Amazonia, it is also a fact that Ludwig and Project Jari never enjoyed an altogether harmonious relationship with the Brazilian government. Their love-hate relationship started with Ludwig's insistence that the Brazilian government must not try to interfere in any way with the internal workings of Jari. Until the last few years of his ownership. Ludwig neither sought nor accepted government aid or input except in three instances. With every foreign investor, the government allowed firms to write off up to 50 percent of their tax bills if they used that money to improve their property or somehow upgrade the surrounding region. In 1975 Ludwig asked the Brazilian government to act as cosignee on the loan used to pay for the construction and delivery of the pulp mill and power plants. Ludwig also petitioned the government for a $5.5 million annual fee to cover the infrastructure and social service costs for his Brazilian work force.

Over the years the list of grievances and misunderstandings between the two parties grew in number. Ludwig was continuously angered by pesky government regulations and the pettiness of minor bureaucrats seeking to exaggerate their own power at his expense. From the government's point of view, Ludwig and his managers created much friction and animosity by routinely bypassing local officials (including the state governors) and dealing only with top officials in Brasília. Ludwig's highhandedness also rankled members of the national government, who became irritated by his influence and power, and by the necessity of treating him more like a statesman than like a businessman.[17]

Another aspect of the jealousy between the two parties was, ironically, the very existence of Jari itself! In spite of—and perhaps *because* of—the fact that Ludwig's endeavors were earning far more in foreign exchange than any other single project in Amazonia, and even though he continuously employed an estimated 30,000 workers, relations between Jari and Brasília remained cool. One possible explanation for this was that this single-minded American entrepreneur was seemingly succeeding in opening up the Amazon, while the national government—for all its various efforts—was not. The avowed aims of the government were to open up the interior, develop its unused resources, generate new revenues, and encourage internal colonialization, but their "grand scheme" was not proving to be an unqualified success. While many commentators on Project Jari were quick to point out that although some of Ludwig's programs and policies, as well as his personal management style, understandably incurred the anger of the government, it was also felt that the government needed a scapegoat to explain away a certain amount of ineptitude on their part.

Whether or not any of this is true, Jari was perceived to be abusing the privileges granted to it. Most Brazilians were initially eager and willing to invite Ludwig to their country and encourage him in his efforts. It was hoped that Ludwig's success would prove to be Brazil's success. And while it is true that he spent his money lavishly and well in creating his industrial enclave in the middle of no man's land, Brazilians began to perceive Jari as a threat to the country's sovereignty. Partially because of his passion for privacy and secrecy, people began to question if Ludwig had any real interest in Brazil's greater well-being. Was Ludwig using the Amazon and Brazil's generosity for the benefit of all, or was he exploiting them only to serve his own personal and financial best interests? It seemed to many that Jari was a vehicle for one man's dream and was not necessarily or primarily concerned with Brazil's ambitions and aspirations.

It is also the case that Ludwig's image suffered because of the close association in people's minds of Jari's activities with the actions and excesses of the other multinational corporations that had been granted or purchased lands in Amazonia. Most of these corporations were primarily interested in the development of vast cattle ranches in order to profit by the world's ever-increasing demands for beef products. Their means of creating these vast ranch-estates were massive, semicontrolled forest fires. For example, in 1975 a United States reconnaissance satellite's heat sensor detected a sudden and intensive warming of the earth in the Amazon Basin, usually associated with an imminent volcanic eruption. A special alert mission was dispatched, and what they found was a German multinational corporation burning down one million acres of tropical forest for a cattle ranch.[18] Unlike Ludwig's plantation project, these forests were destroyed to produce grazing land, and no attempt was made to reforest or rebalance the ecostructure of the damaged area.

Increasingly, Ludwig was depicted by the press as an avaricious gringo out to despoil and control the Amazon. Popular sentiment contended that the government had given away too much in its attempt to open up the Amazon. Ludwig was chided in the media for owning so large a chunk of Brazil. The new-found spirit of patriotism and nationalism was demonstrated throughout the land by such ever-present wall slogans as "The Amazon is Ours!" and "Brazil Doesn't Ask, Doesn't Wait; She Orders!" Alarmists argued that Ludwig's project was only the first step in the takeover of the Amazon. They contended that if Brazilians did not repossess the Amazon, a consortium of foreign corporations might.

Jari eventually became too controversial and too politically risky for the Brazilian government. As a result Brazil never legalized or ceded clear title to all of the Jari property. Moreover, although over 40,000 Brazilians lived and worked in Jari, the government refused to maintain the infrastructure costs in the towns Ludwig had built for his employees. At this point Ludwig and his accountants cried "foul" and "surrender," and began the process of liquidating to a group of twenty-five Brazilian buyers.

In the end Brazilians accused Daniel K. Ludwig of being a carpetbagger and a thief and figuratively rode him out of the country on a rail.

Through it all Ludwig never denied he wanted to make a profit, but he steadfastly denied that he was out to make a profit at the expense of Brazil's best interests. Ludwig was convinced that Amazonia should not and could not remain an "ecological museum" in which the tropical forest would remain a sacred preserve. A sensible middle ground had to be found so that Amazonia's extensive riches could be utilized without doing permanent damage to the overall ecosystem. As one of Ludwig's closest associates stated: "At the end of his life, Mister Ludwig decided to create, in a pioneer area, a work that is entirely new, and is more concerned with achieving something of great socio-economic significance than in reaping quick profits, like most capitalistic enterprises."[19]

NOTES

1. *National Geographic Magazine,* October, 1972, pp. 456, 457.

2. *New York Times Magazine,* November 22, 1981, p. 178.

3. *The Nation,* October 11, 1975, p. 236.

4. *New York Times,* May 14, 1982, p. 2.

5. *Newsweek,* January 25, 1982, p. 42.

6. *New York Times,* September 11, 1982, p. 35.

7. *Time,* September 10, 1979, p. 76.

8. *National Geographic Magazine,* May, 1980, p. 695.

9. *Ibid.*

10. Frances Moore Lappe and Joseph Collins with Cary Fowler, *Food First* (New York: Ballantine Books, 1982), p. 48.

11. *Time,* November 15, 1976, p. 79.

12. *Forbes,* May 14, 1979, p. 130.

13. *Food First,* p. 51.

14. *Ibid.,* p. 52.

15. *New York Times,* August 31, 1980, sec. 4, p. 16.

16. *National Geographic Magazine,* May, 1980, pp. 705, 710.

17. *The Economist,* December, 26, 1981, pp. 86, 87.

18. *Food First,* p. 50.

19. *Forbes,* May 14, 1979, p. 128.

QUESTIONS FOR DISCUSSION

1. Recalling Jacques Cousteau's statement (p. 256), is it possible for a society to effectively balance the economic needs of its people with the requirements of environmental conservation?

2. Was Jari established for the purpose of helping Brazil develop the untapped resources of the Amazon and thereby create long-term wealth and employment in the area? Or was it just another capital venture by an international entrepreneur?

3. Does any developer have the right to alter, use, and often exploit a region and then leave, for whatever reasons, without having designed specific contingency plans for the restoration of the area?

4. Does a foreign investor have the rights to demand extraordinary privileges from a host government or "routinely bypass" local rules and customs?

Case Study
Abbott Laboratories
Puts Restraints on Marketing
Infant Formula in the Third World

Earl A. Molander

On December 10, 1978, Abbott Laboratories received notification that the Religious of Jesus and Mary, a Catholic order holding 100 shares of Abbott stock, would present to company shareholders at the upcoming annual meeting a proposal to establish a review committee to oversee the company's promotion of infant formula in developing nations. The proposal submitted read in part:

> WHEREAS medical testimony before the U.S. Senate linked higher levels of infant mortality and disease to bottle feeding in unsanitary and poverty conditions,
> WHEREAS expert testimony also confirmed that promotion practices of infant formula and milk companies encourage women to abandon breast-feeding in favor of expensive commercial preparations and feeding bottles,
> WHEREAS the management of Abbott/Ross has shown concern for the misuses inherent in marketing baby formula in environments characterized by lack of income, education, sanitation and medical care,
> THEREFORE BE IT RESOLVED that the shareholders request the Board of Directors to establish an Infant Formula Review Committee having the following structures, function and duties . . .

THE COMPANY

Abbott Laboratories is a diversified multinational manufacturer of pharmaceutical, hospital, and health care products headquartered in Chicago, Illinois. In 1977, total Abbott sales were $1.24 billion, of which 33 percent were in 160 countries overseas.

Abbott, through its Ross Laboratories division (hereafter referred to as Abbott/Ross), and the Mead Johnson division of Bristol-Myers dominate

From "Abbott Laboratories Puts Restraints on Marketing Infant Formula in the Third World," in *Responsive Capitalism*, ed. Earl A. Molander (New York: McGraw-Hill, Inc., 1980), pp. 264–76. Reprinted with permission of the publisher.

the United States infant formula industry with 55 and 35 percent of the market, respectively. Overseas, Abbott/Ross faces stiff competition from Mead Johnson, the Myeth Laboratories division of American Home products, and numerous foreign producers. In that part of the overseas infant formula market that is in the developing countries (estimated by Abbot to be about $350 million), Abbott/Ross's market share is only 6 percent. The market in the developing countries is dominated by Nestlé of Switzerland with an estimated 60 percent of all sales.

INFANT FORMULAS: HISTORY[1]

For various physiological and psychological reasons, a small percentage of mothers (variously estimated at between 5 and 20 percent) are unable to provide sufficient breast milk for their newborn infants.[2] (This number rises substantially if the mother is malnourished, in which case the volume of breast milk, not the quality, decreases.) Still other mothers prefer not to breast-feed, either for reasons of convention, because they work, or for personal reasons.

Until the Industrial Revolution, virtually all infants were breast-fed. In limited instances a natural mother's breast-feeding failure was compensated for by the employment of wet nurses. Nevertheless, infant mortality was high. There were attempts at artificially feeding, usually using spouted pots of pottery, pewter, or silver, but in almost all instances the infant eventually died.

Around 1800 the invention of mass-produced glass bottles fitted with nipples of various sorts improved the infant survival rate, but it was not until the last nineteenth and early twentieth centuries that three developments made wide-scale success with bottle-feeding possible: (1) development of safer water supplies and sanitary standards for handling and storing milk; (2) further development of easily cleansed and sterilized bottles and nipples; and (3) alteration of the curd tension of milk through processing to make it more digestible by the infant.

To meet the growing demand for a high-grade infant formula which could as closely as possible approximate a mother's breast milk and be fed to an infant with a nippled bottle, in the 1920s, the company that in 1964 became the Ross Laboratories division of Abbott developed Similac, a product made from skim milk, lactose, and other ingredients.

Even with the development of breast-feeding alternatives, into the 1940s two-thirds of newborn infants in the United States were still breast-fed. Beginning in the late 1940s, breast-feeding became unpopular with many mothers, almost exclusively for reasons of convention. Many infants were bottle-fed with a preparation of evaporated cow's milk, sometimes with carbohydrates added, diluted with water. This feeding was supplemented with cod liver oil for vitamin D and fruit juice for ascorbic acid, the only significant vitamin deficiencies associated with bottle-feeding. With this change went an increased demand for infant formula.

The percentage of women choosing to initiate breast-feeding remained nearly constant at 22 percent from the early 1950s to the early 1970s. However, in the mid-1970s breast-feeding enjoyed a resurgence to where approximately 50 percent of mothers of newborn infants in 1978 were choosing to breast-feed.

CRITICISM OF OVERSEAS MARKETING PRACTICES

For reasons which would eventually become a question of considerable debate among health officials, infant formula manufacturers, and their critics, many mothers in developing countries, especially in urban areas, began to move away from traditional breast-feeding practices and feed their babies with bottles. Among the breast milk substitutes were infant formula, powdered cow's milk (millions of pounds of dried skim milk were donated to developing countries as a part of United States food aid programs), and various mixtures of indigenous foods.

In the late 1960s, health officials in developing countries began to note symptoms of malnutrition and diarrhea in bottle-fed babies, a syndrome that has come to be called "bottle illness." Certain health officials drew a direct connection between this syndrome and the promotional practices of infant formula companies, although in the majority of infant morbidity and mortality cases the contents of the bottle were other than infant formula. These health officials were led by Dr. Derrick B. Jelliffe, then head of the Caribbean Food and Nutrition Institute in Jamaica, who labeled the syndrome "commerciogenic malnutrition."[3]

One consequence of abandonment of breast-feeding and its replacement with bottle-fed infant formula was a loss of protective antibodies from breast milk. Far more serious, however, were the potential misuses of the infant formula by the Third World mother, including: (1) dilution with impure water, and (2) incorrect dilution. Although insufficient dilution was sometimes a problem, a more serious concern was overdilution, brought on either by failure to understand directions or by a desire to "stretch" the formula because of its substantial price (as high as 25 to 40 percent) relative to family income.

Serious concern regarding the effect of prepared infant formula products on infant nutrition and breast-feeding practices in the Third World was first brought to the attention of Abbott/Ross and other infant formula firms by Dr. Jelliffe in 1970 at a meeting in Bogotá, Columbia, sponsored by the United Nations (UN). At the meeting, Dr. Jelliffe presented his charges that infant morbidity and mortality in general were linked in a significant way to the promotion and use of commercial formulas and recommended they be withdrawn from the developing countries entirely. While some of the medical and nutritional experts in attendance agreed with his charges, others took strong exception to them.

A second group of health experts, led by Dr. Fernando Monkeberg, director of the Institute of Nutrition and Food Technology at the University of Chile, took the position that more serious problems would exist if the infant formula alternative were not available. This group argued that while breast-feeding appeared to be declining, particularly in urban centers, this phenomenon was largely independent of prepared infant formula promotion. Further, the group insisted that data on morbidity and mortality had to be examined as part of a much larger picture that included maternal nutrition, sanitation, access to health care, purchasing power, education, lactation failure due to family disruption, urbanization with subsequent life style changes, etc.[4]

The two groups agreed that there was a legitimate need for alternatives to breast-feeding. They also agreed that the use of any type of breast milk supplement or alternative can create problems when combined with poor sanitation, poverty, impure water, or misinformation. But the groups disagreed substantially on the impact of the availability and promotion of infant formulas on a perceived decline in breast-feeding in the developing countries.

At the time of the 1970 Bogotá meeting, most infant formula manufacturers were promoting their products through (1) the mass media—including radio, television, newspaper, and billboards; (2) samples given to health care professionals for free distribution to new mothers; and (3) "mothercraft" nurses, company employees who promoted the product in hospitals and the home. Because Abbott/Ross was a pharmaceutical and health care products firm that traditionally has marketed its products, including infant formula, directly to health care professionals, its infant formula marketing in the developing countries was concentrated originally in sales calls on health care professionals. By contrast, the majority of its competitors were food products companies, like Nestlé, experienced in direct consumer promotion and relying heavily on consumer advertising.

From 1970 to 1973, Abbott/Ross participated in a series of international meetings studying the infant nutrition issue, many under the sponsorship of the United Nations Protein Advisory Group (PAG). These meetings culminated in a 1973 PAG report in which the UN group declared, "It is urgent that infant formulas be developed and introduced to satisfy the special needs of infants who are not breast-fed."[5] The report was also critical of current industry promotion practices, however, and laid down specific "Recommendations to Industry" regarding how infant formulas should be marketed in the Third World.

In order to establish better control over its international sale of infant formula, in the spring of 1974, Abbott/Ross published its own "Code of Marketing Ethics for Developing Countries," the first in the infant formula industry. Following the PAG guidelines, Abbott's code prohibited mass-media marketing and emphasized the need for advice from health care professionals to help the new mother with the choice of whether to breast-feed and the choice among competing infant formulas. (The most recent edition of the code, which contains substantial changes from the first code, is presented as Appendix 22-1.)

Abbott/Ross, after inaugurating its own code of marketing ethics, joined several other companies in an effort to unite all the infant formula companies in adopting a uniform marketing code. This effort eventually led to the founding of the International Council of Infant Food Industries (ICIFI).

A meeting of ICIFI in November 1975 led to the formulation of an industrywide code of ethical conduct. Dave Cox, president of Ross Laboratories, recalled the meeting in Geneva, Switzerland:

> At the meeting, I posed nine minimum conditions under which I thought this problem [criticism of the industry] would be resolved and not get bigger. And I was voted down 8-1 on all of them. I offered to compromise on all of these nine criteria except media promotion to parents, but still could not reach accord with the other companies.[6]

Having failed to resolve so basic an issue, Abbott/Ross opted not to become a member of ICIFI.[7]

INFANT FORMULA MARKETING BECOMES A PUBLIC CONTROVERSY

In 1974, public awareness of the infant formula marketing issue increased dramatically when a Swiss citizens' action organization, Arbeitsgruppe Dritte Welt (Third World Working Group), published a pamphlet entitled *Nestlé Kills Babies*. In response, Nestlé filed a libel suit against the group. Although the group was convicted of the charge and paid small fines, the suit and trial had the effect of drawing worldwide attention to the infant formula companies.[8]

From 1975 onward, articles about the infant formula controversy began to appear with increasing frequency in various United States publications. Many carried striking titles such as, "Baby Formula Abroad: Exporting Infant Malnutrition"; "Bottle Babies: Death and Business Get Their Market"; "Nestlé's Latest Killing in the Bottle Baby Market"; and "The Bottle Baby Scandal: Milking the Third World for All It's Worth."[9]

In these articles, the charges made by Dr. Jelliffe in Bogotá in 1970 were reiterated. (At this point, Dr. Jelliffe had become head of the Division of Population, Family, and International Health in the UCLA School of Public Health and was a leading academic critic of infant formula promotion.) In many instances, the charges were placed in the context of generalized criticism of multinational expansion into the Third World. For example, Leah Margulies, who heads the project on bottle-feeding for the Interfaith Center on Corporate Responsibility (ICCR), wrote in *Christianity and Crisis:*

> Corporate economy needs this vast, unexplored and largely unexploited market [the Third World] for the creation of new customers. Although marketing science has created thousands of little consumption communities at home, there are limitations; some markets, like the refrigerator market, are already approaching saturation. Here lies the motivation for global corporate expan-

sion. Sophisticated techniques are now being applied all over the world to create customers in our own image. . . .

For corporations "development"—the rationale and rallying cry for their penetration of Third World economies—means creating needs their products can fill. For people in the Third World countries, however, development means fulfilling needs that are already there, the goods and services necessary for survival: food, basic community services and industry that is tailored to their national priorities. In creating "needs" that don't exist, corporations are adding to the already existing problems and diverting efforts at real solutions.

This process is demonstrated clearly in the marketing of infant formulas in the Third World. A massive sales campaign presently encourages poor mothers to abandon breast feeding for this more expensive, mechanically complex and less healthful method. There could be no more dramatic illustration of manufacturing a need that wasn't there. It is an important example to examine, both because of the increasing incidence of infant malnutrition and mortality in the Third World, and also so that we understand how products that are relatively benign when used in a developed economy can become dangerous when we export our way of life through our consumer products.[10]

ICCR AND DISSIDENT SHAREHOLDER GROUPS

By 1975, the major criticism of the infant formula manufacturers was coming from ICCR and its member church groups. ICCR is an ecumenical agency of the National Council of Churches, with responsibility for coordinating the work of church groups which, as stockholders in United States corporations, raise social and corporate responsibility issues which they believe arise from the activities of corporations in which they invest.[11]

ICCR interest in infant formula promotion in the Third World dates to 1970, when the organization hired Leah Margulies to study the relationship between the activities of multinational corporations and world hunger. Based on Margulies's studies, in early 1975, the ICCR made promotion of infant formula in the Third World a primary target of its political effort. Simultaneously, ICCR sought to generate interest in the infant formula issue among its member church groups.

What would become one of the ICCR's major strategies also was initiated that same year when the ICCR and a number of its member groups offered resolutions on the 1975 Bristol-Myers and American Home Products proxy statements seeking information on the company's marketing practices in the Third World. The resolutions received less than 3 percent of the votes of the companies' shareholders. Under Securities and Exchange Commission (SEC) rules, this barred the groups from repeating the resolution a second year.

In December 1975, following a meeting with Abbott/Ross representatives to express their concern about the company's overseas marketing practices, the Adrian Dominican Sisters and the Sisters of Mercy filed a shareholder resolution for the April 1976 annual meeting of Abbott Laboratories. The two groups were associated with the Illinois Committee for Responsible Investment (ICRI), a corporate responsibility coalition with ties to ICCR and located in Chicago, not far from Abbott headquarters. The resolution asked for disclosure of the company's overseas infant formula marketing practices to its shareholders.

Abbott/Ross challenged the disclosure resolution with the SEC. The SEC denied the challenge, and recommended inclusion of the disclosure resolution in the proxy statement. Abbott/Ross then contacted both groups of sisters and urged them to withdraw the resolution. The sisters refused.

The sisters formally presented the resolution at the April annual meeting, where it was defeated, securing less than 3 percent of the vote.

INTERNAL REORGANIZATION

As the criticism of infant formula promotion practices grew, Dave Cox, president of Ross, hired Tom McCollough to deal exclusively with this problem. At one time, McCollough had been a vice president with the company. Following a number of positions with the Urban Coalition and various civil rights activities, McCollough had left Ross in 1970 to pursue a new career in educational administration. But in early 1976, Dave Cox persuaded McCollough to return to Ross where he could apply his broad business experience and familiarity with public policy and social conflict to the infant formula issue.

In June 1976, Abbott/Ross formed a permanent work team under the direction of Tom McCollough to study infant nutrition, formula, breast-feeding, and related matters in the Third World. The work team, which now includes a nutritionist, an anthropologist, a medical information specialist, and a pediatric consultant, operates in close cooperation with the Abbott international division and corporate headquarters. The team's role is to "recommend corporate policy change; undertake educational programs for breastfeeding in developing nations; monitor medical, nutritional and social research being conducted around the world related to infant feeding and breastfeeding; and publish monographs and position papers as data emerge."[12]

In the summer of 1976, members of this Abbott/Ross team met with representatives of ICRI and ICCR to discuss the company's overseas promotion practices.

Despite these discussions, the Adrians and two other religious orders, in coordination with the ICCR, decided in the fall of 1976 to offer a second, stronger resolution at the 1977 Abbott annual meeting, this time calling for specific changes in company overseas infant formula promotion practices. A similar resolution had been offered at the Bristol-Myers annual meeting in 1976 and received 5.4 percent of shareholder votes.[13]

In early 1977, Abbott/Ross challenged the practice change resolution with the SEC, which suggested some changes in the resolution. Prior to the scheduled April 1977 annual meeting, Abbott/Ross again met with ICCR/ICRI representatives, substantially the same group which had met the year before, but now also including Sister Cheryl Nichols of the Religious of Jesus and Mary. Abbott/Ross again urged withdrawal of the resolution. In exchange for an opportunity to state its position to company shareholders and in the house organ and other considerations, the group agreed to withdraw.[14]

In February 1977, Abbott disclosed these changes with the publication of a revised code of marketing ethics (Appendix 22-1). The new code contained eight new elements, many of which covered important concerns of ICCR.[15] "Many of these provisions had been observed previously, but were formalized into the code for the first time," said Frank Irving, then vice president of business development for Abbott's international division, which handles the marketing of Similac and other Abbott/Ross products overseas.[16]

In her commentary in the Abbott/Ross house organ on the new code and the company's policies and action regarding marketing infant formula in the Third World, Sister Marilyn Uline of the Adrian Dominican Sisters, the chief liaison between Abbott/Ross and its ICCR critics, noted that two major problems still persisted:

> First, large quantities of free formula samples still flow through health care personnel to mothers who, by this presumed medical endorsement, could be led to use formula under unsafe conditions. Second, formula companies continue to pay representatives both to provide health care and to sell products. By doing this, they unnecessarily merge commercial and professional roles and make themselves vulnerable to charges of self-interest in the guise of providing medical benefits.
>
> Abbott's code of marketing ethics acknowledges these problems by limiting product samples to amounts requested by health care personnel [Appendix 22-2], taking company representatives [who are trained midwives or nurses] out of nurses' uniforms and forbidding employees to visit mothers in their homes. Though such action is certainly commendable, the whole industry must take more substantive action if these problems are to be solved. . . .
>
> The effectiveness of Abbott's progressive code of marketing ethics depends largely on management's successful development of surveillance procedures for its implementation. In addition, though the code invites those responsible for infant care in developing countries to report current deviations, channels for doing this have yet to be created.[17]

In an interview a year and a half later, Sister Uline was more certain of the commitment of Abbott/Ross to control:

> Abbot/Ross is trying to control their people. From Ted Ledder [chairman of the board of Abbott] and Dave Cox—up and down the line, managers have been given to understand this is company policy and they better not be caught doing anything else. Besides, with the church so spread out [in the developing countries] we have an extensive information network and we've detected so many things already that it makes people decide they want to [abide by their codes.][18]

Tom McCollough elaborated on the company's control system:

> We write to our field managers twice a year asking them, "Are you following the code?" The implication is that if you're not, you'll be fired. Further, a

number of key Abbott/Ross executives and I travel extensively in the developing countries and discuss the issue wherever we go.

Two years ago, a lot of people in the company couldn't understand what the hubbub was about. Now the awareness is very high.

Our critics want a surveillance system. We tell them, "You check us. If you see any violation, let us know immediately."[19]

UNITED STATES GOVERNMENT INVOLVEMENT

In early 1977, the United States government became involved in the infant formula issue. The Committee on International Relations of the House of Representatives issued a report encouraging the promotion of breast-feeding in developing nations. In May 1978, Senator Edward Kennedy's Subcommittee on Health and Scientific Research of the Senate Human Resources Committee held hearings on the sale and promotion of infant formula in developing countries. Witnesses included representatives of the four leading manufacturers—Abbott/Ross, Bristol-Myers, American Home Products, and Nestlé—Dr. Jelliffe, and other experts on infant nutrition in developing countries, and representatives from the various special interest groups which had participated in the stockholder actions against Abbott/Ross and other manufacturers, led by Leah Margulies, director of the ICCR's infant formula campaign.

Expert and interest group testimony tended to treat the industry as a whole, only occasionally differentiating among the practices of the individual firms. When firms were cited, Nestlé received far and away the greatest amount of criticism, followed by Bristol-Myers and American Home Products. As a firm, Abbott/Ross received essentially no specific accusations.

In her testimony, Ms. Margulies was particularly critical of the marketing codes of the manufacturers, arguing,

[T]he codes . . . are weak, and . . . legitimize the very practices that we think ought to be stopped. The codes codify how to give out free samples, instead of stopping the free samples. The codes will say that a nurse should have a company insignia on and maybe not be in white uniform, rather than stopping the nurses.[20]

In his testimony, Dr. Jelliffe reviewed the four principal arguments against bottle-fed formulas and in favor of breast-feeding:

1. Economics—the burden which infant formula purchase places on an already poor family.
2. Prevention of infection—the antibodies carried in breast milk.
3. Nutrition—more reliable and better nutrients for the infant.
4. Child spacing and population control—because of the reduced risk of pregnancy to the breast-feeding mother.[21]

Dr. Jelliffe also agreed with Ms. Margulies on the industry's ethical codes, noting: "[T]he chances of them being carried out in the periphery, where the man on the spot is judged by the sales that he makes, are very slight indeed, in my opinion."[22]

In their testimony, prepared statements, and subsequent communications to the subcommittee, Abbott/Ross and the other firms disputed some of the testimony of the expert and interest group witnesses. Nutritional experts from Abbott's Ross division presented a review of the literature on infant-feeding practices in the Third World which suggested that infant formula products had made, and would continue to make, a contribution to infant health and survival.[23] These experts disputed the charge that the availability of infant formula products was a major factor inhibiting the breast-feeding decision of Third World mothers. They also argued that nearly all available data dealt with "bottle-feeding," and not specifically infant formula.

The hearings concluded without any promise of forthcoming legislative proposals. However, Kennedy asked the World Health Organization to convene a conference where these issues could be explored in depth. The conference was scheduled for October 1979.

RELATIONS WITH COMPETITORS

As noted earlier, the infant formula industry in the developing countries is made up of firms from numerous countries and substantially different marketing backgrounds, ranging from a giant Swiss food products firm like Nestlé, experienced in commercial promotion to consumers, to an American pharmaceutical firm like Abbott/Ross that promotes almost exclusively to health care personnel through sales representatives. As such, the companies bring significantly different perspectives to the infant formula issue.

Despite these differences and the Abbott/Ross decision not to participate in ICIFI, there is some contact among the companies as they attempt to deal with a common problem. Following the congressional hearings, the companies met with Senator Kennedy and were urged to find some way of reaching agreement on a universal code all could live with. But inquiries from Kennedy's office to the U.S. Justice Department confirmed that any collaboration on an industrywide code might be a violation of antitrust law and could not be approved a priori. There remains some hope that the World Health Organization conference may generate a code each American company can subscribe to. But in Dave Cox's view, this will not solve the problem in the Third World: "We see no way any [substantive] code is going to be subscribed to by all companies. Even if all of us were to agree to a code, and restrain our dealings, there's a plethora of whole milk, condensed milk, and evaporated milk companies who would jump into the market."[24]

COMPANY ACTIONS

In the last year, Abbott/Ross initiated a number of changes in its overseas activities, partly in response to continued interactions with Sister Uline and others and partly out of its own sense of where it felt change was needed. In addition to the breast-feeding program and the changes outlined in the code (Appendix 22-1) and sample policy (Appendix 22-2), the company now has prepared a "Note to Health Professionals" in developing countries outlining the preferability of breast-feeding and proper use of infant formula (Appendix 22-3) and a notice to distributors and retailers on proper use of infant formulas for inclusion in every case of the product (Appendix 22-4). Abbott/Ross is also market-testing a pictorial representation of proper use of infant formula for inclusion in each package of formula. The company has also modified its product label, which comes in numerous languages.

THE PROBLEM OF RELIABLE DATA

In trying to resolve the complexities of the infant formula promotion issue, one is confronted with very little hard data to support either the contentions of the critics or the defense from industry. There are a number of questions on which the data problem is acute:

1. What is the quantitative impact of (*a*) free samples and (*b*) commercial promotion on the decision of a mother to breast-feed?
2. Given the sociopsychological factors in lactation, what is the effect of consumer promotion on the ability of mothers to lactate?
3. What fraction of the morbidity and mortality of infants in the developing countries is attributable to misuse of infant formula, and what fraction to maternal malnutrition, environmental conditions, and the use of other than infant formula—indigenous foods of various kinds—in bottle-feeding?

Critics cite a number of studies which they contend support their view.[25] But a close scrutiny shows the conclusions to be inferential in many instances. For example, in testifying at the Kennedy hearings, Dr. Manuel Carballo wrote:

> While no attempt has been made in this study to correlate patterns of breast feeding with the type and degree of marketing of industrially processed infant foods, it appears significant that in two of the settings where mothers were provided with free samples of milk there was also a marked low incidence of breast feeding. Similarly the extent to which knowledge about brand products has extended into urban poor and rural communities, and the diverse network of distribution channels utilized in the marketing and distribution of infant foods, would also seem significant. The possible association of these practices with patterns of breast feeding cannot be overlooked.[26]

Industry spokespersons have tended to insist that the critics' contentions be subjected to rigorous analysis. But for critics like Sister Marilyn Uline, this is a weak defense:

> I have ambivalent feelings about what constitutes hard data. What is acknowledged as hard data by industry is that which can be subjected to the rigid canons of social science. For me hard data is doctors in the Third World changing their attitudes toward infant formula marketing. If the evidence convinces them, it convinces me.[27]

Tom McCollough recognizes that the absence of solid data both to support the critics' view and to support the industry's defense is a problem:

> When our work team was first formed, Dave Cox told me he wanted me to do research. We surveyed the literature and very quickly found there was a paucity of good data on infant feeding practices, especially related to infant formula. So we visited overseas sites to try to learn first hand about industry practices and talk to local health care officials and pediatricians. These field visits confirmed not only the absence of good data but the difficulty of doing good studies, especially longitudinal studies, in the fluid world of a developing nation.[28]

To deal with this problem, Abbott/Ross is funding a number of projects to study infant formula feeding practices and their health effects for the baby. These studies include a major field study in the Caribbean designed and conducted by Dr. Judith Gussler, a cultural anthropologist and Ross employee working exclusively on this issue. To monitor the research activities of others and the actions and pronouncements of industry critics, Abbott/Ross has a medical information specialist. Further, Abbott/Ross has commissioned a major study to review all the available literature and information on the subject.

SUMMATION

In spite of these efforts, the 1979 Abbott annual meeting was again the stage for a shareholder's resolution on infant feeding in the Third World. For the infant formula industry, the controversy has expanded, not abated, and has led to a boycott of Nestlé products in the United States and numerous shareholder resolutions at all three major American infant formula manufacturers, including Abbott/Ross.

In 1979, the industry was confronted not just by ICCR but also by the Infant Formula Action Coalition (INFACT), formed in Minneapolis in early 1977 to deal exclusively with the infant formula issue. In the period since its formation, INFACT has organized regional councils throughout the country and has forged alliances with a number of other activist groups, notably the World Hunger Coalition and the social action movements of organized mainline church denominations. Currently, INFACT is coordinating the Nestlé boycott while ICCR concentrates its efforts on the American corporations manufacturing infant formula in which they own stock.

This amorphous but well-connected coalition of infant formula critics has made for a less-than-predictable environment for the companies involved. The Abbott shareholder resolution introducing this case study is a classic example of that unpredictability.

For nearly four years, Abbott/Ross had interacted with Sister Marilyn Uline, the representative of the Adrian Dominican Sisters, and other ICRI/ICCR representatives in Chicago. Late in 1978, Abbott/Ross executives met with this group and INFACT representatives for a frank discussion of differences and recent corporate decisions. The meeting was marked by candor and a cooperative spirit. No shareholder resolution was mentioned to Abbott/Ross, leading the company to believe none would be introduced at the 1979 annual meeting. Subsequent communication between the Chicago group and the company encouraged Abbott/Ross executives in this view, although they were never told specifically that there would be no resolution. Nevertheless, some ICCR members felt that a resolution should be submitted and, seeing none from the Chicago group, arranged for one to be submitted from Maryland (the Religious of Jesus and Mary).

The resolution thus came as an unpleasant surprise to Abbott/Ross. In Tom McCollough's view:

> The shareholder action raises a new question, however, and that is of legitimate negotiation and interaction between the critics and the corporation. If the perceived, authorized agents cannot be counted on, and any dissident member can circumvent the system, is it worth interacting at all if no agreements can be forged?
>
> It's disappointing to see supposedly sophisticated, liberal critics playing zero sum games. They know that "win-win" strategies are possible, but seem not to have the will or skill to make them work.[29]

Appendix 22-1

CODE OF MARKETING ETHICS FOR DEVELOPING COUNTRIES WITH REFERENCE TO INFANT FEEDING (REVISED, WINTER 1977)

INTRODUCTION

Supplying infant formula products in developing nations presents unique marketing problems and opportunities for the Corporation. In these nations it is possible to find the most modern, sophisticated and advanced settings in stark contrast with widespread poverty, illiteracy and inadequate health care. Infant mortality rates can be ten times greater than those of industrialized nations. Most of these infant deaths are caused by diseases such as malaria, measles, malnutrition, etc., which are preventable by applying current medical and nutritional knowhow. Within this context, we are keenly aware of the responsibilities of Abbott Laboratories to make a positive contribution to the health and well-being of infants in developing countries.

THE CENTRAL ROLE OF PROFESSIONAL HEALTH CARE JUDGMENTS

Because good nutrition is an essential factor in proper health care, we believe supervision of the infant's diet should be the sole responsibility of medical and allied health care personnel whose knowledge of nutritional science and understanding of local needs and conditions qualify them to provide this guidance. We conduct our business in cooperation with local health personnel, supporting their work through the provision of appropriate health care products and services. This relationship is especially important in developing countries where delivery of health care to major segments of the population is too often complicated by unfavorable living conditions. Decisions about infant formula should reside solely in the hands of health care professionals. Where no health care counselling is available, the use of our products is inappropriate.

THE PRIORITY OF BREASTFEEDING

Breast milk of healthy, well-nourished mothers is the best feeding to meet the nutritional needs of infants from birth through four to six months of age. At that time, needed and appropriate solid foods should be added to the diet. All mothers should be encouraged to feed their infants at the breast as long as the quantity and quality of milk remains minimally adequate. The recommendation to breastfeed is particularly appropriate for mothers in lower socioeconomic or non-money economic sectors, whose "at-risk" infants may be subjected to malnutrition, unsanitary environments, and endemic diseases. To this end, we pledge to cooperate with local health care personnel, Ministries of Health and concerned international agencies to support health education practices which encourage breastfeeding.

Our product label carries a statement that breast milk is the preferred feeding for infants.

THE VALIDITY OF ALTERNATIVES TO BREAST MILK

Nevertheless, not all mothers lactate successfully, find it practical or desirable for personal reasons. In those cases, the health care profession may be required to recommend a suitable alternative. In that context, we offer Similac® infant formulas, which are patterned as closely after the nutritional qualities of human milk as current knowledge and technology permit. In presenting Similac and other products to the health care professions, our goal is to promote awareness and acceptance of physiologic nutrition as the most desirable alternative when breastfeeding is not possible. Given the scientific evidence in support of our products' efficacy, the health care profession should be free to decide whether our products or other alternatives should be recommended.

We recognize that a valid need for alternative feedings sometimes exists in segments of the population not able to purchase them. Government sponsored programs for public assistance in some form are the best ways to aid mothers who can neither breastfeed, nor afford a suitable replacement.

RESTRICTED PROMOTION OF INFANT FORMULA PRODUCTS

1. We believe that unsupervised, direct promotion of infant feeding products to mothers can unjustly impel them to make decisions concerning the care and nutrition of their babies for which they may lack adequate medical or nutritional knowledge.

   Therefore, we do not advertise our products through general circulation magazines, directories, newspapers, radio, television, billboards, and other public mass media. We believe that no communication to the general public should encroach in any way on the responsibility of health care professionals to provide guidance as their judgment and experience dictate.

2. We do not encourage use of our products where private purchase would impose a financial hardship on the family, or where inadequate facilities for preparation constitute a hazard to infant health. We represent the cost of infant feeding accurately so that professional personnel can better advise mothers according to their economic status.

3. If any contact with mothers is made, either written or oral, it must be with the explicit agreement of a health care professional, so that the responsibility for that contact rests with the profession. If a company representative at any time is permitted to talk with mothers, in hospitals, health clinics, or maternity centers, that permission must be granted in writing, and a non-Abbott health care professional present.

   To help ensure that our infant feeding products are directed only to mothers who need and can afford them and have the capability to prepare them properly and to encourage professional guidance on their use, product samples are supplied only to professional health care personnel at their request. Visiting mothers in their homes is not allowed, even though requested by a health care professional.

4. We employ experienced and professionally knowledgeable company representatives who understand local needs. They are thoroughly taught the preference and value of breastfeeding, the knowledge and proper application of our products, and the influence of social pressures that can lead to unwise purchases and practices by those who cannot afford to buy infant formula.

   They are schooled to perform their duties in a professional manner and with integrity. Deception and other unethical practices are expressly forbidden. Specifically, any implication that our employees are members of a hospital, clinic, or maternity center staff is contrary to company policy. Even in the case of female employees who are qualified nurses, nurses' uniforms are not to be worn. Nurses are reimbursed through adequate salary, not sales commission. The activities of our representatives must be coordinated with those of medical professionals responsible for infant and mother care. They may, under the supervision of responsible health care personnel, furnish "genuine" out-reach services in support of infant care instructions and counselling provided by the clinic, hospital or maternity center, but without any attempt to incur obligation for such services.

5. Our product label and printed instructions, in addition to stressing the importance of breastfeeding, will emphasize the need for accurate, proper proportions in preparing the formula. Pictographs as well as the written word will be included in appropriate languages.

6. While restricting our promotion to health care professionals, we will direct additional company resources to aid their overall mission by providing communications on current health care developments, and by providing them with nonproduct related services for distribution to mothers to:
   a. encourage breastfeeding
   b. promote good overall nutritional practices
   c. improve infant and child care
   d. improve sanitation

7. Further, to insure that the letter and spirit of this revised and strengthened Code of Marketing Ethics is followed, we will distribute it widely in developing countries to appropriate health care agencies and personnel. We invite those directly responsible for infant care in the developing world to report any current deviation from this Code by our employees or distributors. Unless proscribed by law, we will terminate any distributor who does not follow the Code. The company has devised internal procedures and policy to maintain ongoing surveillance of our marketing practices in these nations.

We recognize the variation that exists between countries as to state of development, economic resources and availability of trained health personnel and want our activities in all countries to conform to the spirit and letter of this Code.

Source: Abbott Laboratories, North Chicago, Ill. 60064.

Appendix 22-2

POLICY ON CLINICAL SAMPLES OF INFANT FORMULA IN DEVELOPING COUNTRIES (1 MARCH 1978)

In recent years the infant formula industry has been criticized for alleged abuses of sampling practices in developing nations. The concern is centered on the use of samples as inducements to bottlefeed rather than breastfeed, and of giving samples to mothers who cannot afford to buy infant formula or prepare it safely. Our internal guidelines merit publication so that our position is generally known.

BASIC PRINCIPLES

1. Samples of infant formula are made available in limited quantities for two purposes: the convenience and instruction of a mother for whom Similac® has been selected by a health care professional, and to familiarize health care personnel with the characteristics and performance of the product.
2. Our interest is not served by providing samples for mothers who cannot afford to purchase adequate quantities of the product, or prepare it safely. Neither is it in our commercial interest to have health clinics, hospitals or maternity centers sequester samples, and then provide them in large quantities to specific mothers or food distribution centers as charity donations.
3. The selection, control and use of both nutritional and other health care samples is fundamentally a prerogative and responsibility of health care professionals, who must exercise judgment over their proper distribution and use.

GUIDELINES FOR USE OF INFANT FORMULA CLINICAL SAMPLES

1. Samples should not be used as an inducement to use our products in lieu of breastfeeding. Therefore, samples should not given carte blanche to groups of pregnant women or indiscriminately to all clinic patients at the time of delivery.
2. A sample should be provided only for those specific women for whom a Similac formula has been recommended by a responsible health care professional.
3. Samples should be given to mothers only by health care personnel with complete instructions on their proper use, and never directly by an Abbott employee.
4. Samples to a health clinic, hospital, or maternity center can be provided only at the request of the health care professional in charge.
5. Sampling in the event of "mixed" feeding, i.e., breastfeeding with bottle as supplement, calls for astute management by the health care professional so as not to interfere with the lactation process.
    Supplemental formula should not be recommended until after lactation is established, and quantity of formula carefully monitored.
6. Samples should not be used as a marketing device to encourage mothers to switch brands of formula, if a particular brand has been recommended by a professional.
7. If, in the judgment of the Abbott employee, samples are being misused, the employee has the obligation of correcting the abuse, or terminating the supply.
8. Abbott encourages its employees to have frank discussions with health care professionals about infant formula, our marketing policies and possible abuses of sampling. In the end, mothers, babies, the profession and the industry will benefit from appropriate control of sampling activity.
9. The Corporation would like to be informed of any violations of these Guidelines.

Source: Abbott Laboratories, North Chicago, Ill. 60064.

Appendix 22-3

NOTICE TO HEALTH PROFESSIONALS

On behalf of Abbott Laboratories, manufacturer of Similac Infant Formula, this is to emphasize some important principles of infant feeding, particularly regarding breastfeeding and the use of infant formula.

Abbott recognizes the superiority of breast milk and recommends that all infants be breast-fed for as long as possible. In addition to the proper balance of nutrients, breast milk contains immunological properties not obtainable through any manufactured product. Increasingly sophisticated scientific research has substantiated that "breast is best" for infants.

However, if it is determined that an infant formula is necessary for the partial or total nutrition of an infant under your care, there are special conditions which warrant your attention. Evidence demonstrates that in poverty areas—because of increased risk of contamination and need for economy—the practice of artificial feeding can lead to certain problems.

Successful use of an infant formula depends on proper instruction and preparation. Formula that is diluted incorrectly, or prepared with contaminated water or utensils can cause serious illness or failure to thrive, especially in the very young infant who is particularly vulnerable to infection and undernutrition.

Expressing its concern, the World Health Assembly has twice noted in Resolutions (1974, 1978) that, ". . . even if they (poor parents) can afford such foods the tendency to malnutrition is frequently aggravated because of lack of understanding of the amount and correct and hygienic preparation of the food which should be given to the child."* Therefore, the following guidelines should receive consideration:

1. *Problems of economy:* It is usually more costly to use artificial feeding than breast milk. Where income is low, the cost of purchasing formula can displace family income and encourage overdilution.
   a. Parents must be able to afford the infant formula and understand the total cost of formula for the length of time you expect it to be used. If not, parents may overdilute the formula, thus providing insufficient nutrients.
   b. Parents must have the utensils necessary to prepare the product correctly, as well as understand the expense both of the utensils and the fuel required for boiling the water.
   c. It should be explained that the baby may become ill if formula is diluted to make it last longer.
   d. The family's over-all nutritional needs should be considered. Use of artificial feeding, when it represents a significant proportion of income, may cause a reallocation of food within the family, complicating the delivery of proper diets to other family members.

Source: Abbott Laboratories, North Chicago, Ill. 60064.
*WHA 27.43, 23 May 1974.

2. *Problems of contamination:* Breast milk is sanitary and available to nearly every baby. Special precautions must be followed to assure the safety of formula products. Unsanitary water, coupled with lack of sterile preparation technique, can lead to contaminated formula. When ingested by the infant, this will increase the incidence of gastroenteritis. Aggravated diarrhea can lead to dehydration, especially dangerous to the young infant.
   a. Parents must understand all aspects of formula preparation instructions, including cleaning utensils and boiling water.
   b. In conditions of unsanitary water supply, stress the importance of boiling water at least ten minutes to be used for cleaning utensils or mixing formula.
   c. If refrigeration is not available, explain that only single feedings of infant formula should be prepared. Left-over formula should not be held without refrigeration. (Left-over formula can be consumed by the mother or an older child.)

The interaction of undernutrition and infection is the leading cause of infant morbidity and mortality in the developing world. Since improper artificial feeding can exacerbate these conditions, special precautions must be taken. If, in your opinion, the potential for misuse of infant formula appears probable or possible, the use of artificial feeding should be actively discouraged. In this case, you should recommend the best possible source of local foods, with minimal contamination, to meet the infant's basic needs for protein, calories and vitamins.

We believe that infant formulas can make an important contribution to infant nutrition. Your consideration of these guidelines can help assure the safe, proper use of Similac.

Appendix 22-4

NOTICE TO DISTRIBUTORS AND RETAILERS OF INFANT FORMULA REGARDING YOUR ROLE IN THE DELIVERY OF HEALTH CARE PRODUCTS

Abbott Laboratories, manufacturer of Similac Formulas, want you to know how to help families use infant formula safely.

Because Abbott knows that breast milk is best for babies, we recommend that all babies be breast-fed for as long as possible. If it becomes necessary for mothers to use formula, they sometimes ask those who sell formula about the best way to use it. Knowing what to tell them is an important part of your job.

Using formula carefully helps babies stay healthy. Babies cannot fight germs like older people. Their families need to know that they must work hard to keep germs from babies especially if they feed anything but breast milk.

Source: Abbott Laboratories. North Chicago, Ill. 60064.

When families use formula, they have to know these things:

1. Everything used to mix formula, and the bottles and nipples, must be boiled when they are used. The water to mix with the powder must be boiled too.
2. It is important to use just the right amount of powder and water when mixing the formula. Too much water makes the formula too weak, and the baby will get sick, because the baby will not get enough nourishment. Too much powder makes the formula too strong and may lead to inadequate water intake leading to dehydration, so that will make the baby sick too.
3. Formula costs money. As the baby gets bigger, more formula will be needed to help the baby keep growing. That means more money will be needed to pay for increased amounts of formula. The family must understand this plan so everyone can eat as well as possible.
4. When the family does not have a refrigerator, only one bottle of formula must be made at a time. When the baby does not drink all the formula, the mother or another child should drink the formula rather than save it or throw it away.
5. If a baby should show signs of sickness, the baby should be brought to a health worker right away. Little babies are not strong, and when they get sick, they have a better chance to get well if they get help right away.

If you believe families cannot use infant formula correctly, you should consult your local health authorities about what other foods will best meet the infant's needs for protein, calories and vitamins, with a minimum risk of contamination.

Our Similac formulas can help babies grow and be healthy only if families use them correctly. An important part of your job is helping families use formula safely. Those who buy formula are often your friends and neighbors. It is right to help them feed their babies the safe way so they will be well and strong.

NOTES

1. Much of this history is drawn from H. F. Meyer, *Infant Foods and Feeding Practice* (Springfield, Ill.: Charles C. Thomas, Publisher, 1960), especially chap. 1.

2. To observe the problems in this measurement, see Helen Deem and Murray McGeorge, "Breast-Feeding," *New Zealand Medical Journal*, 57:539–556, 1958.

3. Quoted in Barbara Garson, "The Bottle Baby Scandal: Milking the Third World for All It's Worth," *Mother Jones*, December 1977, p. 33.

4. *Marketing and Promotion of Infant Formula in the Developing Nations, Hearings before the Senate Committee on Human Resources, Subcommittee on Health and Scientific Research*, 95th Cong., 2d Sess., 1978, report by David O. Cox, president of the Ross Division of Abbott Laboratories, pp. 198–199.

5. United Nations, Protein-Calorie Advisory Group, "Promotion of Special Foods (Infant Formula and Processed Protein Foods) for Vulnerable Groups," PAG Statement No. 23, 18 July 1972, revised November 1973.

6. Interview with Dave Cox, president, Ross Laboratories, Columbus, Ohio, 2 February 1979.

7. "Infant Formula in Third World," *Commitment* (Abbott house organ), Spring 1976, p. 12.

8. "The Nestlé Libel Suit," *Business International*, October 8, 1976, p. 323.

9. Leah Margulies, "Baby Formula Abroad: Exporting Infant Malnutrition," *Christianity and Crisis*, November 10, 1975, pp. 264–67; Leah Margulies, "Bottle Babies: Death and Business Get Their Market," *Business & Society Review*, Spring 1978, pp. 43–49; Douglas Clement, "Nestlé's Latest Killing in the Bottle Baby Market," *Business & Society Review*, Summer 1978, pp. 60–64; Barbara Garson, "Bottle Baby Scandal," pp. 33–40.

10. Margulies, "Baby Formula Abroad," pp. 264 and 265.

11. See Bristol-Myers Co., *Statements of the Sisters of the Precious Blood and Bristol-Myers Company on Infant Formula Marketing Practices Overseas*, distributed to Bristol-Myers shareholders, undated, p. 3.

12. Quoted in "Abbott Program Supports Breastfeeding," *Commitment*, Summer 1977, p. 7.

13. Bristol-Myers Co., *Statements*, p. 3.

14. "Abbott Program," *Commitment*, p. 8.

15. For an enumeration of these changes, see ibid.

16. Ibid., p. 7.

17. Ibid., p. 7.

18. Interview with Sister Marilyn Uline, Adrian Dominican Sisters, Chicago, Ill., 1 February 1979.

19. Interview with Tom McCollough, research specialist, Third World, Ross Laboratories, Columbus, Ohio, 2 February 1979.

20. *Marketing and Promotion of Infant Formula in the Developing Nations, Hearings before the Senate Committee on Human Resources, Subcommittee on Health and Scientific Research*, 95th Cong., 2d Sess., 1978, p. 39.

21. Ibid., pp. 42–43.

22. Ibid., pp. 68–69.

23. Ibid., pp. 248–81.

24. Interview with Dave Cox, president, Ross Laboratories, Columbus, Ohio, 2 February 1979.

25. See for example, T. Greiner, *The Promotion of Bottle Feeding by Multinational Corporations: How Advertising and the Health Professions Have Contributed*, Publication 2 (Ithaca, N.Y.: Cornell International Nutrition Monograph Series, 1975); T. Greiner, *Regulation and Education: Strategies for Solving the Bottle Feeding Problem*, Publication 4 (Ithaca, N.Y.: Cornell International Nutrition Monograph Series, 1977); and *U.S. Senate Hearings*, 95th Cong., 2d Sess., 23 May 1978, statement of Dr. Manuel Carballo, scientist, maternal and child health, division of family health of the World Health Organization, pp. 103–15.

26. *U.S. Senate Hearings*, p. 112.

27. Interview with Sister Marilyn Uline, Adrian Dominican Sisters, Chicago, Ill., 1 February 1979.

28. Interview with Tom McCollough, research specialist, Third World, Ross Laboratories, Columbus, Ohio, 2 February 1979.

29. Letter from Tom McCollough, Ross Laboratories, Columbus, Ohio, to the author, March 14, 1979.

QUESTIONS FOR DISCUSSION*

1. In Sister Marilyn Uline's commentary on Abbott/Ross's new code, she notes that two "problems" still remain: (1) that free samples of the formula are still given to mothers who may misuse them, and (2) that formula companies con-

tinue to pay representatives both to provide health care and to sell products. Did Abbott/Ross respond sufficiently to these two criticisms? If not, how *should* it have responded?

2. Evaluate Tom McCollough's remark at the end of the case that Abbott/Ross's critics failed to play fair by introducing a last-minute shareholder resolution.